Shojo Beat

Time Stranger Kyoko

Vol. **3**
Story & Art by
Arina Tanemura

Cast of Characters

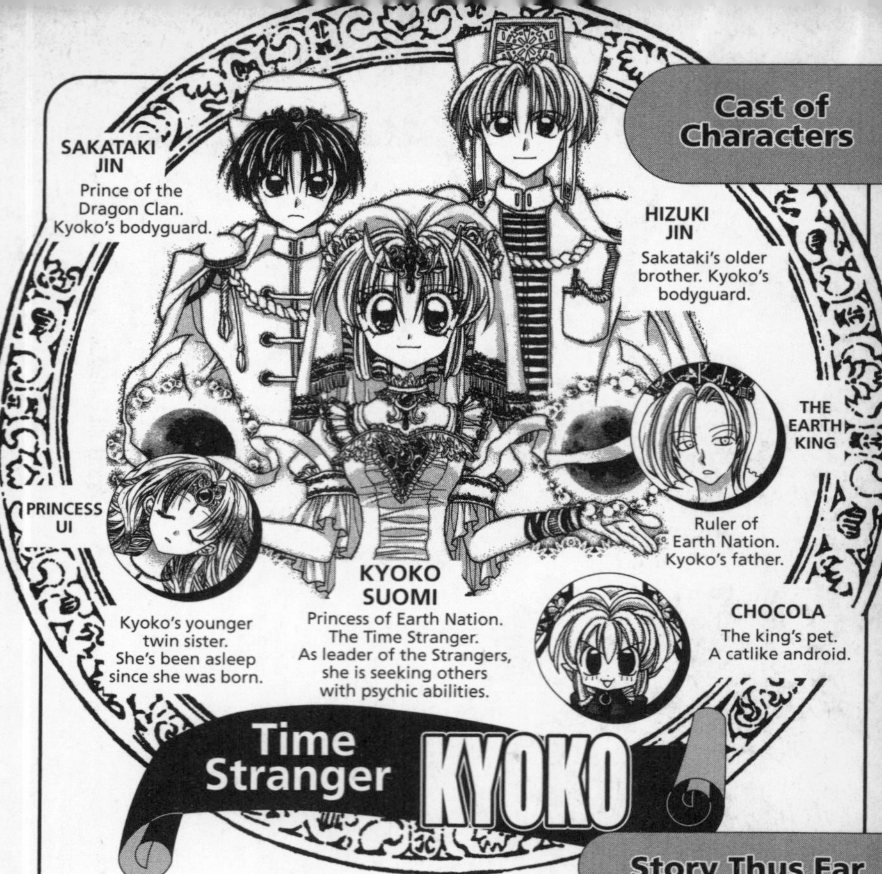

SAKATAKI JIN
Prince of the Dragon Clan. Kyoko's bodyguard.

HIZUKI JIN
Sakataki's older brother. Kyoko's bodyguard.

THE EARTH KING
Ruler of Earth Nation. Kyoko's father.

PRINCESS UI
Kyoko's younger twin sister. She's been asleep since she was born.

KYOKO SUOMI
Princess of Earth Nation. The Time Stranger. As leader of the Strangers, she is seeking others with psychic abilities.

CHOCOLA
The king's pet. A catlike android.

Time Stranger KYOKO

Story Thus Far

It is the 30th century. The planet has united into one country called Earth Nation. The princess of Earth Nation, Kyoko, wishes to live as an ordinary girl and not take up the duties of a ruler. The king tells Kyoko that if she can awaken her younger sister, Princess Ui, who has been asleep for 16 years, she can have her freedom. To awaken Princess Ui, Kyoko must gather the 12 God Stones and the 12 psychics who control them, known as Strangers.

When the Time-Space Stone reacts to Kyoko, she awakens to her role as the Time Stranger. Kyoko finds four other Strangers—Sakataki of the Dragon Tribe, Karen of the Flower Tribe, Sarai of the Snake Tribe and Mizuno of the Fish Tribe—and sends them to the castle to give strength to Princess Ui. However, Princess Ui shows no sign of waking up.

Kyoko confesses to her friends that she knows she's not the King's biological daughter. Fearing that she's one of the evil Demon Tribe and that continuing to live as a princess will destroy Earth Nation, she flees the castle.

But if Princess Ui is not awakened, the royal line will end. Having second thoughts, Kyoko returns to the castle to take up the task of protecting Earth Nation.

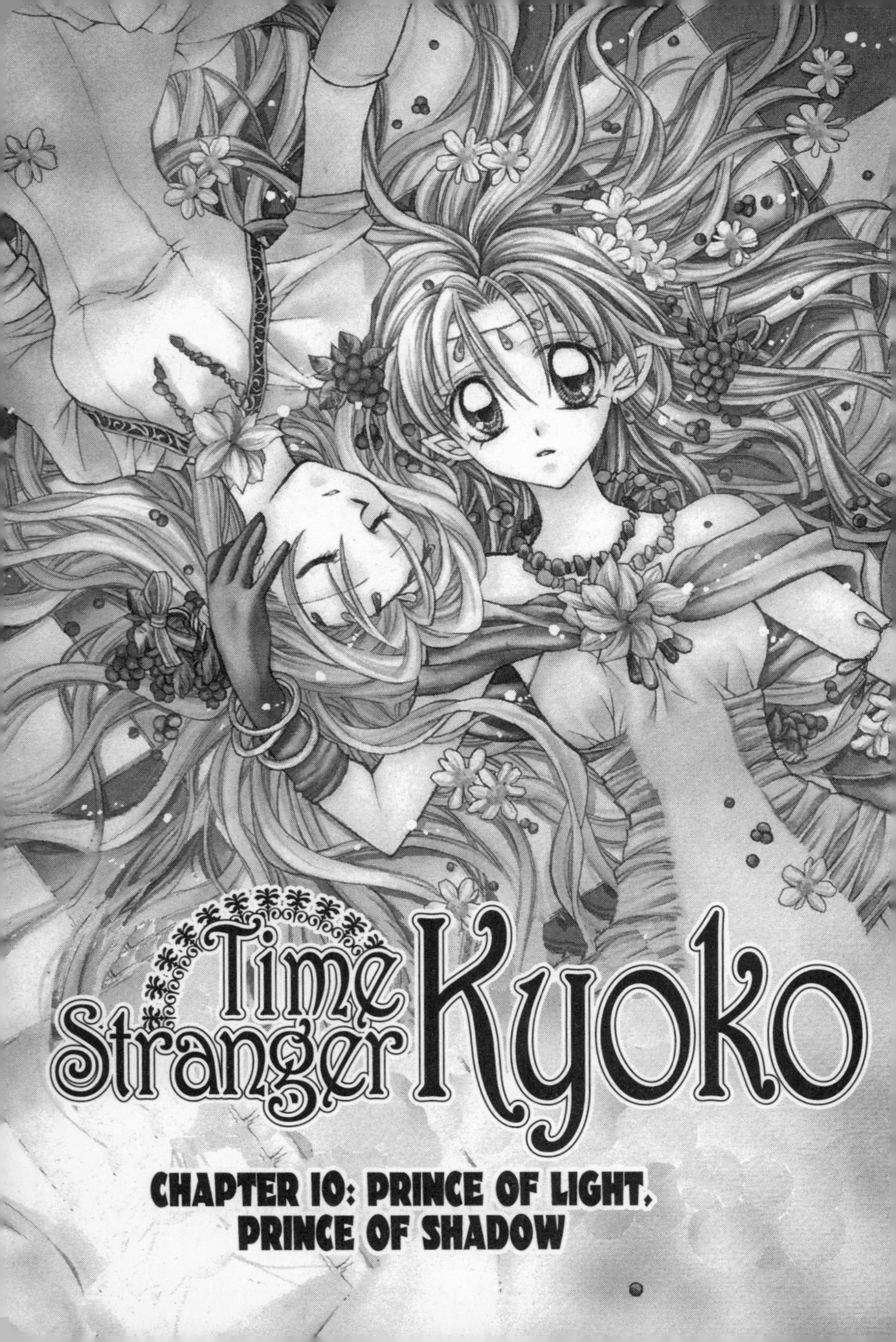
Time Stranger Kyoko
CHAPTER 10: PRINCE OF LIGHT, PRINCE OF SHADOW

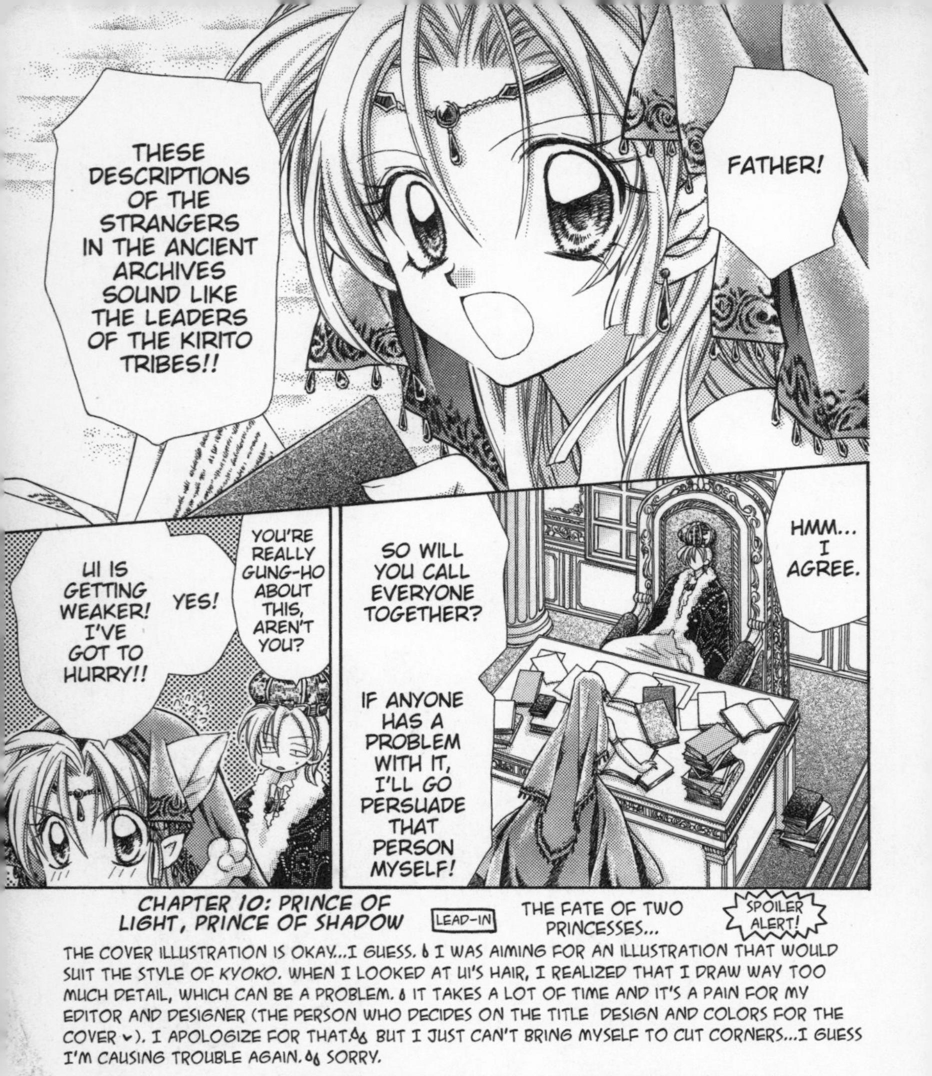
FATHER!
THESE DESCRIPTIONS OF THE STRANGERS IN THE ANCIENT ARCHIVES SOUND LIKE THE LEADERS OF THE KIRITO TRIBES!!
HMM... I AGREE.
SO WILL YOU CALL EVERYONE TOGETHER?
IF ANYONE HAS A PROBLEM WITH IT, I'LL GO PERSUADE THAT PERSON MYSELF!
YOU'RE REALLY GUNG-HO ABOUT THIS, AREN'T YOU?
YES!
UI IS GETTING WEAKER! I'VE GOT TO HURRY!!

CHAPTER 10: PRINCE OF LIGHT, PRINCE OF SHADOW

LEAD-IN THE FATE OF TWO PRINCESSES... SPOILER ALERT!

THE COVER ILLUSTRATION IS OKAY...I GUESS. I WAS AIMING FOR AN ILLUSTRATION THAT WOULD SUIT THE STYLE OF KYOKO. WHEN I LOOKED AT UI'S HAIR, I REALIZED THAT I DRAW WAY TOO MUCH DETAIL, WHICH CAN BE A PROBLEM. IT TAKES A LOT OF TIME AND IT'S A PAIN FOR MY EDITOR AND DESIGNER (THE PERSON WHO DECIDES ON THE TITLE DESIGN AND COLORS FOR THE COVER). I APOLOGIZE FOR THAT. BUT I JUST CAN'T BRING MYSELF TO CUT CORNERS...I GUESS I'M CAUSING TROUBLE AGAIN. SORRY.

THE STORY STARTED MOVING REALLY QUICKLY ALL OF A SUDDEN. I WONDER IF A LOT OF MY READERS WERE SURPRISED. TO BE FRANK, BEFORE I EVEN WROTE THE ROUGH DRAFT FOR THIS CHAPTER, I HAD DECIDED TO END THE STORY SOON. MORE THAN ANYTHING ELSE, I WANTED TO TELL HIZUKI'S STORY, SO MAYBE THE REST OF THE STRANGERS GOT THE SHORT END OF THE STICK.

OF ALL THE CHAPTERS IN *KYOKO*, THIS IS ONE OF THE TWO THAT SATISFIES ME THE MOST. (THE OTHER ONE IS CHAPTER 12.) I FEEL THAT KYOKO-CHAN'S PERSONALITY REALLY SHINES THROUGH... THANK GOODNESS.

LET'S SEE...MY MEMORIES OF THIS CHAPTER... I DREW THE PAGES IN NAGOYA, AND I HAD TO DELIVER THEM BY BULLET TRAIN. I WASN'T QUITE FINISHED, THOUGH. THEY STILL NEEDED SCREENTONE. BUT NONE OF MY ASSISTANTS WOULD COME WITH ME, SO, HALF-CRYING AND SICK TO MY STOMACH, I LAID ALL THE TONE MYSELF. (I WAS IN A FIRST-CLASS CAR, AND THE FAMOUS SOCCER PLAYER RAMOS WAS SITTING BEHIND ME.) HA HA...FIVE OF MY TEN ASSISTANTS ARE FROM TOKYO! WHY COULDN'T JUST ONE OF THEM HAVE COME OUT?

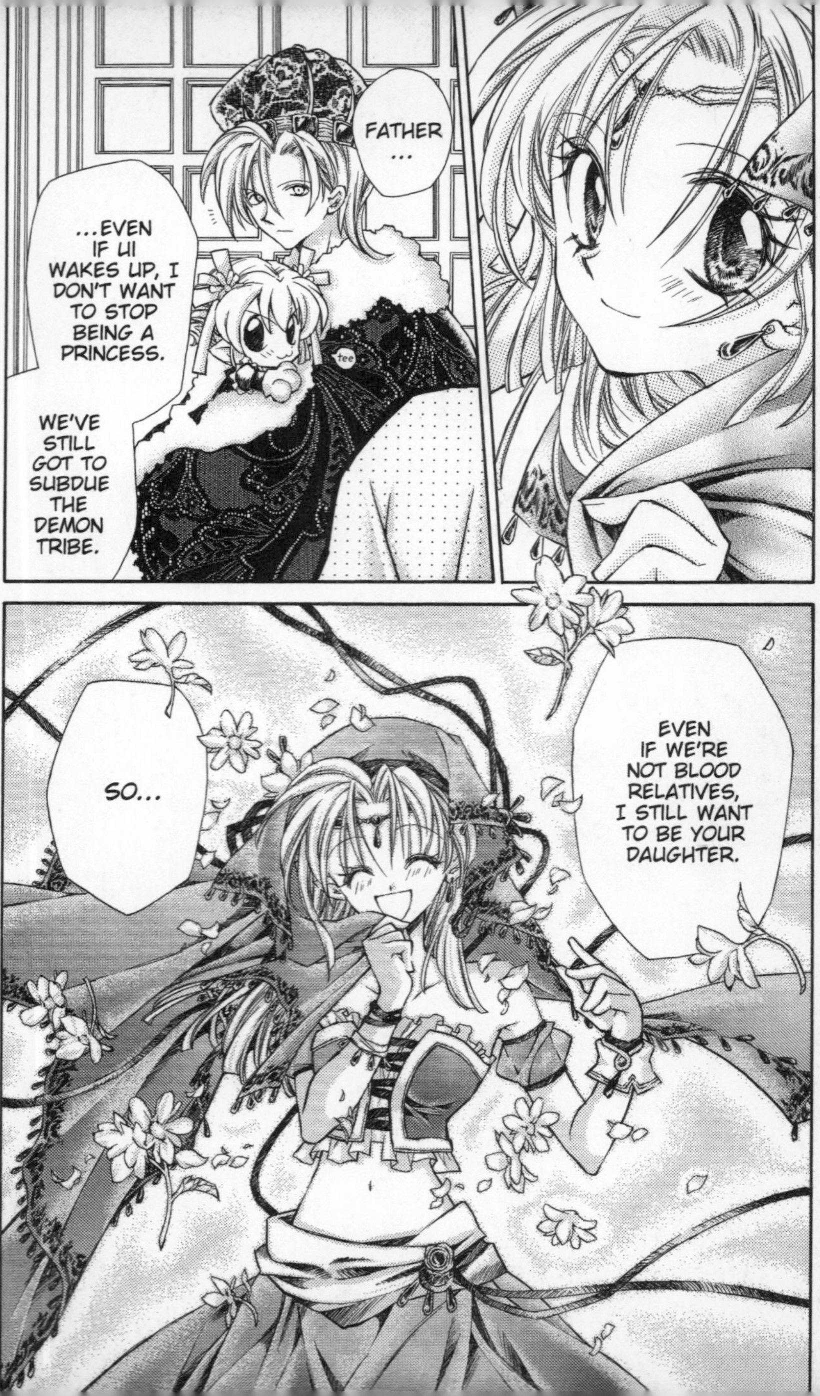
FATHER ...
...EVEN IF UI WAKES UP, I DON'T WANT TO STOP BEING A PRINCESS.
tee
WE'VE STILL GOT TO SUBDUE THE DEMON TRIBE.
EVEN IF WE'RE NOT BLOOD RELATIVES, I STILL WANT TO BE YOUR DAUGHTER.
SO...

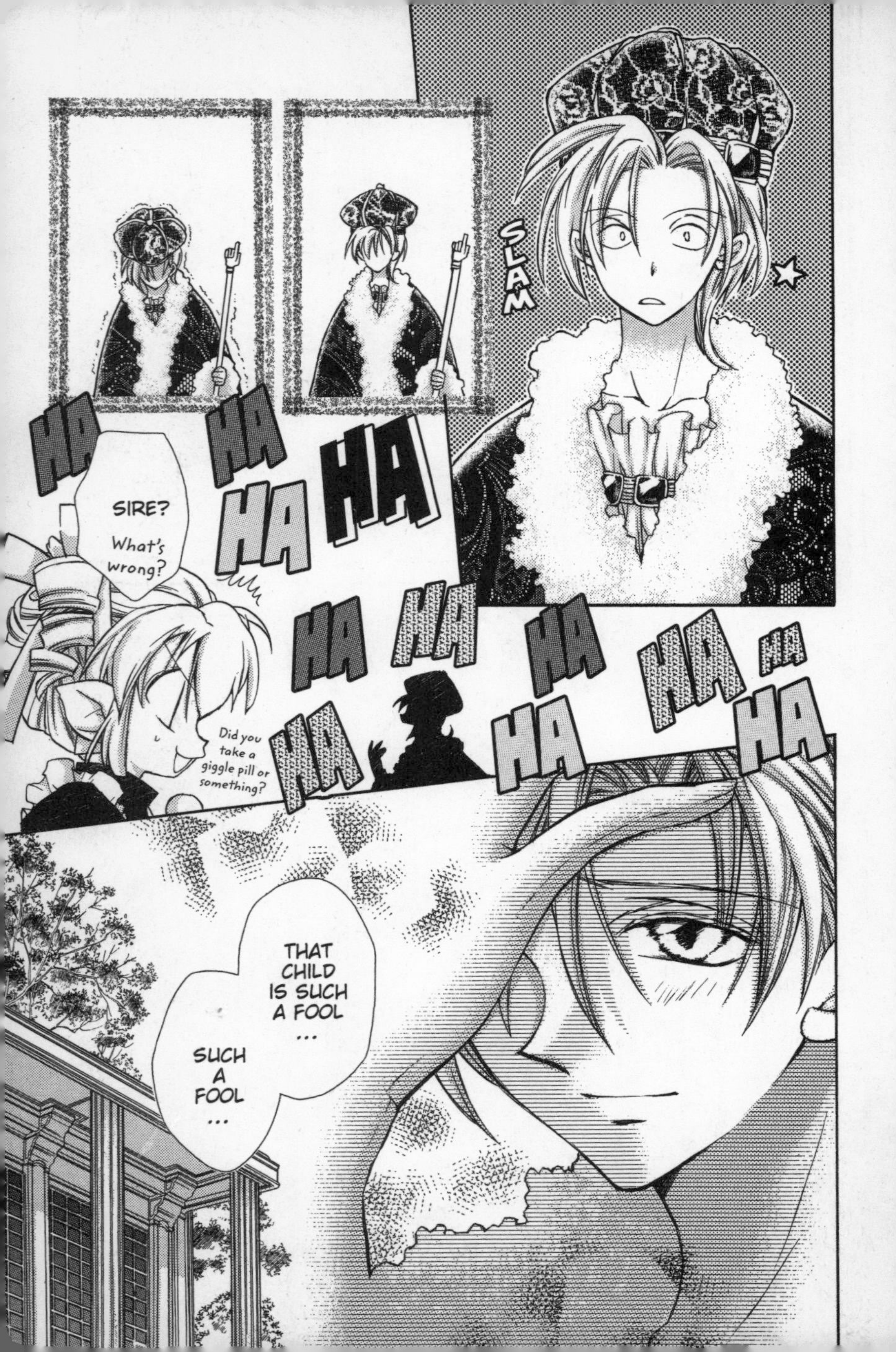
SLAM
HA HA HA HA
SIRE? What's wrong?
HA HA HA HA HA HA HA HA HA HA
Did you take a giggle pill or something?
THAT CHILD IS SUCH A FOOL ...
SUCH A FOOL ...

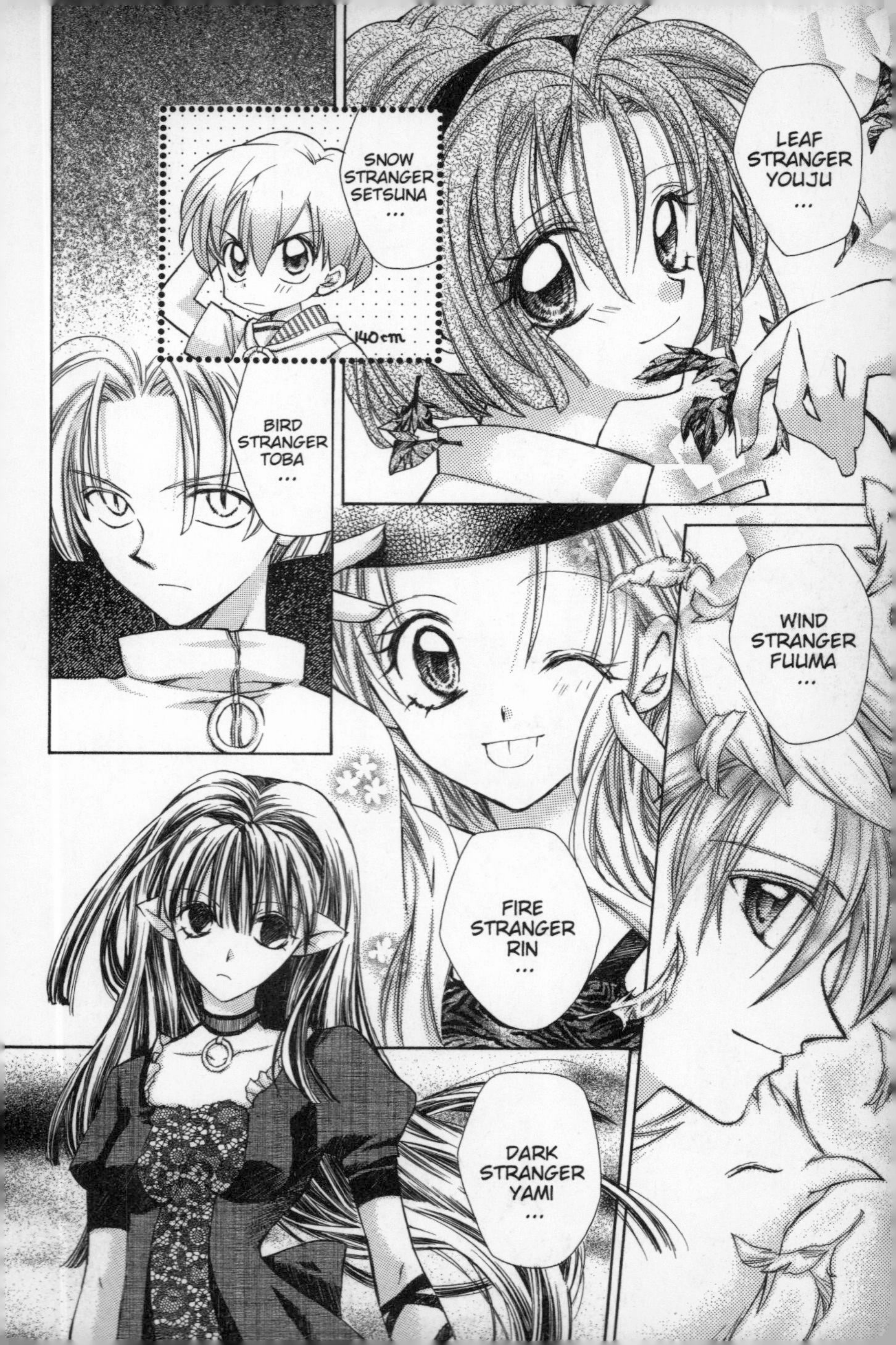
LEAF STRANGER YOUJU ...
SNOW STRANGER SETSUNA ...
140cm
BIRD STRANGER TOBA ...
WIND STRANGER FUUMA ...
FIRE STRANGER RIN ...
DARK STRANGER YAMI ...

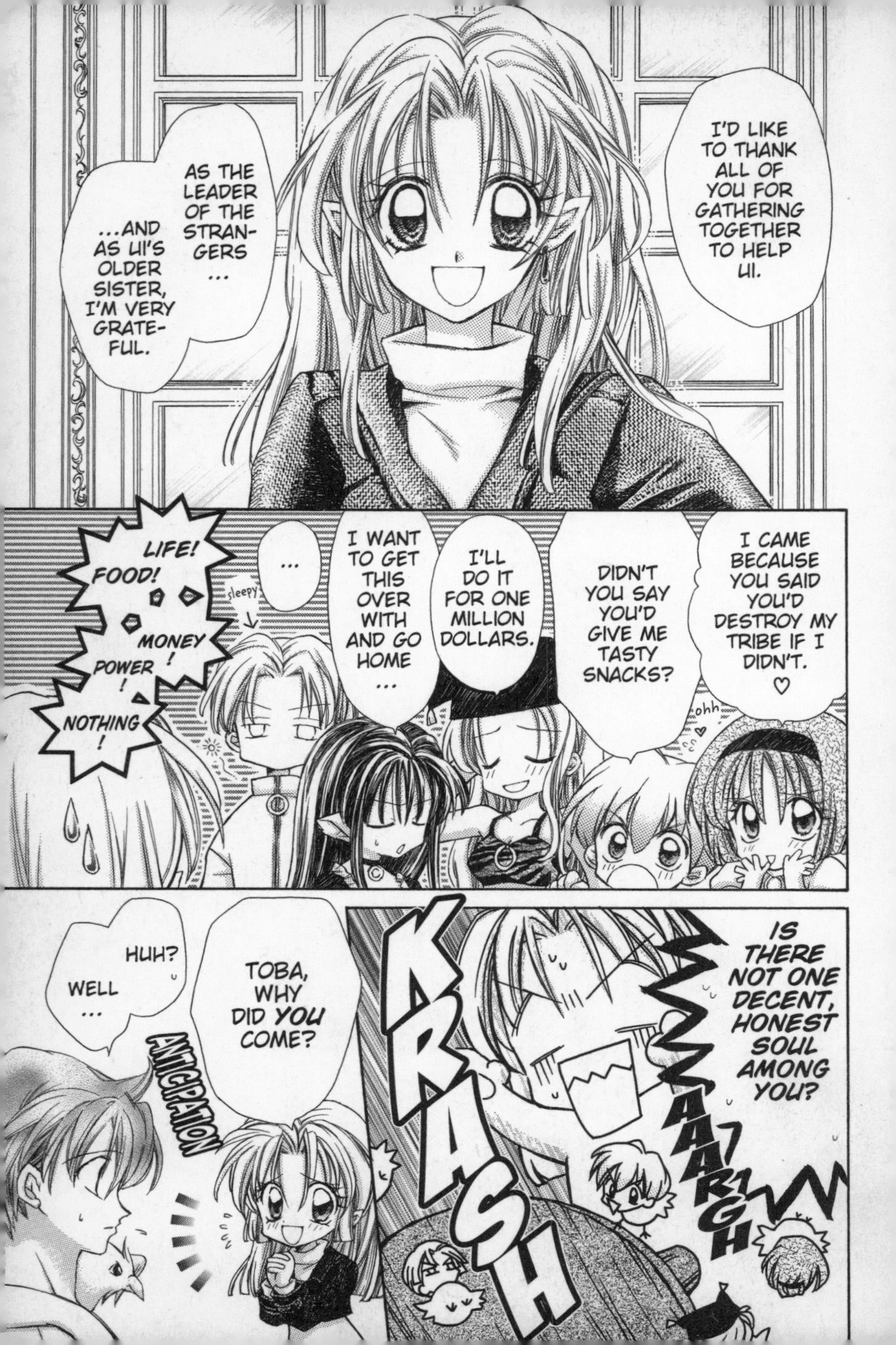
I'D LIKE TO THANK ALL OF YOU FOR GATHERING TOGETHER TO HELP UI.
AS THE LEADER OF THE STRANGERS ...
...AND AS UI'S OLDER SISTER, I'M VERY GRATEFUL.
I CAME BECAUSE YOU SAID YOU'D DESTROY MY TRIBE IF I DIDN'T. ♡
ohh
DIDN'T YOU SAY YOU'D GIVE ME TASTY SNACKS?
I'LL DO IT FOR ONE MILLION DOLLARS.
I WANT TO GET THIS OVER WITH AND GO HOME ...
...
sleepy
LIFE! FOOD! MONEY! POWER! NOTHING!
IS THERE NOT ONE DECENT, HONEST SOUL AMONG YOU?
AAAARGH
KRASH
TOBA, WHY DID YOU COME?
HUH? WELL ...
ANTICIPATION

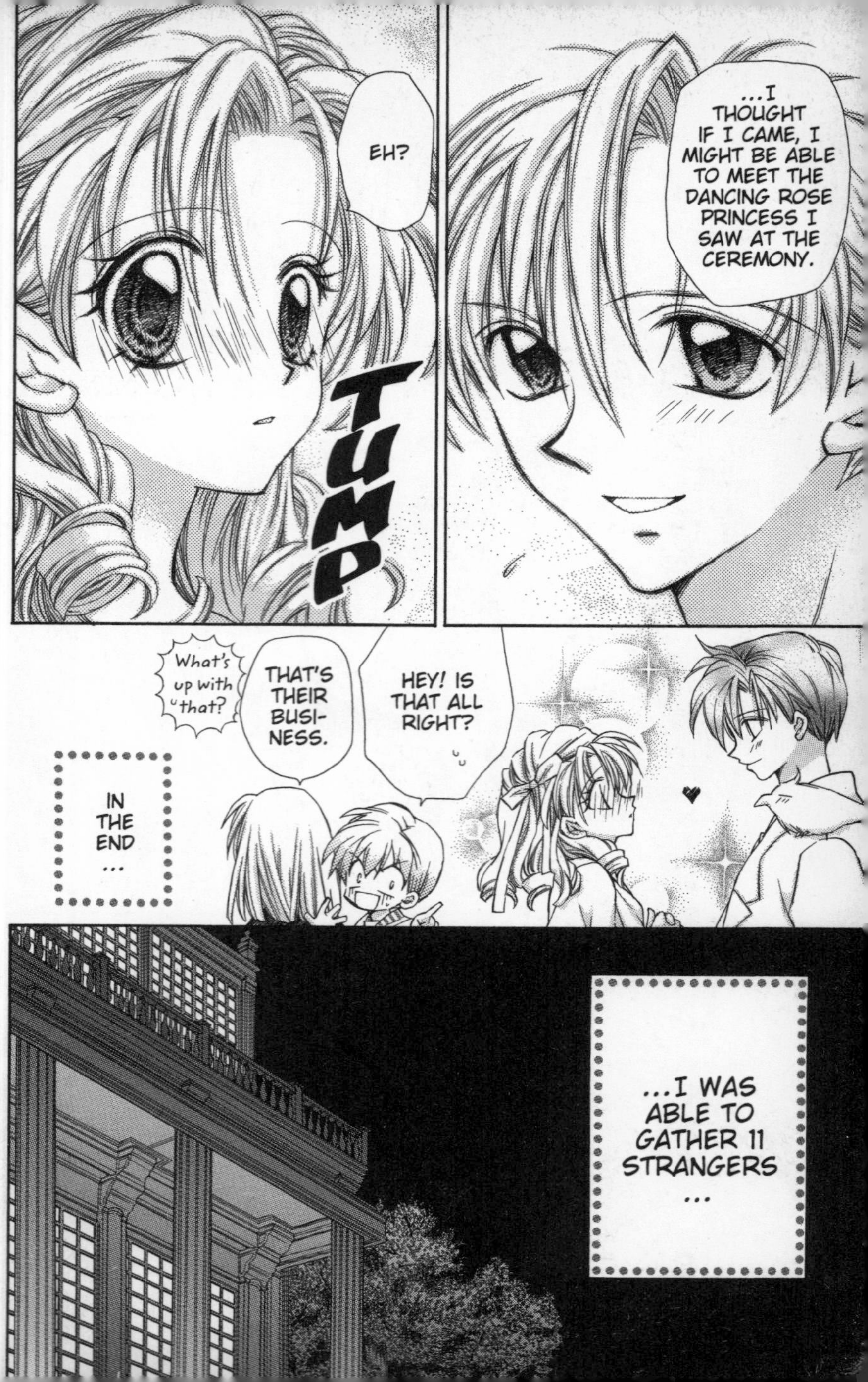
...I THOUGHT IF I CAME, I MIGHT BE ABLE TO MEET THE DANCING ROSE PRINCESS I SAW AT THE CEREMONY.
EH?
TUMP
HEY! IS THAT ALL RIGHT?
THAT'S THEIR BUSI-NESS.
What's up with that?
IN THE END ...
...I WAS ABLE TO GATHER 11 STRANGERS ...

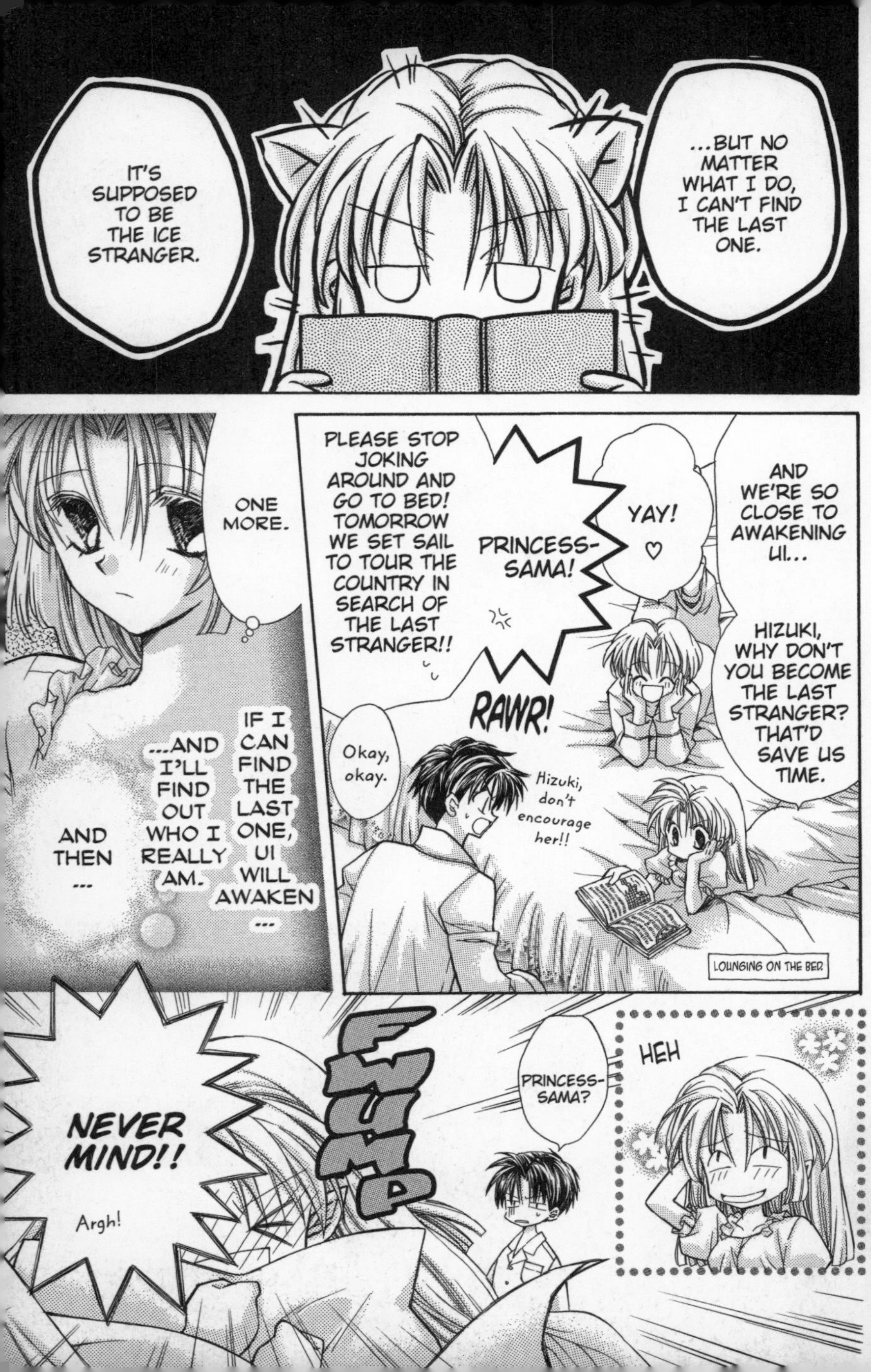
...BUT NO MATTER WHAT I DO, I CAN'T FIND THE LAST ONE.
IT'S SUPPOSED TO BE THE ICE STRANGER.
AND WE'RE SO CLOSE TO AWAKENING UI...
HIZUKI, WHY DON'T YOU BECOME THE LAST STRANGER? THAT'D SAVE US TIME.
YAY! ♡
PRINCESS-SAMA!
PLEASE STOP JOKING AROUND AND GO TO BED! TOMORROW WE SET SAIL TO TOUR THE COUNTRY IN SEARCH OF THE LAST STRANGER!!
RAWR!
Hizuki, don't encourage her!!
Okay, okay.
LOUNGING ON THE BED
ONE MORE.
IF I CAN FIND THE LAST ONE, UI WILL AWAKEN...
...AND I'LL FIND OUT WHO I REALLY AM.
AND THEN...
HEH
PRINCESS-SAMA?
FWUMP
NEVER MIND!!
Argh!

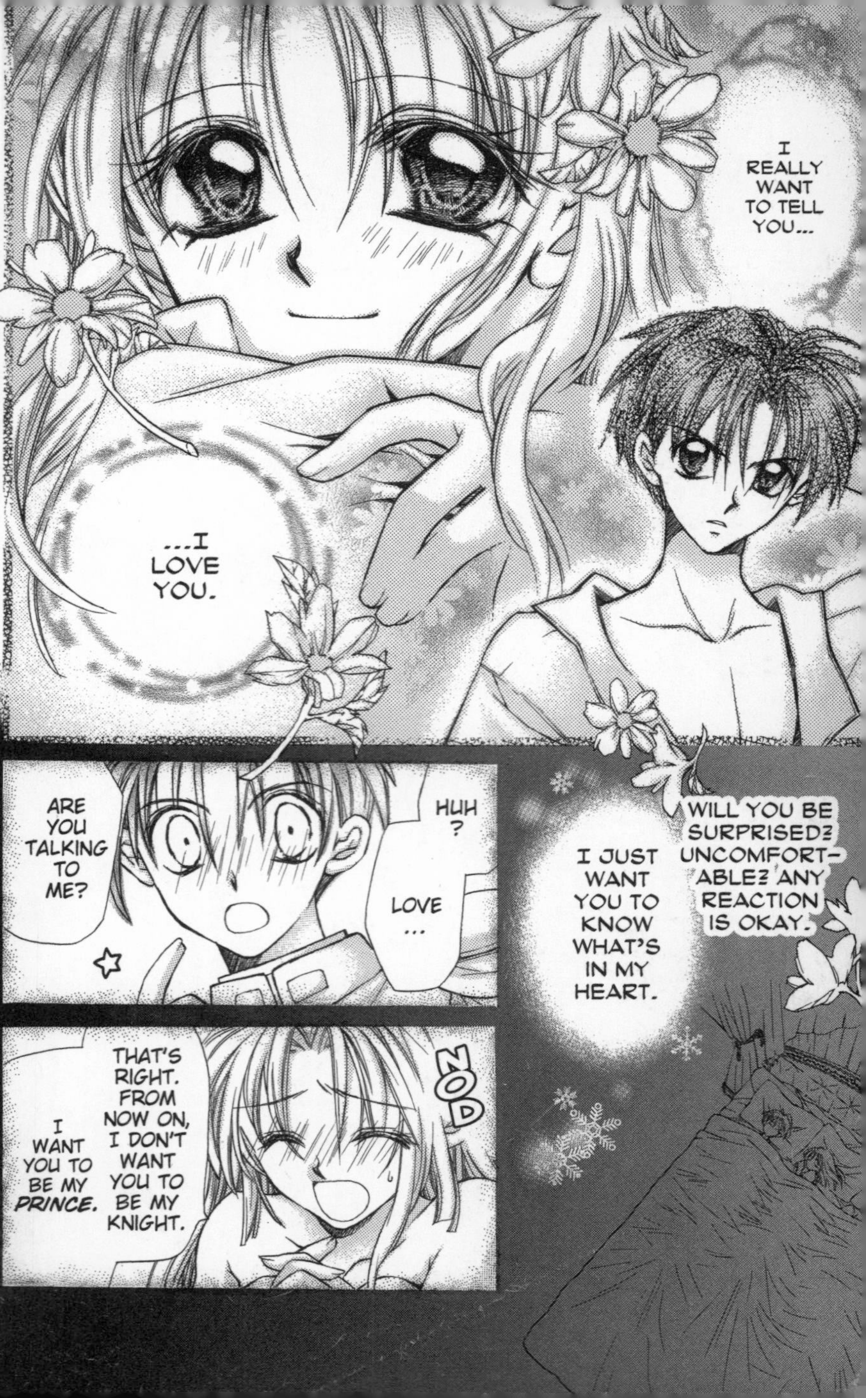

I REALLY WANT TO TELL YOU...
...I LOVE YOU.
WILL YOU BE SURPRISED? UNCOMFORT-ABLE? ANY REACTION IS OKAY.
I JUST WANT YOU TO KNOW WHAT'S IN MY HEART.
HUH?
LOVE ...
ARE YOU TALKING TO ME?
NOD
THAT'S RIGHT. FROM NOW ON, I DON'T WANT YOU TO BE MY KNIGHT.
I WANT YOU TO BE MY *PRINCE*.

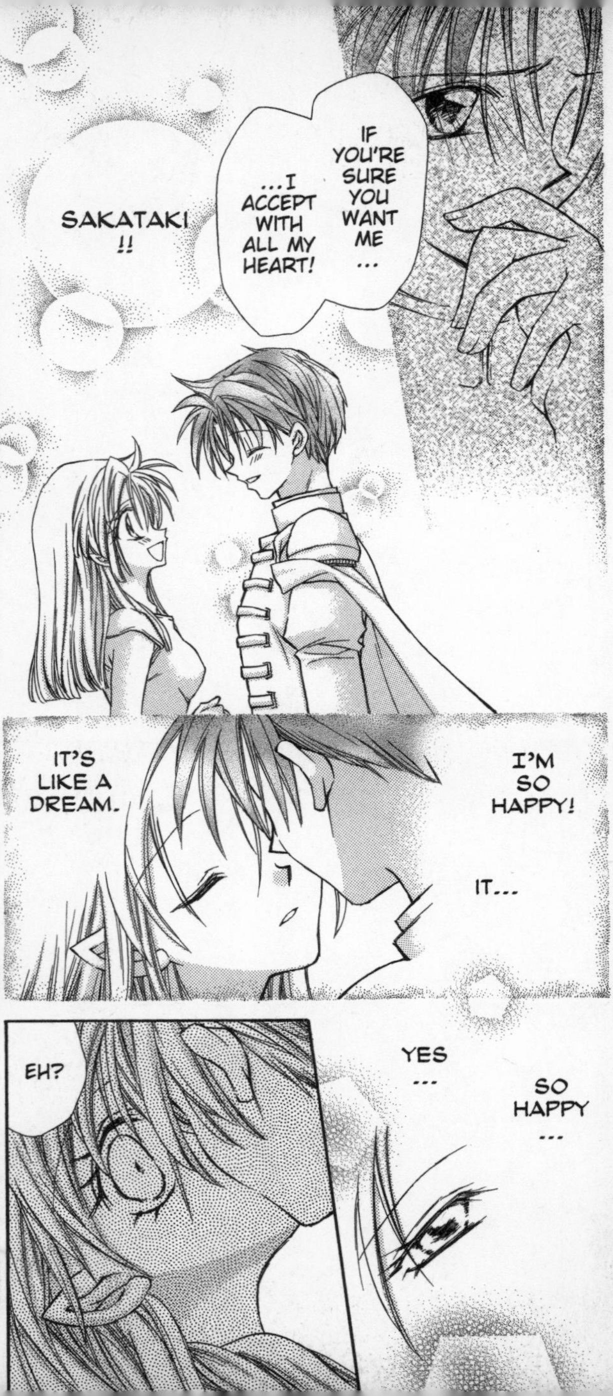
IF YOU'RE SURE YOU WANT ME ...
...I ACCEPT WITH ALL MY HEART!
SAKATAKI !!
I'M SO HAPPY!
IT...
IT'S LIKE A DREAM.
YES ...
SO HAPPY ...
EH?

ARINA TANEMURA'S

PENCHI DE SHAKIN

CHAPTER 45 (I THINK)

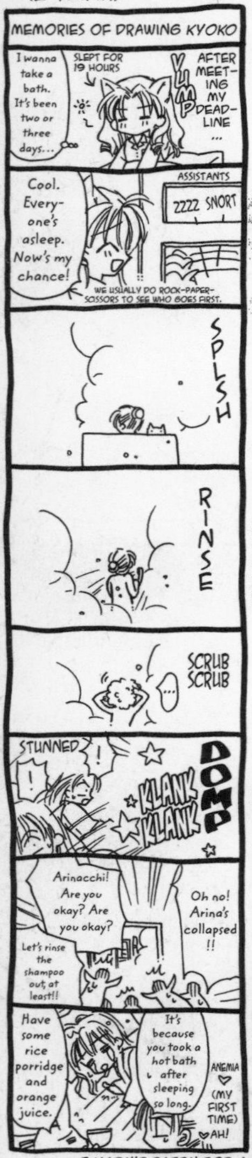
MEMORIES OF DRAWING KYOKO
AFTER MEETING MY DEADLINE ...
VUMP
SLEPT FOR 19 HOURS
I wanna take a bath. It's been two or three days...
ASSISTANTS
ZZZZ SNORT
Cool. Everyone's asleep. Now's my chance!
WE USUALLY DO ROCK-PAPER-SCISSORS TO SEE WHO GOES FIRST.
SPLSH
RINSE
SCRUB SCRUB
...
DOMP
KLANK KLANK
STUNNED
!
!
Oh no! Arina's collapsed !!
Arinacchi! Are you okay? Are you okay?
Let's rinse the shampoo out, at least!!
ANEMIA ♥ (MY FIRST TIME) ♥ AH!
It's because you took a hot bath after sleeping so long.
Have some rice porridge and orange juice.

I HADN'T EATEN FOR A LONG TIME EITHER.

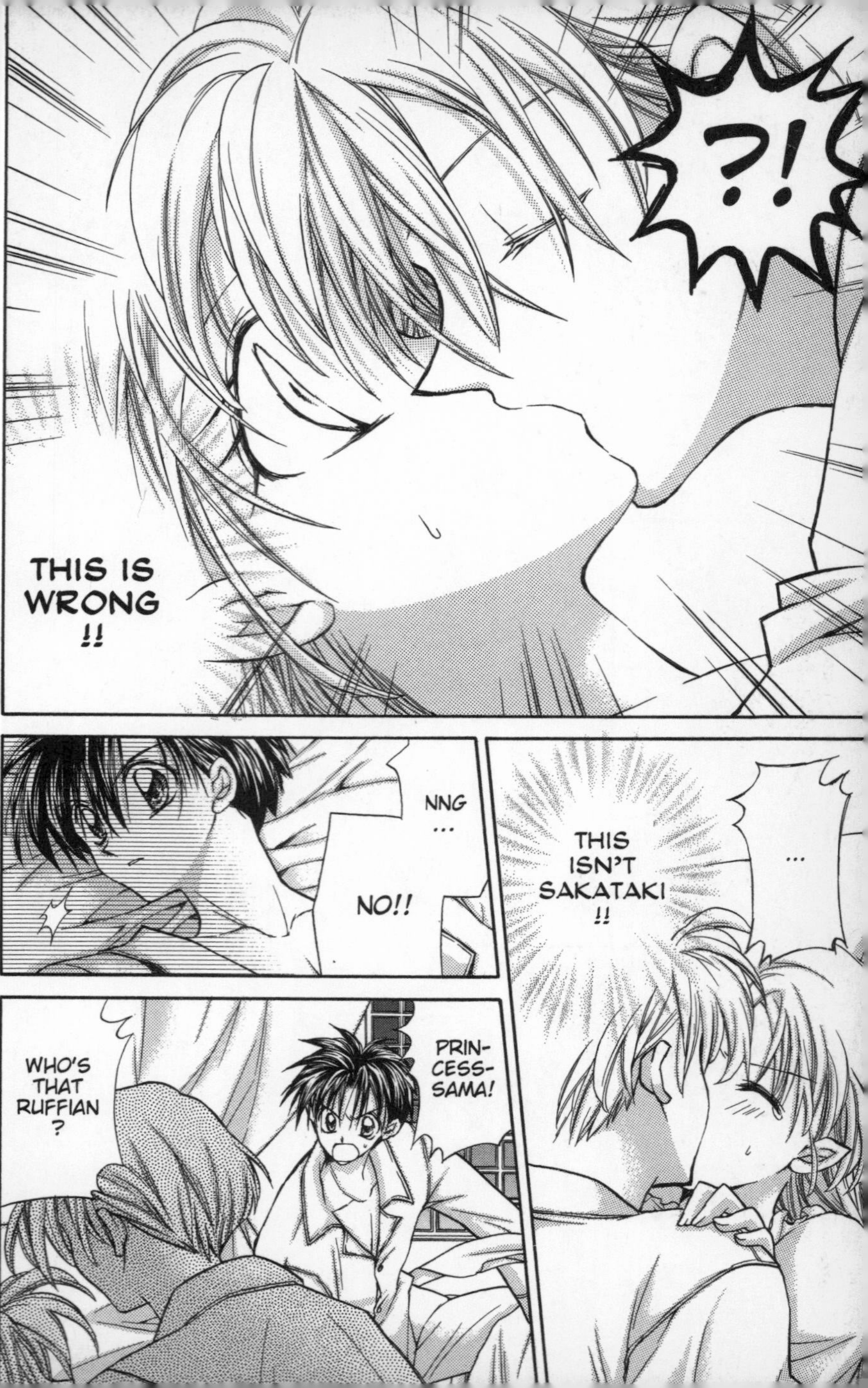
?!
THIS IS WRONG !!
...
THIS ISN'T SAKATAKI !!
NNG ...
NO!!
PRIN-CESS-SAMA!
WHO'S THAT RUFFIAN ?

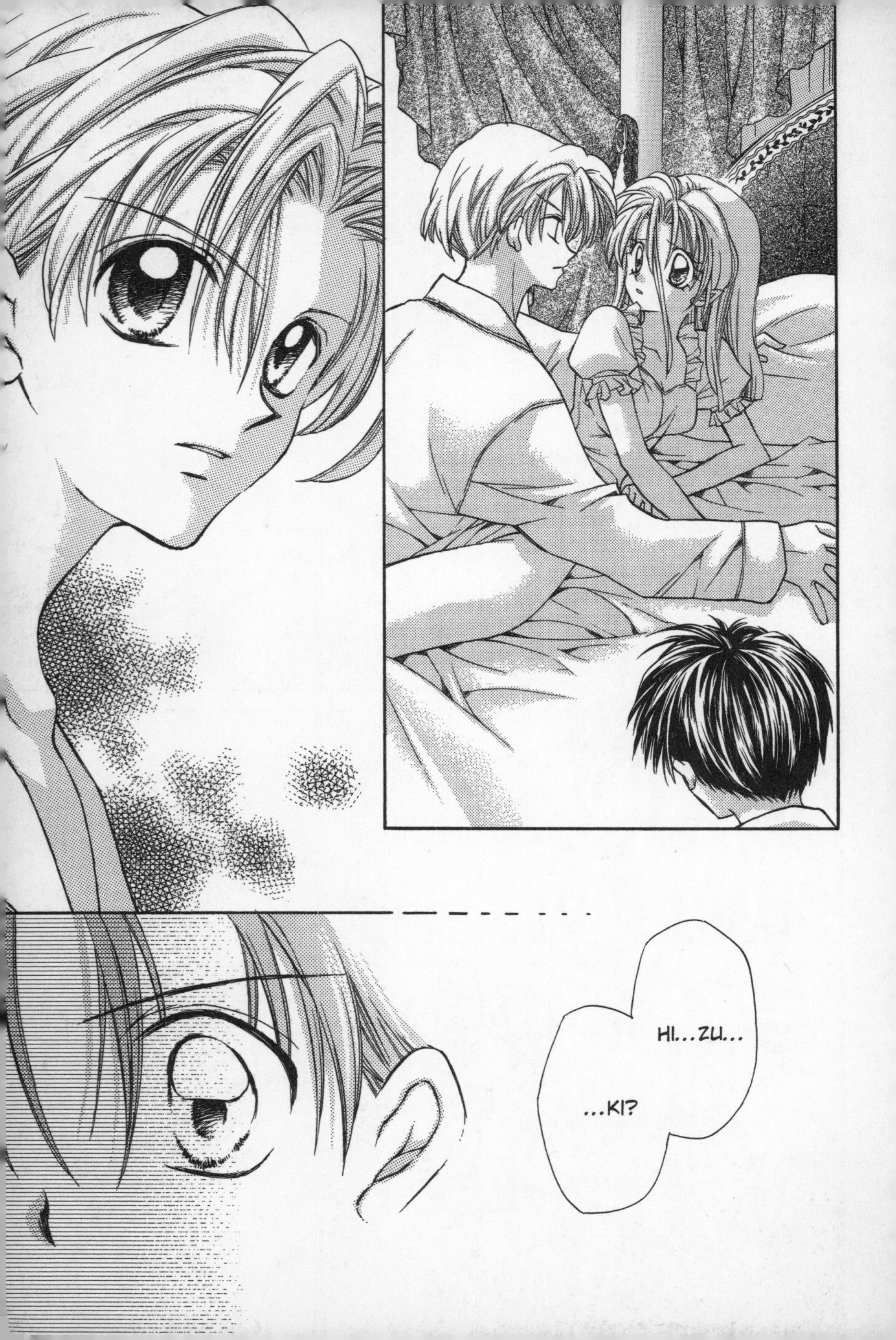
HI...ZU...
...KI?

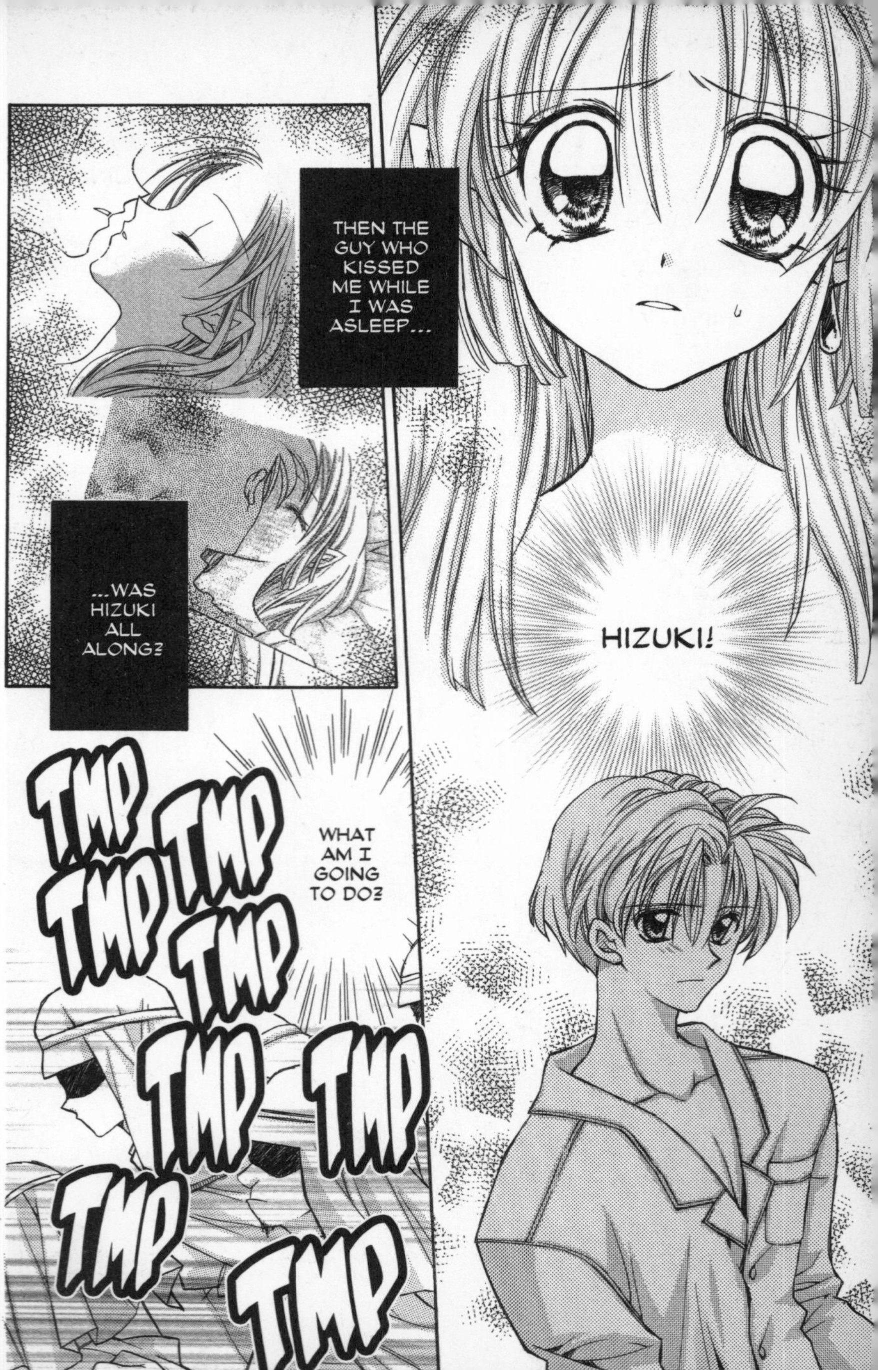
HIZUKI!
THEN THE GUY WHO KISSED ME WHILE I WAS ASLEEP...
...WAS HIZUKI ALL ALONG?
WHAT AM I GOING TO DO?
TMP TMP TMP TMP TMP TMP TMP TMP

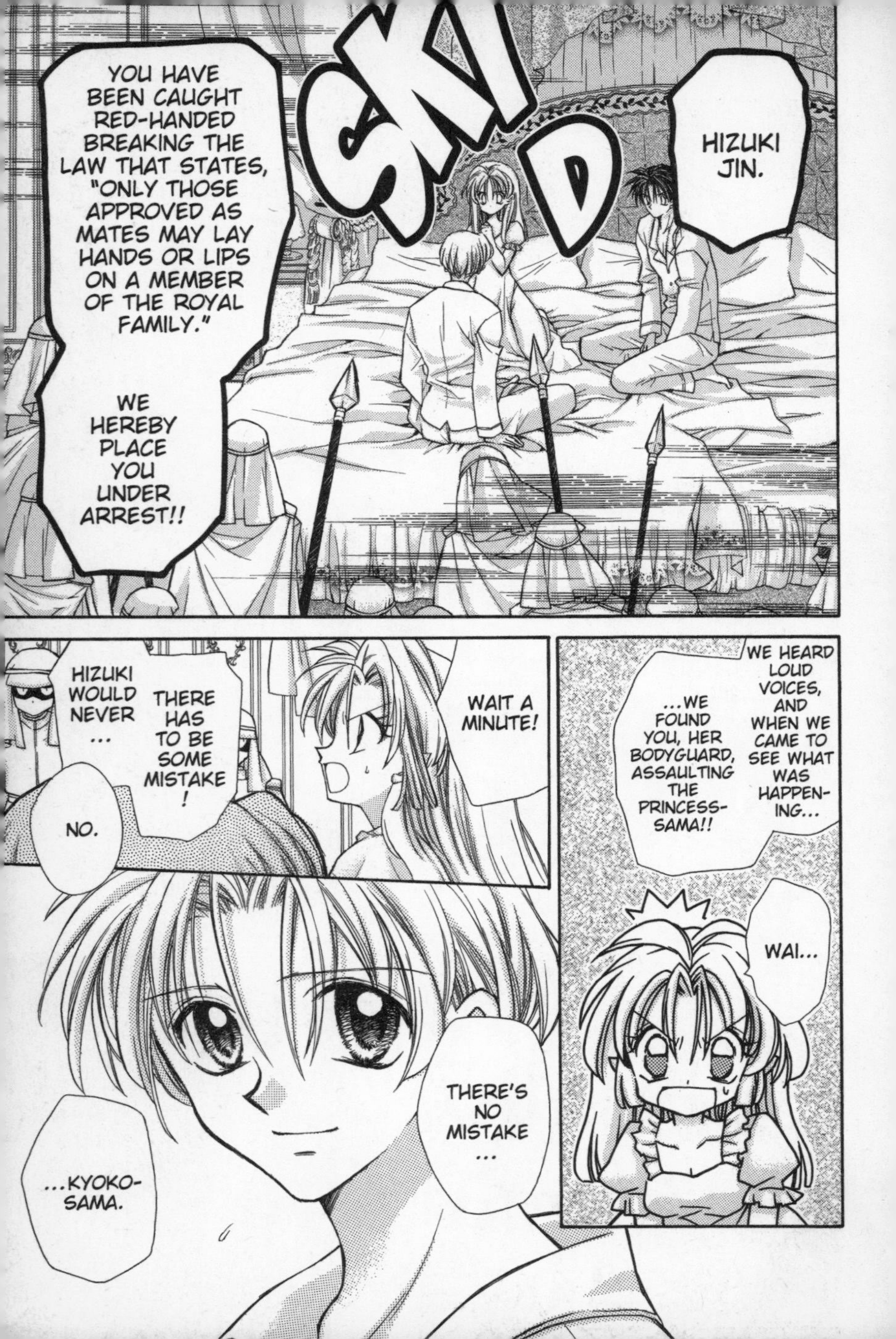
HIZUKI JIN.
YOU HAVE BEEN CAUGHT RED-HANDED BREAKING THE LAW THAT STATES, "ONLY THOSE APPROVED AS MATES MAY LAY HANDS OR LIPS ON A MEMBER OF THE ROYAL FAMILY."
WE HEREBY PLACE YOU UNDER ARREST!!
WE HEARD LOUD VOICES, AND WHEN WE CAME TO SEE WHAT WAS HAPPEN-ING...
...WE FOUND YOU, HER BODYGUARD, ASSAULTING THE PRINCESS-SAMA!!
WAI...
WAIT A MINUTE!
THERE HAS TO BE SOME MISTAKE!
HIZUKI WOULD NEVER...
NO.
THERE'S NO MISTAKE...
...KYOKO-SAMA.

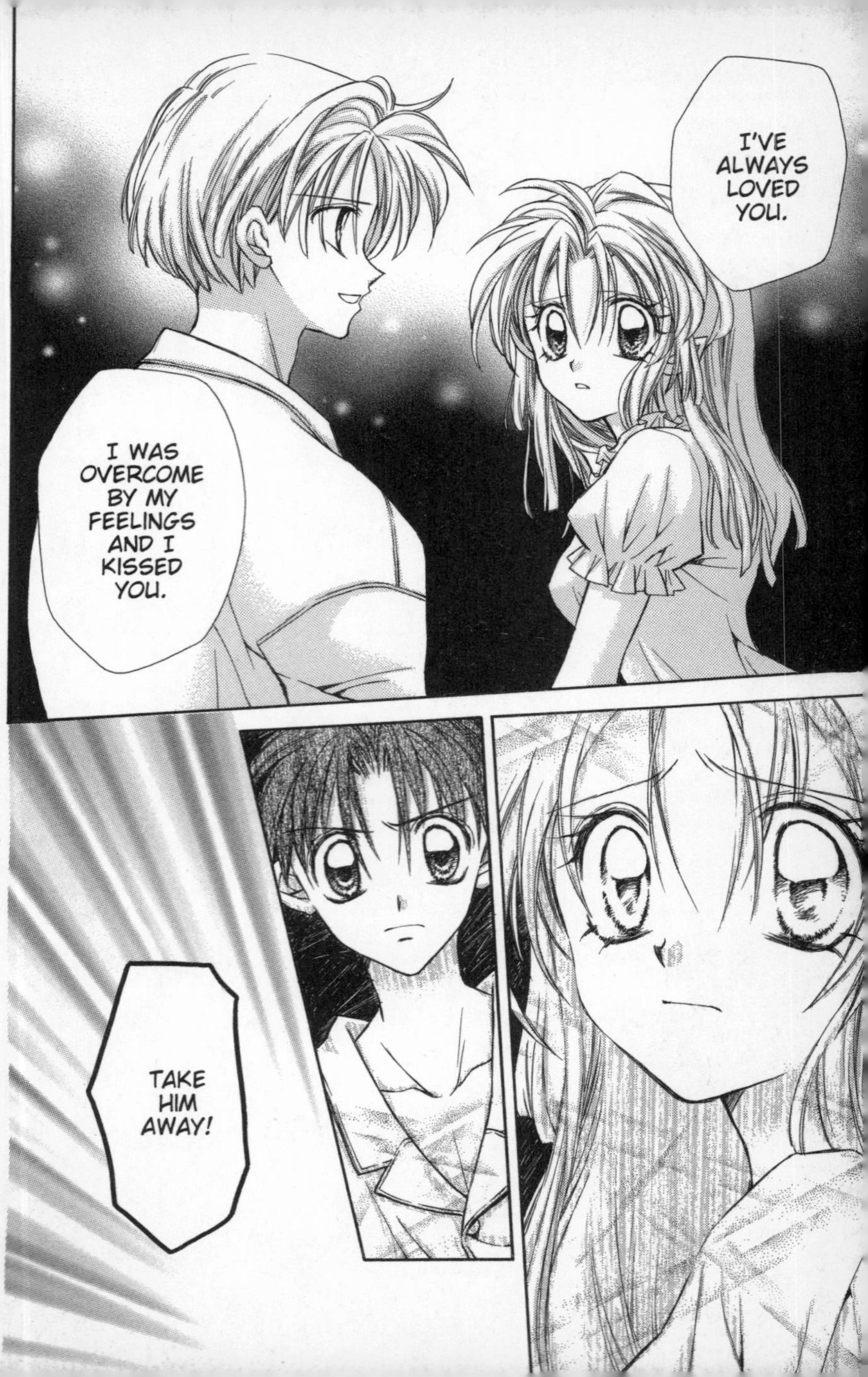
I'VE ALWAYS LOVED YOU.
I WAS OVERCOME BY MY FEELINGS AND I KISSED YOU.
TAKE HIM AWAY!

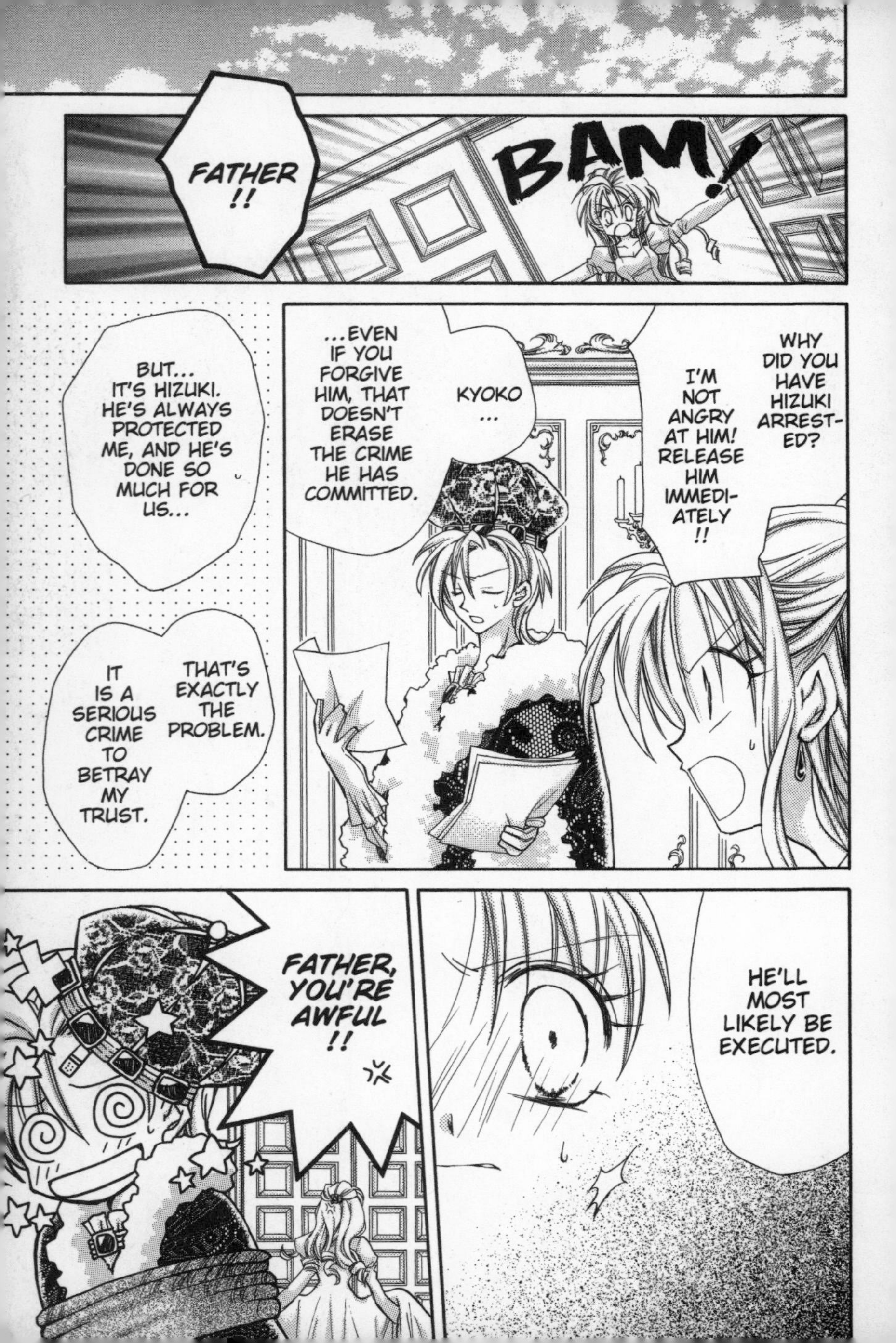
BAM!
FATHER !!
WHY DID YOU HAVE HIZUKI ARREST-ED?
I'M NOT ANGRY AT HIM! RELEASE HIM IMMEDI-ATELY !!
KYOKO ...
...EVEN IF YOU FORGIVE HIM, THAT DOESN'T ERASE THE CRIME HE HAS COMMITTED.
BUT... IT'S HIZUKI. HE'S ALWAYS PROTECTED ME, AND HE'S DONE SO MUCH FOR US...
THAT'S EXACTLY THE PROBLEM.
IT IS A SERIOUS CRIME TO BETRAY MY TRUST.
HE'LL MOST LIKELY BE EXECUTED.
FATHER, YOU'RE AWFUL !!

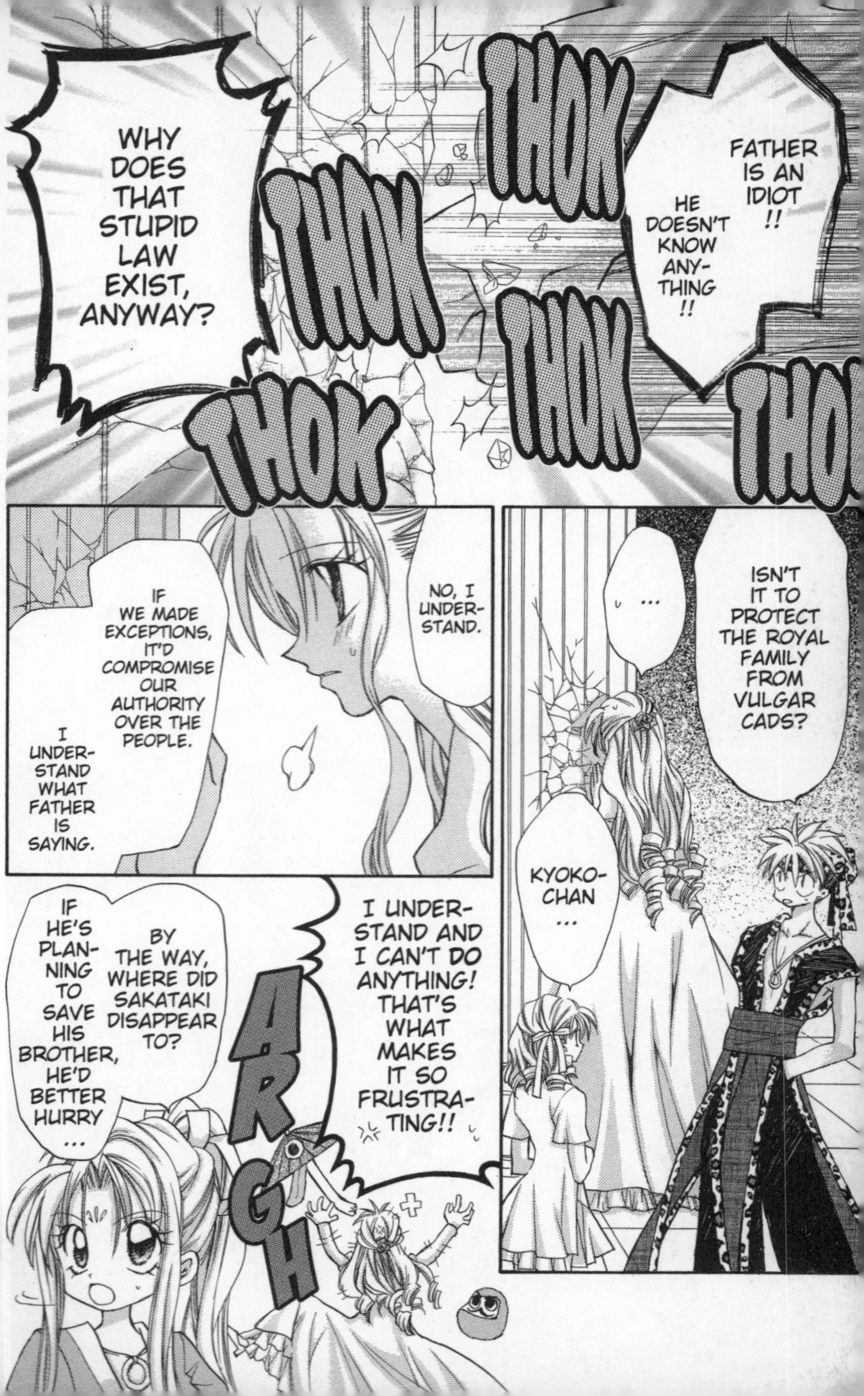
FATHER IS AN IDIOT!!
HE DOESN'T KNOW ANYTHING!!
THOK
THOK
THOK
THOK
THOK
WHY DOES THAT STUPID LAW EXIST, ANYWAY?
ISN'T IT TO PROTECT THE ROYAL FAMILY FROM VULGAR CADS?
...
KYOKO-CHAN...
NO, I UNDERSTAND.
IF WE MADE EXCEPTIONS, IT'D COMPROMISE OUR AUTHORITY OVER THE PEOPLE.
I UNDERSTAND WHAT FATHER IS SAYING.
I UNDERSTAND AND I CAN'T DO ANYTHING! THAT'S WHAT MAKES IT SO FRUSTRATING!!
ARGH
BY THE WAY, WHERE DID SAKATAKI DISAPPEAR TO?
IF HE'S PLANNING TO SAVE HIS BROTHER, HE'D BETTER HURRY...

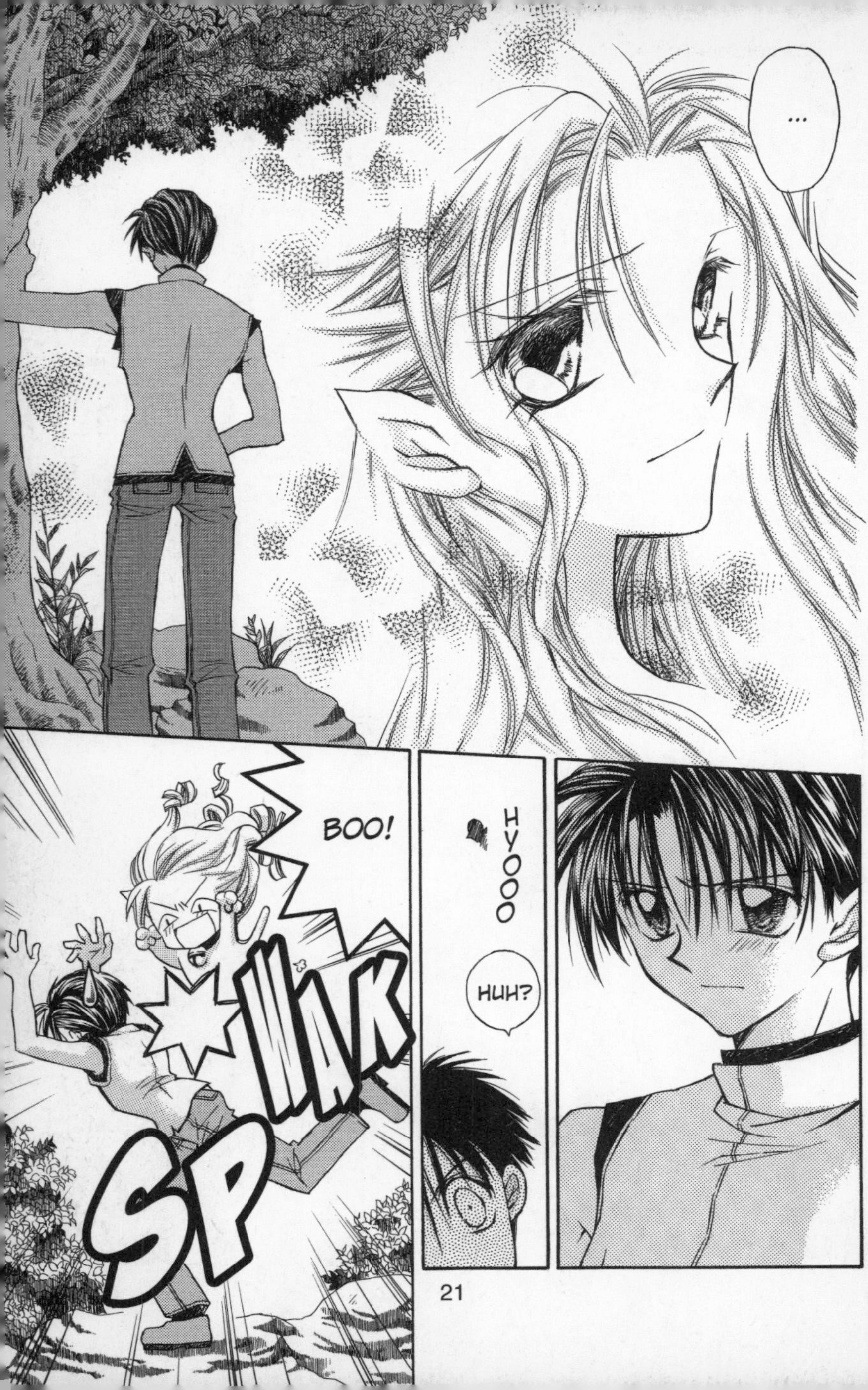
...
HYOOOO
HUH?
BOO!
SPWAK

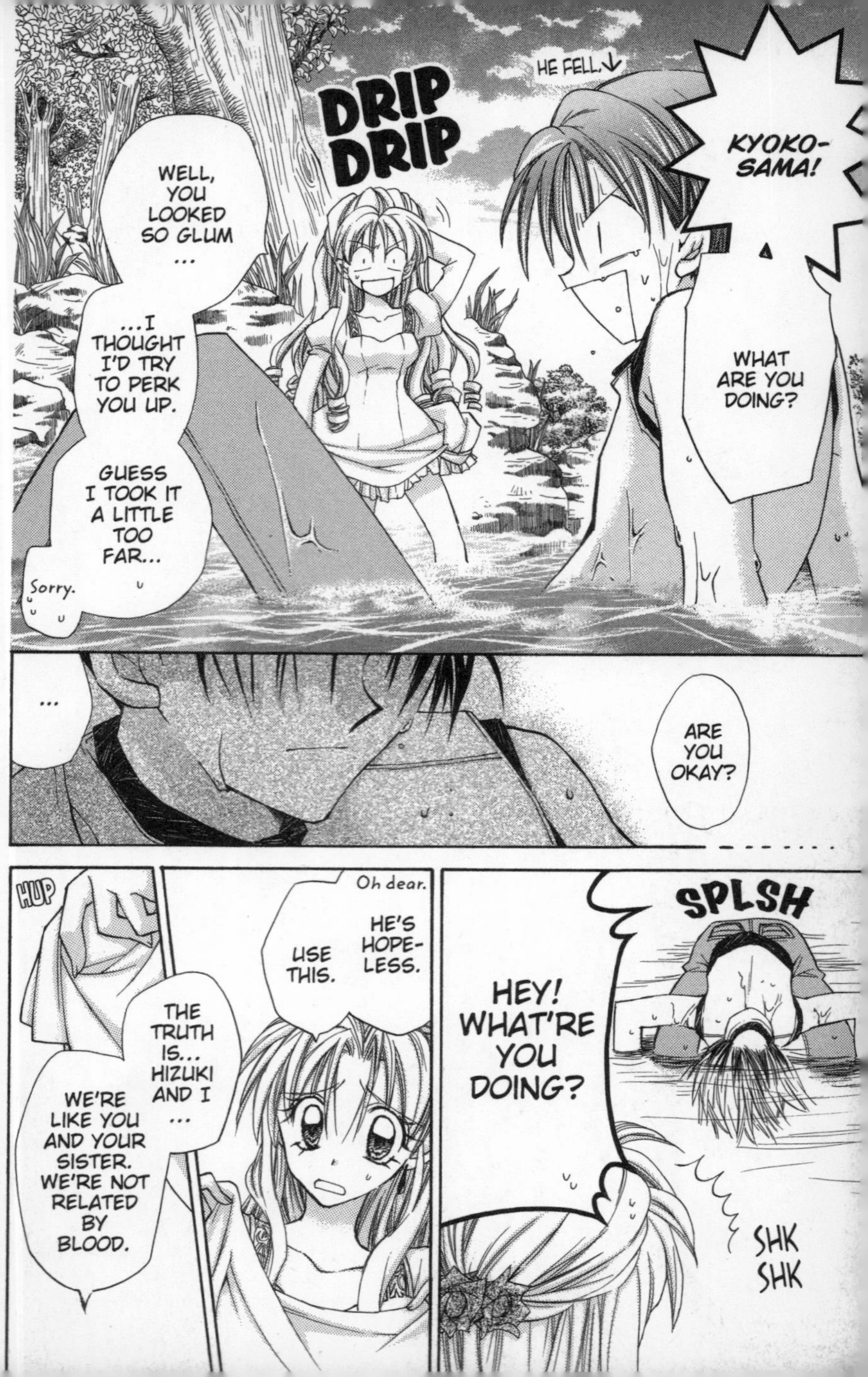
KYOKO-SAMA!
HE FELL.↓
DRIP DRIP
WHAT ARE YOU DOING?
WELL, YOU LOOKED SO GLUM ...
...I THOUGHT I'D TRY TO PERK YOU UP.
GUESS I TOOK IT A LITTLE TOO FAR...
Sorry.
ARE YOU OKAY?
...
SPLSH
HEY! WHAT'RE YOU DOING?
SHK SHK
Oh dear.
HE'S HOPE-LESS.
USE THIS.
THE TRUTH IS... HIZUKI AND I ...
WE'RE LIKE YOU AND YOUR SISTER. WE'RE NOT RELATED BY BLOOD.
HUP

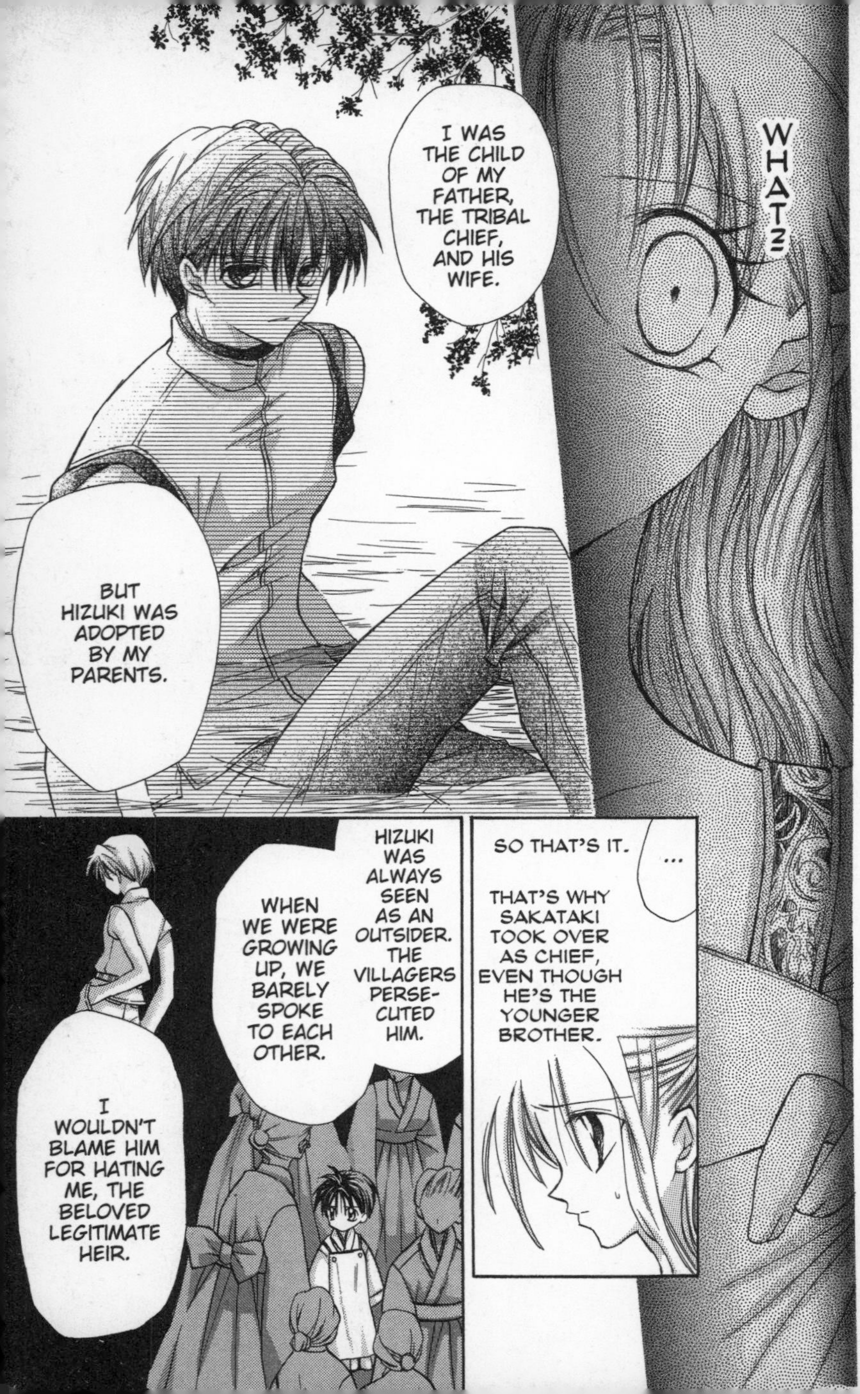
WHAT?
I WAS THE CHILD OF MY FATHER, THE TRIBAL CHIEF, AND HIS WIFE.
BUT HIZUKI WAS ADOPTED BY MY PARENTS.
...
SO THAT'S IT.
THAT'S WHY SAKATAKI TOOK OVER AS CHIEF, EVEN THOUGH HE'S THE YOUNGER BROTHER.
HIZUKI WAS ALWAYS SEEN AS AN OUTSIDER. THE VILLAGERS PERSE-CUTED HIM.
WHEN WE WERE GROWING UP, WE BARELY SPOKE TO EACH OTHER.
I WOULDN'T BLAME HIM FOR HATING ME, THE BELOVED LEGITIMATE HEIR.

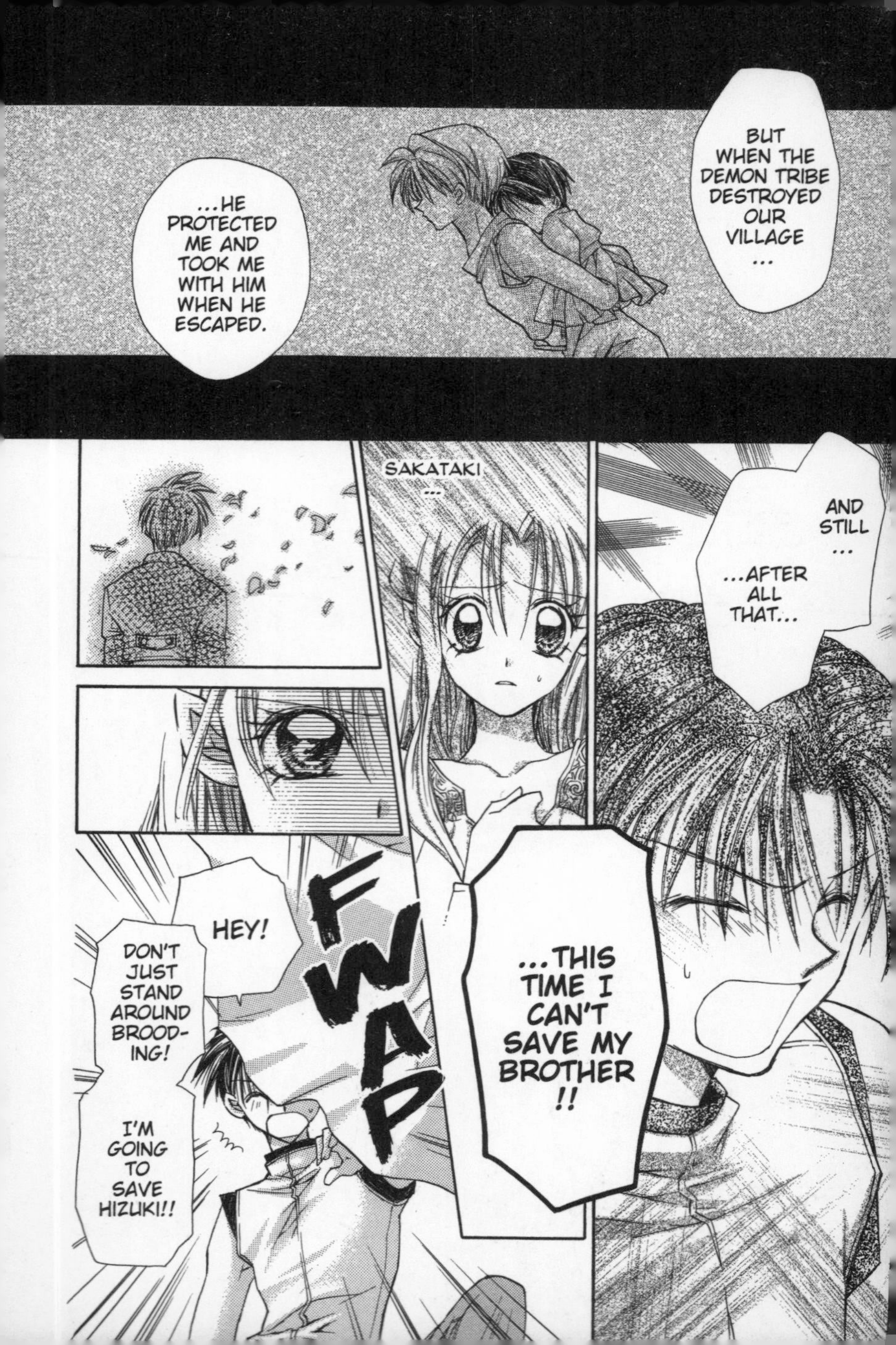
BUT WHEN THE DEMON TRIBE DESTROYED OUR VILLAGE ...
...HE PROTECTED ME AND TOOK ME WITH HIM WHEN HE ESCAPED.
AND STILL ...
...AFTER ALL THAT...
...THIS TIME I CAN'T SAVE MY BROTHER !!
SAKATAKI ...
HEY!
FWAP
DON'T JUST STAND AROUND BROOD-ING!
I'M GOING TO SAVE HIZUKI!!

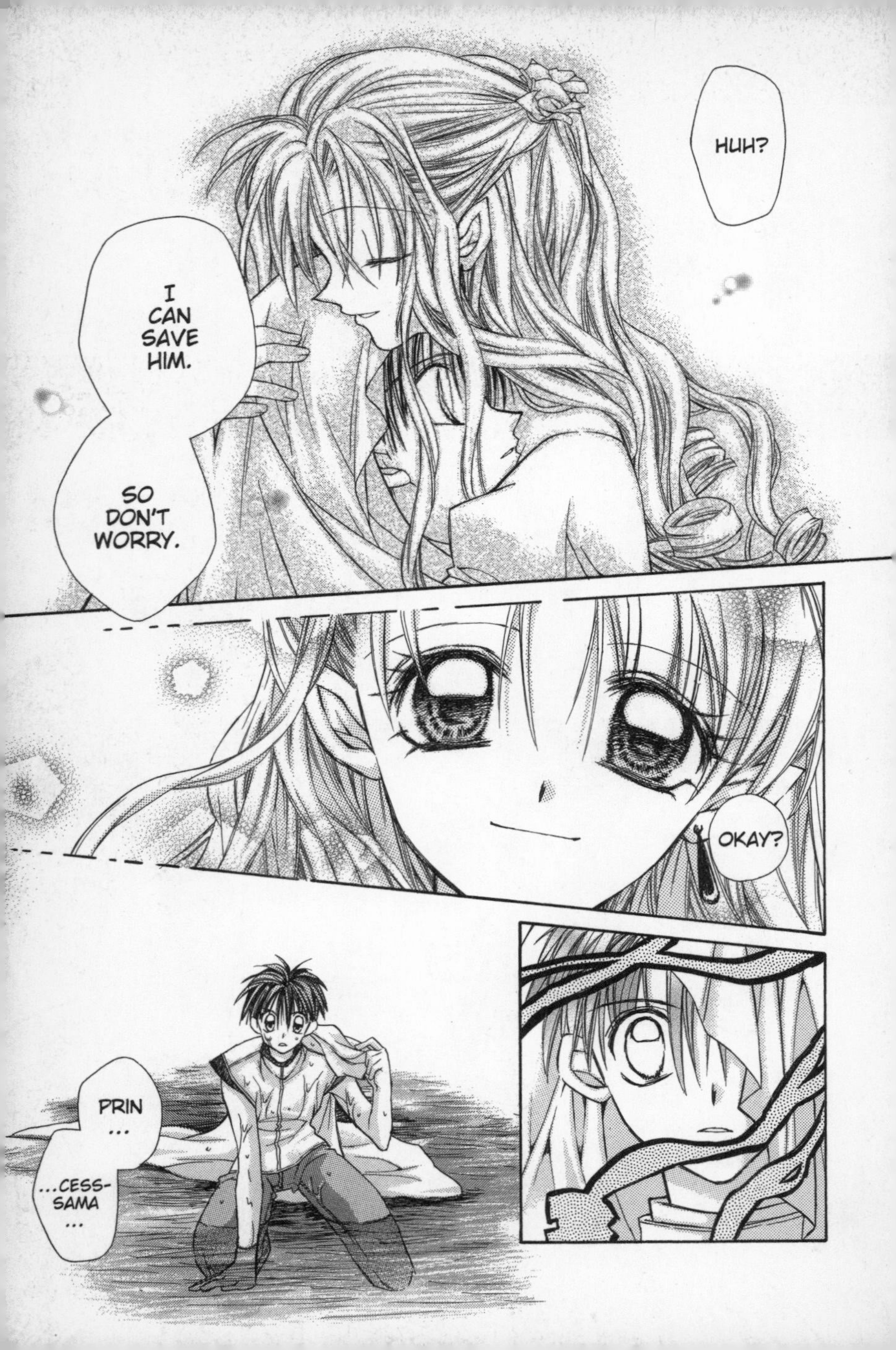
HUH?
I CAN SAVE HIM.
SO DON'T WORRY.
OKAY?
PRIN ...
...CESS-SAMA ...

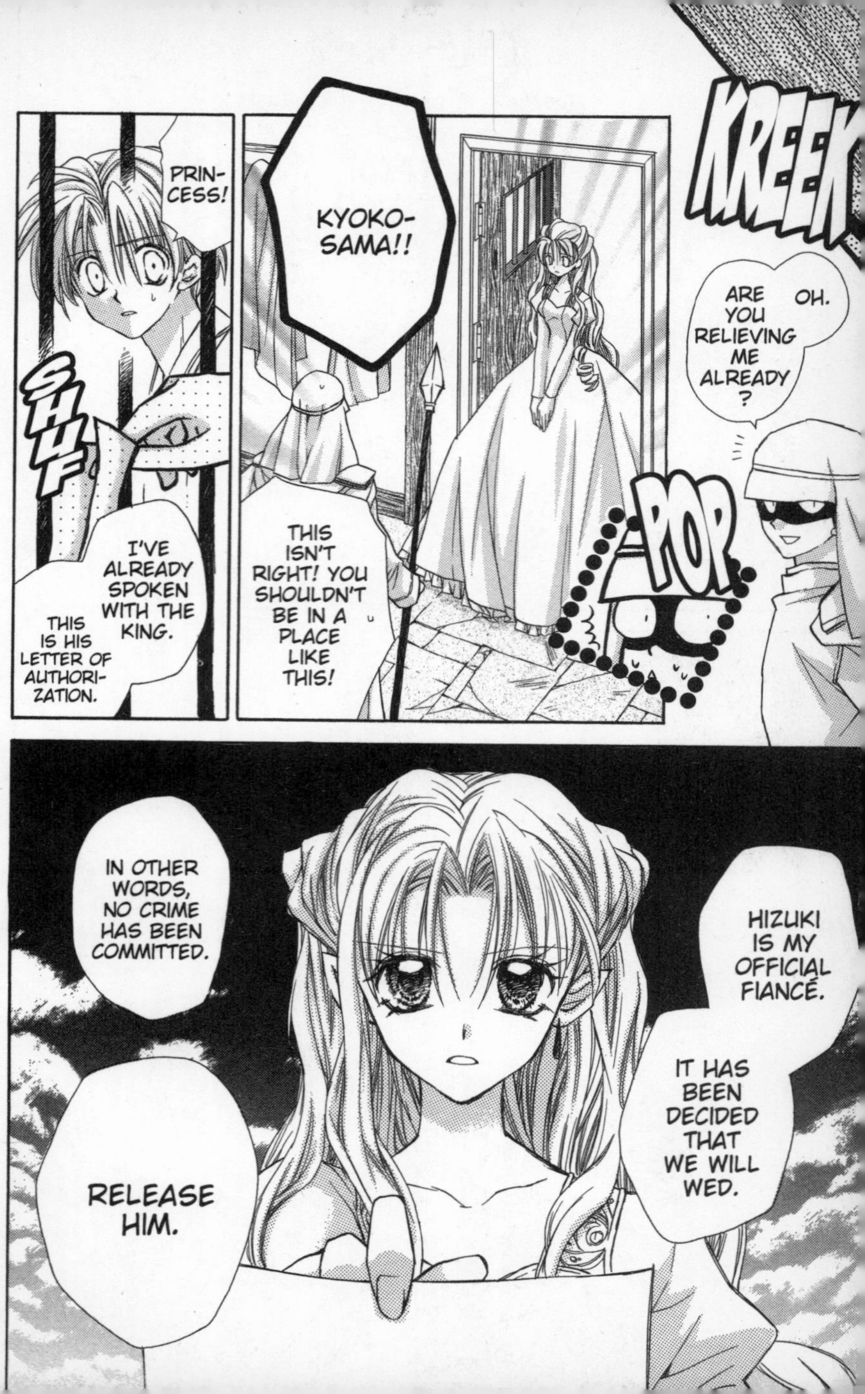
KREEK
OH. ARE YOU RELIEVING ME ALREADY?
POP
KYOKO-SAMA!!
THIS ISN'T RIGHT! YOU SHOULDN'T BE IN A PLACE LIKE THIS!
PRIN-CESS!
SHUF
I'VE ALREADY SPOKEN WITH THE KING.
THIS IS HIS LETTER OF AUTHORI-ZATION.
HIZUKI IS MY OFFICIAL FIANCÉ.
IT HAS BEEN DECIDED THAT WE WILL WED.
IN OTHER WORDS, NO CRIME HAS BEEN COMMITTED.
RELEASE HIM.

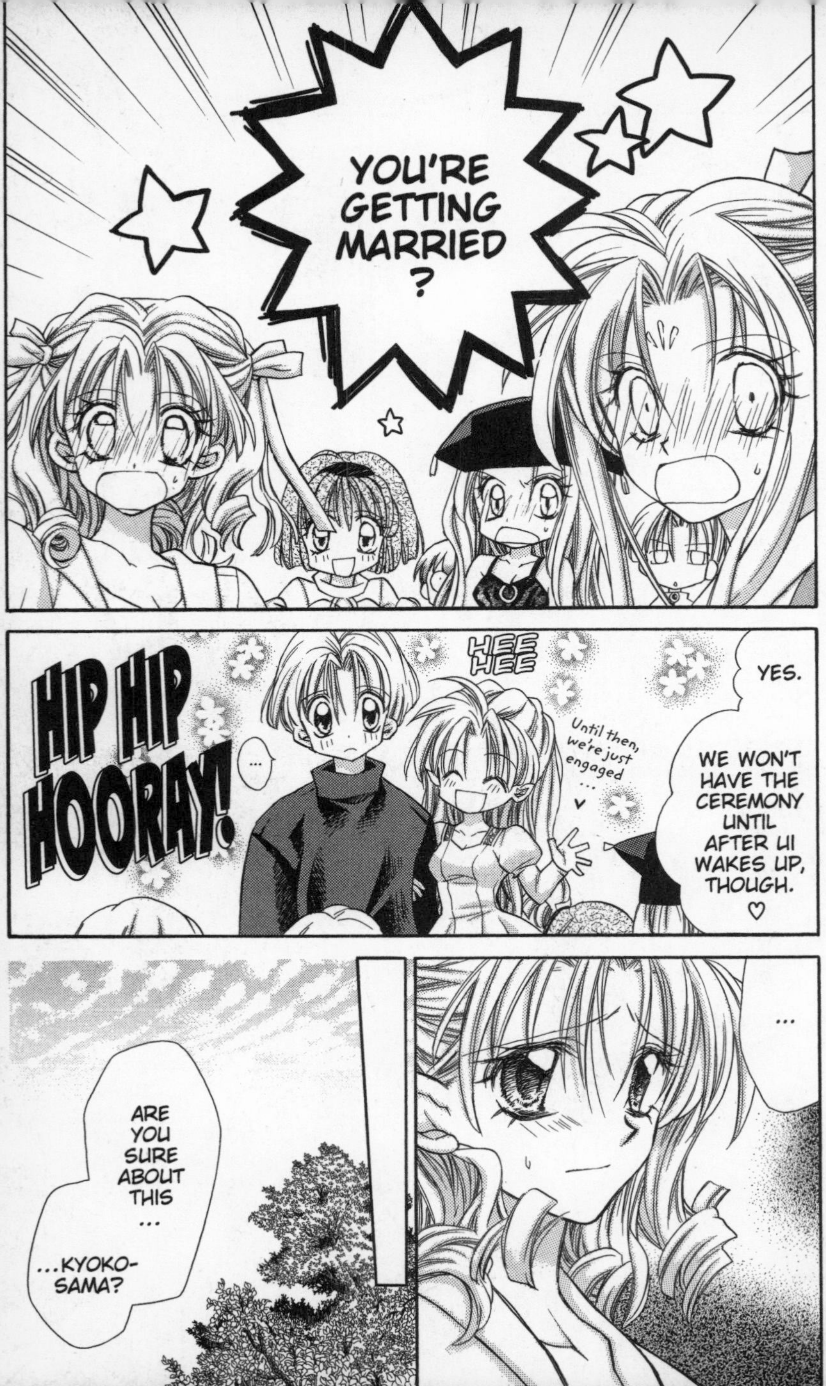
YOU'RE GETTING MARRIED?
YES.
WE WON'T HAVE THE CEREMONY UNTIL AFTER UI WAKES UP, THOUGH. ♡
HEE HEE
Until then, we're just engaged... ♥
...
HIP HIP HOORAY!
...
ARE YOU SURE ABOUT THIS...
...KYOKO-SAMA?

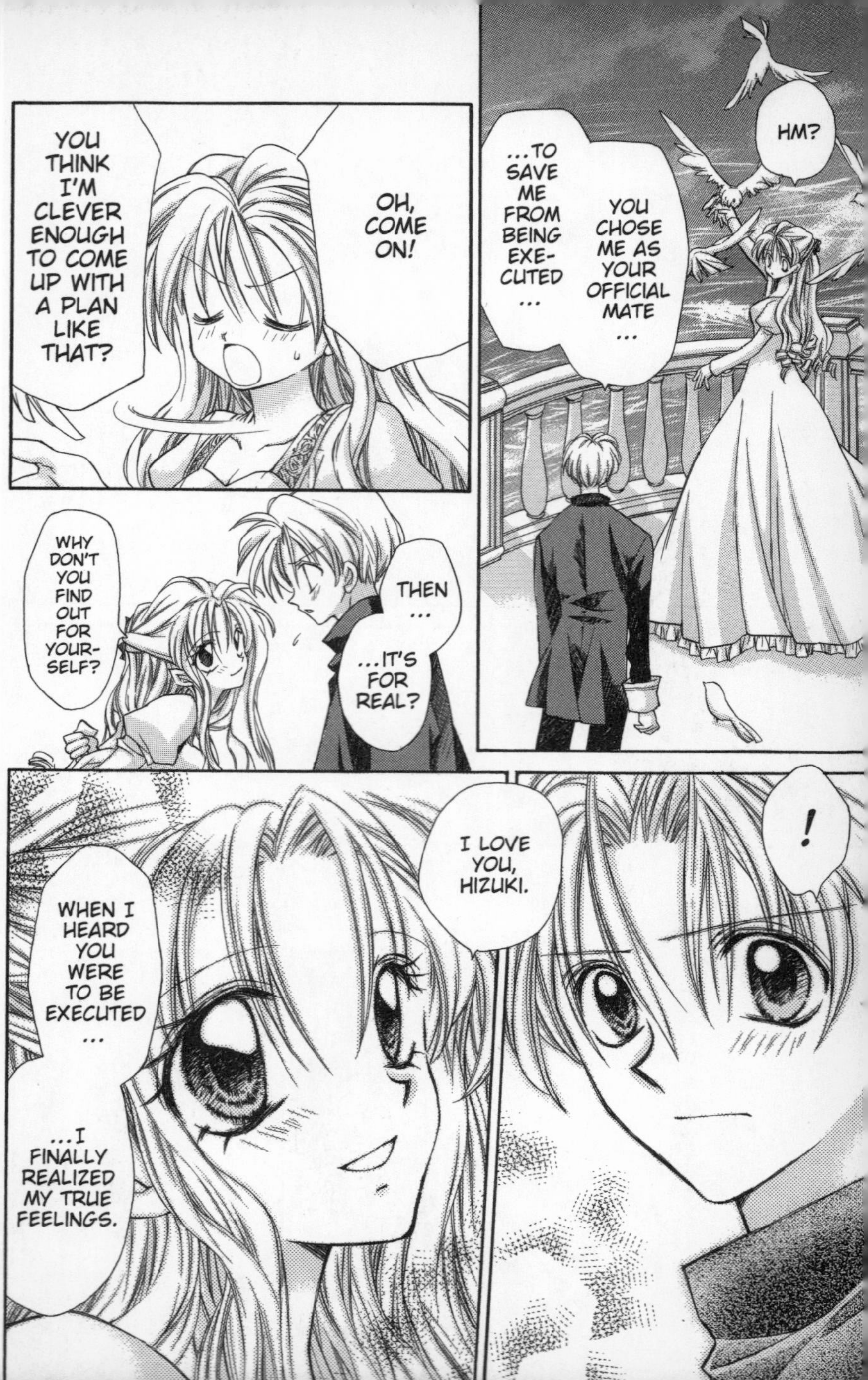
HM?
YOU CHOSE ME AS YOUR OFFICIAL MATE...
...TO SAVE ME FROM BEING EXE-CUTED...
OH, COME ON!
YOU THINK I'M CLEVER ENOUGH TO COME UP WITH A PLAN LIKE THAT?
THEN...
...IT'S FOR REAL?
WHY DON'T YOU FIND OUT FOR YOUR-SELF?
!
I LOVE YOU, HIZUKI.
WHEN I HEARD YOU WERE TO BE EXECUTED...
...I FINALLY REALIZED MY TRUE FEELINGS.

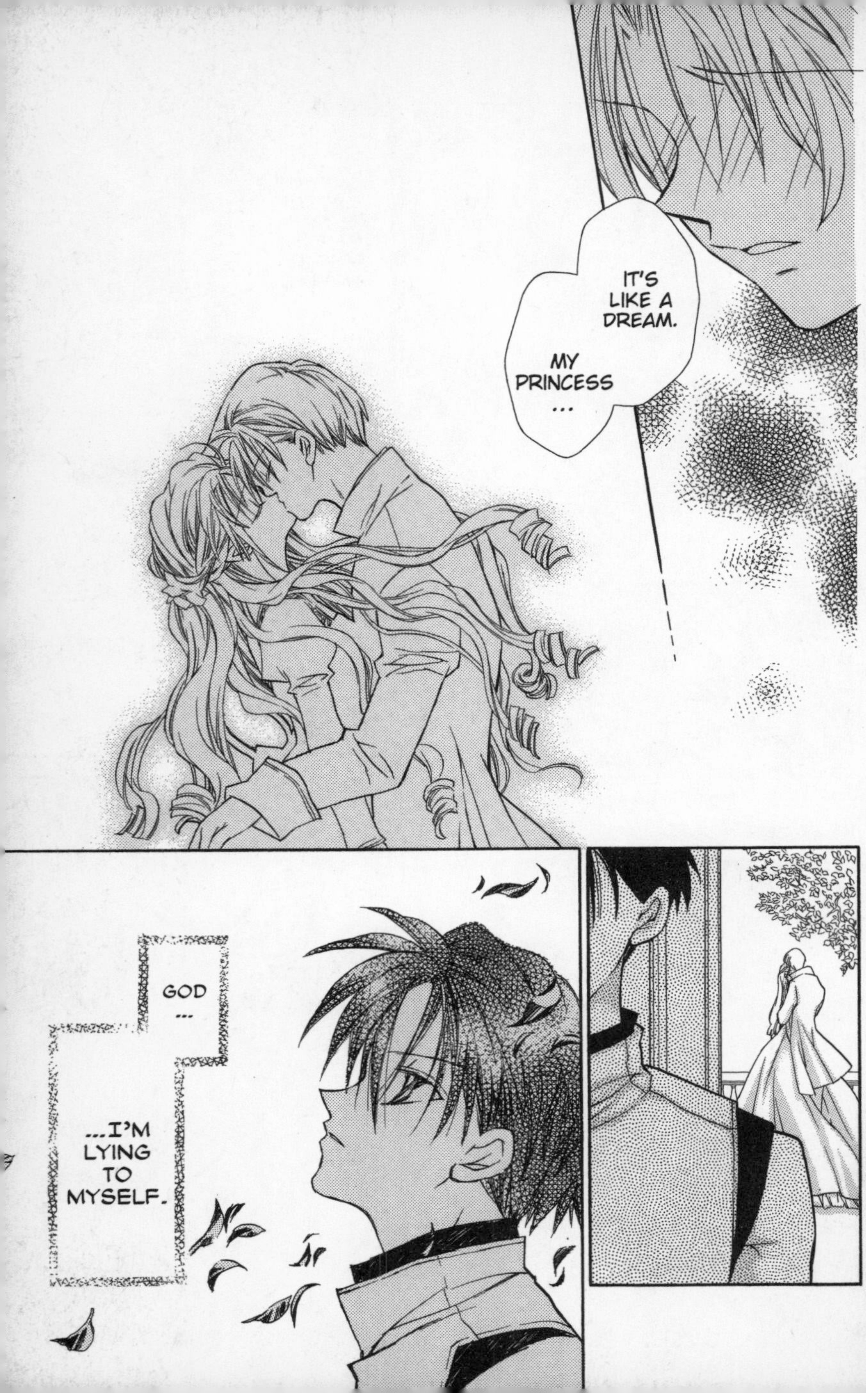
IT'S LIKE A DREAM.
MY PRINCESS...
GOD...
...I'M LYING TO MYSELF.

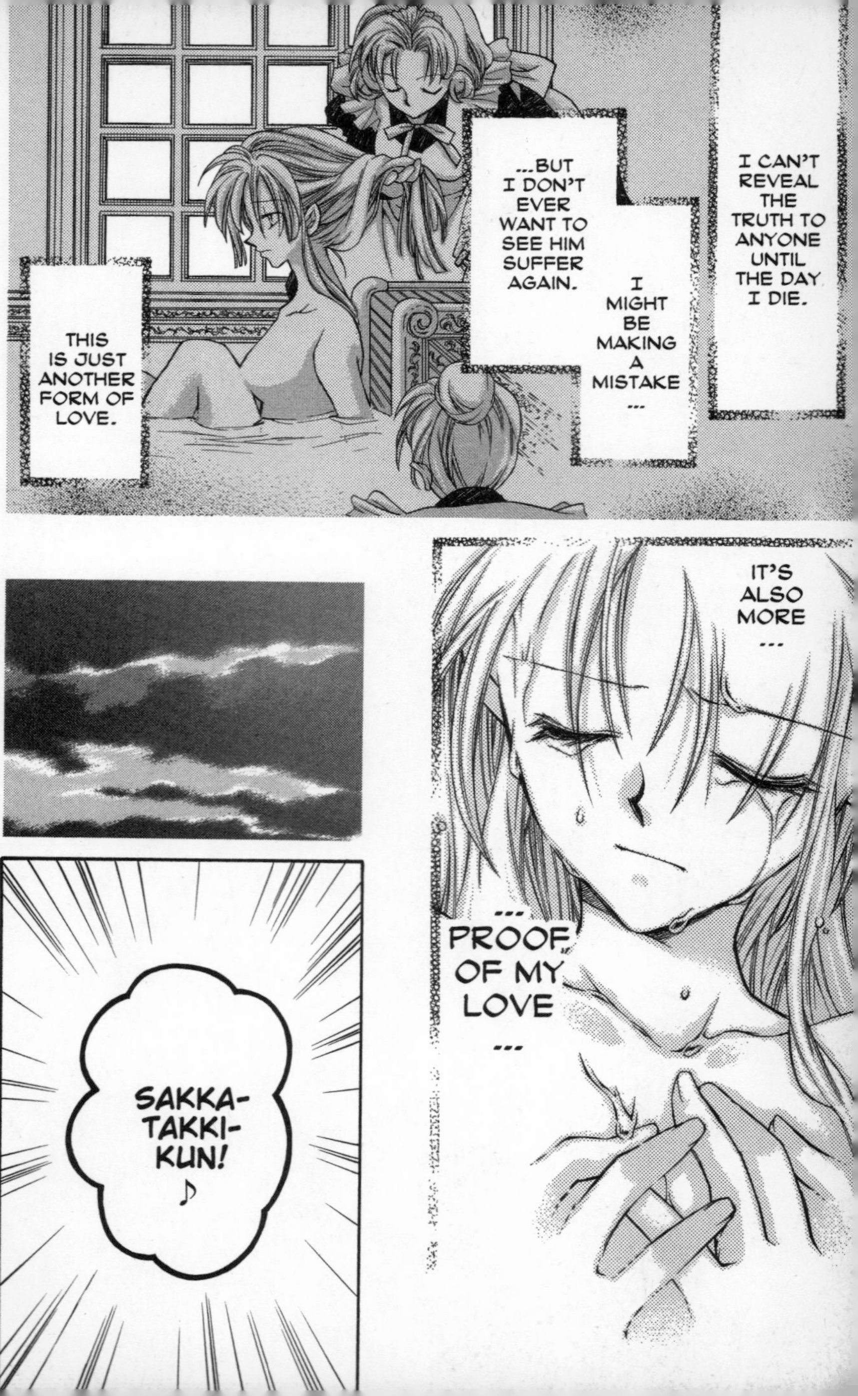
I CAN'T REVEAL THE TRUTH TO ANYONE UNTIL THE DAY I DIE.
I MIGHT BE MAKING A MISTAKE...
...BUT I DON'T EVER WANT TO SEE HIM SUFFER AGAIN.
THIS IS JUST ANOTHER FORM OF LOVE.
IT'S ALSO MORE...
...PROOF OF MY LOVE...
SAKKA-TAKKI-KUN! ♪

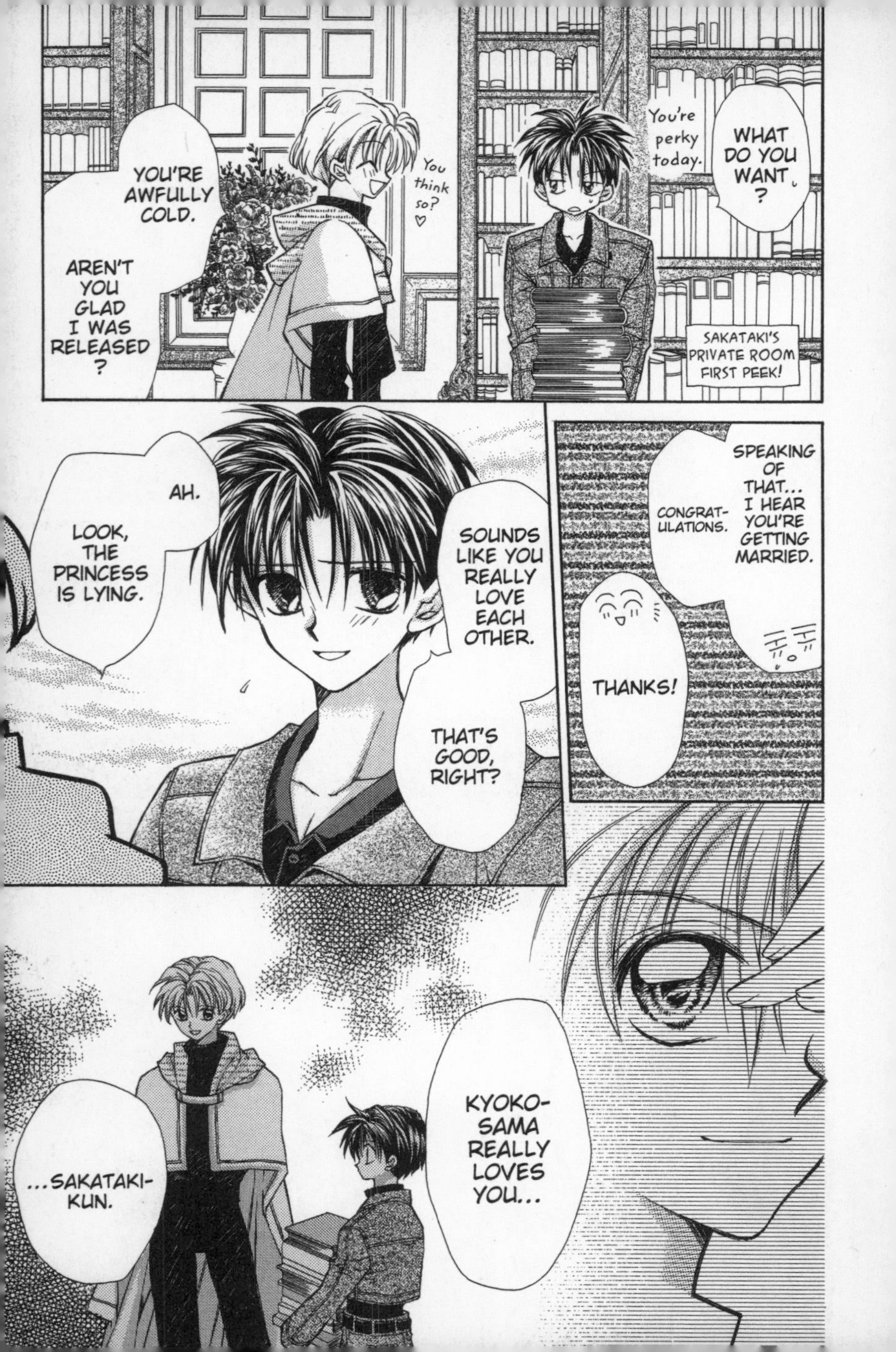
WHAT DO YOU WANT?
You're perky today.
SAKATAKI'S PRIVATE ROOM FIRST PEEK!
You think so? ♡
YOU'RE AWFULLY COLD.
AREN'T YOU GLAD I WAS RELEASED?
SPEAKING OF THAT... I HEAR YOU'RE GETTING MARRIED.
CONGRATULATIONS.
THANKS!
SOUNDS LIKE YOU REALLY LOVE EACH OTHER.
THAT'S GOOD, RIGHT?
AH.
LOOK, THE PRINCESS IS LYING.
KYOKO-SAMA REALLY LOVES YOU...
...SAKATAKI-KUN.

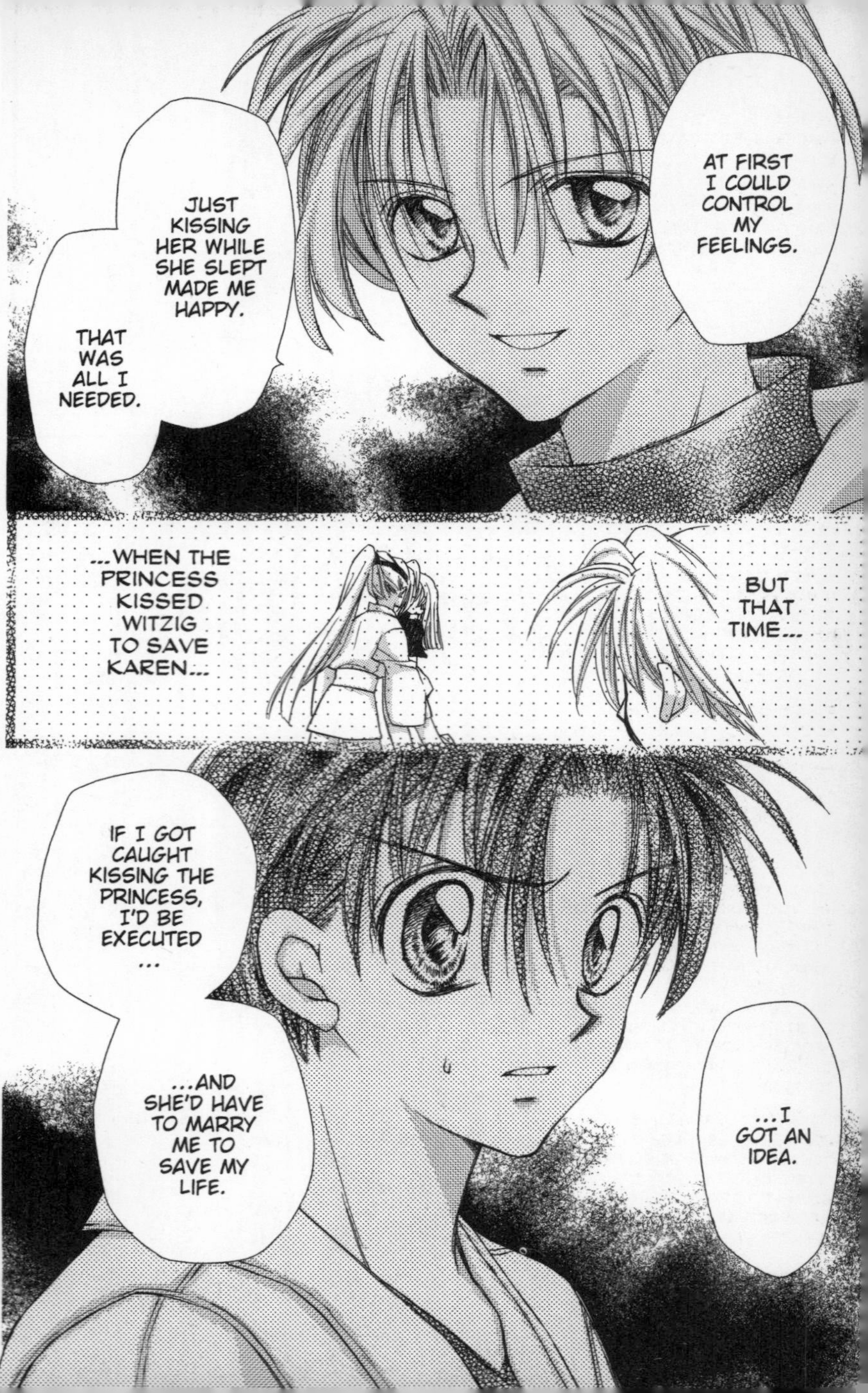
AT FIRST I COULD CONTROL MY FEELINGS.
JUST KISSING HER WHILE SHE SLEPT MADE ME HAPPY.
THAT WAS ALL I NEEDED.
BUT THAT TIME...
...WHEN THE PRINCESS KISSED WITZIG TO SAVE KAREN...
...I GOT AN IDEA.
IF I GOT CAUGHT KISSING THE PRINCESS, I'D BE EXECUTED...
...AND SHE'D HAVE TO MARRY ME TO SAVE MY LIFE.

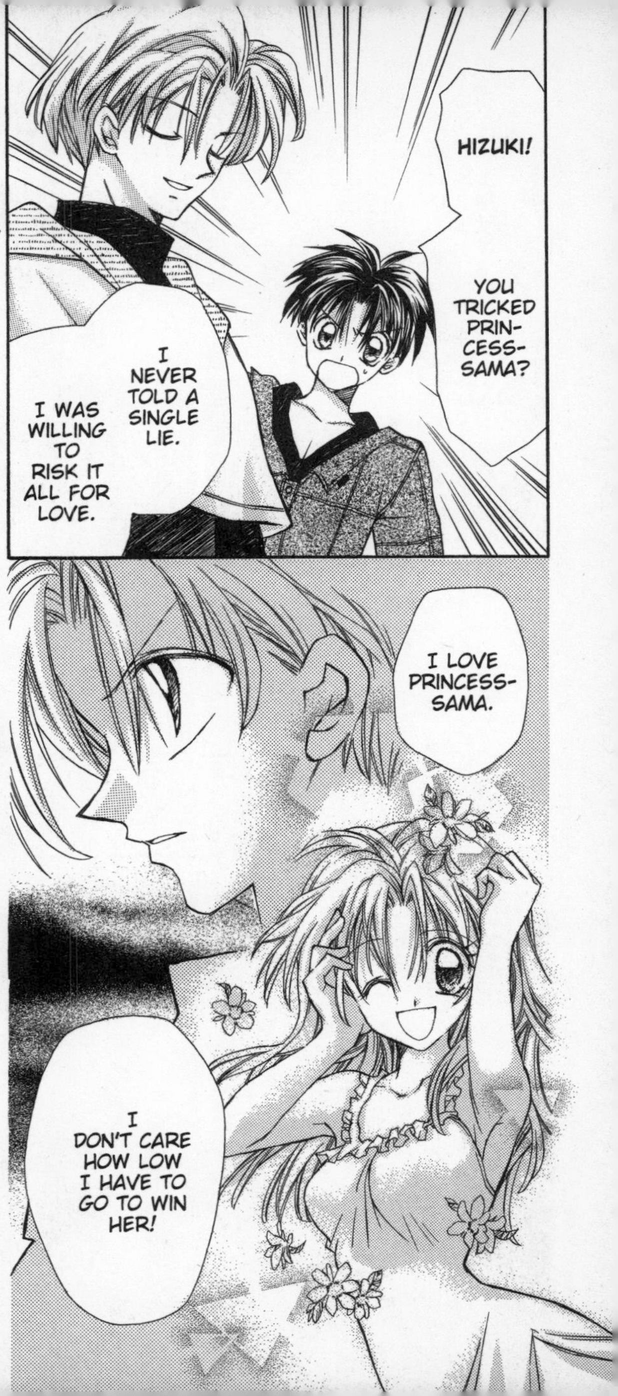
HIZUKI!
YOU TRICKED PRINCESS-SAMA?
I NEVER TOLD A SINGLE LIE.
I WAS WILLING TO RISK IT ALL FOR LOVE.
I LOVE PRINCESS-SAMA.
I DON'T CARE HOW LOW I HAVE TO GO TO WIN HER!

HELLO.

HI! ARINA HERE! THANK YOU FOR READING *TIME STRANGER KYOKO* VOLUME 3.

THE COVER ILLUSTRATION IS A POSTER I DREW TO MEMORIALIZE THE BIG FINALE. (TWELVE PEOPLE... THAT'S A LOT TO DRAW.) BY THE WAY, I FIRST DREW KYOKO-CHAN IN MY SECOND OR THIRD YEAR OF JUNIOR HIGH. THE KYOKO-CHAN OF TODAY IS BASED ON THOSE DRAWINGS.

WELL, WITH THIS VOLUME, *KYOKO* IS FINISHED. AT THE TIME I STARTED THIS SERIES, I HAD A LOT OF PSYCHOLOGICAL PROBLEMS, AND I WAS UNABLE TO CONCENTRATE ON MY MANGA. THEREFORE, I COULDN'T PLOT IT AS CAREFULLY AS I WOULD HAVE LIKED. I'M BEING COMPLETELY HONEST HERE.

SOMETIMES I WASN'T SURE HOW IT WAS GOING TO TURN OUT. I THINK ALL MY WORRYING PROBABLY HAD AN EFFECT ON THE FINISHED PRODUCT.

That's a weird way to put it...

FRANKLY, I DECIDED IT WAS WRONG TO CONTINUE THE SERIES, SO I ASKED MY EDITORS TO LET ME END IT.

Think of me as a potter who destroys pot after pot until she makes a perfect one.

MY EDITORS SEEMED TO UNDERSTAND, AND THEY GAVE IN WITHOUT TOO MUCH RESISTANCE. I'M THE KIND OF PERSON WHO CAN'T HESITATE ONCE I'VE DECIDED ON SOMETHING. ONCE IT WAS AGREED THAT I'D END THE SERIES, I WANTED TO END IT RIGHT AWAY, WHICH CAUSED PROBLEMS FOR A LOT OF PEOPLE. I WOULD LIKE TO APOLOGIZE TO THEM.

HOWEVER, I WAS ABLE TO RECUPERATE (IT HELPED THAT *KYOKO* WASN'T A VERY STRESSFUL COMIC TO DRAW), AND I'M GOING TO ATTACK MY NEW SERIES WITH ENERGY, SO PLEASE READ IT!

IT'S STARTING IN THIS MONTH'S ISSUE OF *RIBON* IN JAPAN.

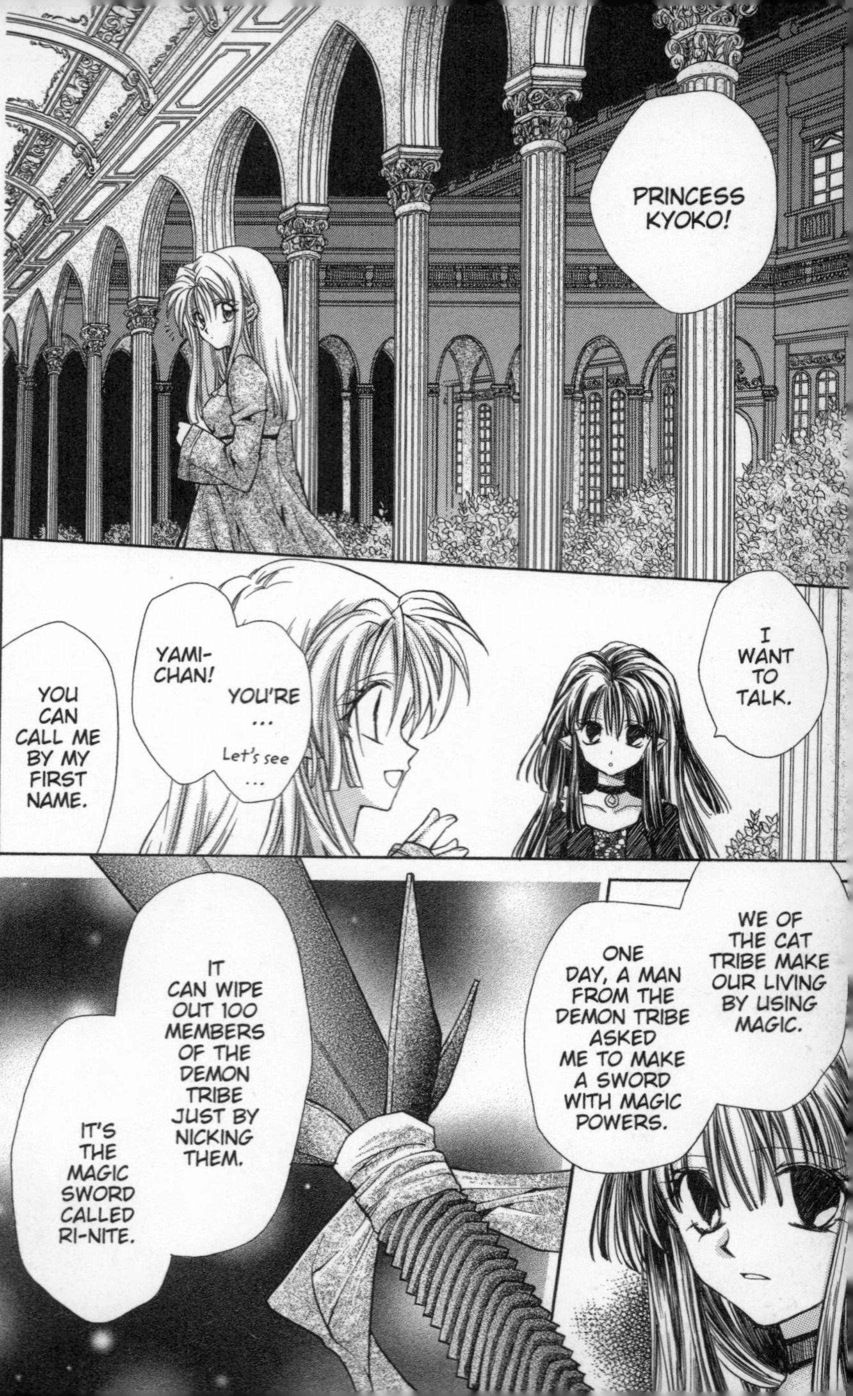
PRINCESS KYOKO!
I WANT TO TALK.
YAMI-CHAN!
YOU'RE ... Let's see ...
YOU CAN CALL ME BY MY FIRST NAME.
WE OF THE CAT TRIBE MAKE OUR LIVING BY USING MAGIC.
ONE DAY, A MAN FROM THE DEMON TRIBE ASKED ME TO MAKE A SWORD WITH MAGIC POWERS.
IT CAN WIPE OUT 100 MEMBERS OF THE DEMON TRIBE JUST BY NICKING THEM.
IT'S THE MAGIC SWORD CALLED RI-NITE.

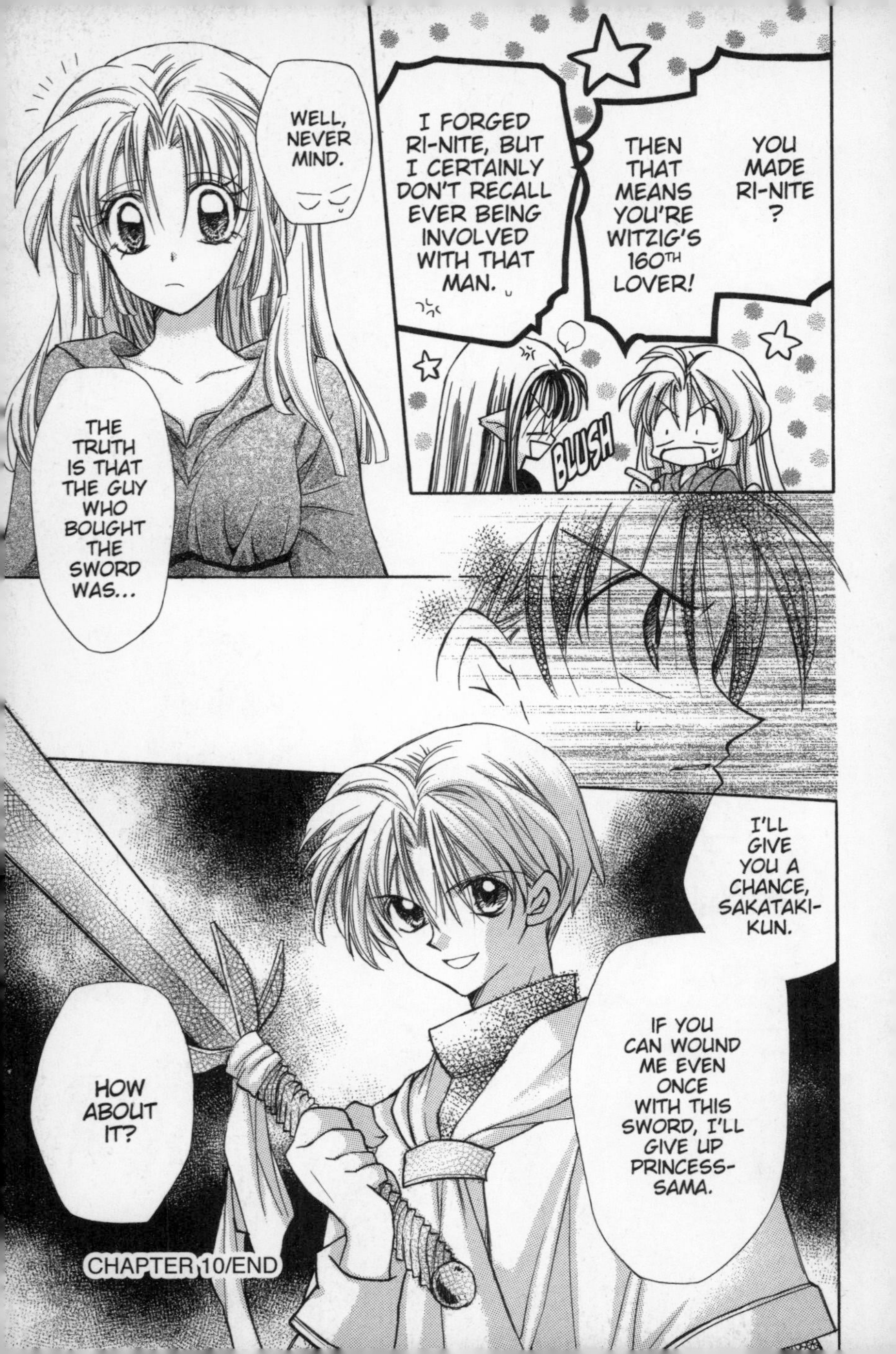
YOU MADE RI-NITE?
THEN THAT MEANS YOU'RE WITZIG'S 160TH LOVER!
I FORGED RI-NITE, BUT I CERTAINLY DON'T RECALL EVER BEING INVOLVED WITH THAT MAN.
BLUSH
WELL, NEVER MIND.
THE TRUTH IS THAT THE GUY WHO BOUGHT THE SWORD WAS...
I'LL GIVE YOU A CHANCE, SAKATAKI-KUN.
IF YOU CAN WOUND ME EVEN ONCE WITH THIS SWORD, I'LL GIVE UP PRINCESS-SAMA.
HOW ABOUT IT?
CHAPTER 10/END

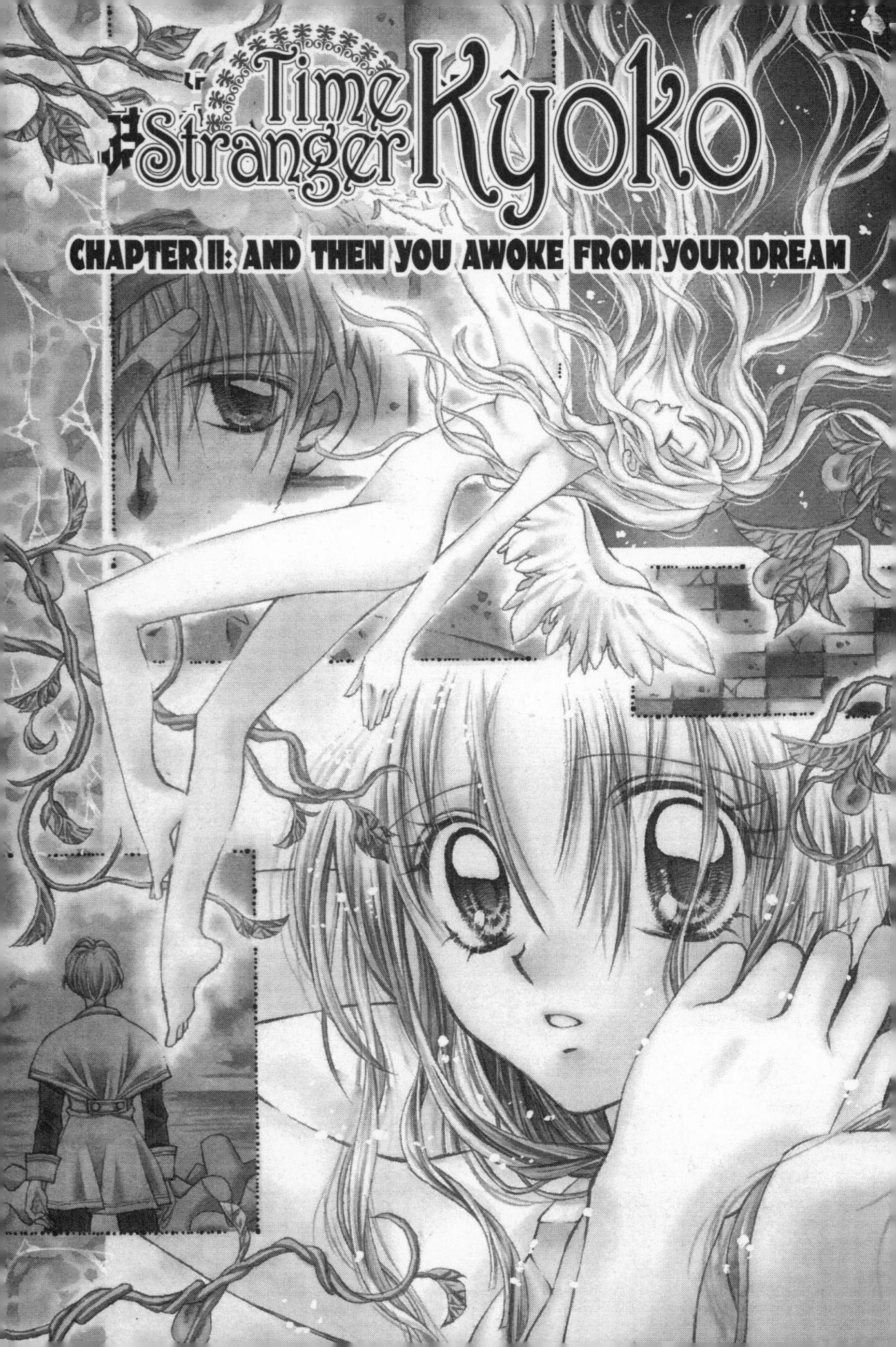
Time Stranger Kyôko
CHAPTER 11: AND THEN YOU AWOKE FROM YOUR DREAM

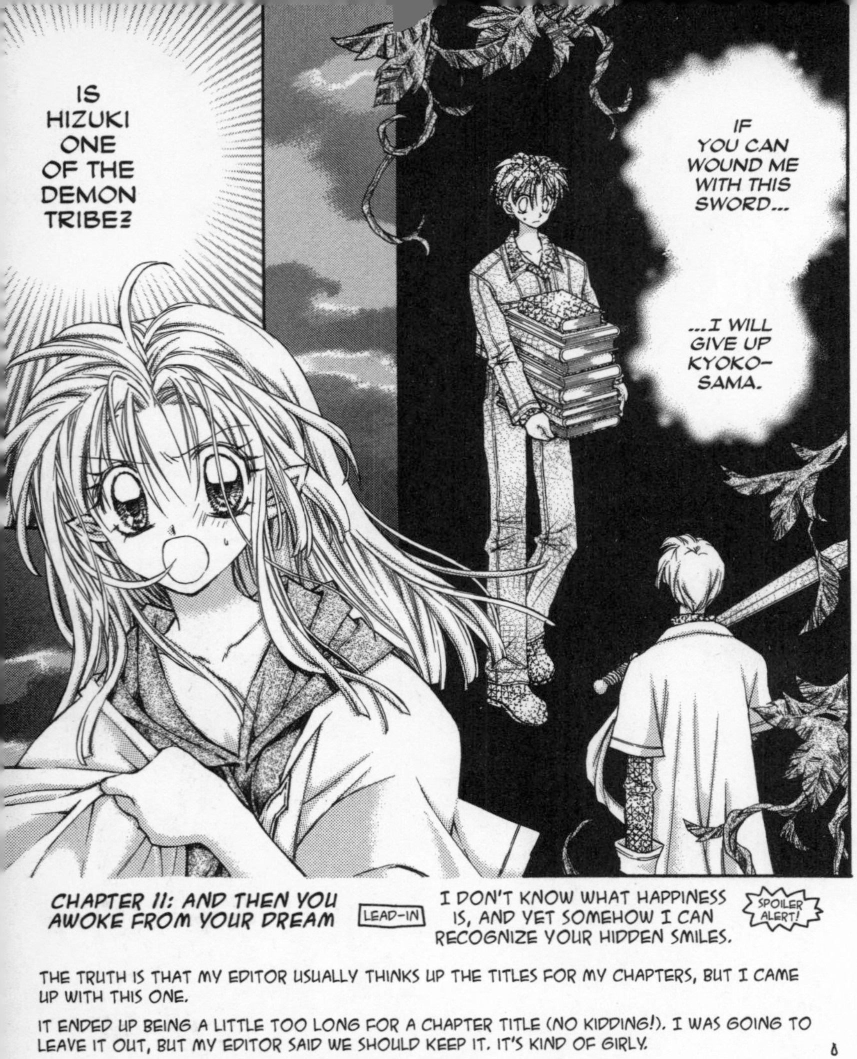
IF YOU CAN WOUND ME WITH THIS SWORD...
...I WILL GIVE UP KYOKO-SAMA.
IS HIZUKI ONE OF THE DEMON TRIBE?

CHAPTER 11: AND THEN YOU AWOKE FROM YOUR DREAM

LEAD-IN I DON'T KNOW WHAT HAPPINESS IS, AND YET SOMEHOW I CAN RECOGNIZE YOUR HIDDEN SMILES. SPOILER ALERT!

THE TRUTH IS THAT MY EDITOR USUALLY THINKS UP THE TITLES FOR MY CHAPTERS, BUT I CAME UP WITH THIS ONE.

IT ENDED UP BEING A LITTLE TOO LONG FOR A CHAPTER TITLE (NO KIDDING!). I WAS GOING TO LEAVE IT OUT, BUT MY EDITOR SAID WE SHOULD KEEP IT. IT'S KIND OF GIRLY.

BUT I REALLY LIKE THE REAL TITLE ↑. IT MEANS THAT UI'S SITUATION AND KYOKO-CHAN'S DREAM-LIKE LIFE ARE BOTH COMING TO AN END.

WITH THE TITLE PAGE ILLUSTRATION, I WAS HOPING TO EXPRESS ALL THOSE COMPLEX FEELINGS... OKAY, BACK TO THE STORY. READING IT OVER AGAIN NOW, I FIND IT REALLY INTERESTING. (SUCH COMPOSURE!) FRANKLY, I DON'T USUALLY READ MY OWN MANGA CRITICALLY, AND I'M SURE SOME PEOPLE WILL THINK IT'S ODD FOR ME TO TALK ABOUT MY WORK LIKE THIS. OH WELL. AT LEAST I WAS SOMEHOW ABLE TO GET ACROSS WHAT I'D HOPED TO EXPRESS.

FOR THIS CHAPTER IN PARTICULAR, I HAVE TO SAY, "VIVA ASANO KAKA!!" THANKS FOR THE MANY GREAT BACKGROUNDS!! YOU'RE GREAT! WHEN YOU FIRST CAME HERE AS AN ASSISTANT, ALL YOU DID WAS CUT THE SCREENTONE... YOU COULDN'T EVEN DRAW A PLAIN WAFFLE-PATTERNED CEILING... IT'S AMAZING!! THE LITTLE ILLUSTRATIVE TOUCHES IN KYOKO ARE MY FAVORITE OUT OF ALL MY MANGA, AND IT'S ALL BECAUSE OF THE BACKGROUNDS. AND THE SCREENTONE.

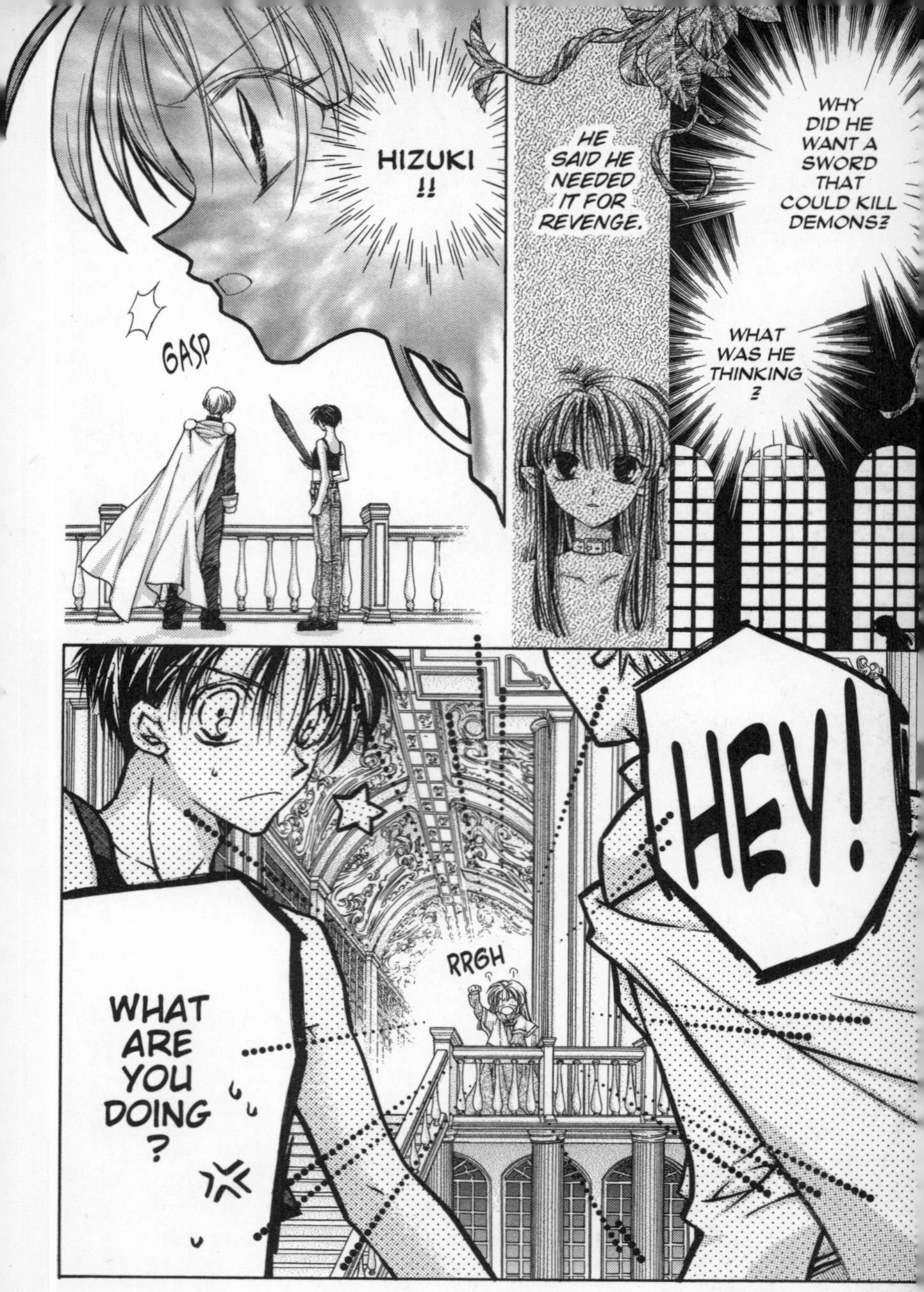
WHY DID HE WANT A SWORD THAT COULD KILL DEMONS?
WHAT WAS HE THINKING?
HE SAID HE NEEDED IT FOR REVENGE.
HIZUKI!!
GASP
HEY!
RRGH
WHAT ARE YOU DOING?

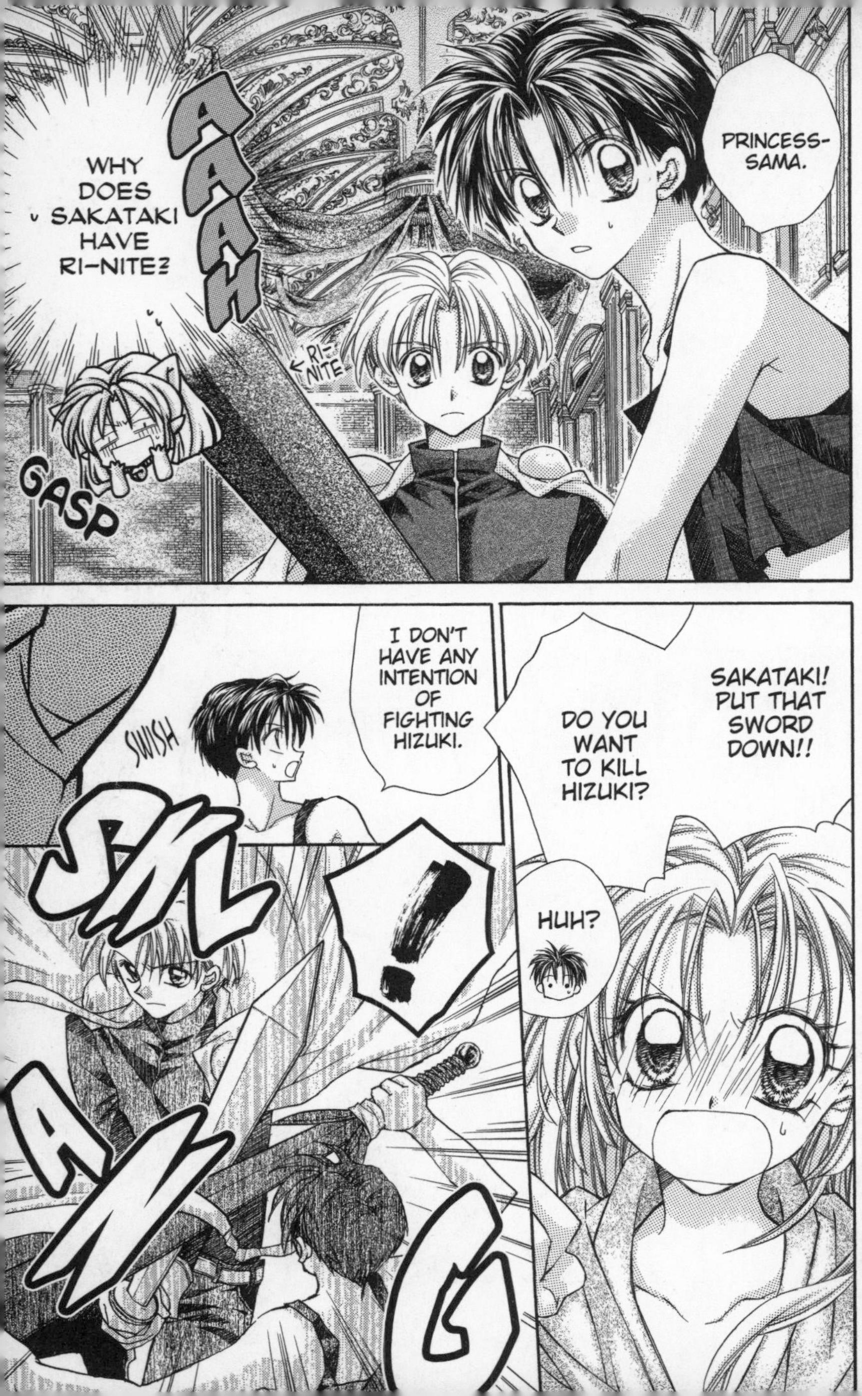
PRINCESS-SAMA.
RI-NITE
AAAH
WHY DOES SAKATAKI HAVE RI-NITE?
GASP
SAKATAKI! PUT THAT SWORD DOWN!!
DO YOU WANT TO KILL HIZUKI?
HUH?
I DON'T HAVE ANY INTENTION OF FIGHTING HIZUKI.
SWISH
!

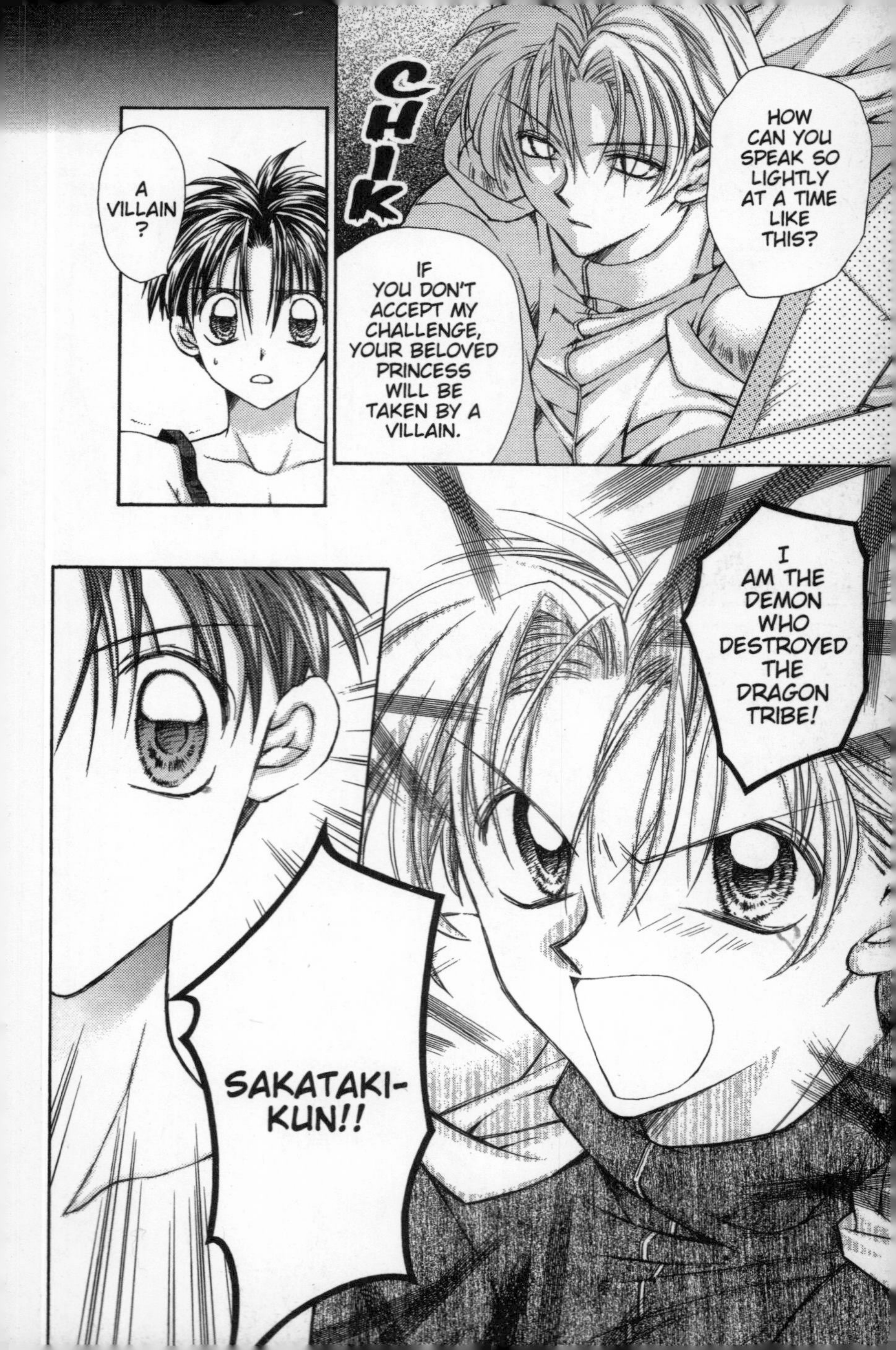
HOW CAN YOU SPEAK SO LIGHTLY AT A TIME LIKE THIS?
CHIK
IF YOU DON'T ACCEPT MY CHALLENGE, YOUR BELOVED PRINCESS WILL BE TAKEN BY A VILLAIN.
A VILLAIN?
I AM THE DEMON WHO DESTROYED THE DRAGON TRIBE!
SAKATAKI-KUN!!

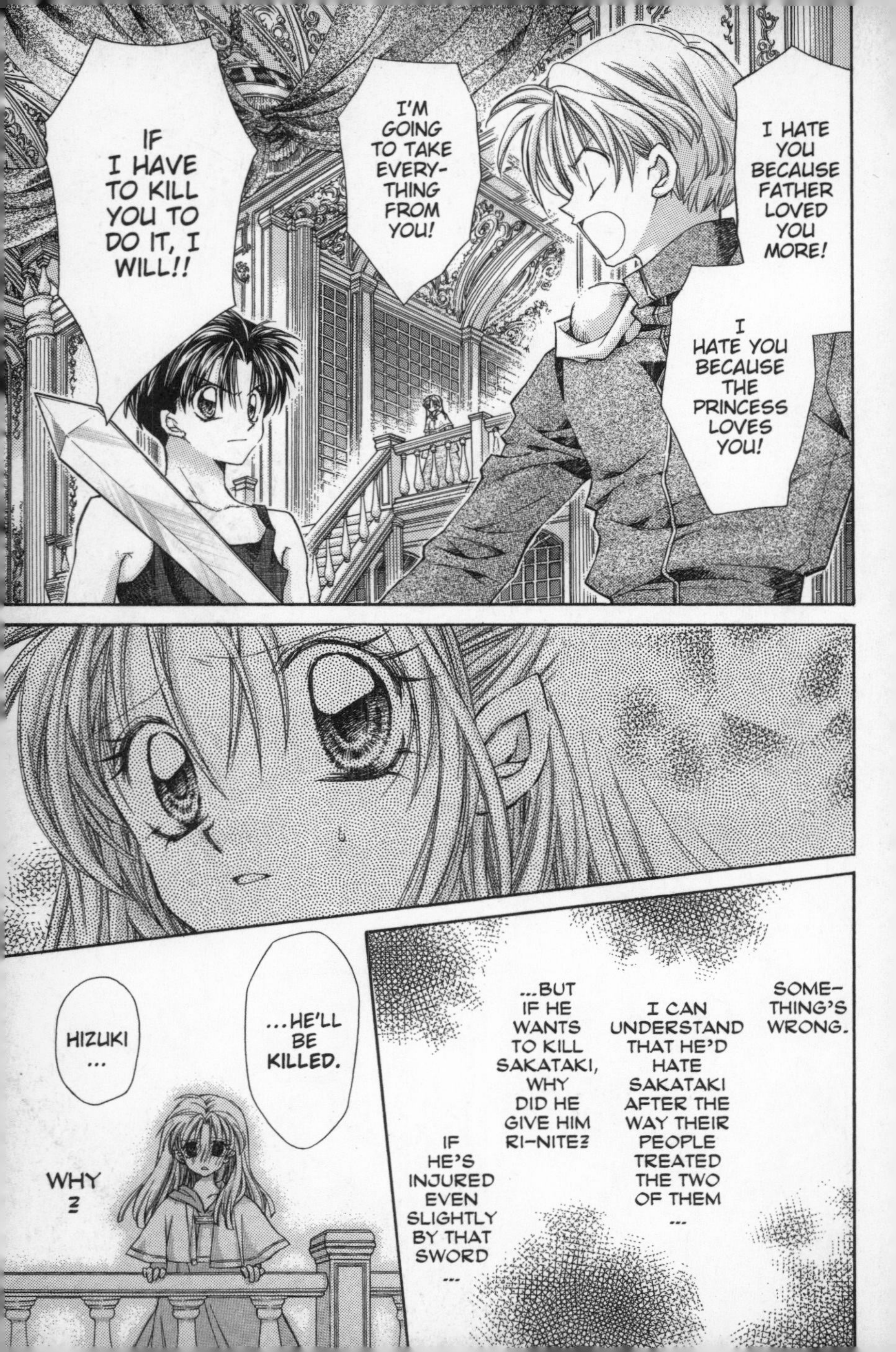
I HATE YOU BECAUSE FATHER LOVED YOU MORE!
I HATE YOU BECAUSE THE PRINCESS LOVES YOU!
I'M GOING TO TAKE EVERY-THING FROM YOU!
IF I HAVE TO KILL YOU TO DO IT, I WILL!!
SOME-THING'S WRONG.
I CAN UNDERSTAND THAT HE'D HATE SAKATAKI AFTER THE WAY THEIR PEOPLE TREATED THE TWO OF THEM ...
...BUT IF HE WANTS TO KILL SAKATAKI, WHY DID HE GIVE HIM RI-NITE?
IF HE'S INJURED EVEN SLIGHTLY BY THAT SWORD ...
...HE'LL BE KILLED.
HIZUKI ...
WHY ?

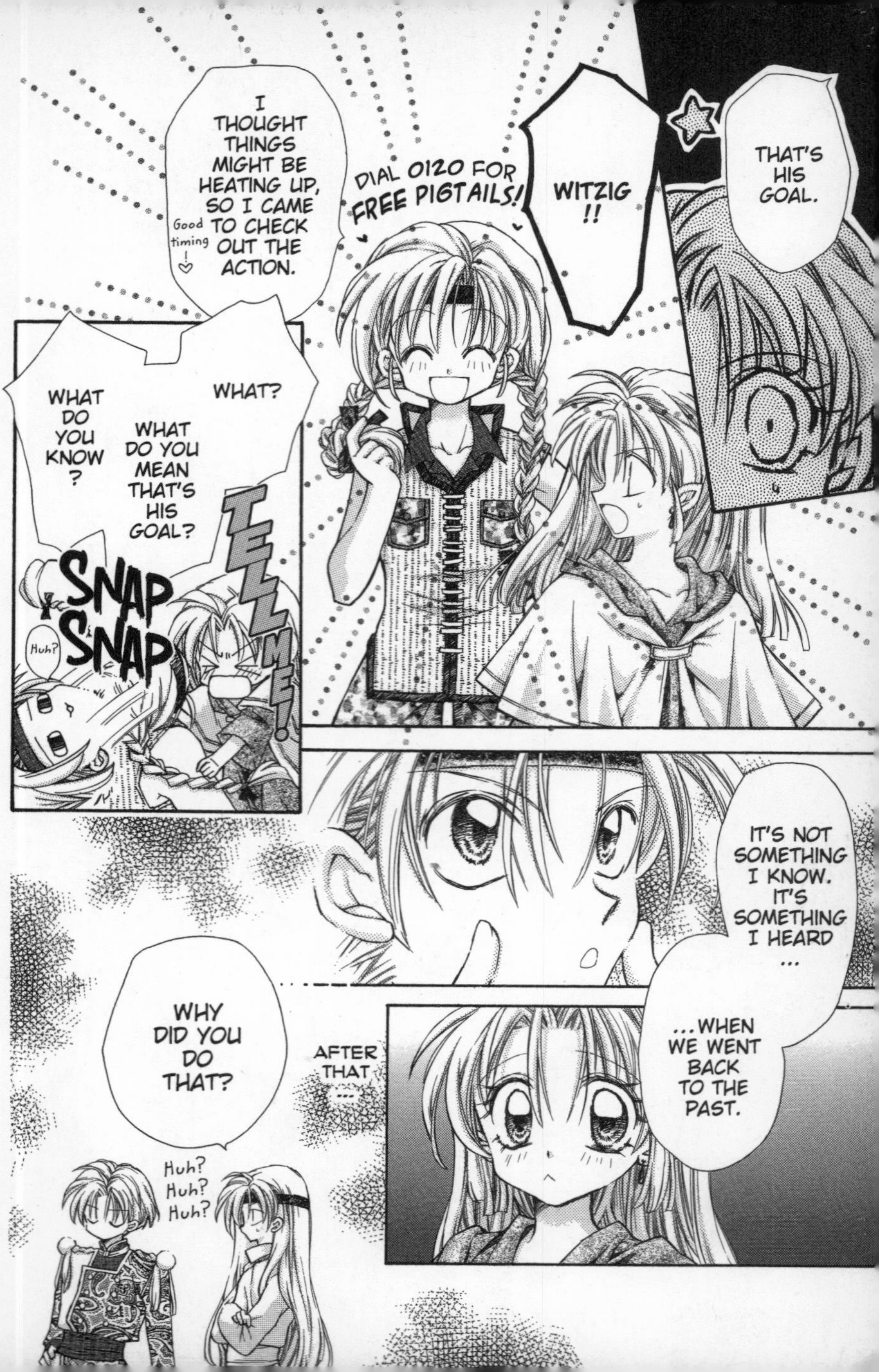
THAT'S HIS GOAL.
WITZIG !!
DIAL 0120 FOR FREE PIGTAILS!
I THOUGHT THINGS MIGHT BE HEATING UP, SO I CAME TO CHECK OUT THE ACTION.
Good timing ! ♡
WHAT?
WHAT DO YOU MEAN THAT'S HIS GOAL?
WHAT DO YOU KNOW?
TELL ME!
SNAP SNAP
Huh?
IT'S NOT SOMETHING I KNOW. IT'S SOMETHING I HEARD...
...WHEN WE WENT BACK TO THE PAST.
AFTER THAT...
WHY DID YOU DO THAT?
Huh? Huh? Huh?

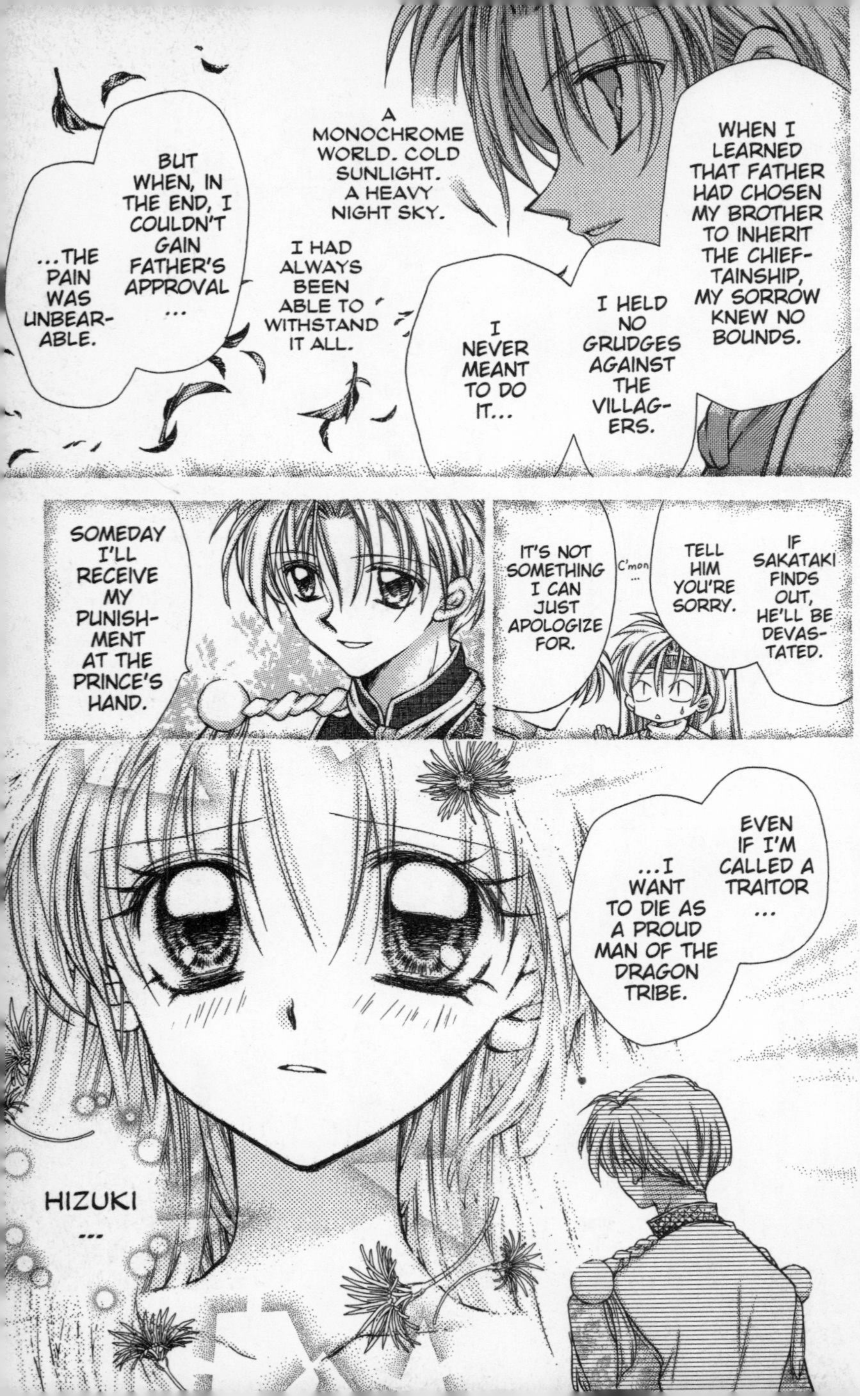
WHEN I LEARNED THAT FATHER HAD CHOSEN MY BROTHER TO INHERIT THE CHIEF-TAINSHIP, MY SORROW KNEW NO BOUNDS.
I HELD NO GRUDGES AGAINST THE VILLAG-ERS.
I NEVER MEANT TO DO IT...
A MONOCHROME WORLD. COLD SUNLIGHT. A HEAVY NIGHT SKY.
I HAD ALWAYS BEEN ABLE TO WITHSTAND IT ALL.
BUT WHEN, IN THE END, I COULDN'T GAIN FATHER'S APPROVAL...
...THE PAIN WAS UNBEAR-ABLE.
IF SAKATAKI FINDS OUT, HE'LL BE DEVAS-TATED.
TELL HIM YOU'RE SORRY.
C'mon...
IT'S NOT SOMETHING I CAN JUST APOLOGIZE FOR.
SOMEDAY I'LL RECEIVE MY PUNISH-MENT AT THE PRINCE'S HAND.
EVEN IF I'M CALLED A TRAITOR...
...I WANT TO DIE AS A PROUD MAN OF THE DRAGON TRIBE.
HIZUKI...

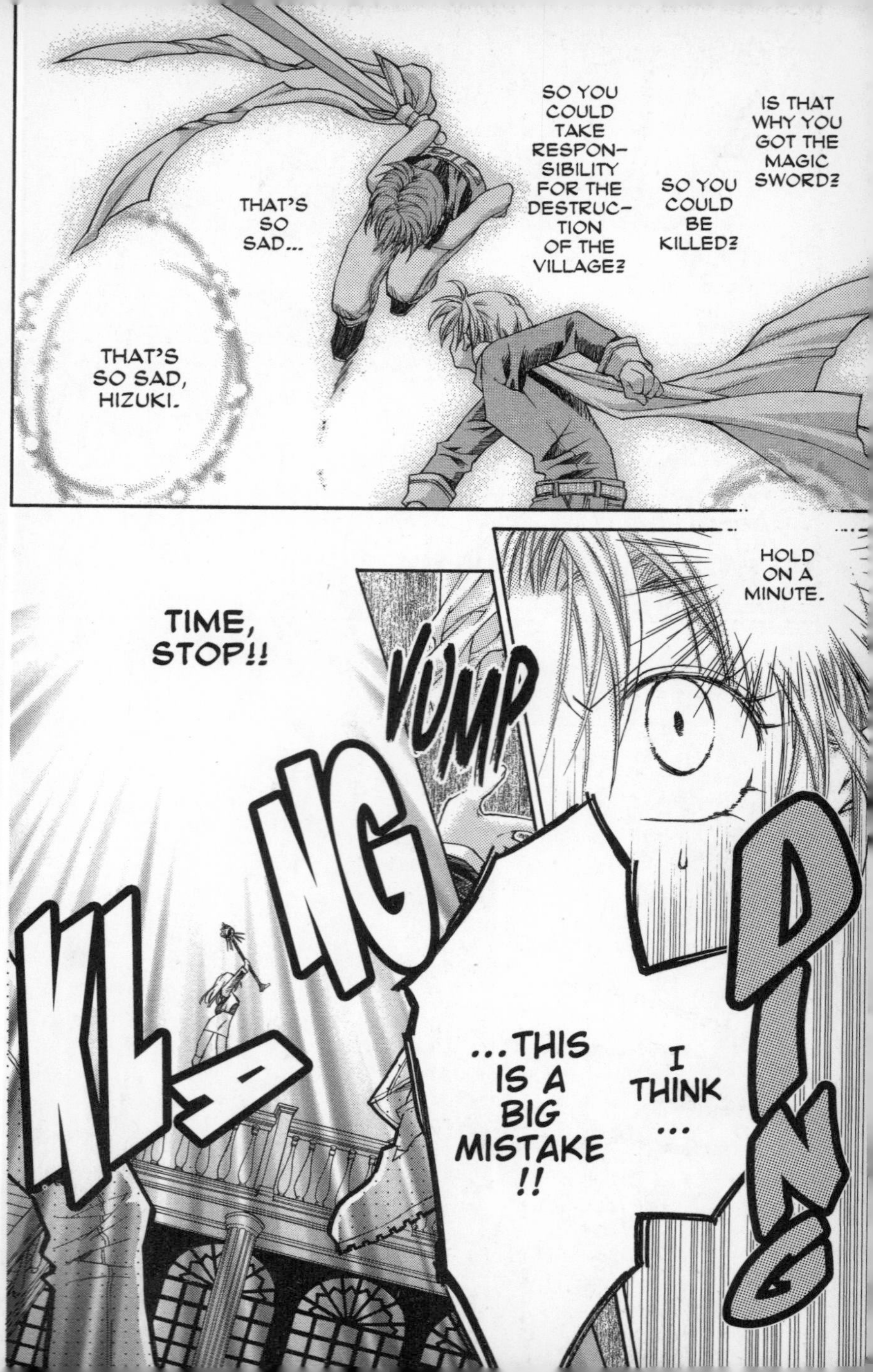
IS THAT WHY YOU GOT THE MAGIC SWORD?
SO YOU COULD BE KILLED?
SO YOU COULD TAKE RESPONSIBILITY FOR THE DESTRUCTION OF THE VILLAGE?
THAT'S SO SAD...
THAT'S SO SAD, HIZUKI.
HOLD ON A MINUTE.
VUMP
TIME, STOP!!
DING
I THINK...
...THIS IS A BIG MISTAKE!!
KL-A-NG

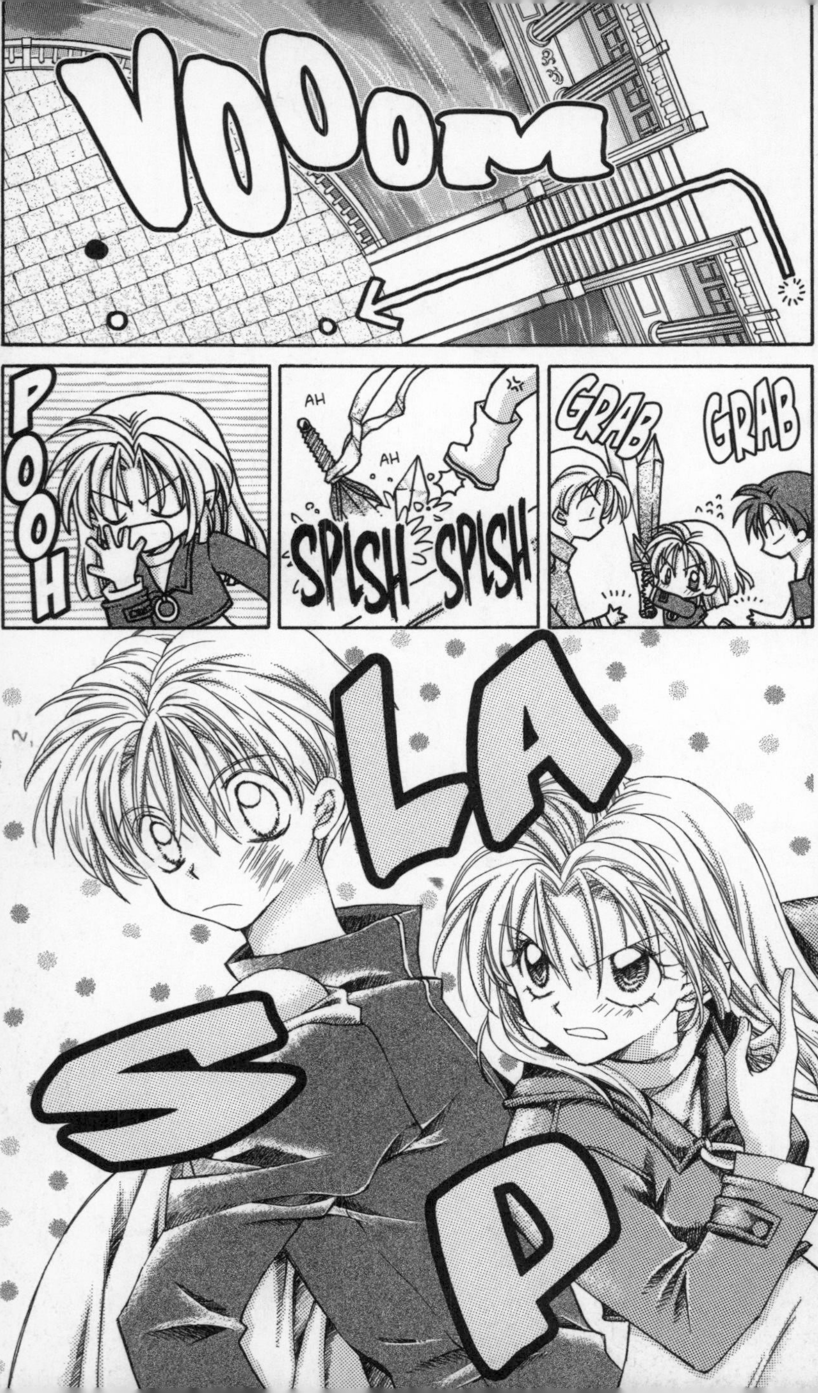
VOOOM
GRAB
GRAB
AH
AH
SPLSH
SPLSH
POOH
SLAP

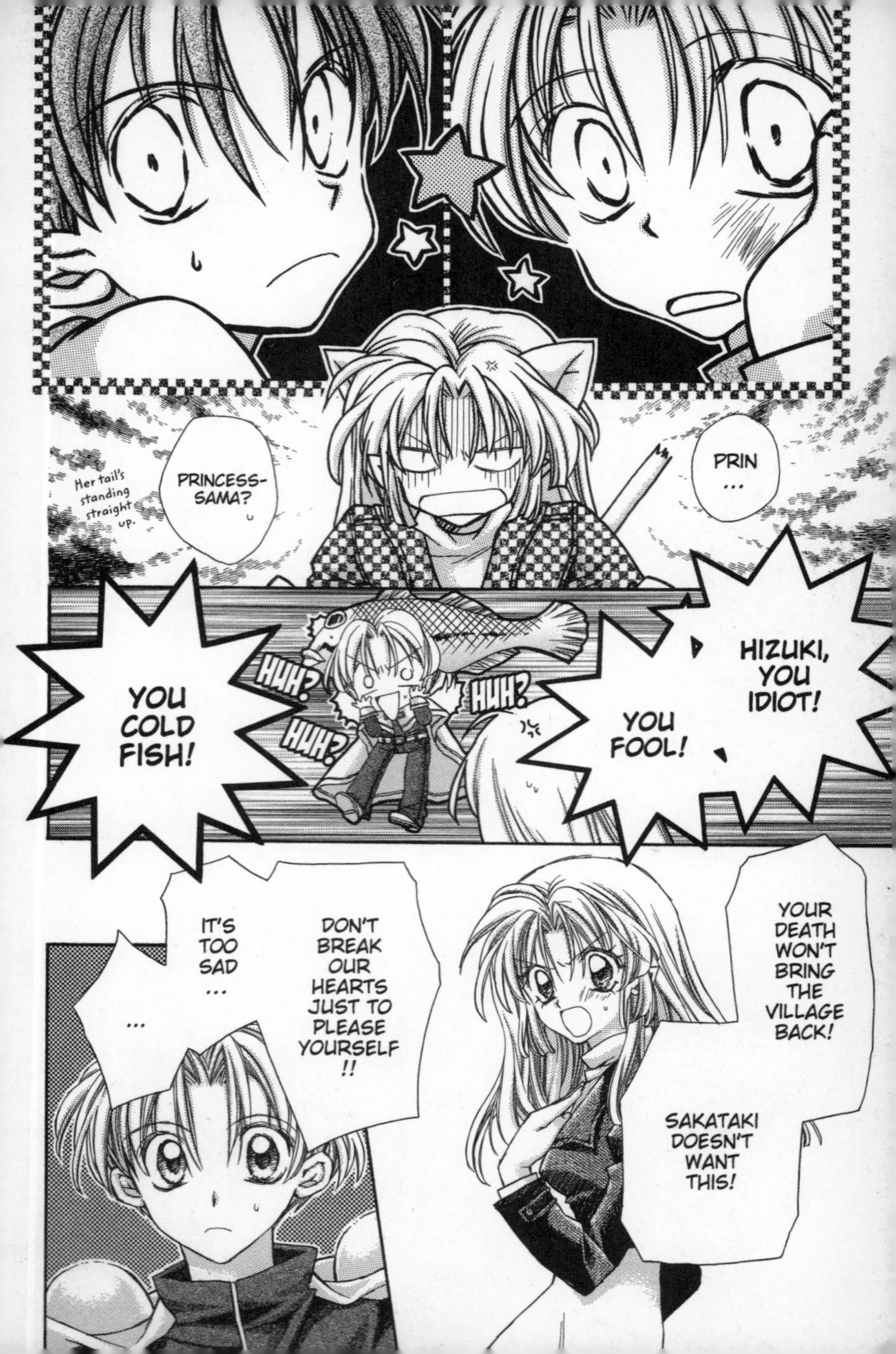
PRIN...
PRINCESS-SAMA?
Her tail's standing straight up.
HIZUKI, YOU IDIOT!
YOU FOOL!
HUH?
HUH?
HUH?
YOU COLD FISH!
YOUR DEATH WON'T BRING THE VILLAGE BACK!
SAKATAKI DOESN'T WANT THIS!
DON'T BREAK OUR HEARTS JUST TO PLEASE YOURSELF!!
IT'S TOO SAD...
...

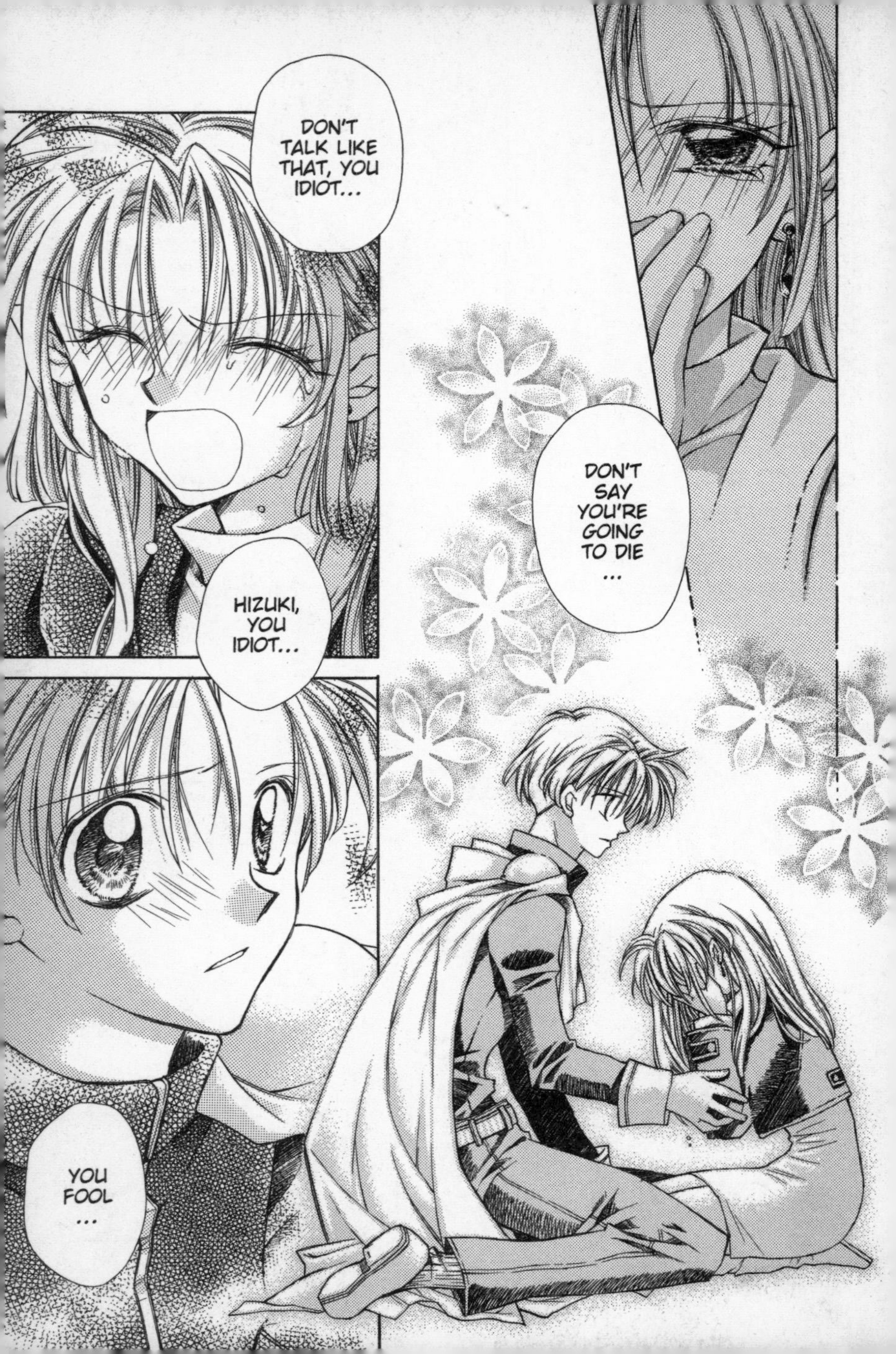
DON'T SAY YOU'RE GOING TO DIE ...
DON'T TALK LIKE THAT, YOU IDIOT...
HIZUKI, YOU IDIOT...
YOU FOOL ...

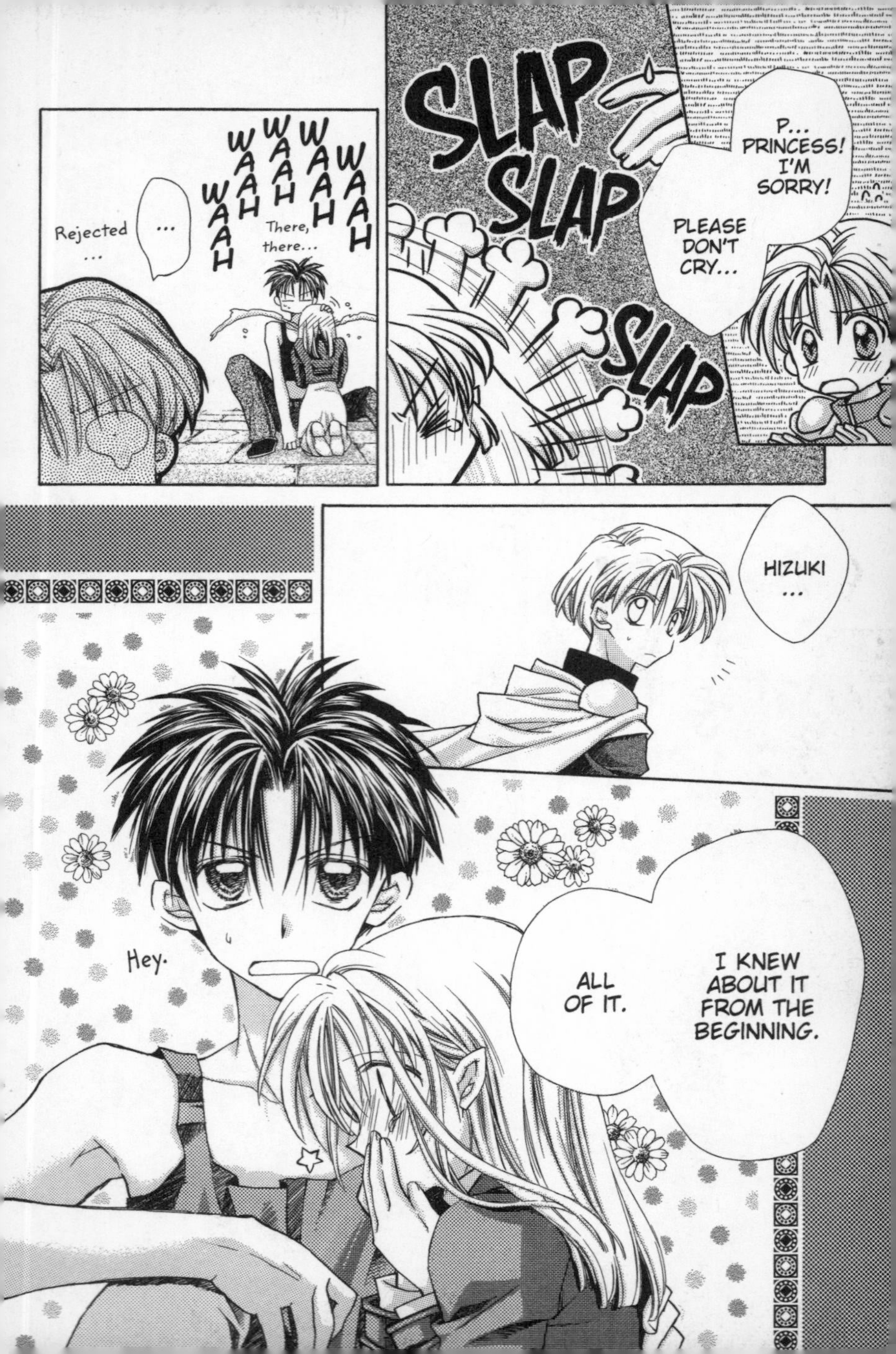
P... PRINCESS! I'M SORRY!
PLEASE DON'T CRY...
SLAP
SLAP
SLAP
WAAH
WAAH
WAAH
WAAH
WAAH
There, there...
...
Rejected...
HIZUKI...
I KNEW ABOUT IT FROM THE BEGINNING.
ALL OF IT.
Hey.

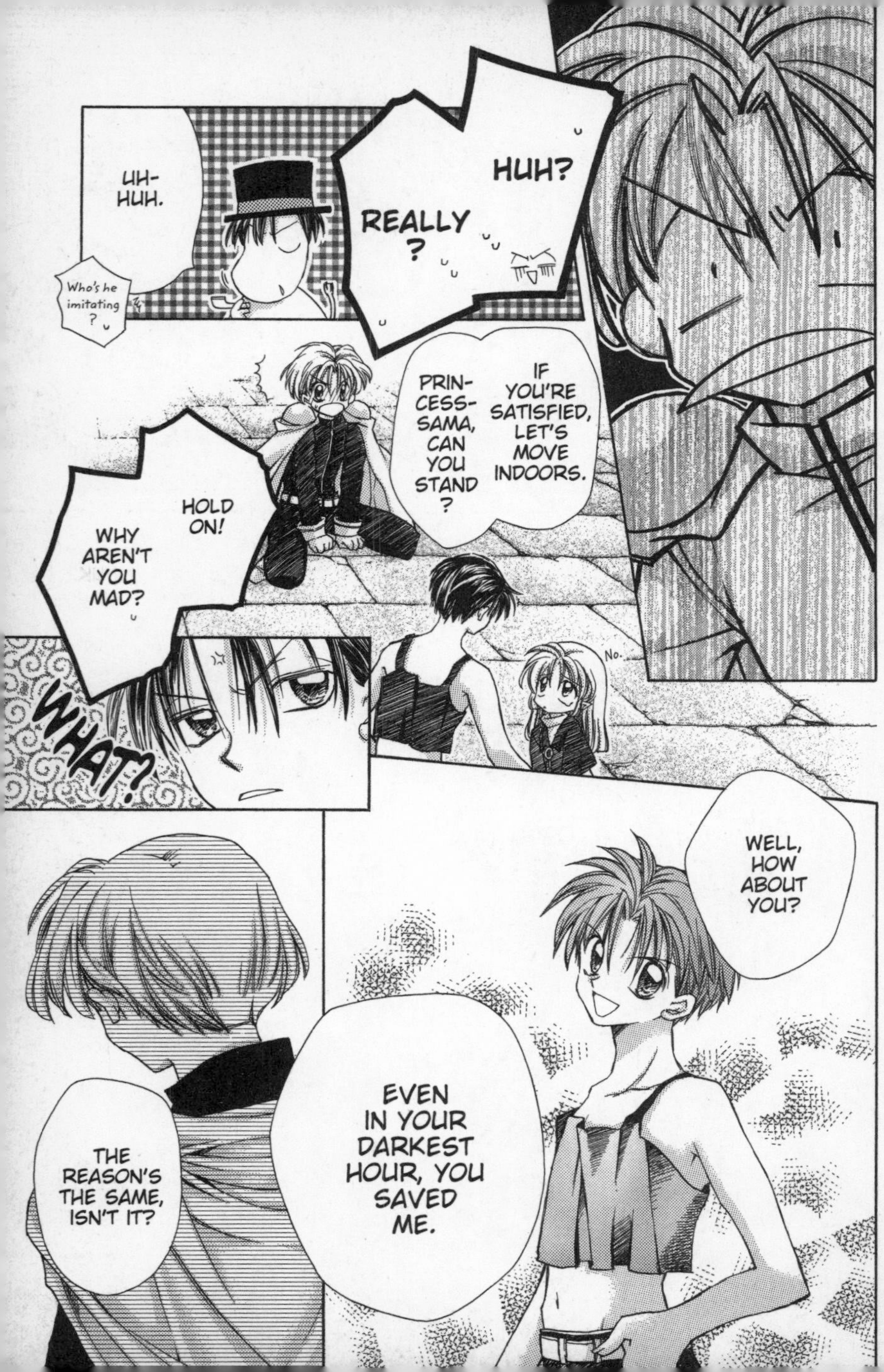
HUH? REALLY?
UH-HUH.
Who's he imitating?
IF YOU'RE SATISFIED, LET'S MOVE INDOORS.
PRINCESS-SAMA, CAN YOU STAND?
HOLD ON! WHY AREN'T YOU MAD?
No.
WHAT!?
WELL, HOW ABOUT YOU?
EVEN IN YOUR DARKEST HOUR, YOU SAVED ME.
THE REASON'S THE SAME, ISN'T IT?

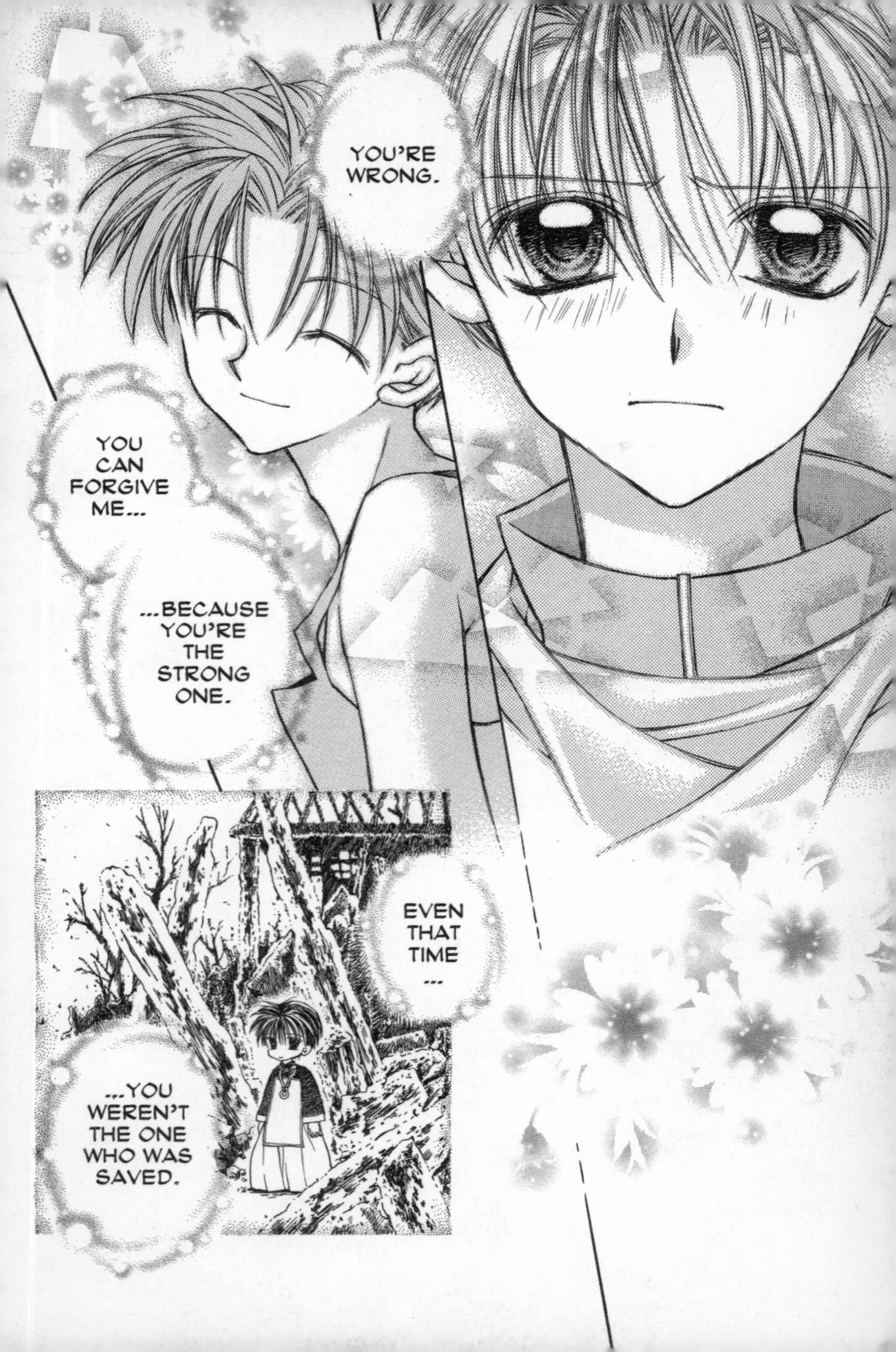
YOU'RE WRONG.
YOU CAN FORGIVE ME...
...BECAUSE YOU'RE THE STRONG ONE.
EVEN THAT TIME...
...YOU WEREN'T THE ONE WHO WAS SAVED.

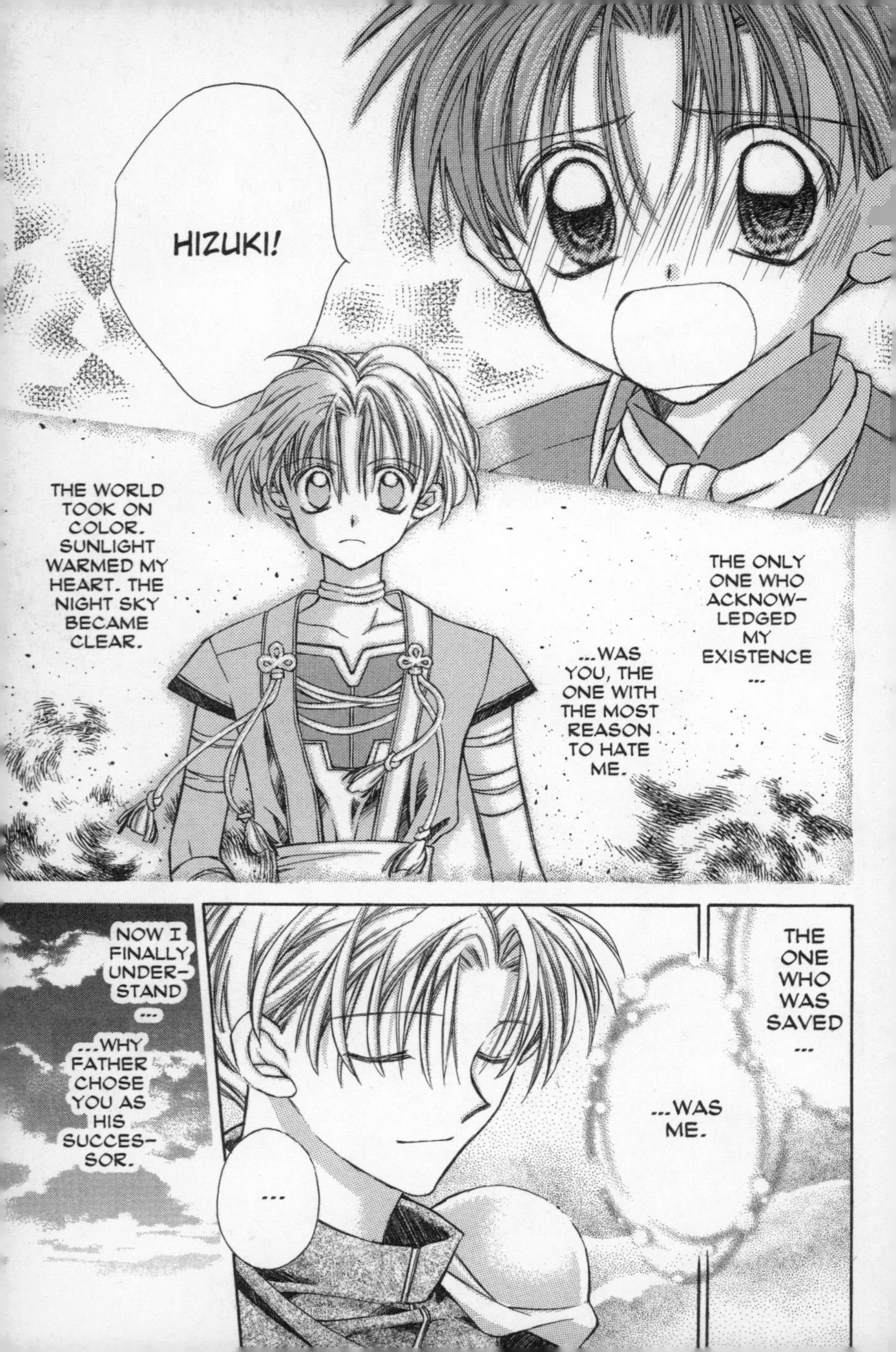
HIZUKI!
THE ONLY ONE WHO ACKNOW-LEDGED MY EXISTENCE...
...WAS YOU, THE ONE WITH THE MOST REASON TO HATE ME.
THE WORLD TOOK ON COLOR. SUNLIGHT WARMED MY HEART. THE NIGHT SKY BECAME CLEAR.
THE ONE WHO WAS SAVED...
...WAS ME.
...
NOW I FINALLY UNDER-STAND...
...WHY FATHER CHOSE YOU AS HIS SUCCES-SOR.

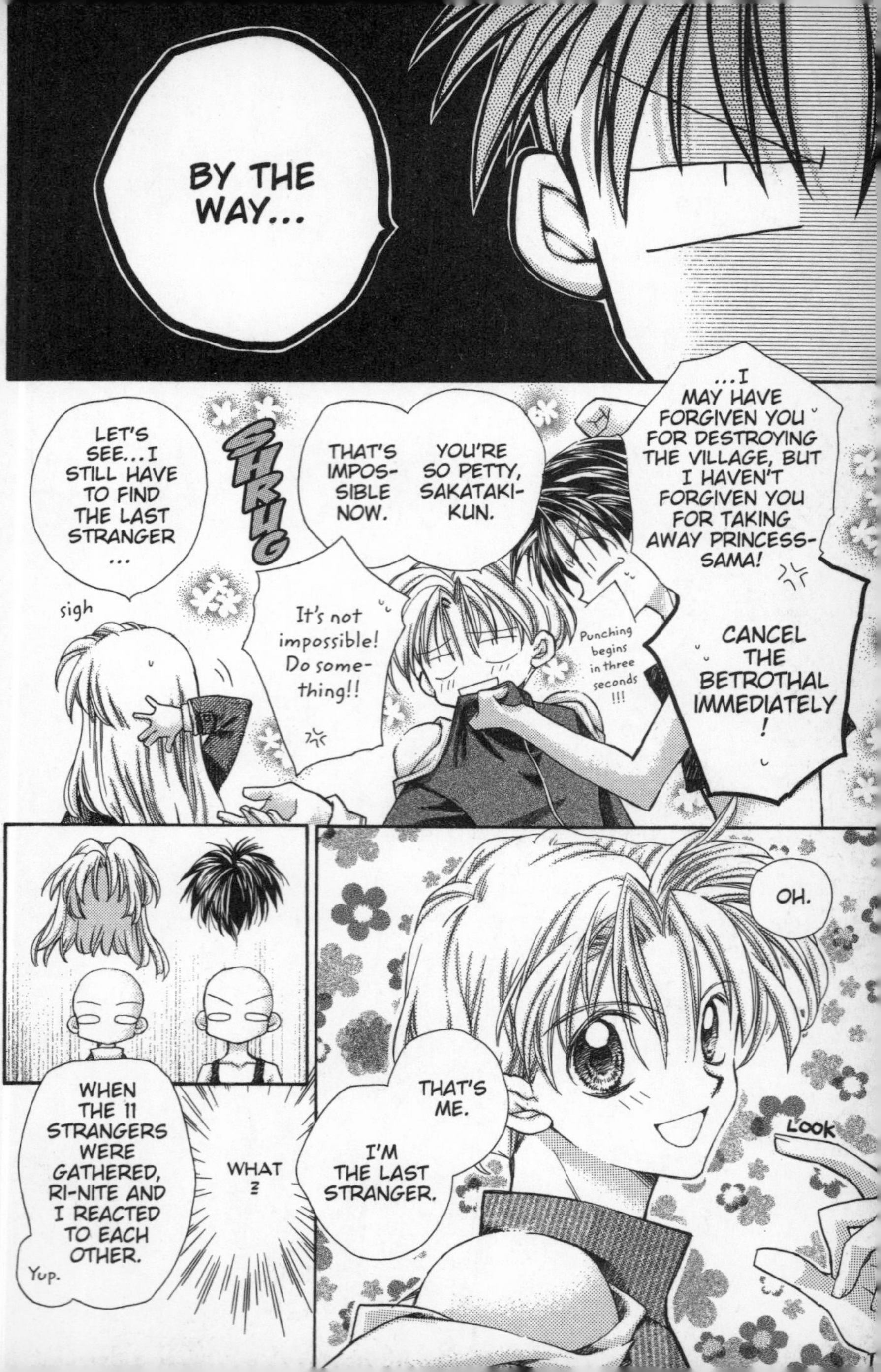
BY THE WAY...
...I MAY HAVE FORGIVEN YOU FOR DESTROYING THE VILLAGE, BUT I HAVEN'T FORGIVEN YOU FOR TAKING AWAY PRINCESS-SAMA!
CANCEL THE BETROTHAL IMMEDIATELY!
Punching begins in three seconds!!!
YOU'RE SO PETTY, SAKATAKI-KUN.
THAT'S IMPOSSIBLE NOW.
It's not impossible! Do something!!
SHRUG
LET'S SEE...I STILL HAVE TO FIND THE LAST STRANGER...
sigh
OH.
THAT'S ME.
I'M THE LAST STRANGER.
LOOK
WHAT?
WHEN THE 11 STRANGERS WERE GATHERED, RI-NITE AND I REACTED TO EACH OTHER.
Yup.

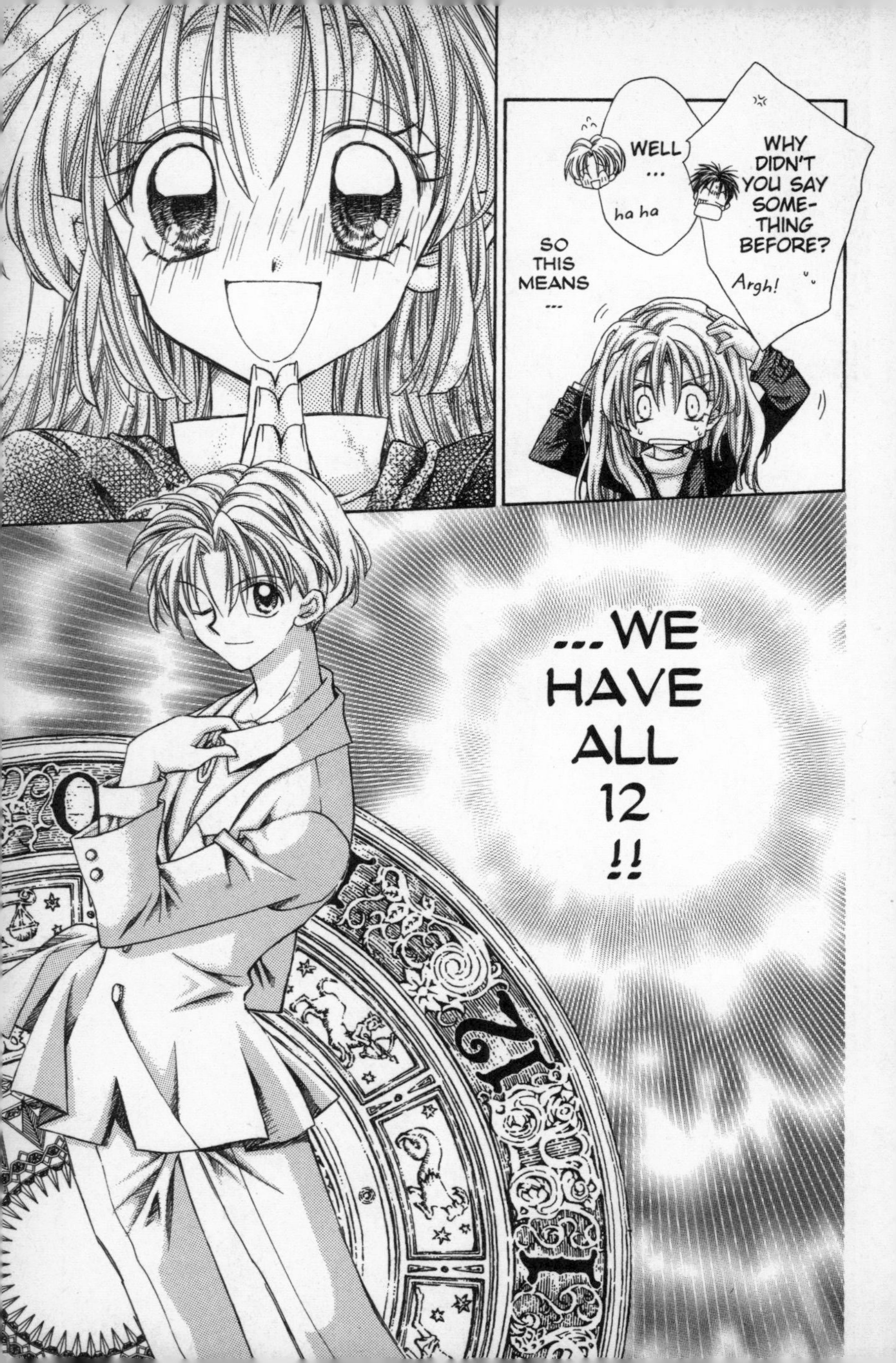
WHY DIDN'T YOU SAY SOME-THING BEFORE?
Argh!
WELL ...
ha ha
SO THIS MEANS ...
...WE HAVE ALL 12 !!

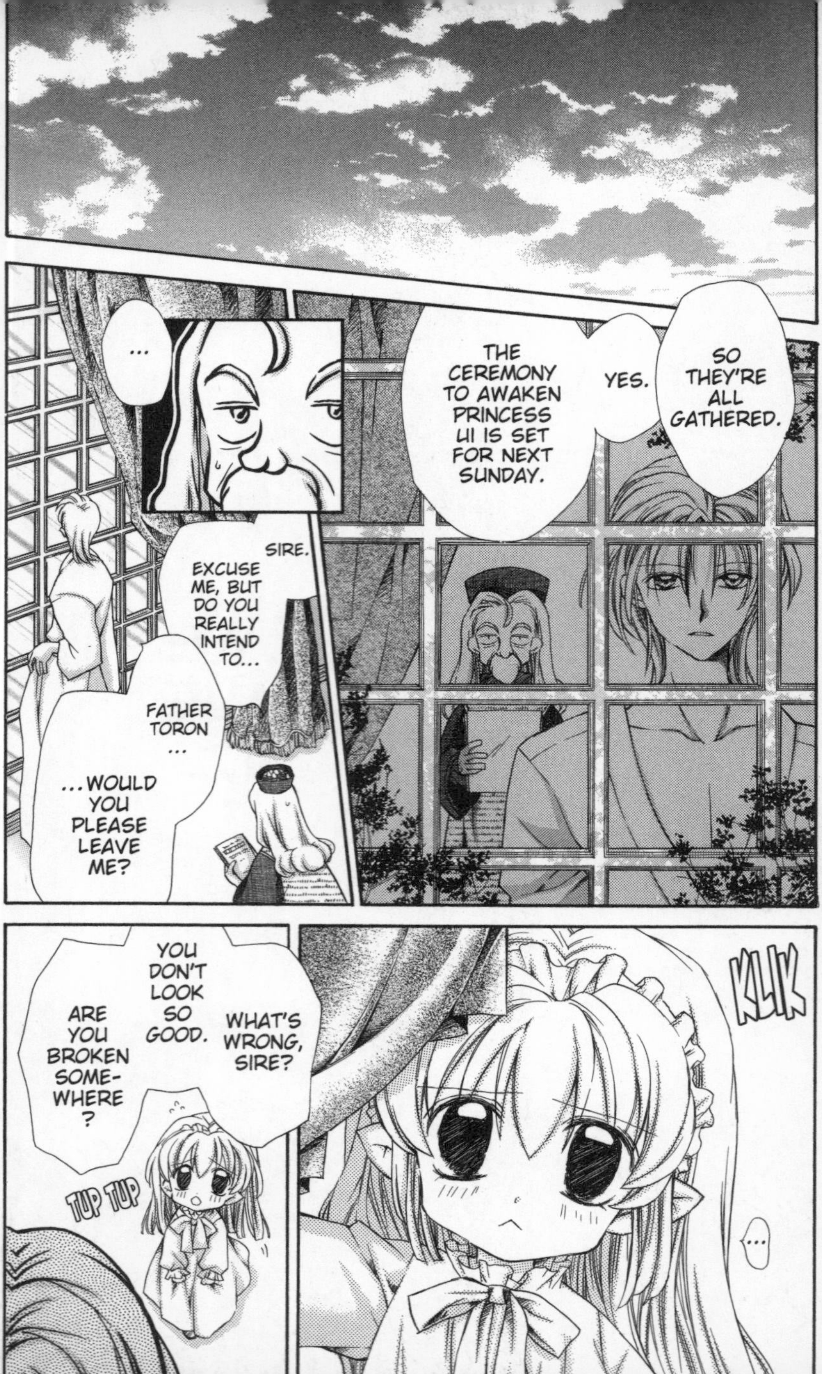

SO THEY'RE ALL GATHERED.
YES.
THE CEREMONY TO AWAKEN PRINCESS UI IS SET FOR NEXT SUNDAY.
...
SIRE.
EXCUSE ME, BUT DO YOU REALLY INTEND TO...
FATHER TORON ...
...WOULD YOU PLEASE LEAVE ME?
KLIK
...
WHAT'S WRONG, SIRE?
YOU DON'T LOOK SO GOOD.
ARE YOU BROKEN SOME-WHERE?
TUP TUP

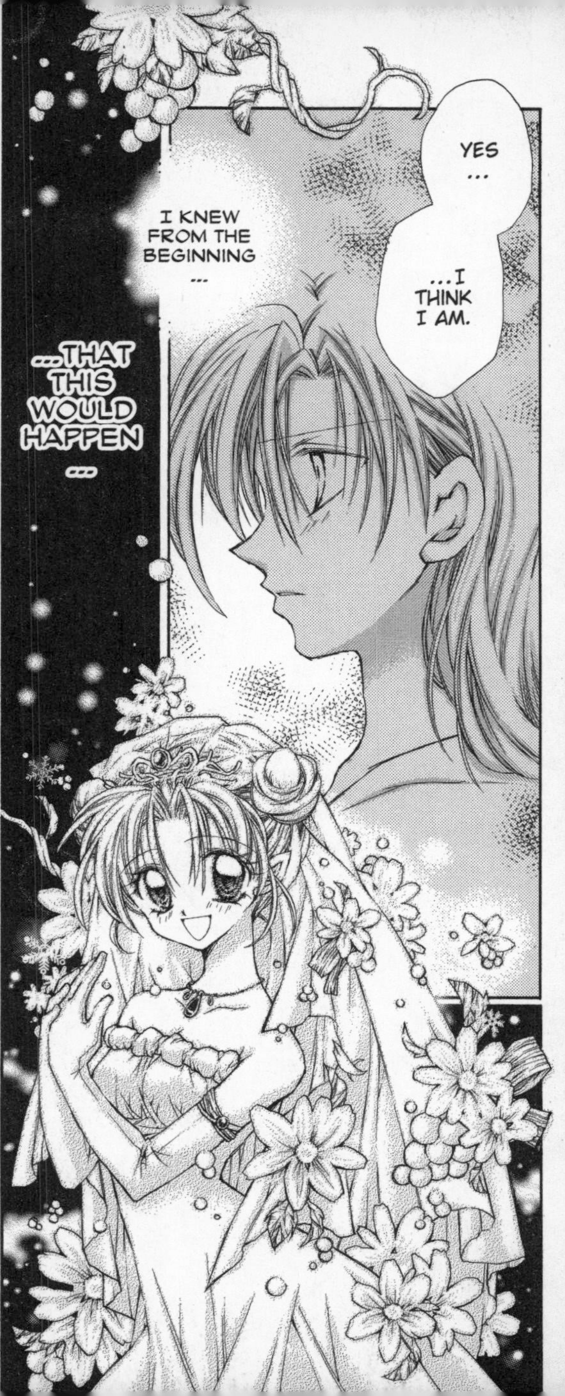
YES ... ...I THINK I AM.
I KNEW FROM THE BEGINNING ...
...THAT THIS WOULD HAPPEN ...

HO-CHAN AND ME

DOKADON! (WHAT SOUND IS THAT?) I, ARINA TANEMURA, RECENTLY APPEARED ON A DVD FEATURING VOICE ACTOR KUWASHIMA HOUKO.

He plays Maron in *Kamikaze Kaito Jeanne*.

FOR SOME REASON I WAS INVITED TO BE A GUEST ON THE TV VERSION OF NIPPON CULTURAL BROADCASTING'S RADIO PROGRAM *CLUB DB*. (WHEN THE *JEANNE* ANIME WAS AIRING ON TV, I WAS A GUEST ON THE RADIO SHOW FROM TIME TO TIME.) SO I WENT! (THAT WAS THE PHOTO SHOOT I WAS TALKING ABOUT IN VOLUME 2!!)

I REALLY HATE MY OWN FACE.

I WORRIED THAT IF I SHOWED MY FACE ON TV, MY FANS AND EVERYBODY ELSE WOULD BE GROSSED OUT.
IT WAS A SPECIAL INVITATION FROM HO-CHAN, AND MY STAFF ASSURED ME THAT I RECEIVED MANY POSTCARDS FROM FANS ASKING ME TO APPEAR ON SHOWS MORE OFTEN...BUT THE MAIN REASON I DECIDED TO DO IT WAS THAT I WANTED TO SEE HO-CHAN AGAIN!

My staff members went too.

ON THE DAY OF THE SHOOT, I WENT INTO A TRAILER, AND A PROFESSIONAL MAKE-UP ARTIST DID MY MAKE-UP. (THIS MADE ME VERY HAPPY.)
SHE WAS VERY FAST AND VERY GOOD. THEN I CHANGED INTO THE YUKATA THEY'D PREPARED FOR ME (OR RATHER, I WAS CHANGED INTO IT), BUT WHEN I WENT TO MEET HO-CHAN...

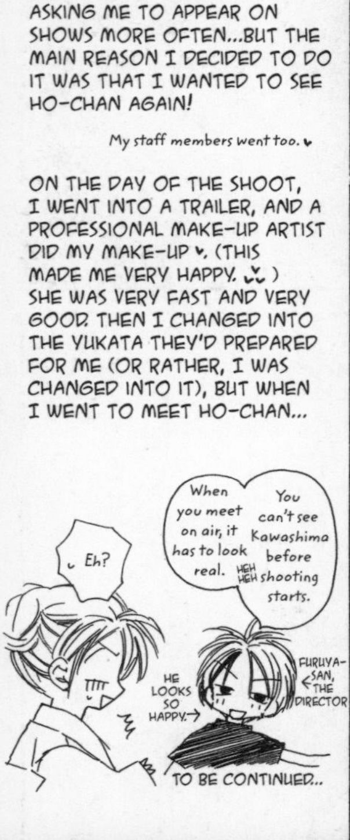
You can't see Kawashima before shooting starts.
When you meet on air, it has to look real.
HEH HEH
Eh?
FURUYA-SAN, THE DIRECTOR
HE LOOKS SO HAPPY.
TO BE CONTINUED..

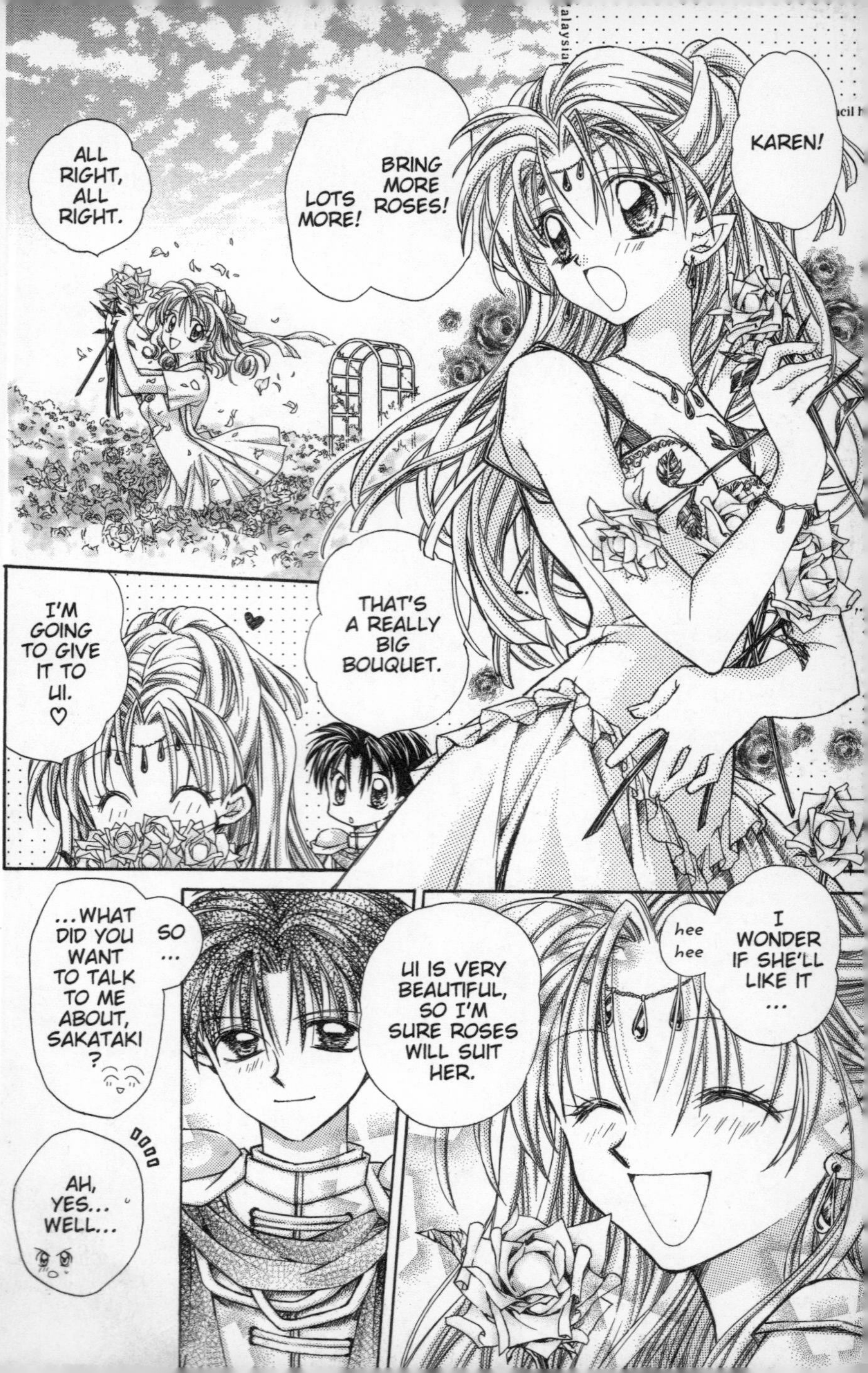
KAREN!
BRING MORE ROSES! LOTS MORE!
ALL RIGHT, ALL RIGHT.
THAT'S A REALLY BIG BOUQUET.
I'M GOING TO GIVE IT TO UI. ♡
hee hee
I WONDER IF SHE'LL LIKE IT ...
UI IS VERY BEAUTIFUL, SO I'M SURE ROSES WILL SUIT HER.
SO ...
...WHAT DID YOU WANT TO TALK TO ME ABOUT, SAKATAKI?
AH, YES... WELL...

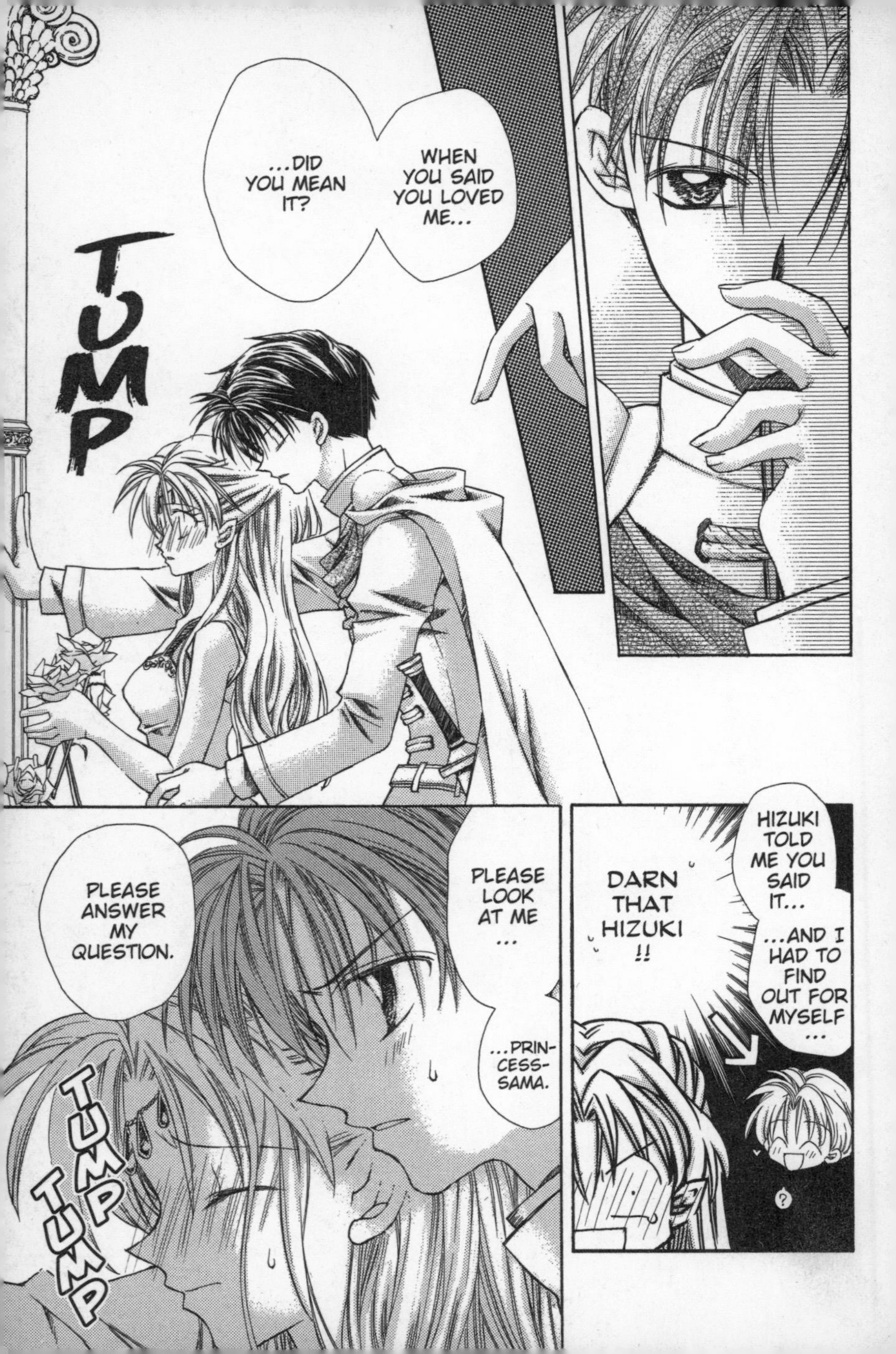
WHEN YOU SAID YOU LOVED ME...
...DID YOU MEAN IT?
TUMP
HIZUKI TOLD ME YOU SAID IT...
...AND I HAD TO FIND OUT FOR MYSELF...
DARN THAT HIZUKI !!
PLEASE LOOK AT ME ...
...PRIN-CESS-SAMA.
PLEASE ANSWER MY QUESTION.
TUMP TUMP

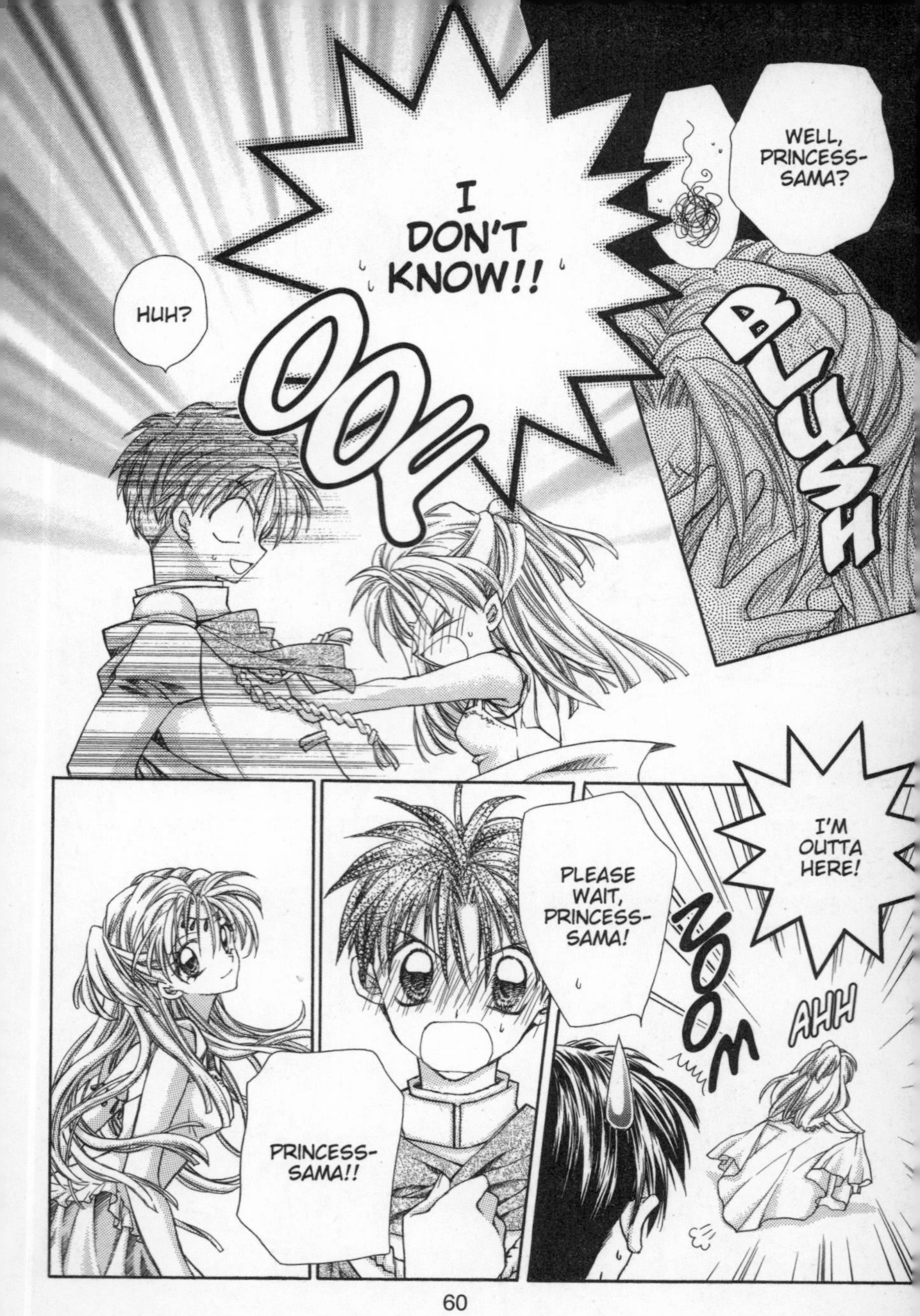
WELL, PRINCESS-SAMA?
BLUSH
I DON'T KNOW!!
HUH?
I'M OUTTA HERE!
AHH
PLEASE WAIT, PRINCESS-SAMA!
PRINCESS-SAMA!!

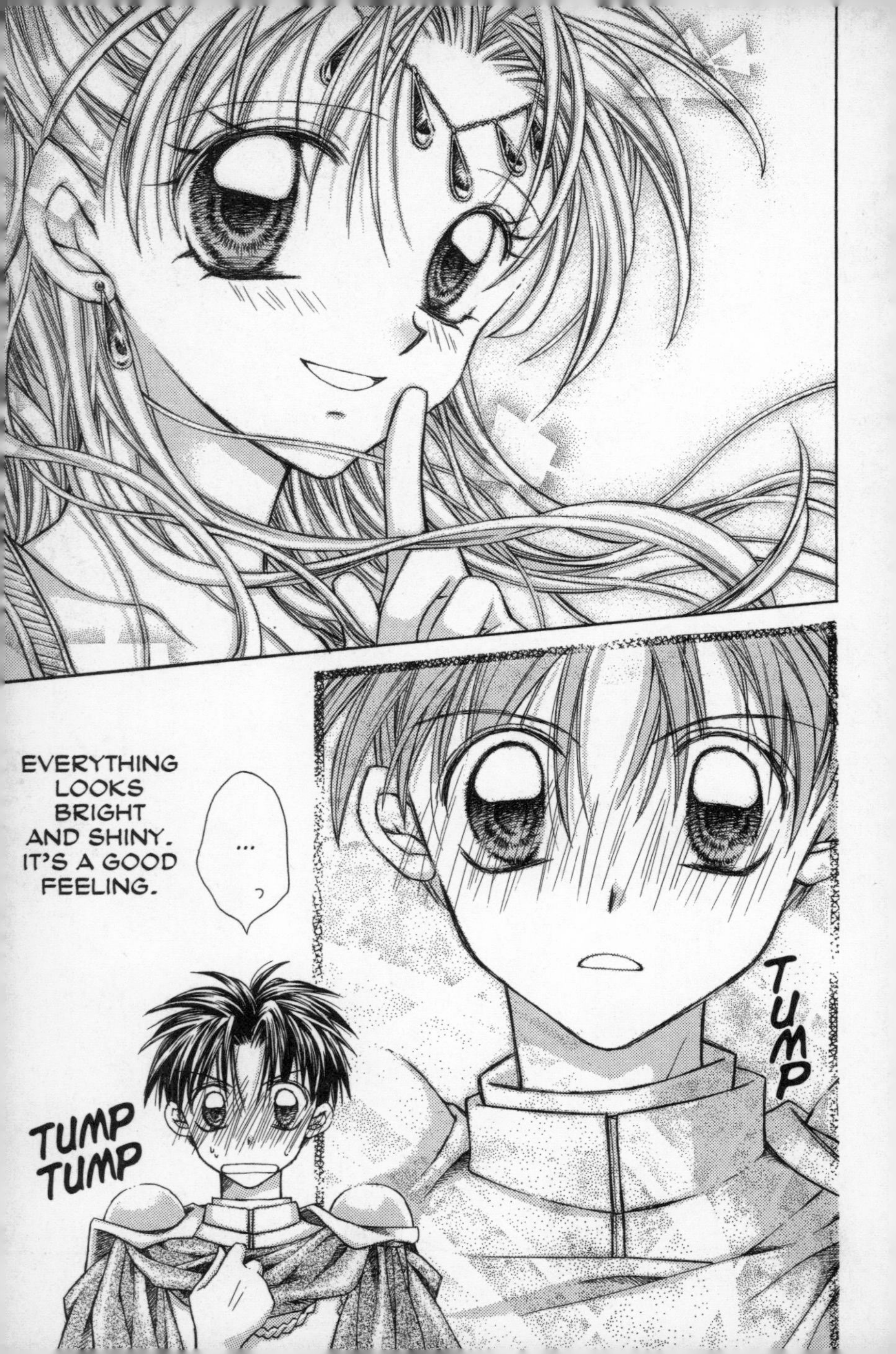
TUMP
EVERYTHING LOOKS BRIGHT AND SHINY. IT'S A GOOD FEELING.
...
TUMP TUMP

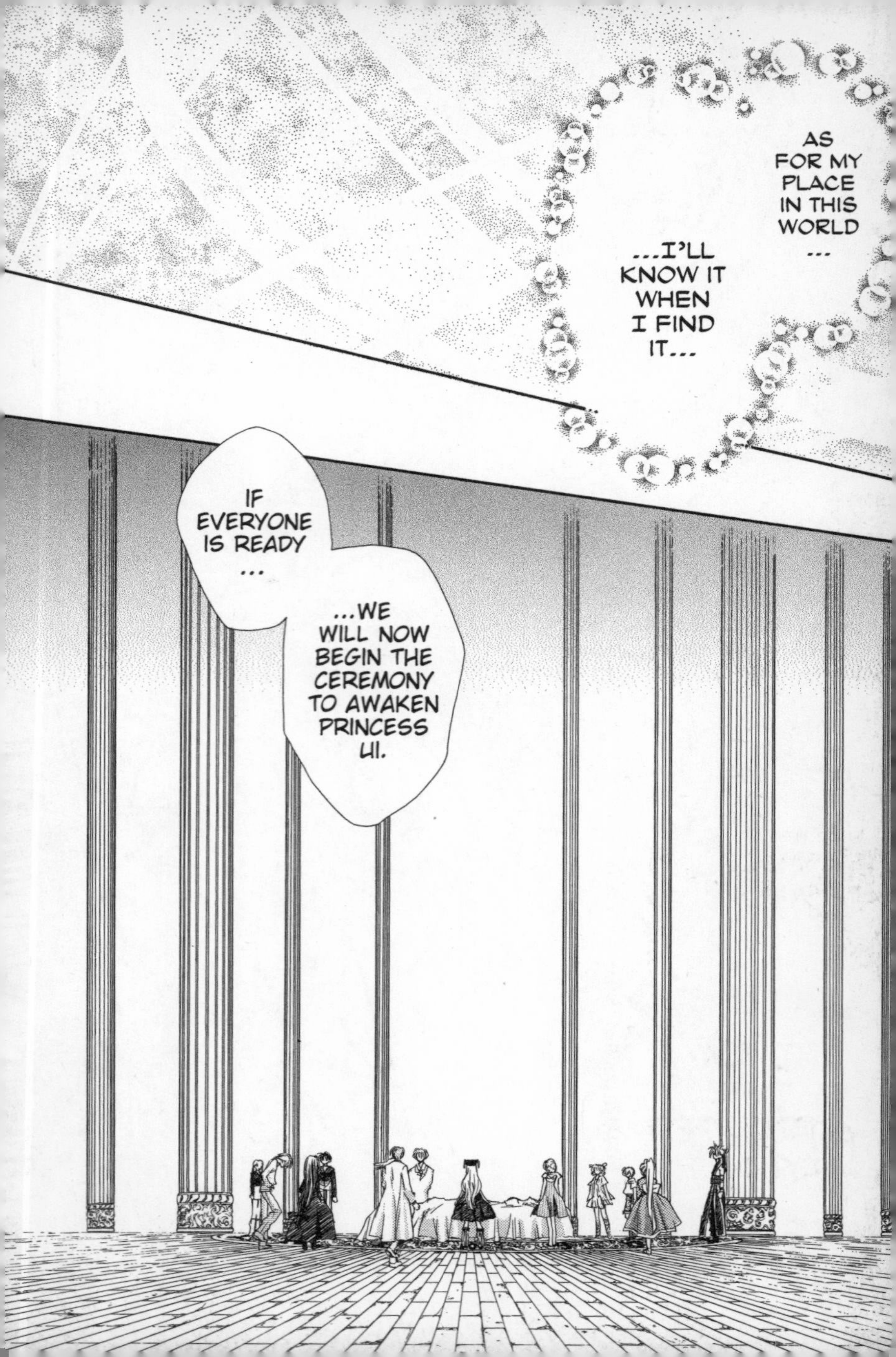
AS FOR MY PLACE IN THIS WORLD ...
...I'LL KNOW IT WHEN I FIND IT...
IF EVERYONE IS READY ...
...WE WILL NOW BEGIN THE CEREMONY TO AWAKEN PRINCESS UI.

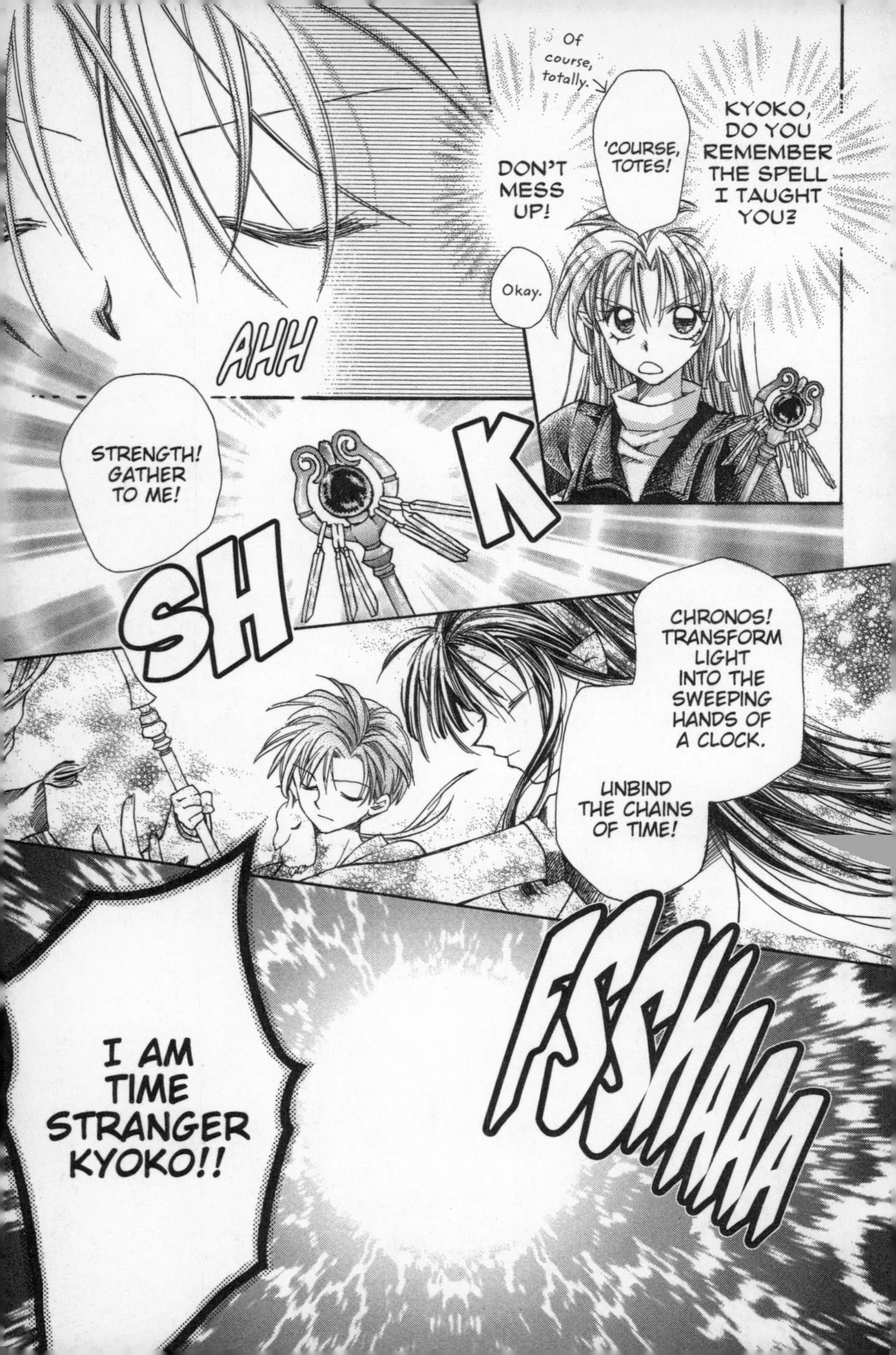
KYOKO, DO YOU REMEMBER THE SPELL I TAUGHT YOU?
'COURSE, TOTES!
Of course, totally.
DON'T MESS UP!
Okay.
AHH
STRENGTH! GATHER TO ME!
SHK
CHRONOS! TRANSFORM LIGHT INTO THE SWEEPING HANDS OF A CLOCK.
UNBIND THE CHAINS OF TIME!
FSHAAA
I AM TIME STRANGER KYOKO!!

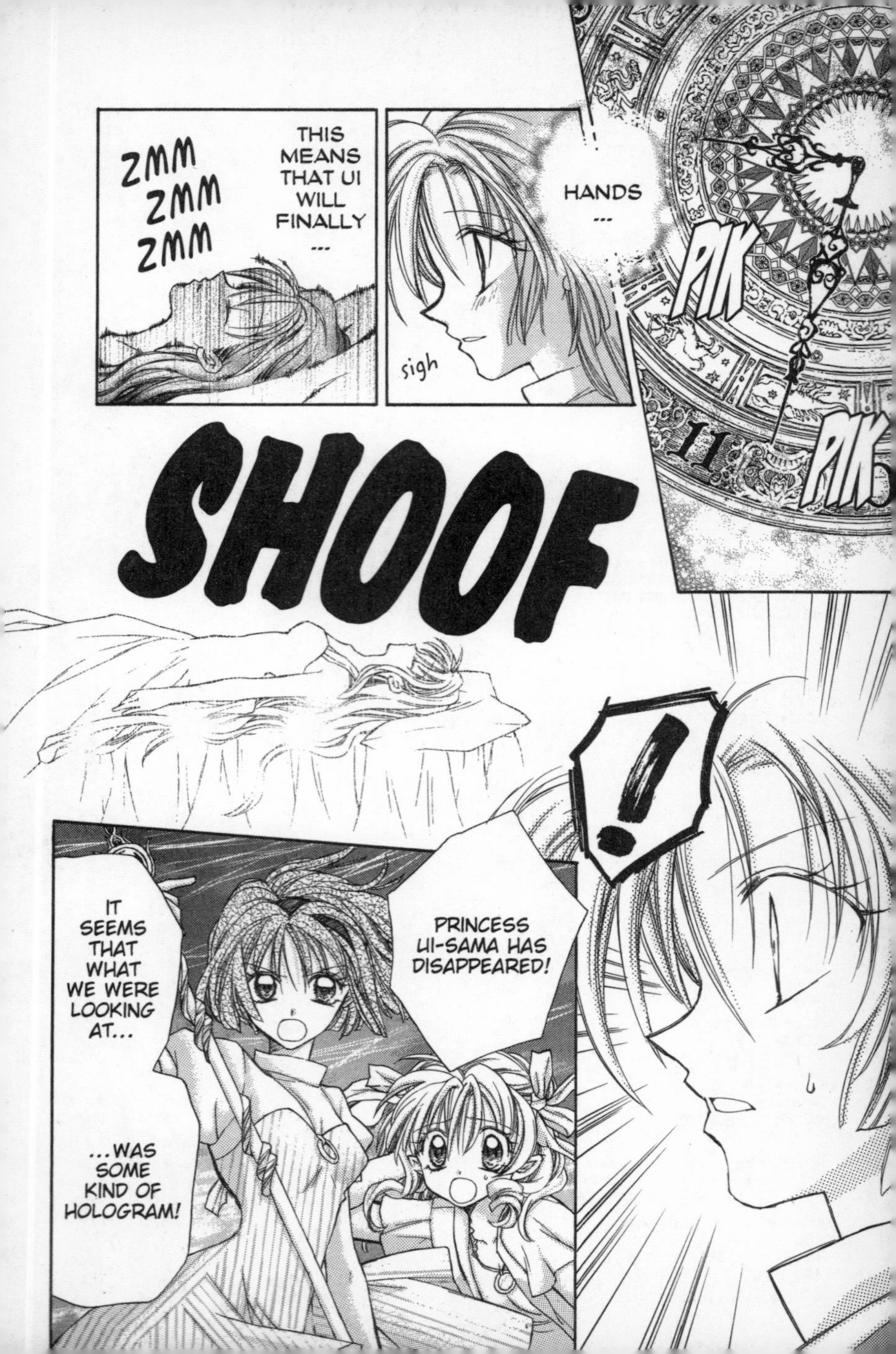

HANDS ---
PIK
11
PIK
sigh
THIS MEANS THAT UI WILL FINALLY ---
ZMM ZMM ZMM
SHOOF
!
PRINCESS UI-SAMA HAS DISAPPEARED!
IT SEEMS THAT WHAT WE WERE LOOKING AT...
...WAS SOME KIND OF HOLOGRAM!

HO-CHAN AND ME②

→CONTINUED

FIRST THEY RECORDED MY GREETING. (IT'S AN EASTER EGG ON THE DVD.) THEN I BOARDED A *YAKATABUNE* AND FINALLY MET HO-CHAN AGAIN.

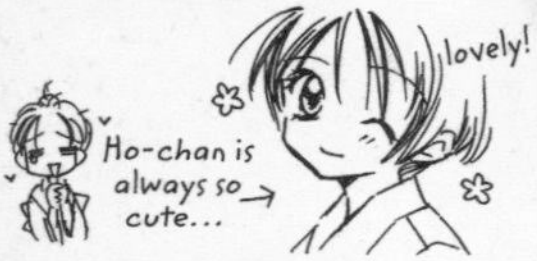
lovely!
Ho-chan is always so cute...

I HADN'T SEEN HER FOR ABOUT A YEAR AND A HALF, SINCE THE MEETING ABOUT THE *JEANNE* ANIME (OR WAS IT WHEN I WAS A GUEST ON ONE OF THE RADIO PROGRAMS...), SO I WAS SUPER HAPPY.

IF YOU WANT TO KNOW WHAT WE TALKED ABOUT, YOU'LL JUST HAVE TO WATCH THE DVD. FOR NOW, LET ME TELL YOU ABOUT SOME OF THE STUFF THAT DOESN'T APPEAR ON THE DVD. THE LAST THING I DID WAS DRAW A SELF-PORTRAIT AND A PICTURE THAT HO-CHAN REQUESTED...BUT I WAS REALLY SEASICK.

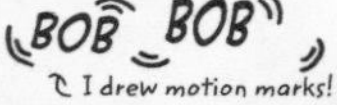
BOB BOB
I drew motion marks!

I SUPPOSE IT WAS ONLY TO BE EXPECTED. (I HADN'T HAD ENOUGH SLEEP, AND THEY FED ME TEMPURA, AND THEN I HAD TO LOOK DOWN A LOT TO DRAW.) I FELT TERRIBLE. BUT...

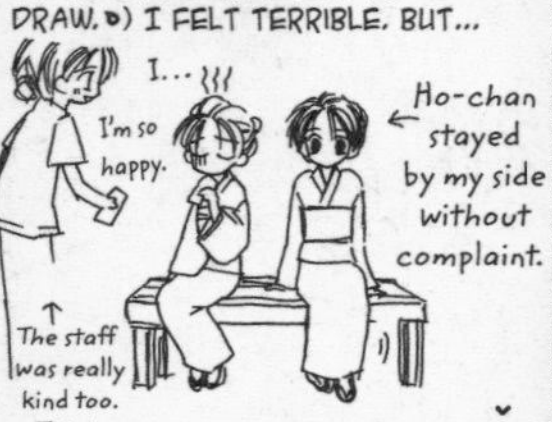
I...
I'm so happy.
Ho-chan stayed by my side without complaint.
The staff was really kind too. This is Ho-chan's manager.
Somehow, through all of this, I was totally content.

JUST MEETING HO-CHAN GAVE ME A LOT OF ENERGY. (IT'S THE SAME WITH MAMI-NE AND NAO-NI...I REALLY LOVE PEOPLE WHO ALWAYS TRY HARD!) I WOULD LIKE TO THANK HER FOR AN UNFORGETTABLE TIME...

The phone call made me happy too...Let's have another long talk sometime, okay?

TO THE STAFF AND THE PEOPLE FROM KONAMI, I REALLY ENJOYED MYSELF. (EVEN GETTING SEASICK WAS A GOOD MEMORY.)

THANK YOU VERY MUCH.

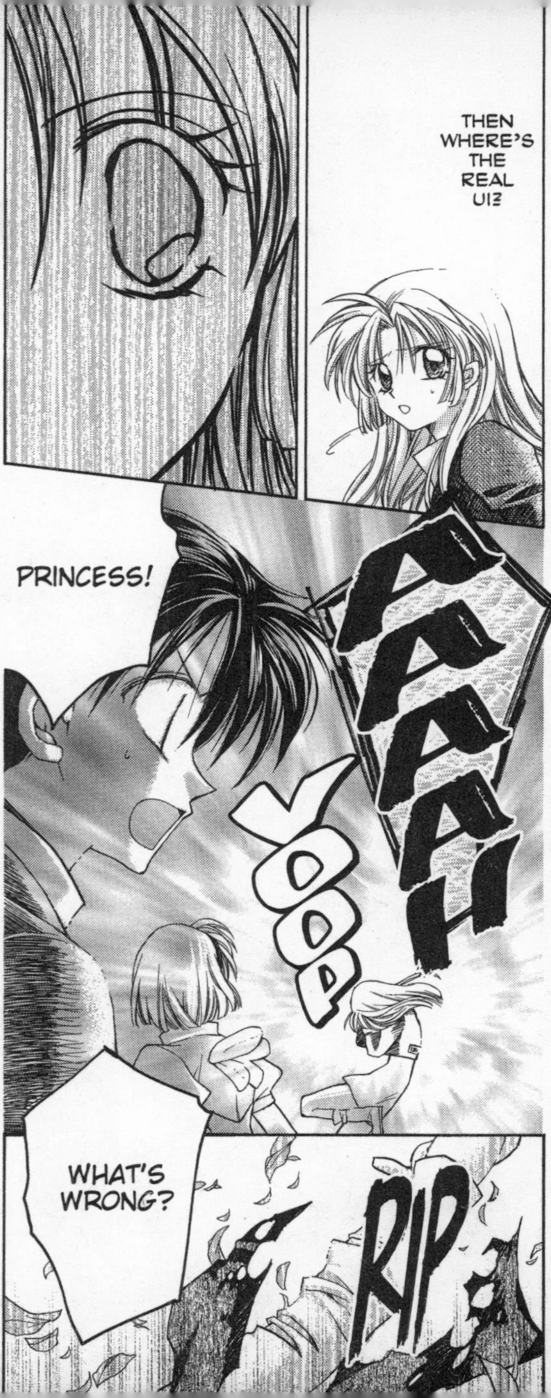
THEN WHERE'S THE REAL UI?
PRINCESS!
AAAAH
WOOP
WHAT'S WRONG?
RIP

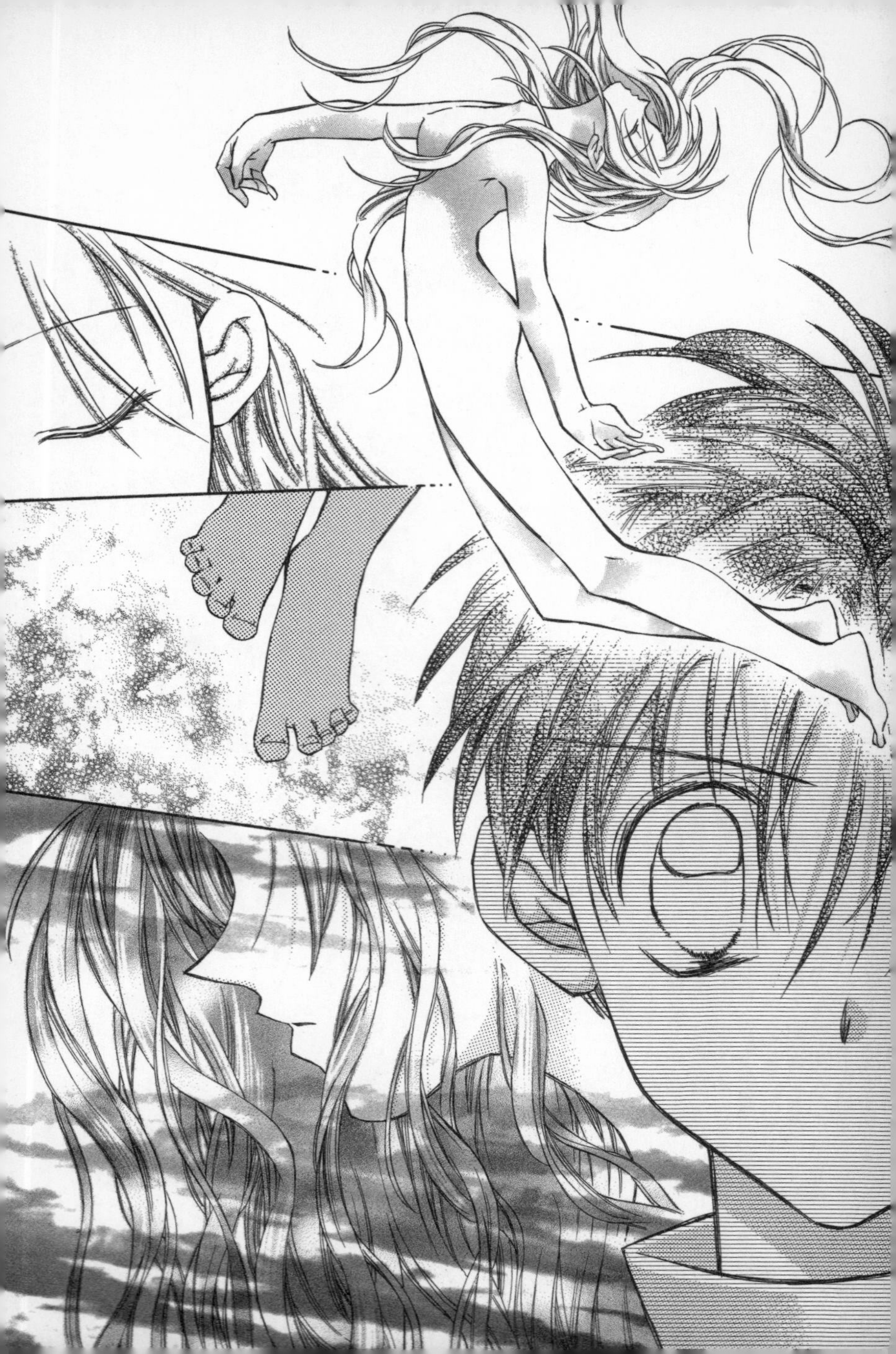

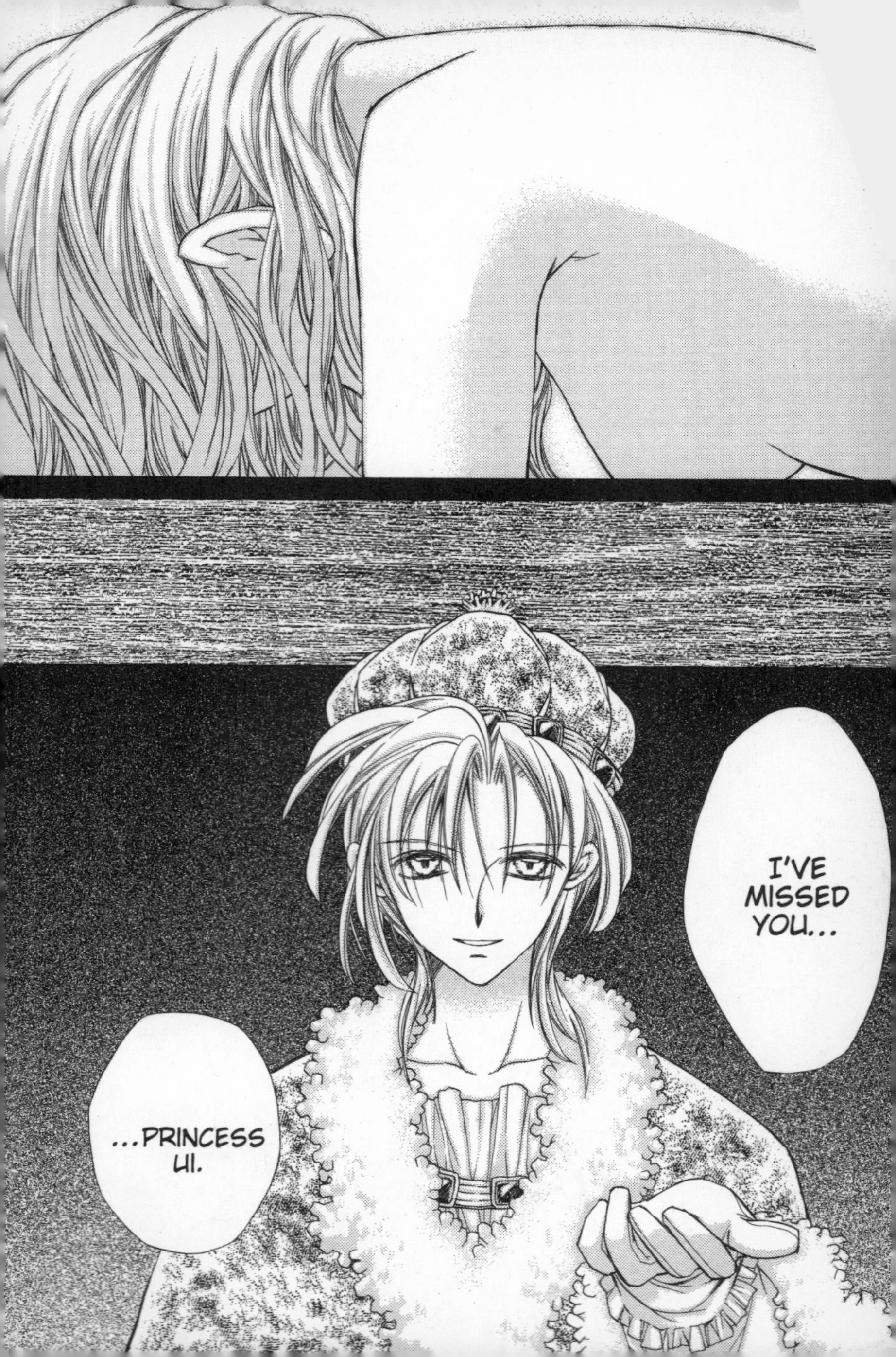
I'VE MISSED YOU...
...PRINCESS UI.

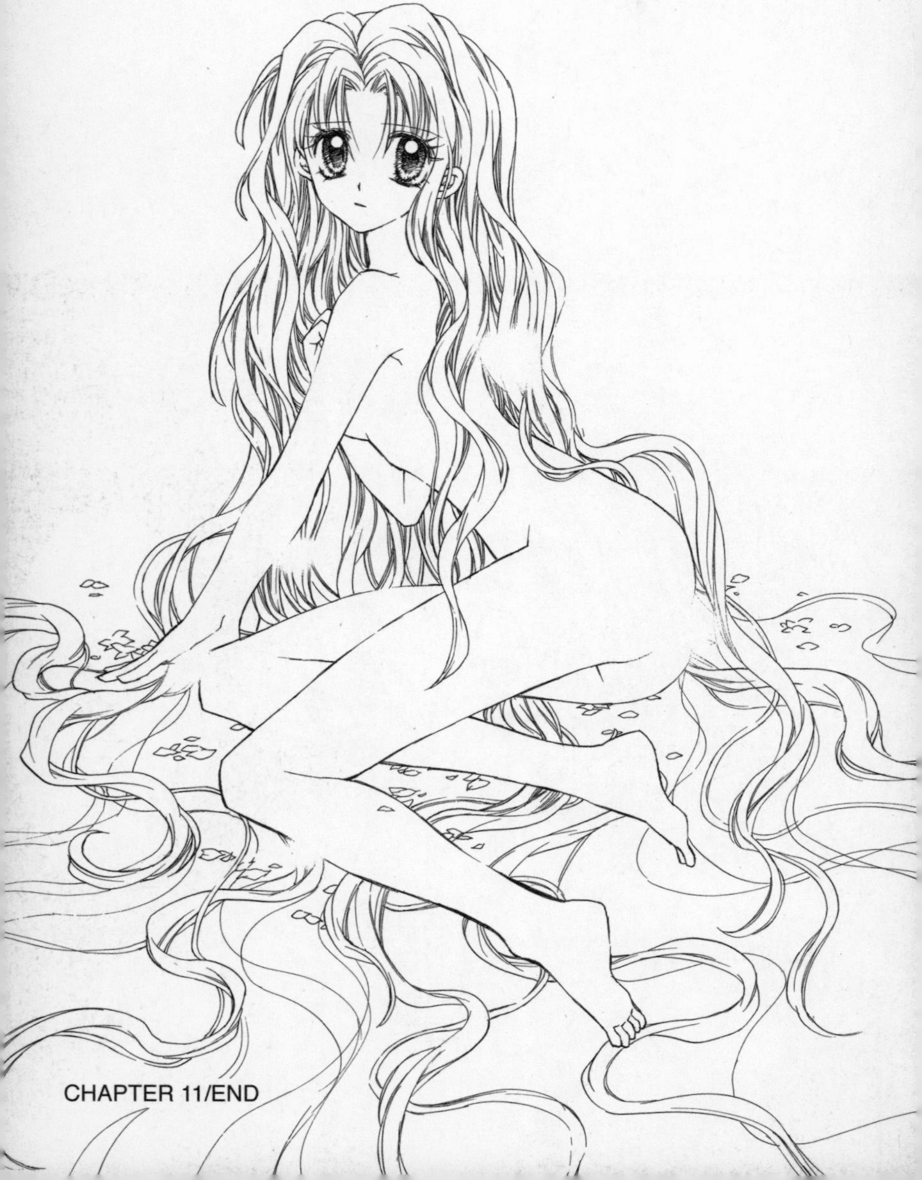

CHAPTER 11/END

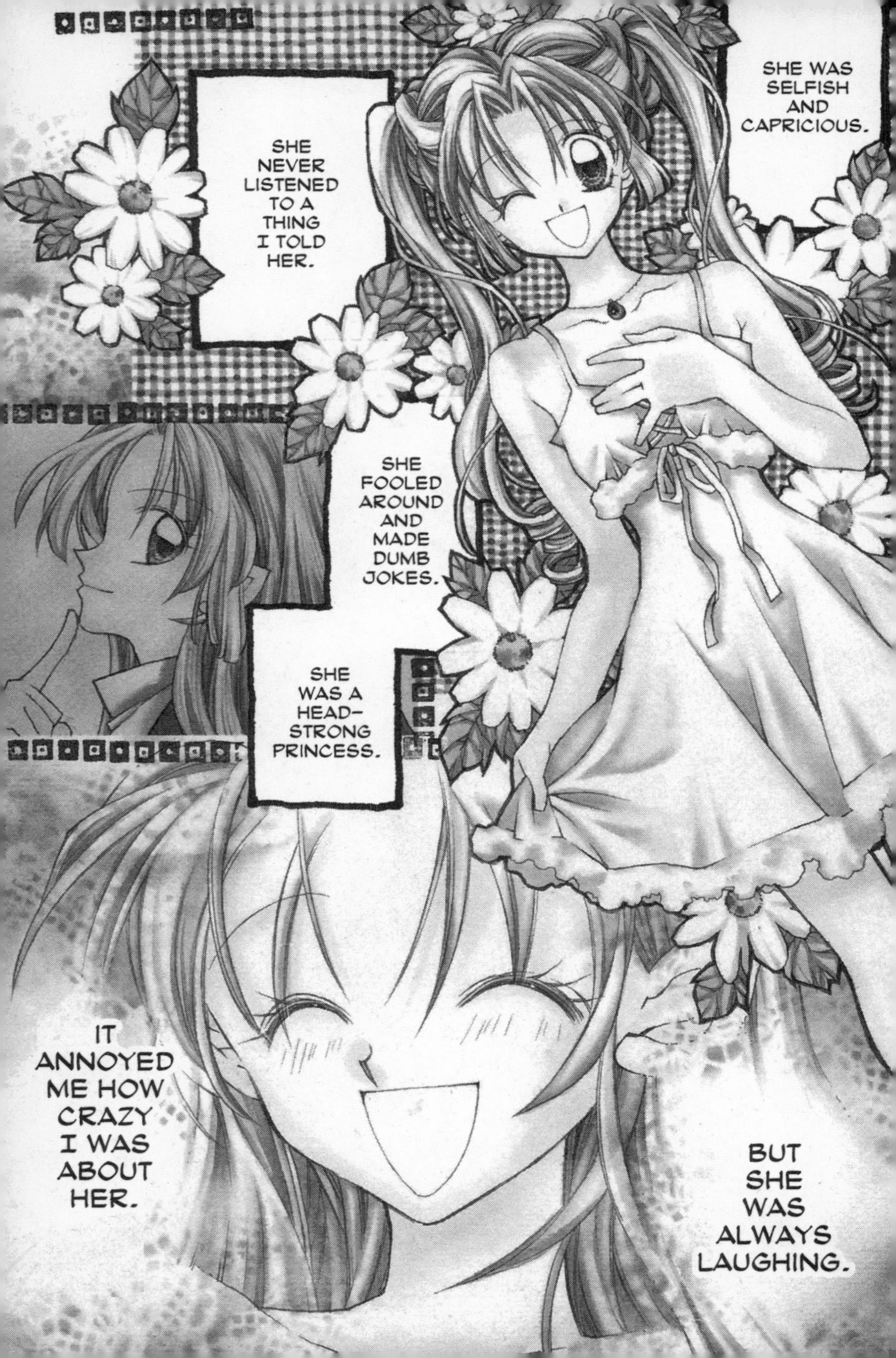
SHE WAS SELFISH AND CAPRICIOUS.
SHE NEVER LISTENED TO A THING I TOLD HER.
SHE FOOLED AROUND AND MADE DUMB JOKES.
SHE WAS A HEAD-STRONG PRINCESS.
IT ANNOYED ME HOW CRAZY I WAS ABOUT HER.
BUT SHE WAS ALWAYS LAUGHING.

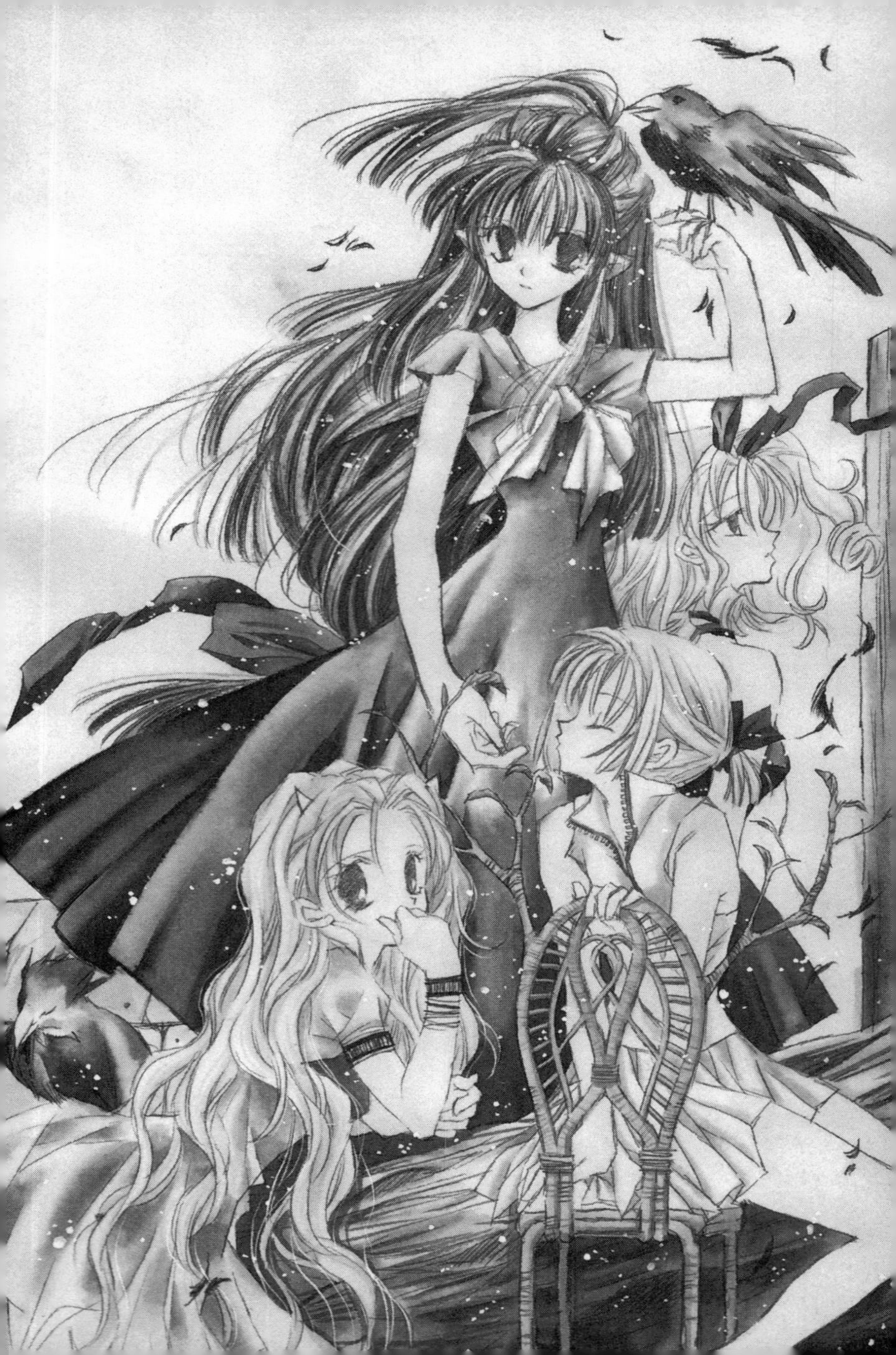

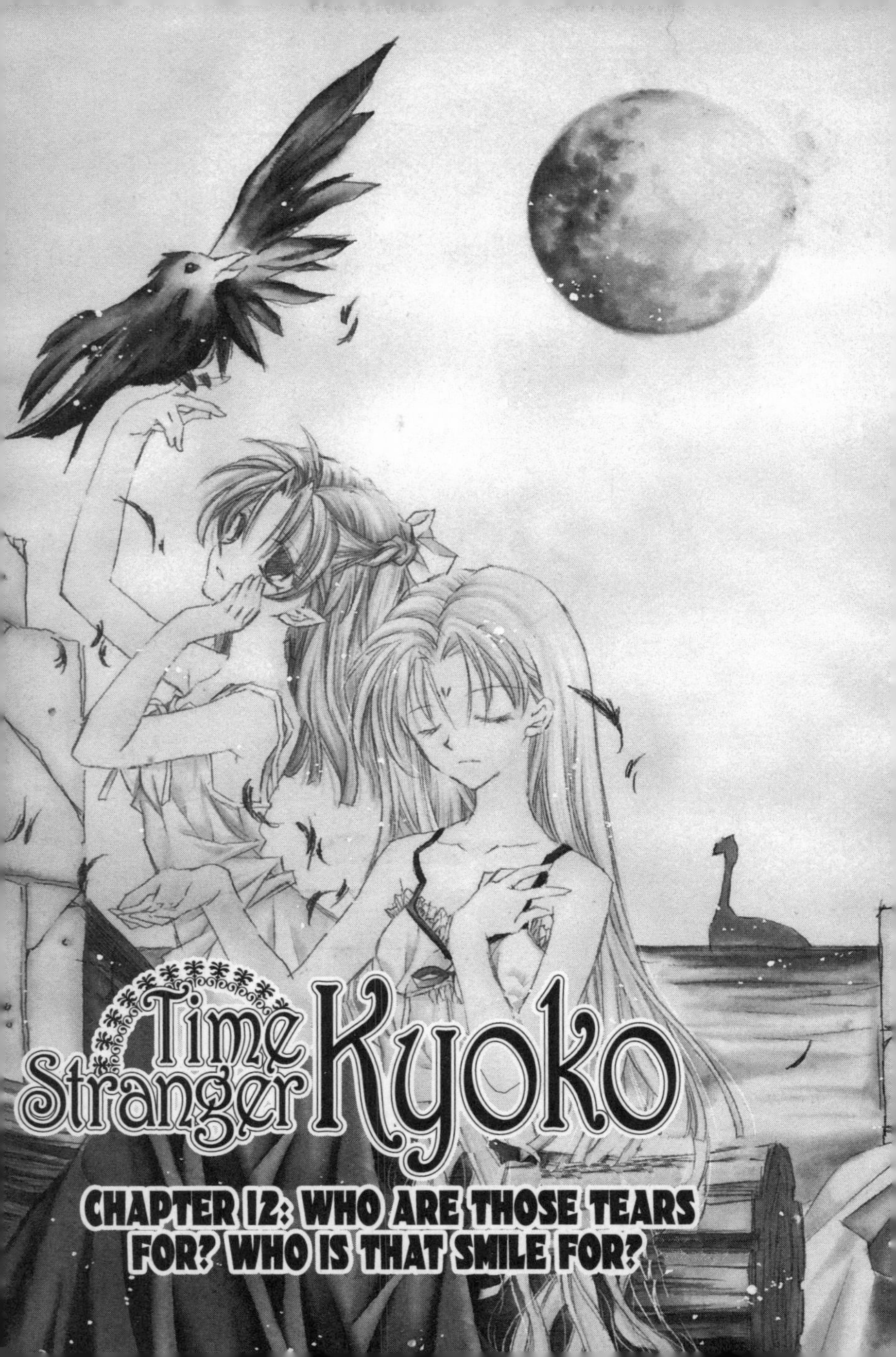
Time Stranger Kyoko
CHAPTER 12: WHO ARE THOSE TEARS FOR? WHO IS THAT SMILE FOR?

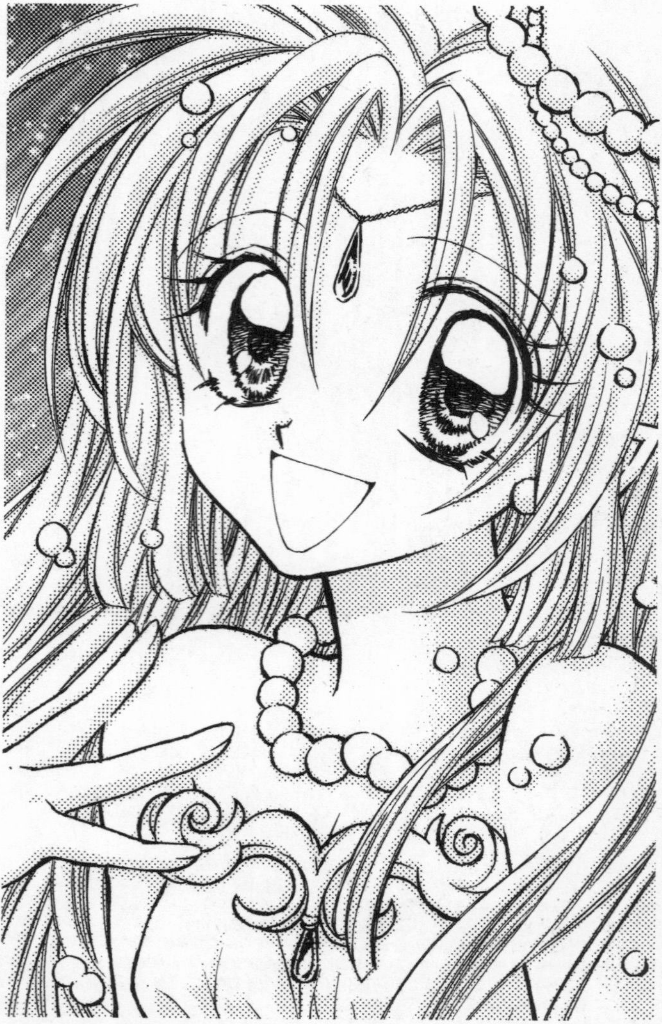

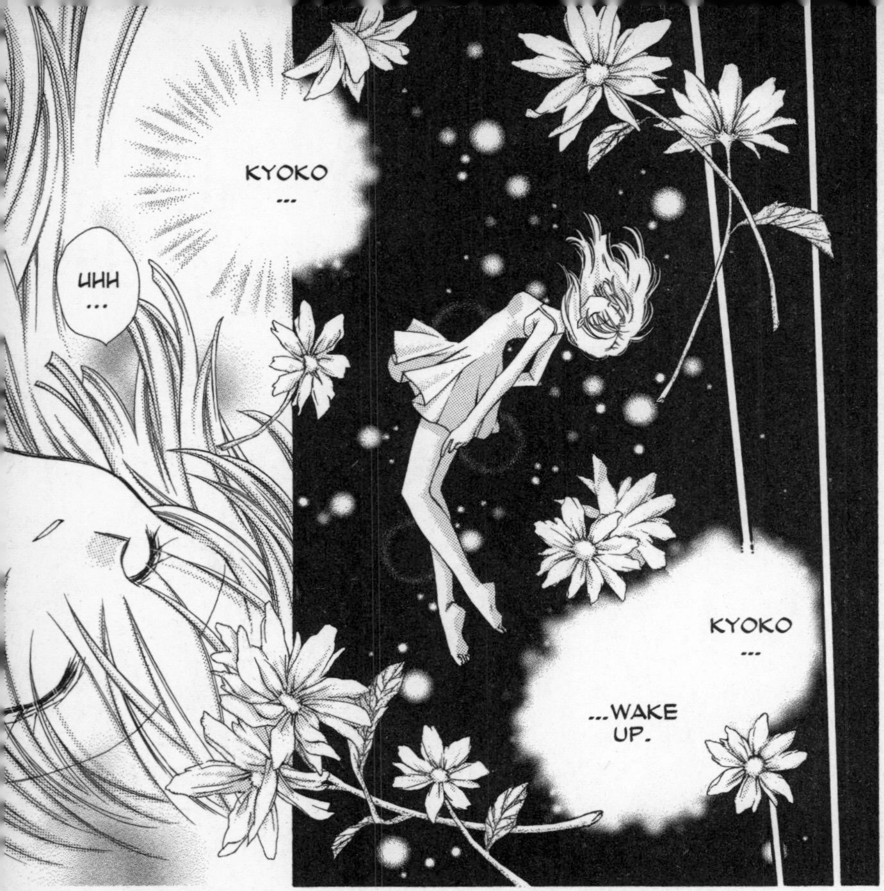
KYOKO ...
...WAKE UP.
KYOKO ...
UHH ...

CHAPTER 12: WHO ARE THOSE TEARS FOR? WHO IS THAT SMILE FOR? LEAD-IN

WHAT LIES AHEAD FOR THE STRANGERS NOW THAT THEY'VE ACCOMPLISHED THEIR MISSION?

(SPOILER ALERT!)

THIS TITLE PAGE ILLUSTRATION IS ONE I WANTED TO DRAW AT LEAST ONCE: JUST THE FEMALE STRANGERS. IT WAS USED AS A POSTER IN AN EXTRA EDITION OF *KYOKO*. I COULDN'T DECIDE WHETHER TO USE IT AS A POSTER OR A TITLE PAGE IMAGE. (EITHER WOULD BE OKAY.) THE SOLID LINES WERE DRAWN WITH A LEAD PENCIL. I WANTED IT TO LOOK POSED...I REALLY LIKE THE DRAWINGS OF RIN-CHAN AND YOUJU-CHAN. I WANTED IT TO LOOK LIKE THE PALE BLUE SKY JUST BEFORE DAWN.

BACK TO THE STORY...THIS WAS THE SCENE I WANTED TO WRITE THE MOST, SO I REALLY ENJOYED IT. LOVE IS GREAT, ISN'T IT? ♥ YUP, THIS IS MY FAVORITE PART OF THE STORY! AWESOME TIMES TWO. IT SEEMS UI'S CHARACTER WAS DIFFERENT FROM WHAT THE FANS EXPECTED, AND THEY WERE REALLY SURPRISED. HER IMAGE KEPT CHANGING IN MY MIND... SHE WAS ASLEEP FOR 16 YEARS, SO I THOUGHT THAT WHEN SHE FINALLY WOKE SHE'D BE LIKE A BABY. BUT THEN I THOUGHT SHE SHOULD HAVE SOME AWARENESS OR UNDERSTANDING OF WHAT WAS GOING ON. IN THIS CHAPTER, DRAWING THE CLOCK BROUGHT ASA-CHAN ALMOST TO TEARS. THIS TIME THE CLOCK CAME OUT A LITTLE FUNKY, WITH SNAKES AROUND THE EDGES, COURTESY OF KACCHI. WELL DONE. THE SCREENTONE TEAM HAD IT ROUGH TOO. PLEASE KEEP UP THE GOOD WORK!

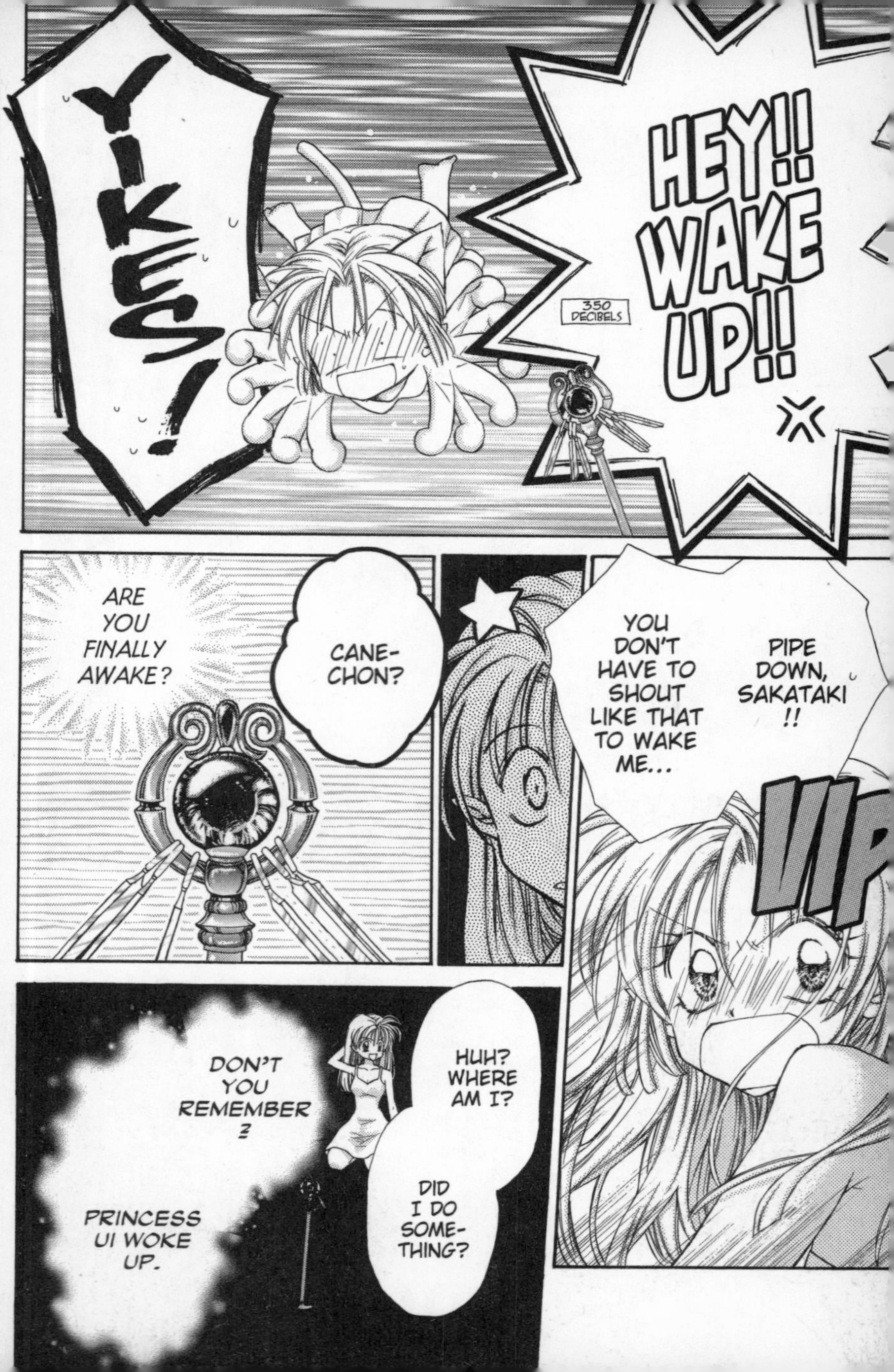
HEY!! WAKE UP!!
350 DECIBELS
YIKES!
PIPE DOWN, SAKATAKI!!
YOU DON'T HAVE TO SHOUT LIKE THAT TO WAKE ME...
CANE-CHON?
ARE YOU FINALLY AWAKE?
HUH? WHERE AM I?
DID I DO SOMETHING?
DON'T YOU REMEMBER?
PRINCESS UI WOKE UP.

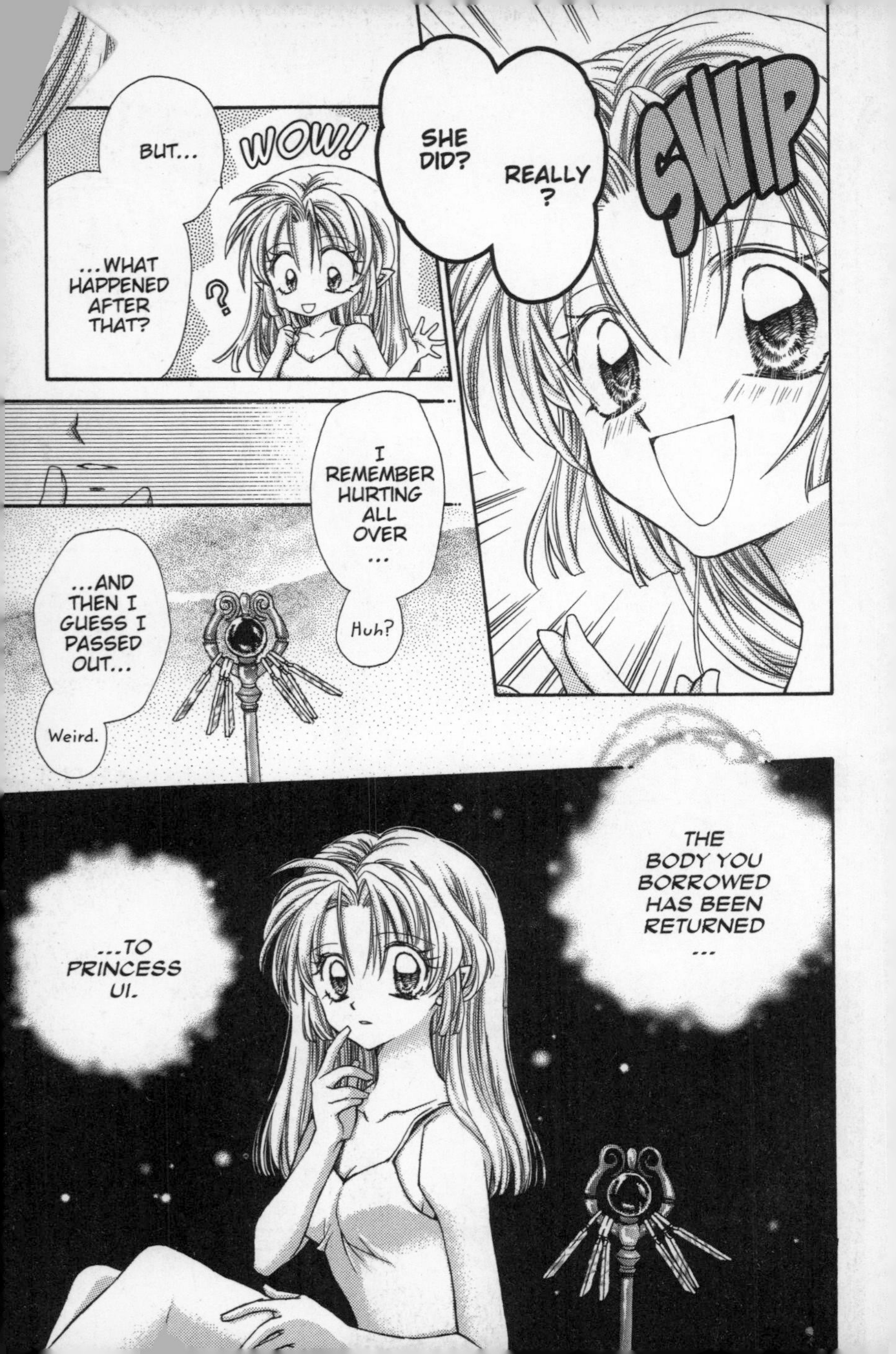
SHE DID?
REALLY?
SWIP
WOW!
BUT...
...WHAT HAPPENED AFTER THAT?
I REMEMBER HURTING ALL OVER...
Huh?
...AND THEN I GUESS I PASSED OUT...
Weird.
THE BODY YOU BORROWED HAS BEEN RETURNED...
...TO PRINCESS UI.

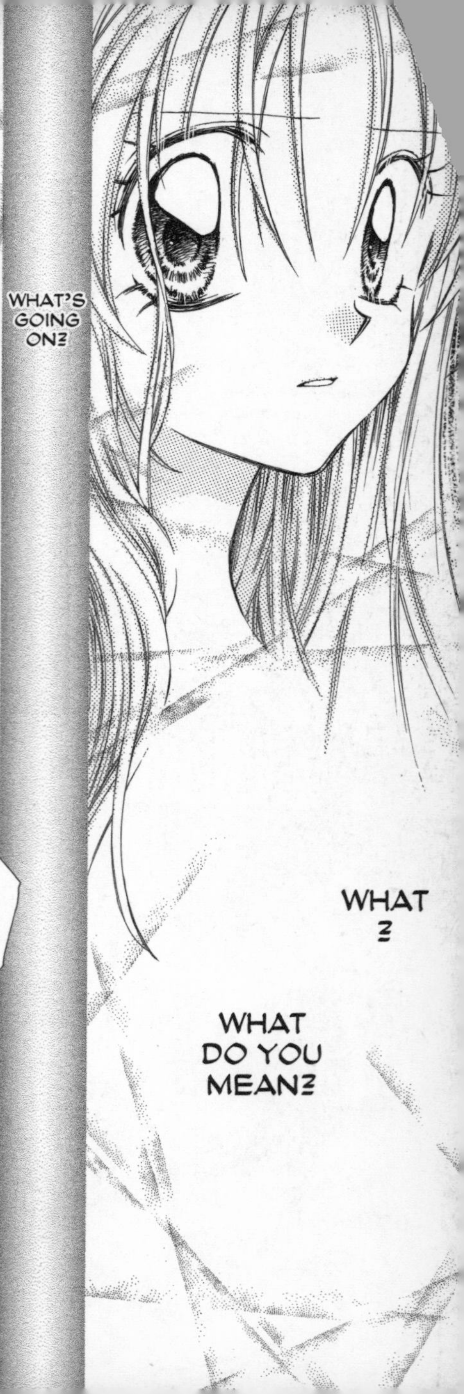
WHAT'S GOING ON?
WHAT ?
WHAT DO YOU MEAN?

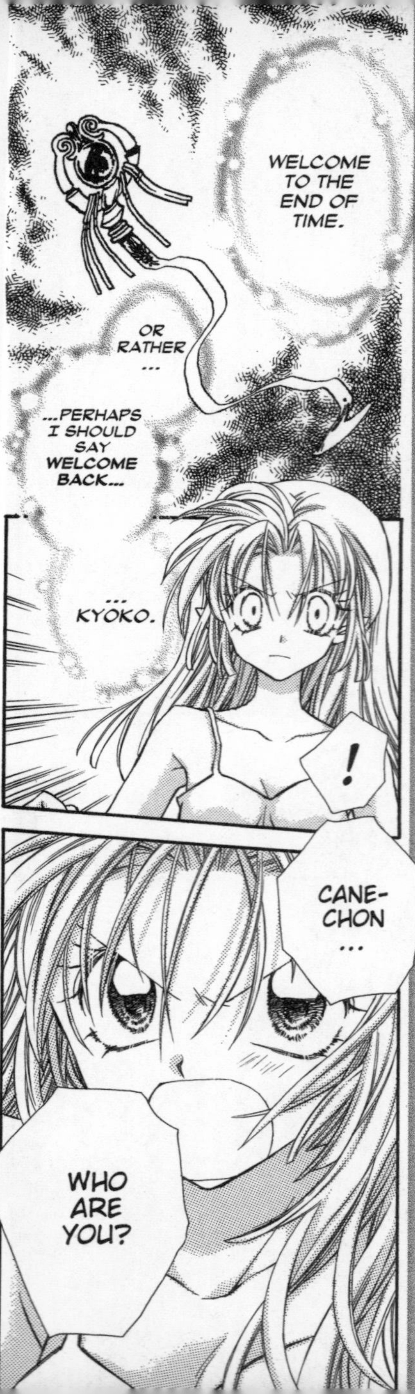
WELCOME TO THE END OF TIME.
OR RATHER ...
...PERHAPS I SHOULD SAY WELCOME BACK...
... KYÔKO.
!
CANE-CHON ...
WHO ARE YOU?

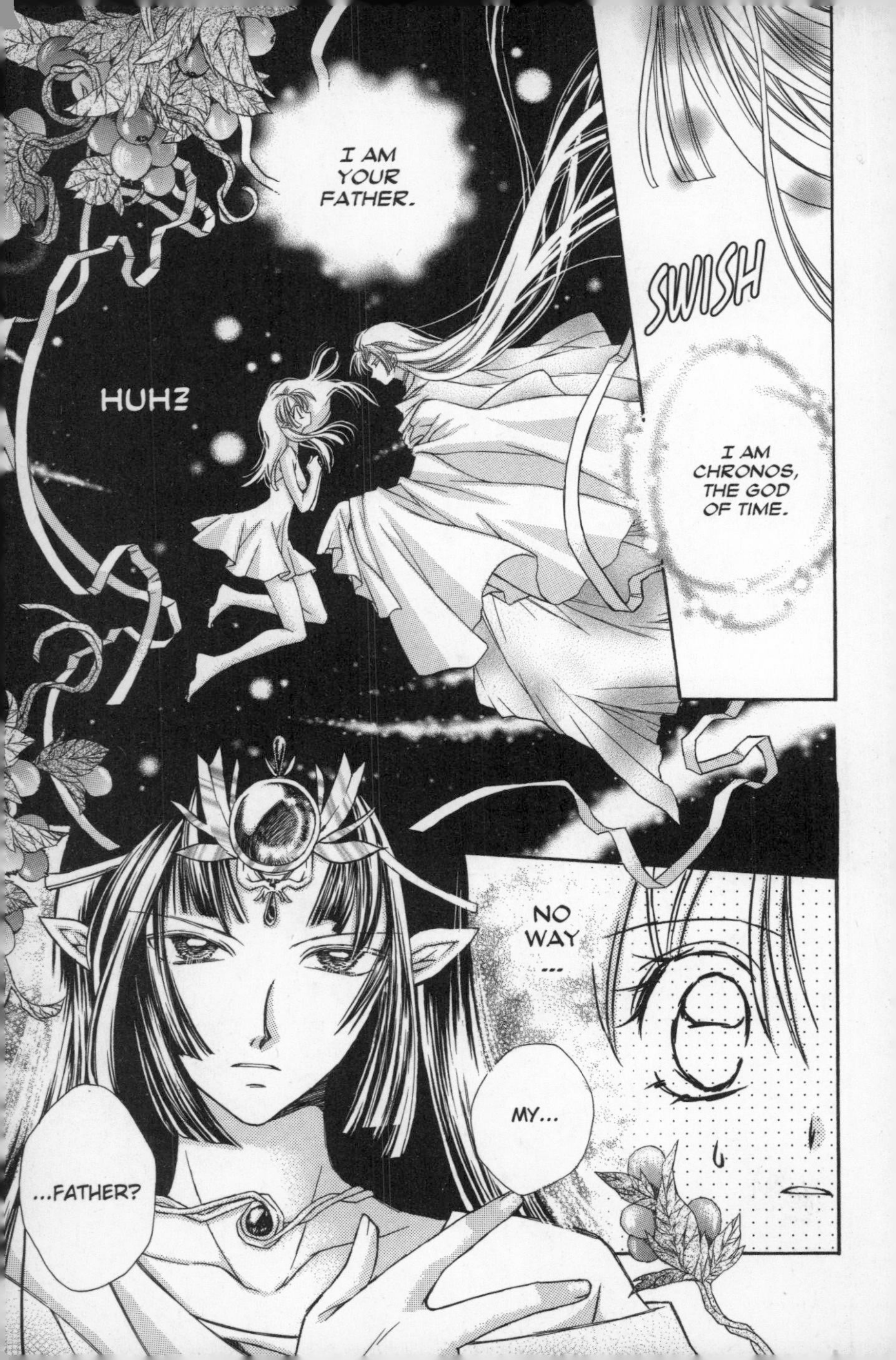
SWISH
I AM CHRONOS, THE GOD OF TIME.
I AM YOUR FATHER.
HUH?
NO WAY ...
MY...
...FATHER?

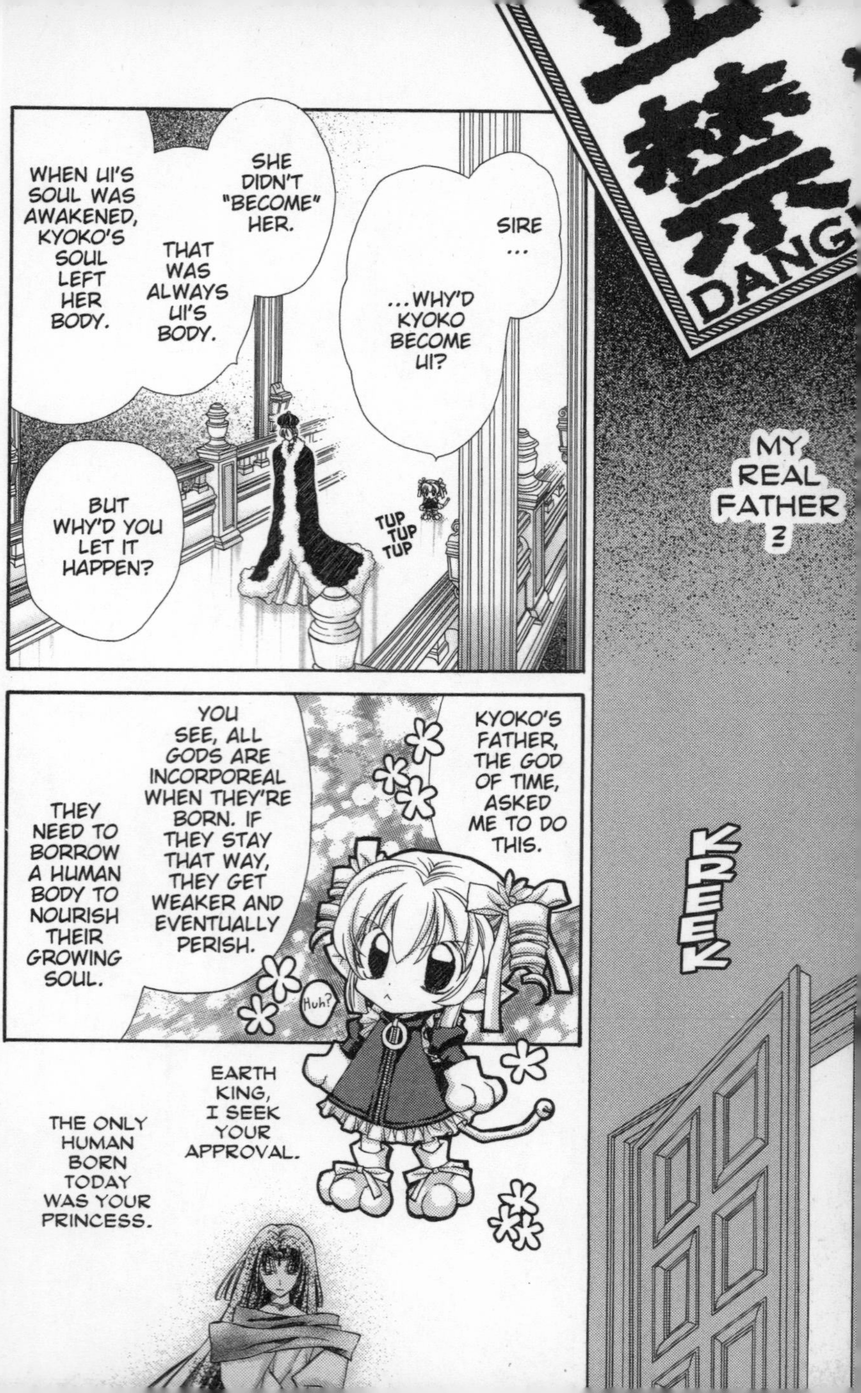
DANG
MY REAL FATHER?
KREEK
SIRE...
...WHY'D KYOKO BECOME UI?
SHE DIDN'T "BECOME" HER.
THAT WAS ALWAYS UI'S BODY.
WHEN UI'S SOUL WAS AWAKENED, KYOKO'S SOUL LEFT HER BODY.
TUP TUP TUP
BUT WHY'D YOU LET IT HAPPEN?
KYOKO'S FATHER, THE GOD OF TIME, ASKED ME TO DO THIS.
YOU SEE, ALL GODS ARE INCORPOREAL WHEN THEY'RE BORN. IF THEY STAY THAT WAY, THEY GET WEAKER AND EVENTUALLY PERISH.
THEY NEED TO BORROW A HUMAN BODY TO NOURISH THEIR GROWING SOUL.
Huh?
EARTH KING, I SEEK YOUR APPROVAL.
THE ONLY HUMAN BORN TODAY WAS YOUR PRINCESS.

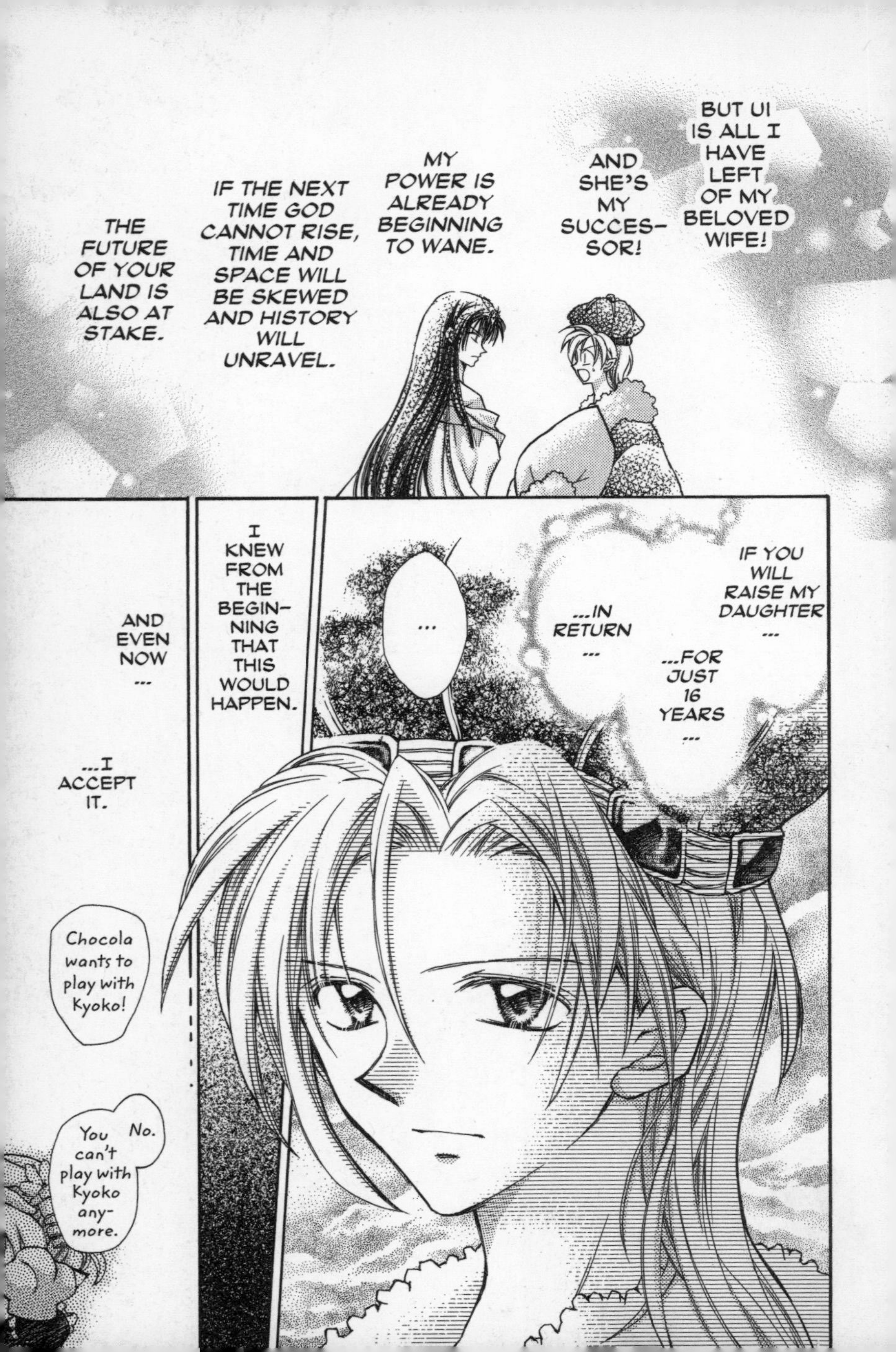
BUT UI IS ALL I HAVE LEFT OF MY BELOVED WIFE!
AND SHE'S MY SUCCES-SOR!
MY POWER IS ALREADY BEGINNING TO WANE.
IF THE NEXT TIME GOD CANNOT RISE, TIME AND SPACE WILL BE SKEWED AND HISTORY WILL UNRAVEL.
THE FUTURE OF YOUR LAND IS ALSO AT STAKE.
IF YOU WILL RAISE MY DAUGHTER...
...FOR JUST 16 YEARS...
...IN RETURN...
...
I KNEW FROM THE BEGIN-NING THAT THIS WOULD HAPPEN.
AND EVEN NOW...
...I ACCEPT IT.
Chocola wants to play with Kyoko!
No. You can't play with Kyoko any-more.

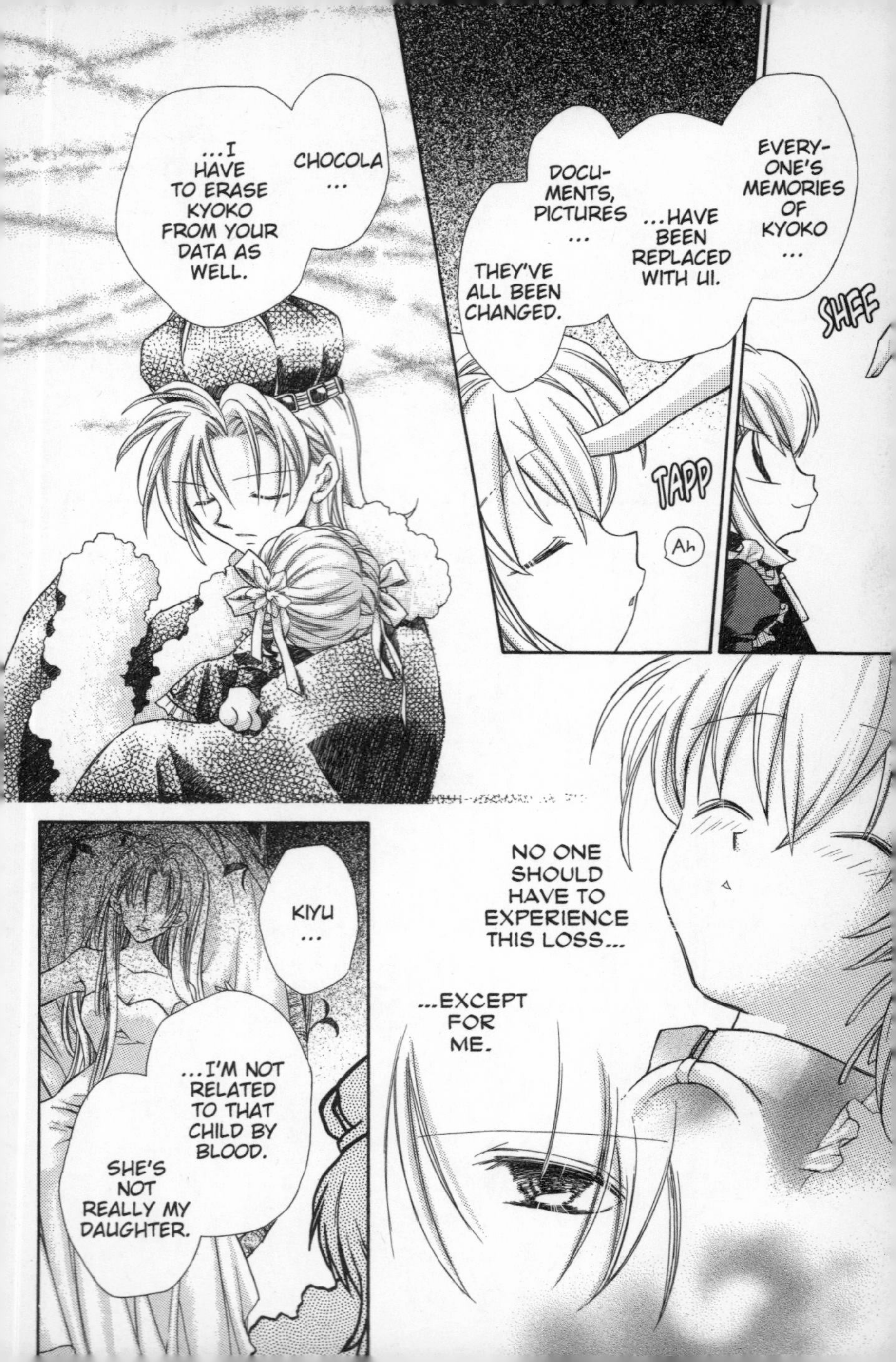
EVERY-ONE'S MEMORIES OF KYOKO ...
...HAVE BEEN REPLACED WITH UI.
DOCU-MENTS, PICTURES ...
THEY'VE ALL BEEN CHANGED.
SHFF
TAPP
Ah
CHOCOLA ...
...I HAVE TO ERASE KYOKO FROM YOUR DATA AS WELL.
NO ONE SHOULD HAVE TO EXPERIENCE THIS LOSS...
...EXCEPT FOR ME.
KIYU ...
...I'M NOT RELATED TO THAT CHILD BY BLOOD.
SHE'S NOT REALLY MY DAUGHTER.

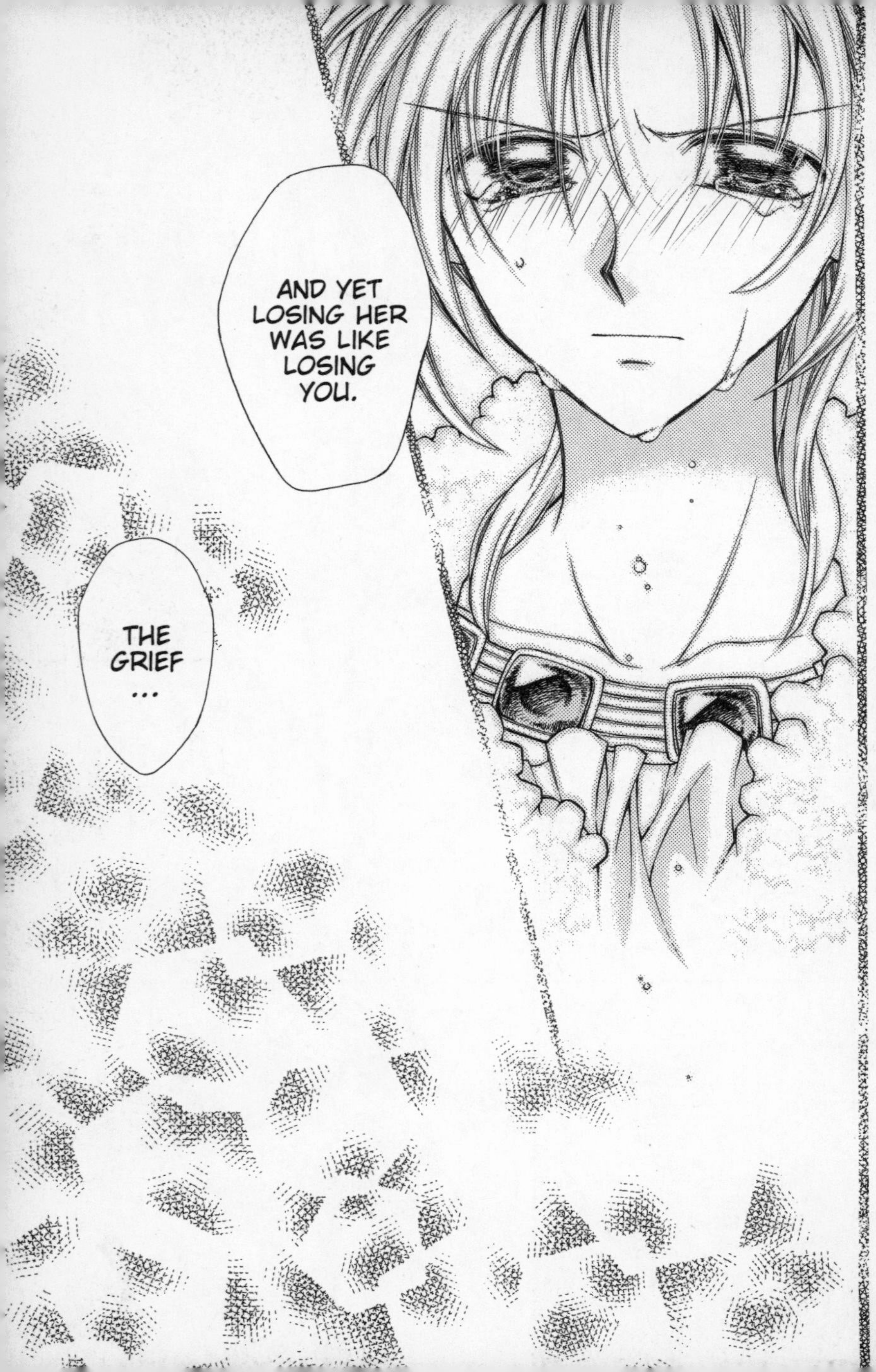
AND YET LOSING HER WAS LIKE LOSING YOU.
THE GRIEF ...

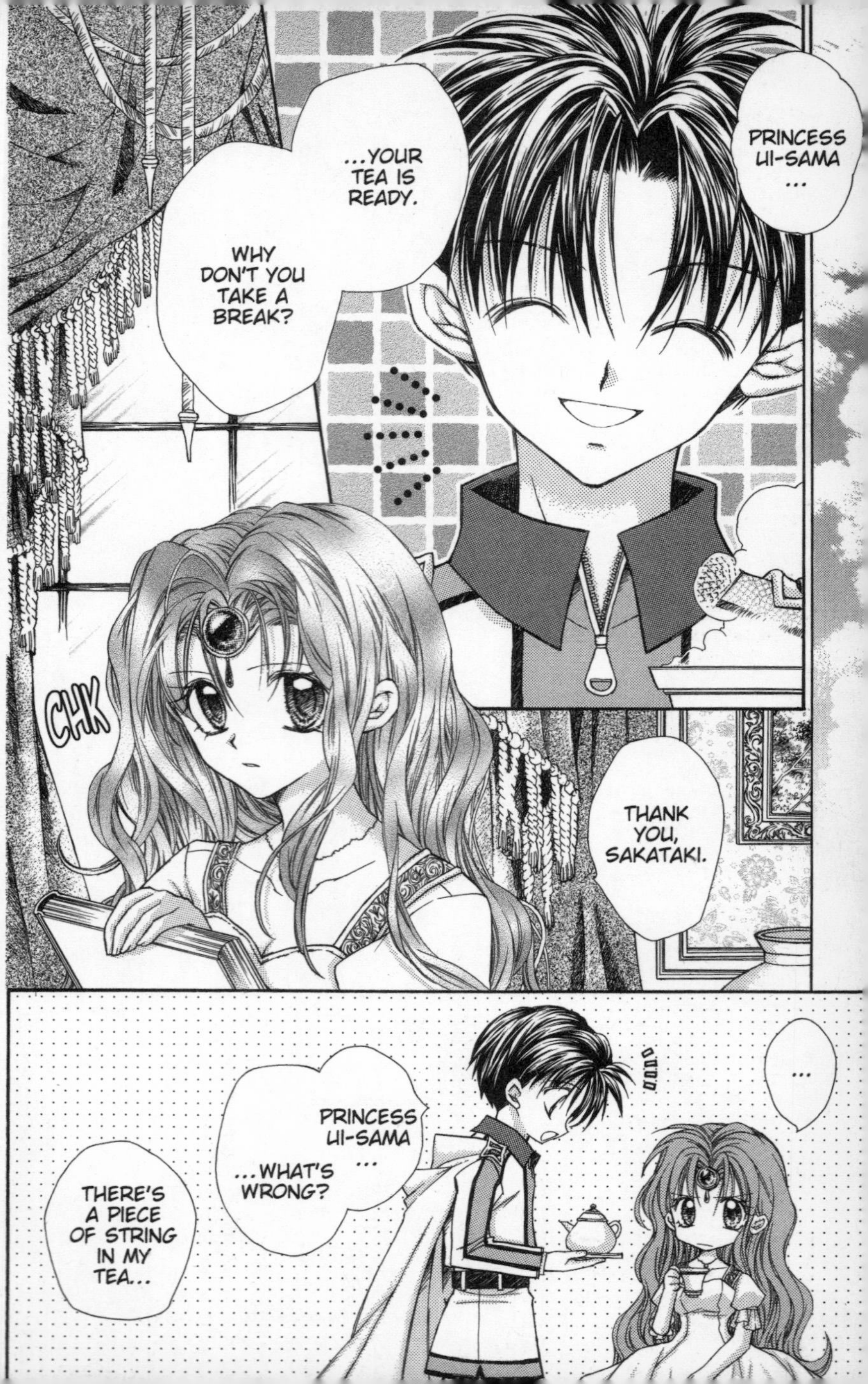
PRINCESS UI-SAMA ...
...YOUR TEA IS READY.
WHY DON'T YOU TAKE A BREAK?
CHK
THANK YOU, SAKATAKI.
...
PRINCESS UI-SAMA ...
...WHAT'S WRONG?
THERE'S A PIECE OF STRING IN MY TEA...

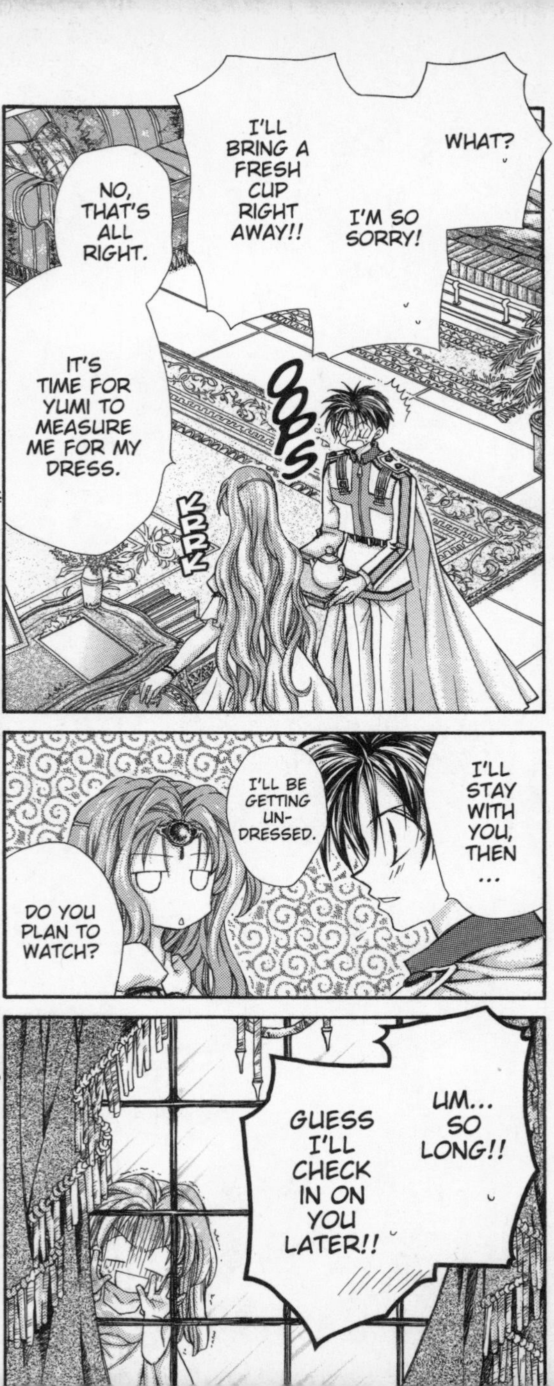
WHAT?
I'M SO SORRY!
I'LL BRING A FRESH CUP RIGHT AWAY!!
NO, THAT'S ALL RIGHT.
OOPS
IT'S TIME FOR YUMI TO MEASURE ME FOR MY DRESS.
KRRK
I'LL STAY WITH YOU, THEN...
I'LL BE GETTING UN-DRESSED.
DO YOU PLAN TO WATCH?
UM... SO LONG!!
GUESS I'LL CHECK IN ON YOU LATER!!

FF10.

WE BEAT IT! I USED WHAT LITTLE DOWNTIME I HAD, AND I MADE THE NEW ASSISTANT JOIN IN TOO, AND THE FOUR OF US BEAT IT TOGETHER. ← WHENEVER I HAD A DEADLINE, I PASSED THE CONTROLLER TO SOMEONE ELSE...

AT FIRST THERE WEREN'T MANY BATTLES, AND THE FIRST FIVE OR SIX HOURS WERE KIND OF BORING (YOU COULD FINISH WITHOUT VANQUISHING THE ENEMY). BUT AS I KEPT GOING THE BATTLES GOT MORE FUN, AND THE ULTIMATE WEAPONS HAVE THE BEST DAMAGE LIMITS!! YOU CAN GIVE YOUR ENEMIES MORE THAN **9,999** HIT POINTS.

I THINK THIS WILL BE EVEN MORE EXCITING FOR THOSE WHO HAVE PLAYED PREVIOUS *FINAL FANTASY* GAMES. THE SPHERE BOARD IS REALLY INTERESTING! ONE OF THE MAJOR ATTRACTIONS IS THAT YOU CAN DEVELOP THE CHARACTERS AS YOU LIKE.

I also like the Sabotender miniquests.

THE SCENARIO AND SETTING ARE VERY GOOD. IT MADE MY HEART POUND. I CAN'T SAY ANY MORE BECAUSE I DON'T WANT TO GIVE ANYTHING AWAY. I WAS MOST CAUGHT UP DURING THE BIG BATTLE HALFWAY THROUGH. MY HEART KEPT BEATING FASTER AS I WONDERED HOW IT WAS GOING TO TURN OUT.

IT'S BEEN A LONG TIME SINCE I BEAT A VIDEO GAME.

Auronji is great! (It's really just Auron. I just felt like adding the "ji"...)

THE END...SORRY, WHEN I FIRST SAW IT, ALL I COULD SAY WAS, "WHAT THE HECK IS THIS?"

Why? It's okay...it's okay...but it's so short. My only moment of dissatisfaction (bitter laugh).

I WORKED SO HARD, AND THIS IS ALL I GET? (SOB) I WANTED TO AT LEAST SEE WHAT HAPPENED TO THE CHARACTERS AFTERWARD. I DIDN'T LIKE THAT IT LEFT SO MUCH UP TO THE IMAGINATION, BUT I GUESS THAT'S A PERSONAL PET PEEVE.

I feel the same way about manga.

BUT THE SECOND TIME I SAW IT, I LIKED IT BETTER. IT WAS MY FAULT FOR EXPECTING TOO MUCH FROM THE BEGINNING.

I guess I still haven't totally accepted it...

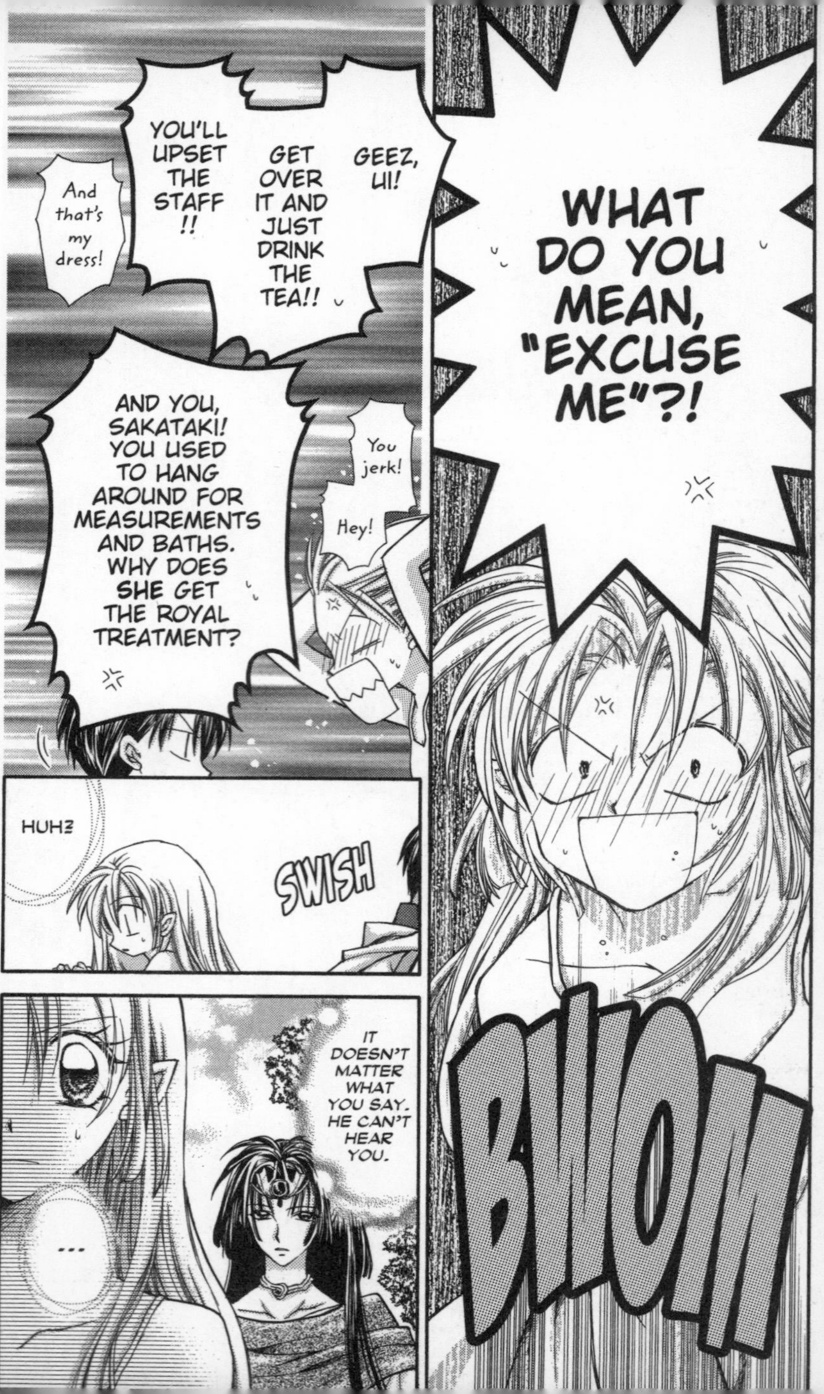
WHAT DO YOU MEAN, "EXCUSE ME"?!
BWOM
GEEZ, UI!
GET OVER IT AND JUST DRINK THE TEA!!
YOU'LL UPSET THE STAFF!!
And that's my dress!
You jerk!
Hey!
AND YOU, SAKATAKI! YOU USED TO HANG AROUND FOR MEASUREMENTS AND BATHS. WHY DOES SHE GET THE ROYAL TREATMENT?
SWISH
HUH?
IT DOESN'T MATTER WHAT YOU SAY. HE CAN'T HEAR YOU.
...

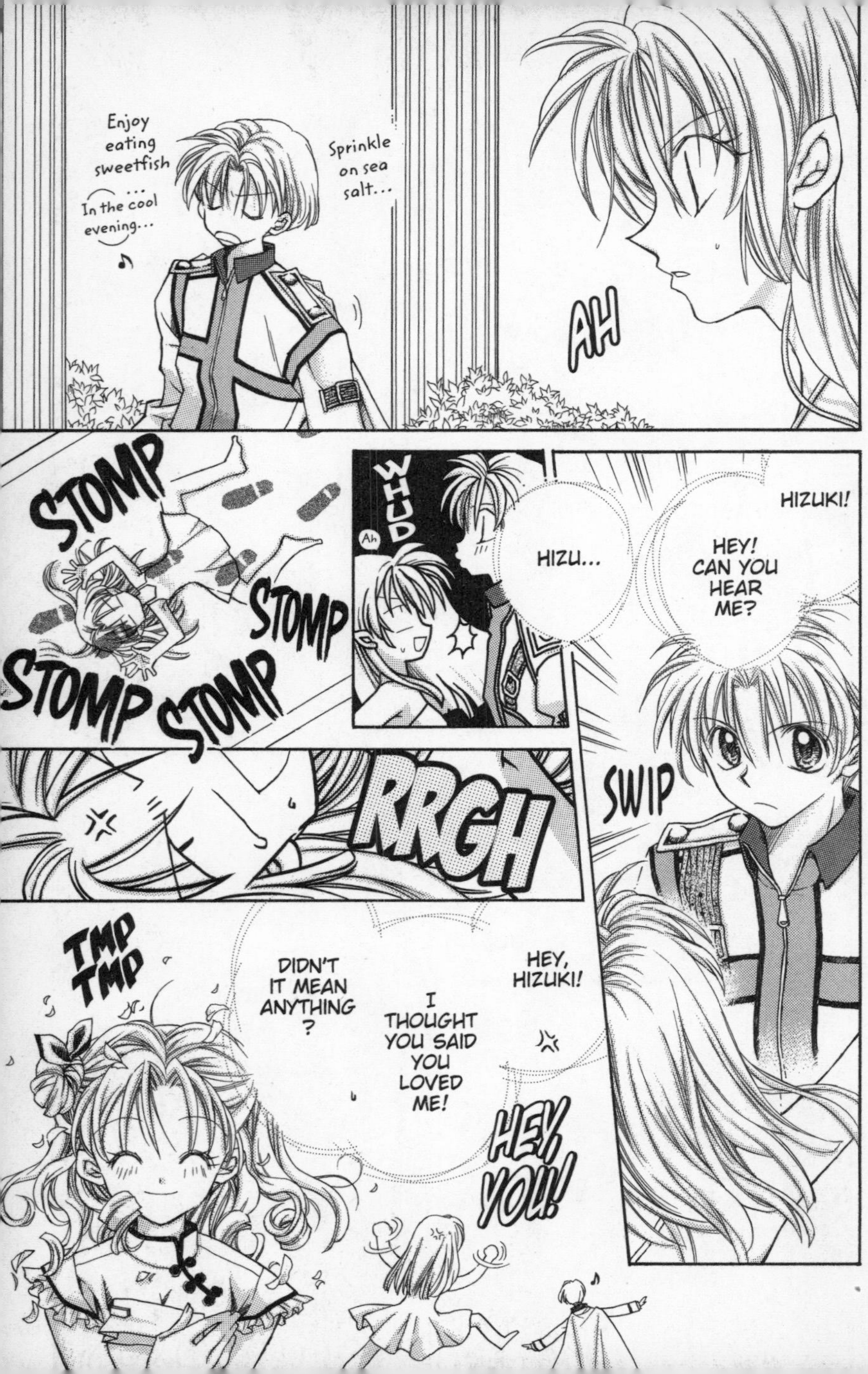
AH
Sprinkle on sea salt...
Enjoy eating sweetfish ... In the cool evening...
HIZUKI!
HEY! CAN YOU HEAR ME?
SWIP
HIZU...
WHUD
Ah
STOMP
STOMP
STOMP
STOMP
RRGH
HEY, HIZUKI!
I THOUGHT YOU SAID YOU LOVED ME!
DIDN'T IT MEAN ANYTHING?
HEY, YOU!!
TMP TMP

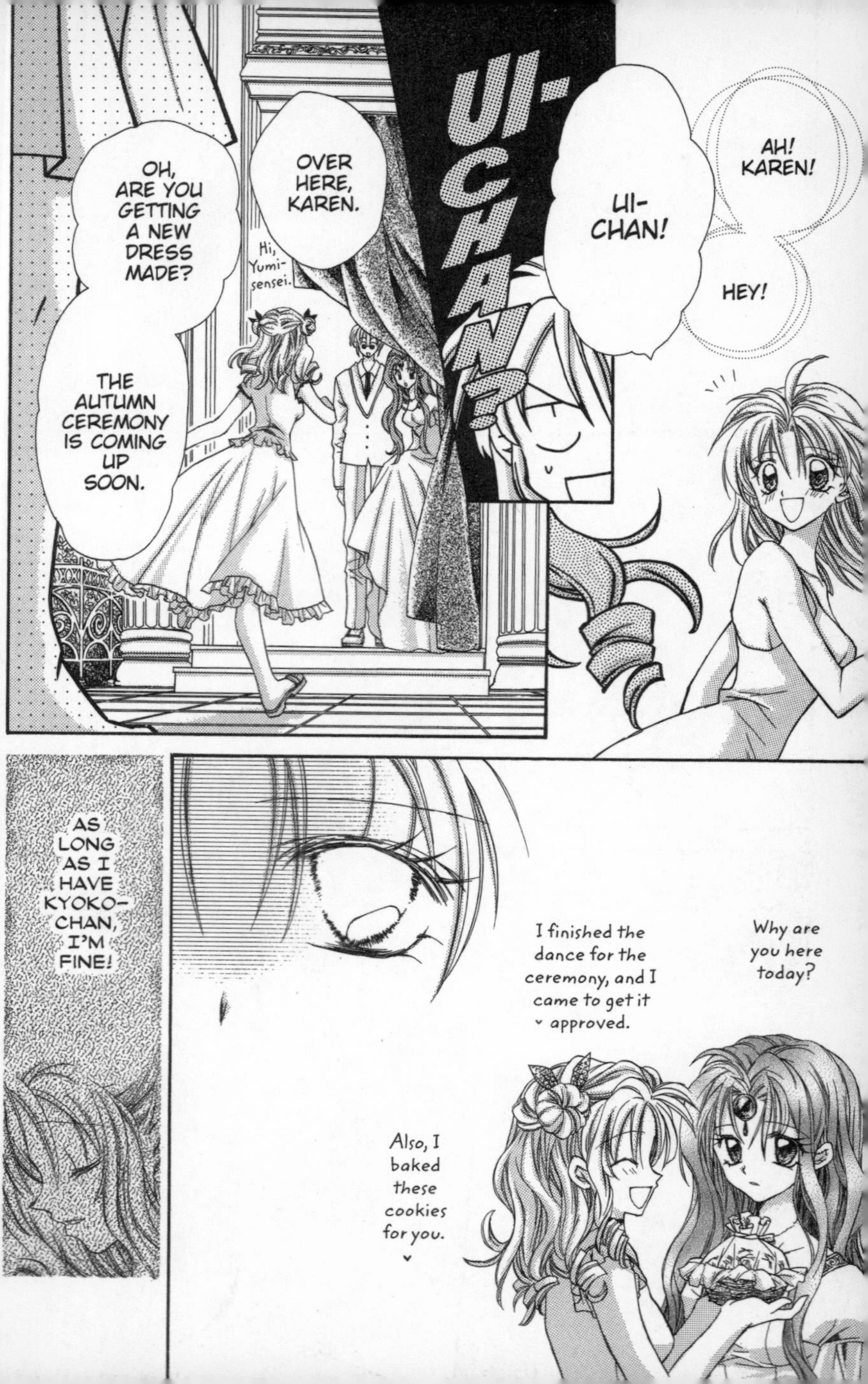
AH! KAREN!
HEY!
UI-CHAN!
UI-CHAN!
OVER HERE, KAREN.
Hi, Yumi-sensei.
OH, ARE YOU GETTING A NEW DRESS MADE?
THE AUTUMN CEREMONY IS COMING UP SOON.
Why are you here today?
I finished the dance for the ceremony, and I came to get it approved.
Also, I baked these cookies for you.
AS LONG AS I HAVE KYOKO-CHAN, I'M FINE!

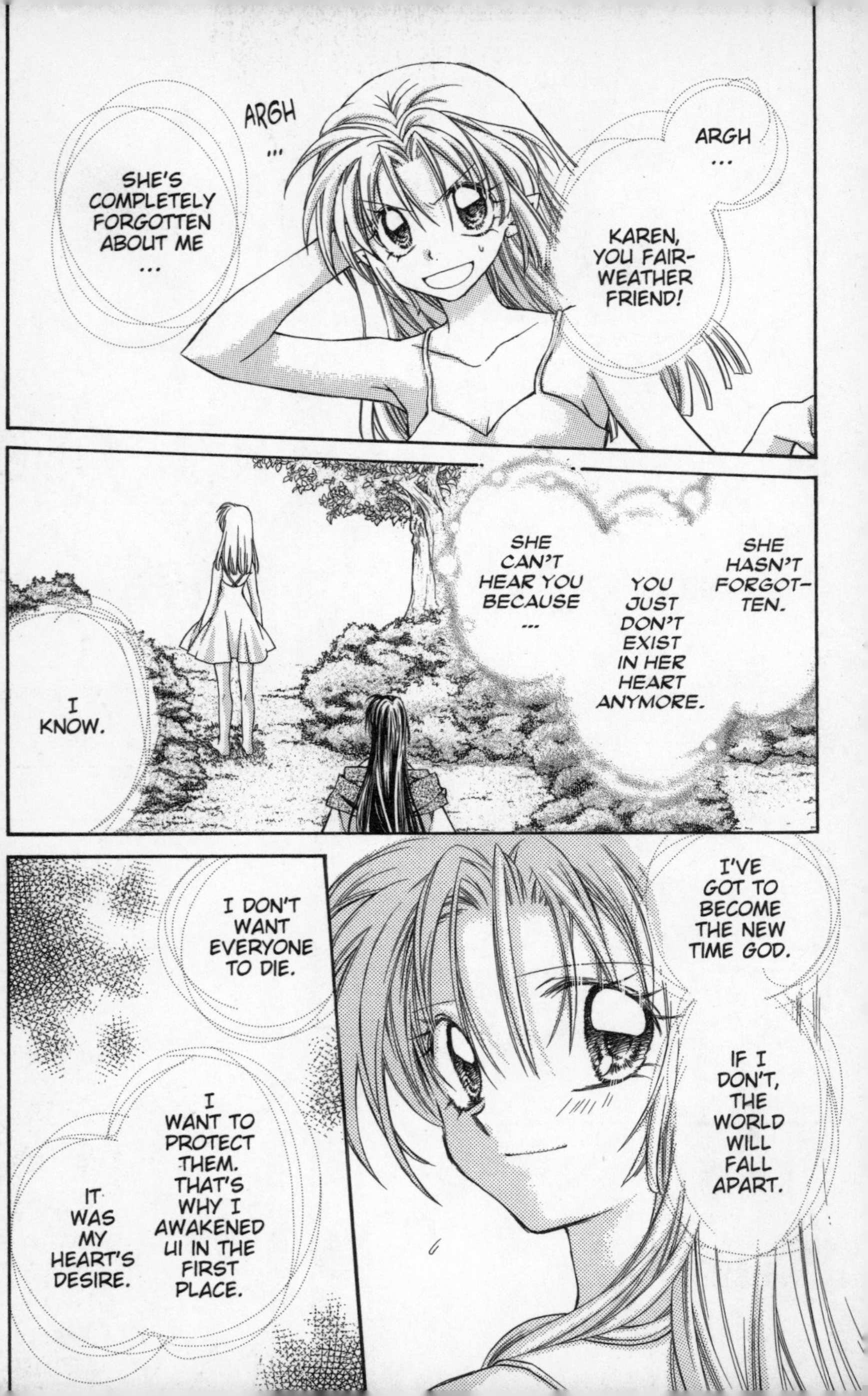
ARGH ...
KAREN, YOU FAIR-WEATHER FRIEND!
ARGH ...
SHE'S COMPLETELY FORGOTTEN ABOUT ME ...
SHE HASN'T FORGOT-TEN.
SHE CAN'T HEAR YOU BECAUSE ...
YOU JUST DON'T EXIST IN HER HEART ANYMORE.
I KNOW.
I'VE GOT TO BECOME THE NEW TIME GOD.
I DON'T WANT EVERYONE TO DIE.
IF I DON'T, THE WORLD WILL FALL APART.
I WANT TO PROTECT THEM. THAT'S WHY I AWAKENED UI IN THE FIRST PLACE.
IT WAS MY HEART'S DESIRE.

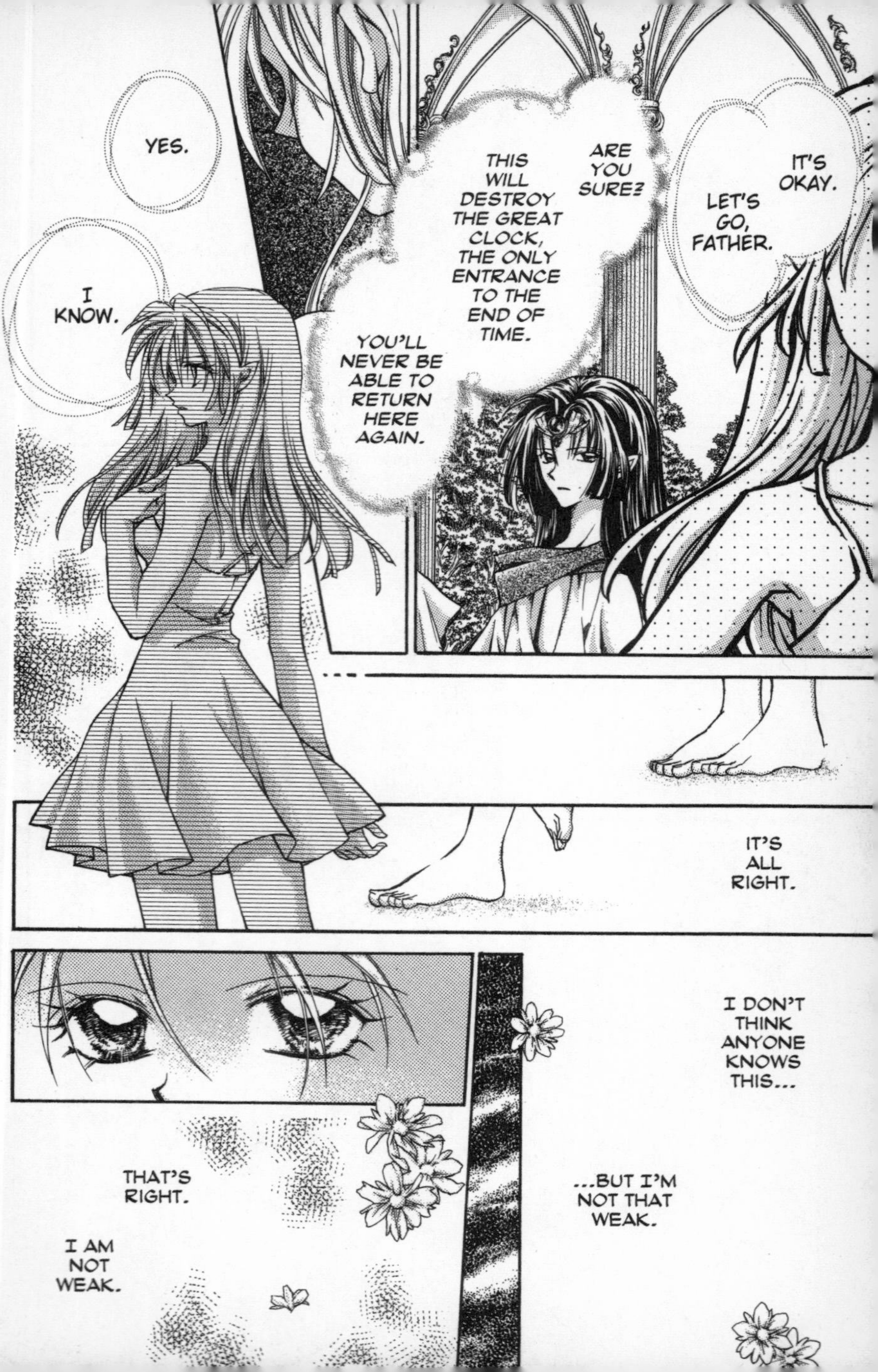
IT'S OKAY.
LET'S GO, FATHER.
ARE YOU SURE?
THIS WILL DESTROY THE GREAT CLOCK, THE ONLY ENTRANCE TO THE END OF TIME.
YOU'LL NEVER BE ABLE TO RETURN HERE AGAIN.
YES.
I KNOW.
IT'S ALL RIGHT.
I DON'T THINK ANYONE KNOWS THIS...
...BUT I'M NOT THAT WEAK.
THAT'S RIGHT.
I AM NOT WEAK.

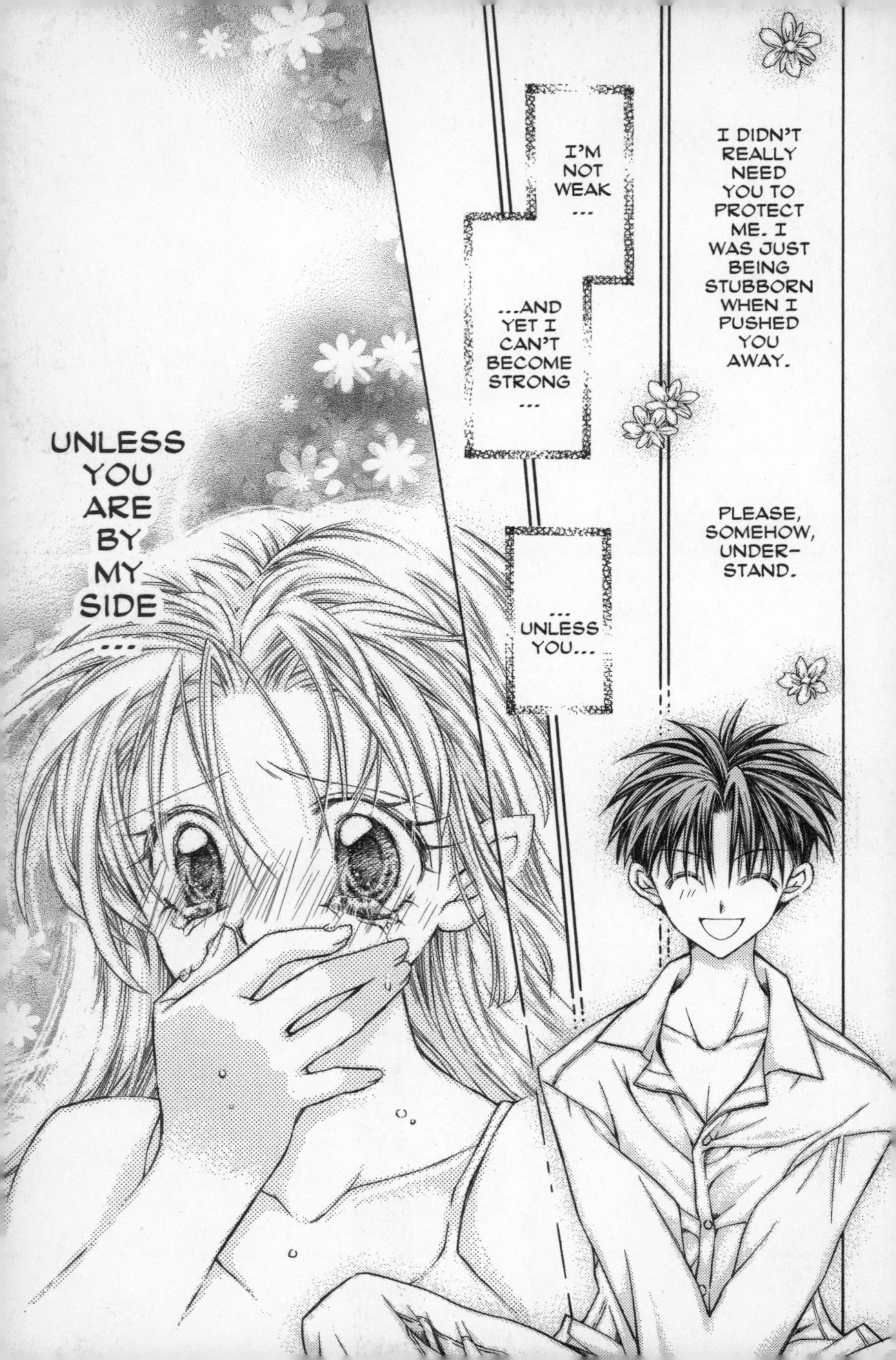
I DIDN'T REALLY NEED YOU TO PROTECT ME. I WAS JUST BEING STUBBORN WHEN I PUSHED YOU AWAY.
PLEASE, SOMEHOW, UNDER-STAND.
I'M NOT WEAK...
...AND YET I CAN'T BECOME STRONG...
...UNLESS YOU...
UNLESS YOU ARE BY MY SIDE...

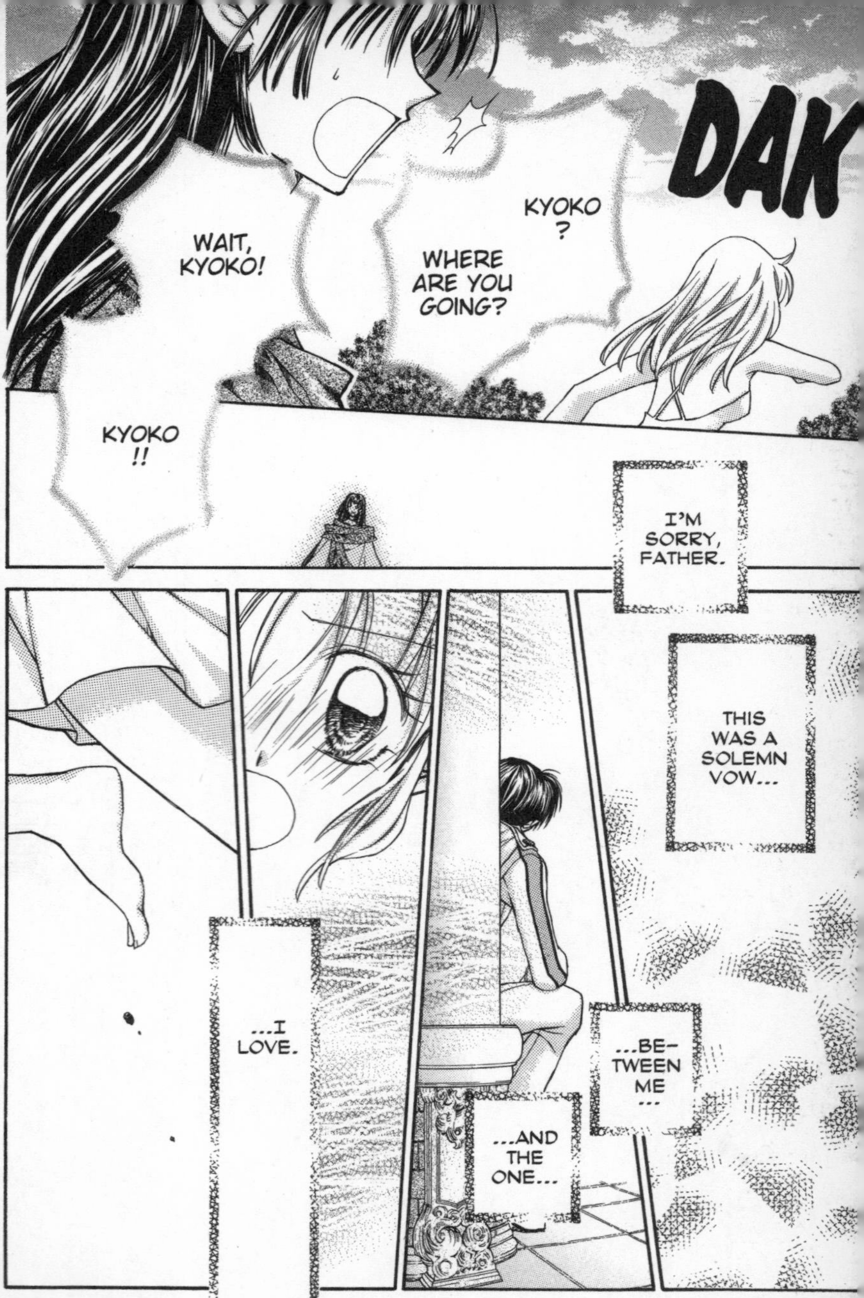
DAK
KYOKO ?
WHERE ARE YOU GOING?
WAIT, KYOKO!
I'M SORRY, FATHER.
KYOKO !!
THIS WAS A SOLEMN VOW...
...BE- TWEEN ME ...
...AND THE ONE...
...I LOVE.

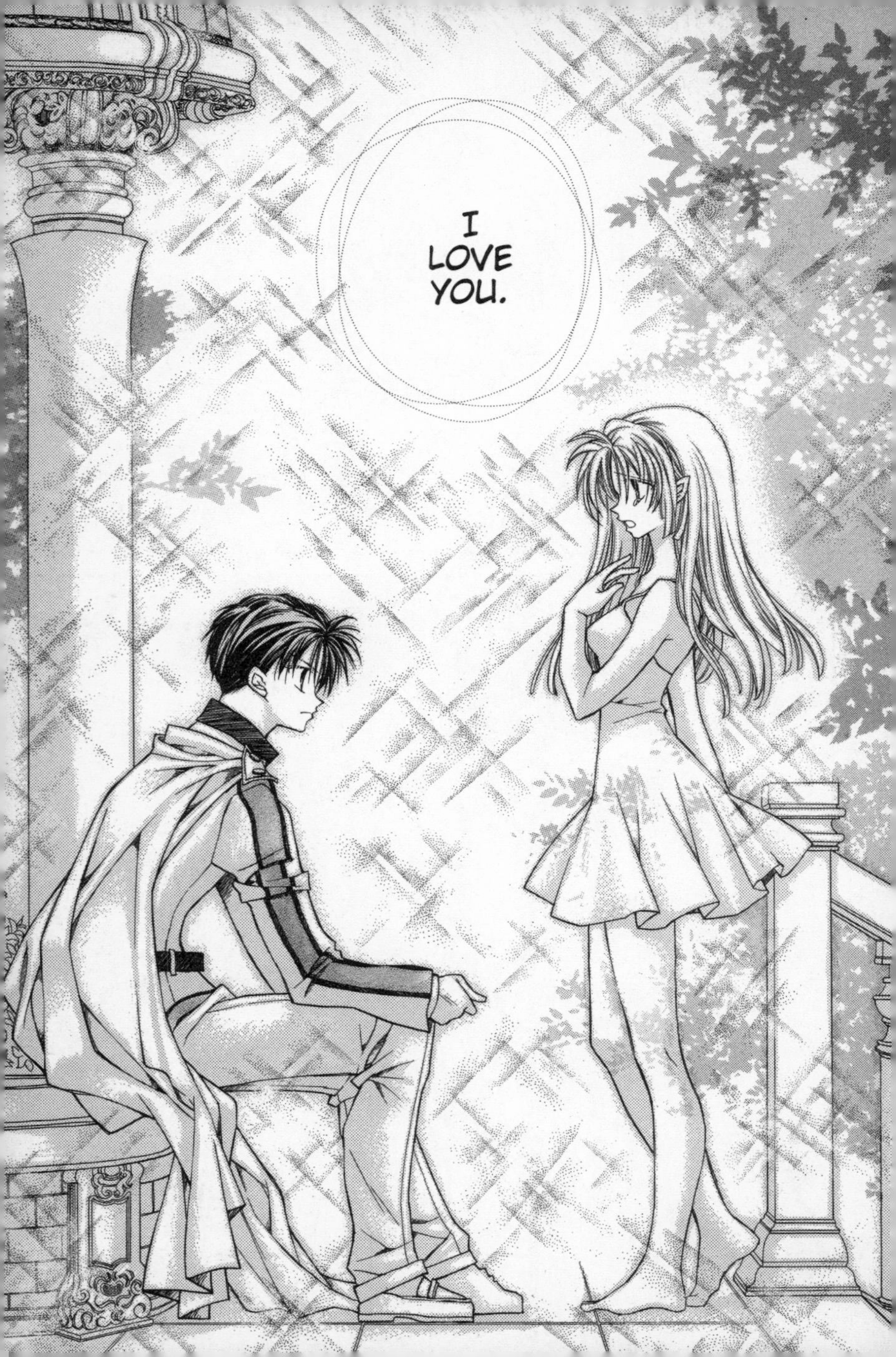
I LOVE YOU.

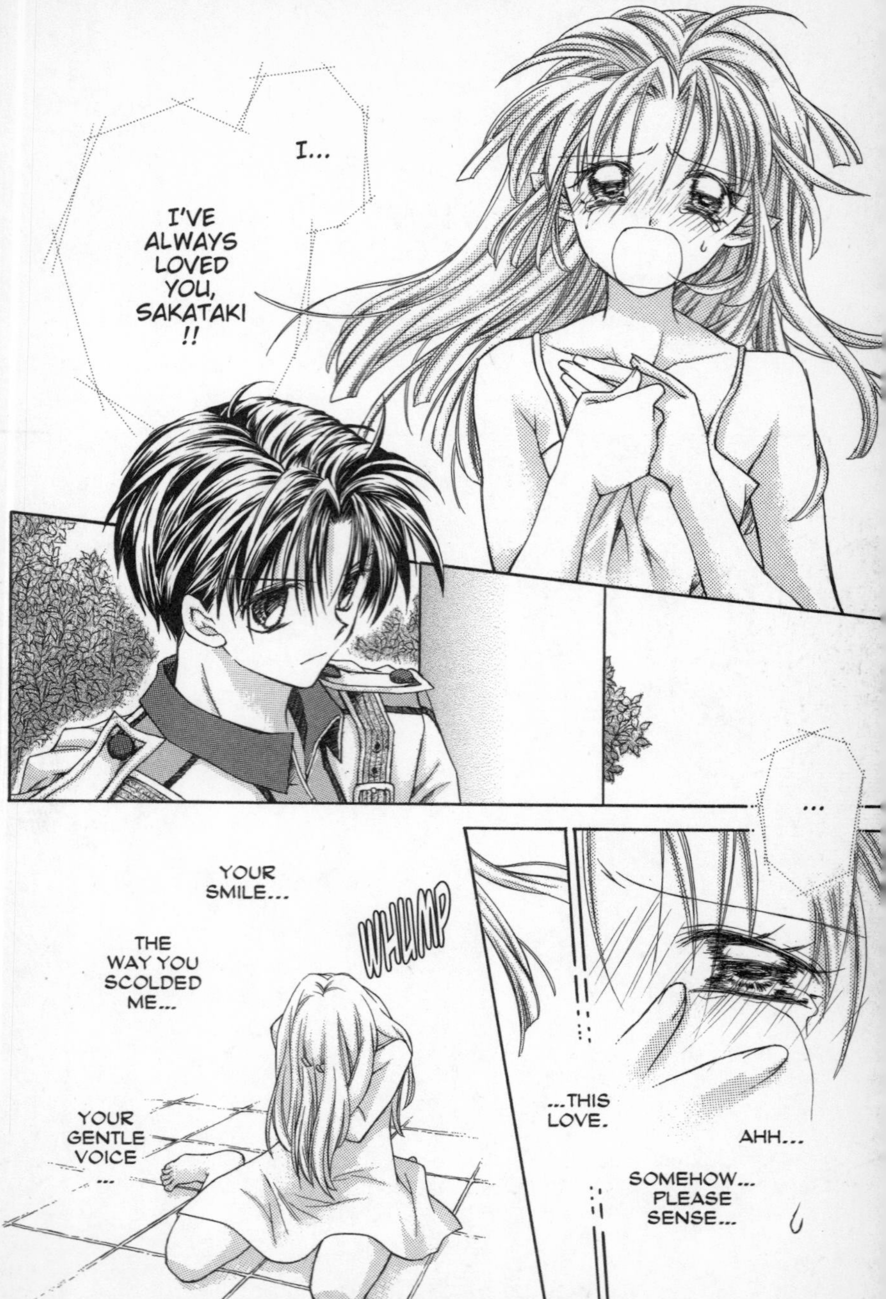

I...
I'VE ALWAYS LOVED YOU, SAKATAKI !!
...
AHH...
SOMEHOW... PLEASE SENSE...
...THIS LOVE.
YOUR SMILE...
WHUMP
THE WAY YOU SCOLDED ME...
YOUR GENTLE VOICE ...

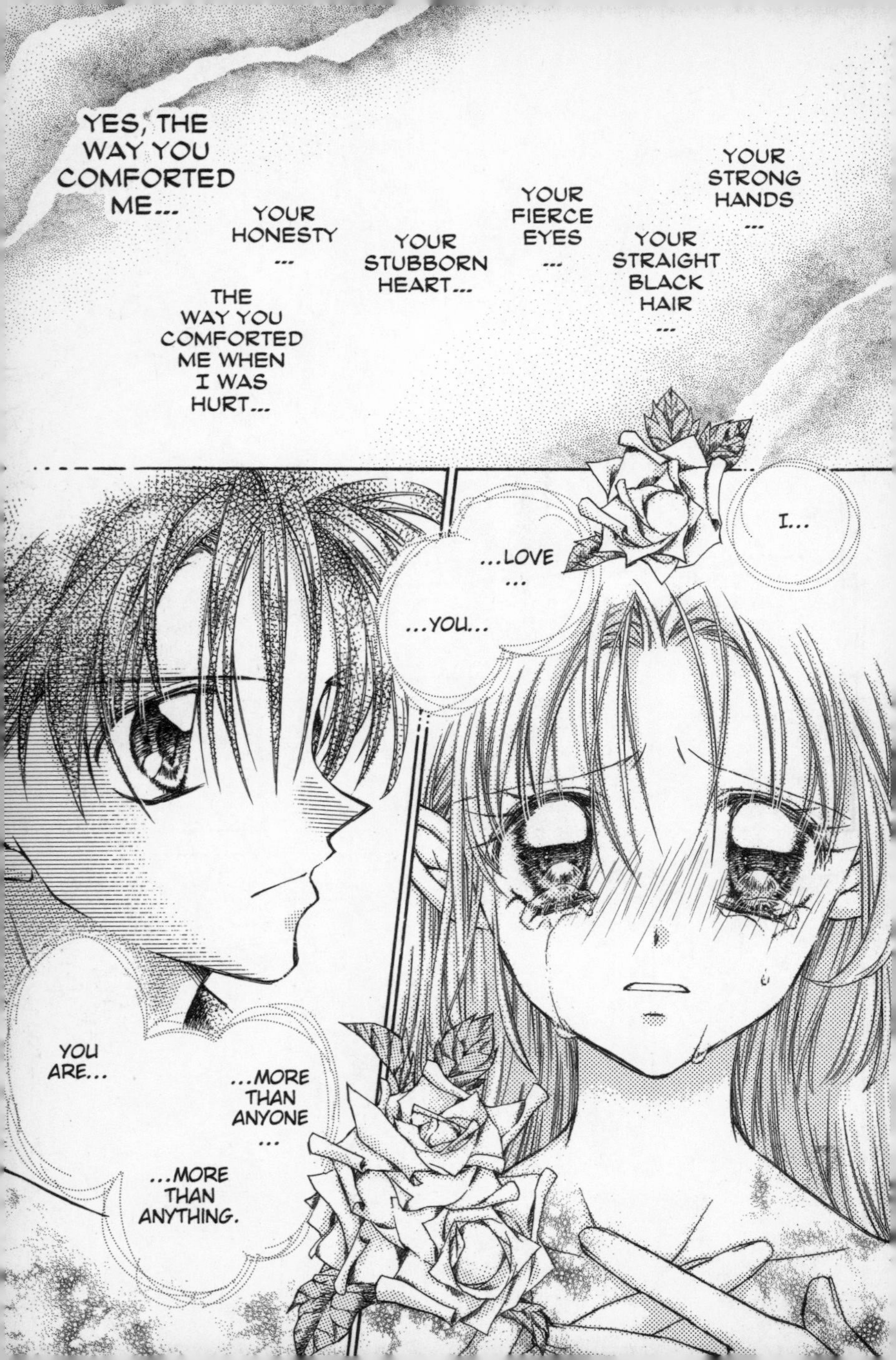
YOUR STRONG HANDS...
YOUR STRAIGHT BLACK HAIR...
YOUR FIERCE EYES...
YOUR STUBBORN HEART...
YOUR HONESTY...
THE WAY YOU COMFORTED ME WHEN I WAS HURT...
YES, THE WAY YOU COMFORTED ME...
I...
...LOVE...
...YOU...
YOU ARE...
...MORE THAN ANYONE...
...MORE THAN ANYTHING.

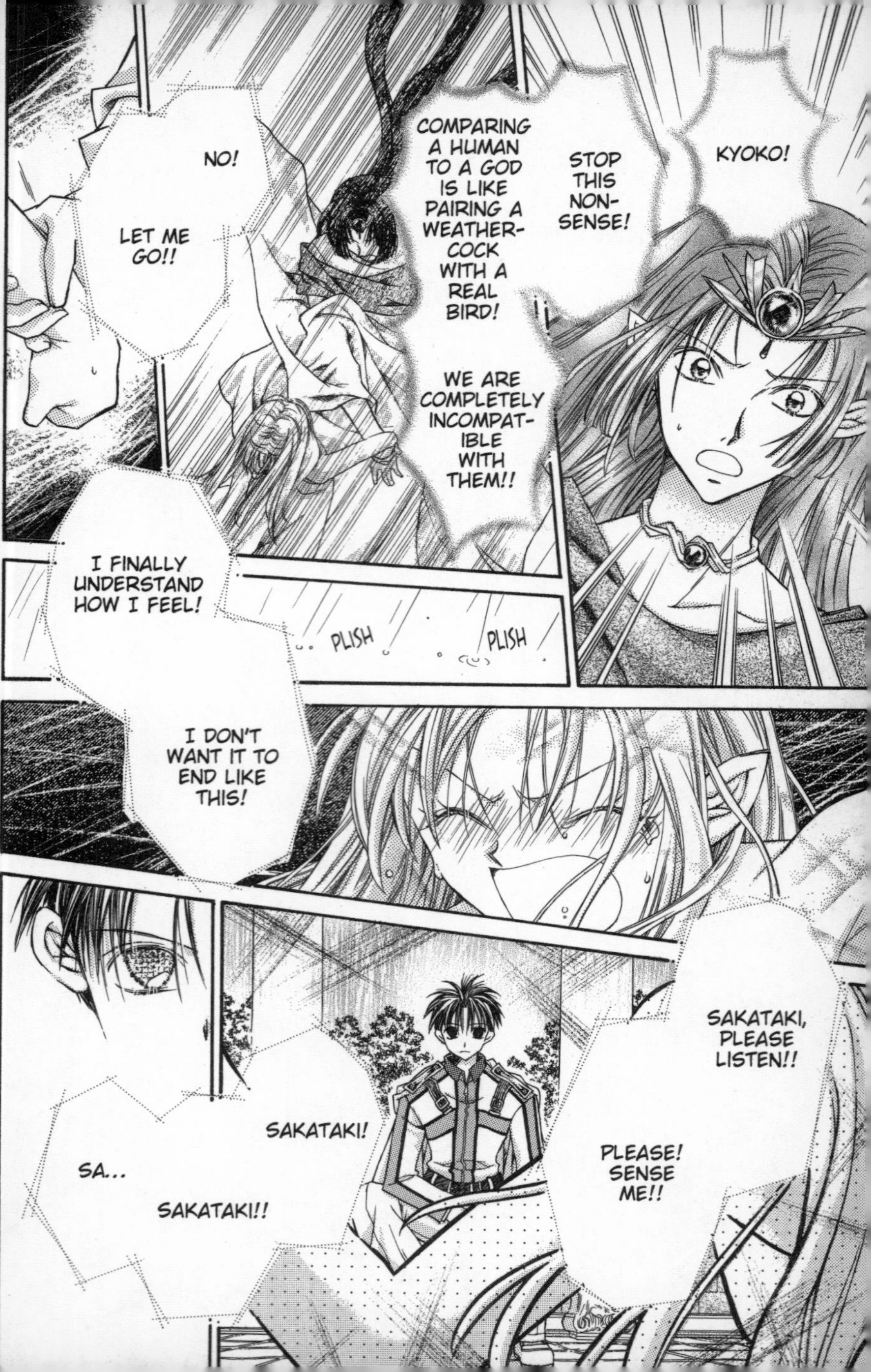
KYOKO!
STOP THIS NON-SENSE!
COMPARING A HUMAN TO A GOD IS LIKE PAIRING A WEATHER-COCK WITH A REAL BIRD!
WE ARE COMPLETELY INCOMPAT-IBLE WITH THEM!!
NO!
LET ME GO!!
PLISH
PLISH
I FINALLY UNDERSTAND HOW I FEEL!
I DON'T WANT IT TO END LIKE THIS!
SAKATAKI, PLEASE LISTEN!!
PLEASE! SENSE ME!!
SAKATAKI!
SA...
SAKATAKI!!

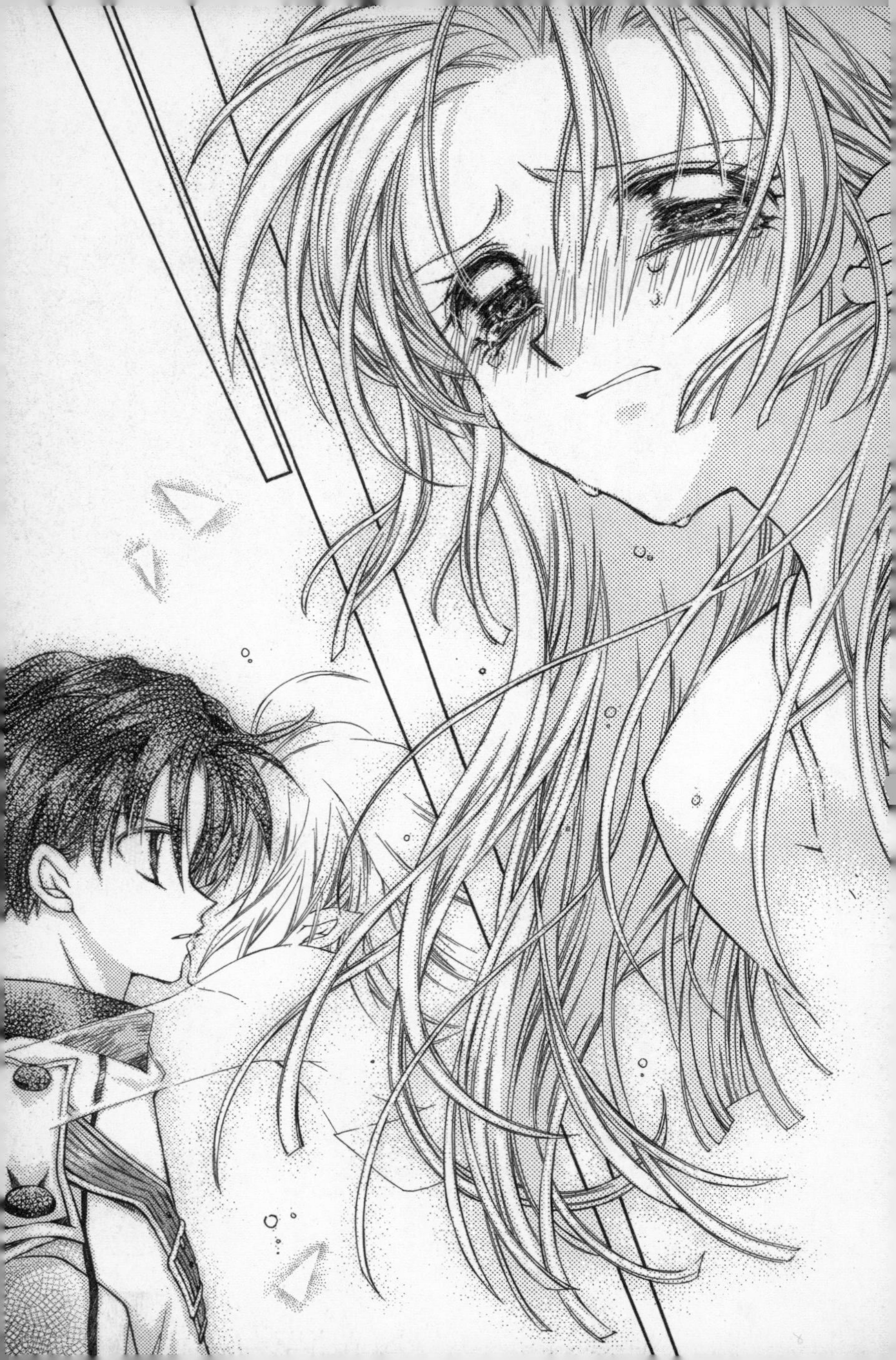

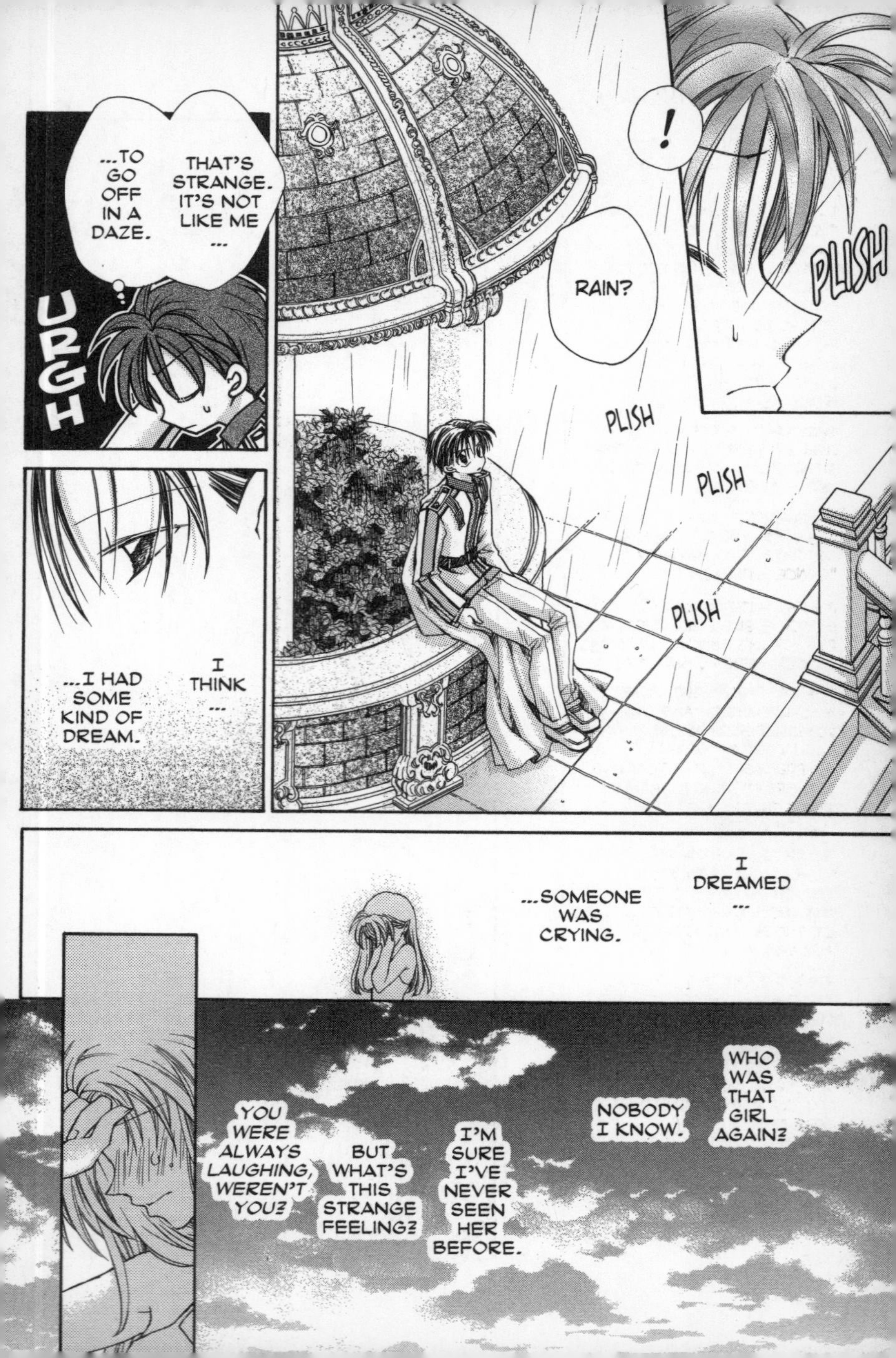
!
PLISH
RAIN?
PLISH
PLISH
PLISH
THAT'S STRANGE. IT'S NOT LIKE ME ...
...TO GO OFF IN A DAZE.
URGH
I THINK ...
...I HAD SOME KIND OF DREAM.
I DREAMED ...
...SOMEONE WAS CRYING.
WHO WAS THAT GIRL AGAIN?
NOBODY I KNOW.
I'M SURE I'VE NEVER SEEN HER BEFORE.
BUT WHAT'S THIS STRANGE FEELING?
YOU WERE ALWAYS LAUGHING, WEREN'T YOU?

I LOVE MOMUSU○!

BUT THAT ISN'T WHY I PUT A BIG CIRCLE AT THE END OF MY SENTENCES. HEH...

I LOVE MOMUSU○. I WATCHED THEM BEFORE I STARTED MY MANGA CAREER, BUT IT'S ONLY RECENTLY THAT I'VE BECOME A REALLY BIG FAN. I THINK IT STARTED WHEN I BOUGHT A COLLECTION OF THEIR BEST PROMOTIONAL VIDEOS. THEN I BOUGHT THEIR BEST-OF ALBUM. I THOUGHT, "AHH...IT MUST BE GOOD TO BE A MUSUME.♥"

THEY'RE CUTE AND REALLY LIVELY, AND THEY ALWAYS GIVE IT THEIR ALL...THAT'S WHAT I LOVE ABOUT THEM.

MY FAVORITE SONG IS "I WISH." I ALSO LIKE "HAPPY SUMMER WEDDING," "SAY YEAH!" AND "DANCE SURU NO DA!"♥

MY FAVORITE MEMBER IS GOCCHIN, BUT I LIKE THEM ALL.♥ RIKA-CHAN'S DANCING IN "MY☆PEACE" IS GREAT, ISN'T IT?♥♥

THE KAGO AND TSUJI COMBO IS ALSO EXCELLENT, AND WHEN YOSSUI DRESSED AS A MAN IT REALLY SET MY HEART FLUTTERING. ("MR. MOONLIGHT" WAS GREAT!) KAORIN AND KANACCHI ARE VERY GIRLY, SO I LIKE THEM TOO.♥

I LIKE KEI-CHAN BECAUSE SHE'S SUCH A GOOD DANCER.♥ YAGUCHI IS VERY CHEERFUL, AND MINI MONI IS WONDERFUL.♥♥ OF THE NEW MEMBERS, I LOVE AI-CHAN.♥

THEIR RECENT "MECHA IKE" VIDEO WITH THE SCHOOL TRIP WAS GREAT, WASN'T IT? AND OKAMURA-SAN'S "LOVE REVOLUTION 21" WAS THE BEST!!

IF YOU SEE ME AT THE MOMUSU○ LIVE CONCERT IN TOKYO, GIVE ME A SHOUT.

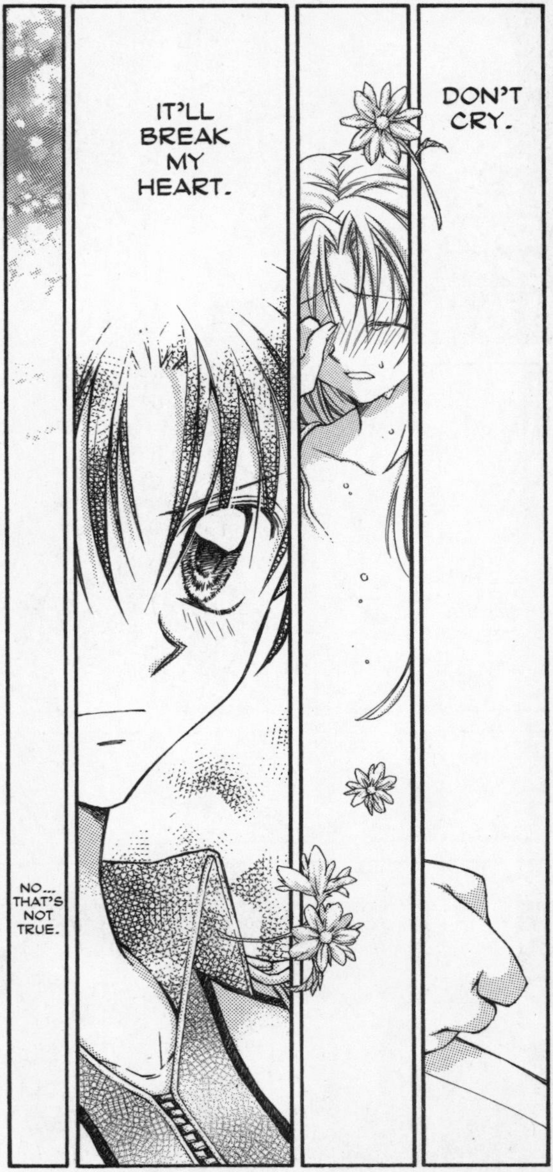
DON'T CRY.
IT'LL BREAK MY HEART.
NO... THAT'S NOT TRUE.

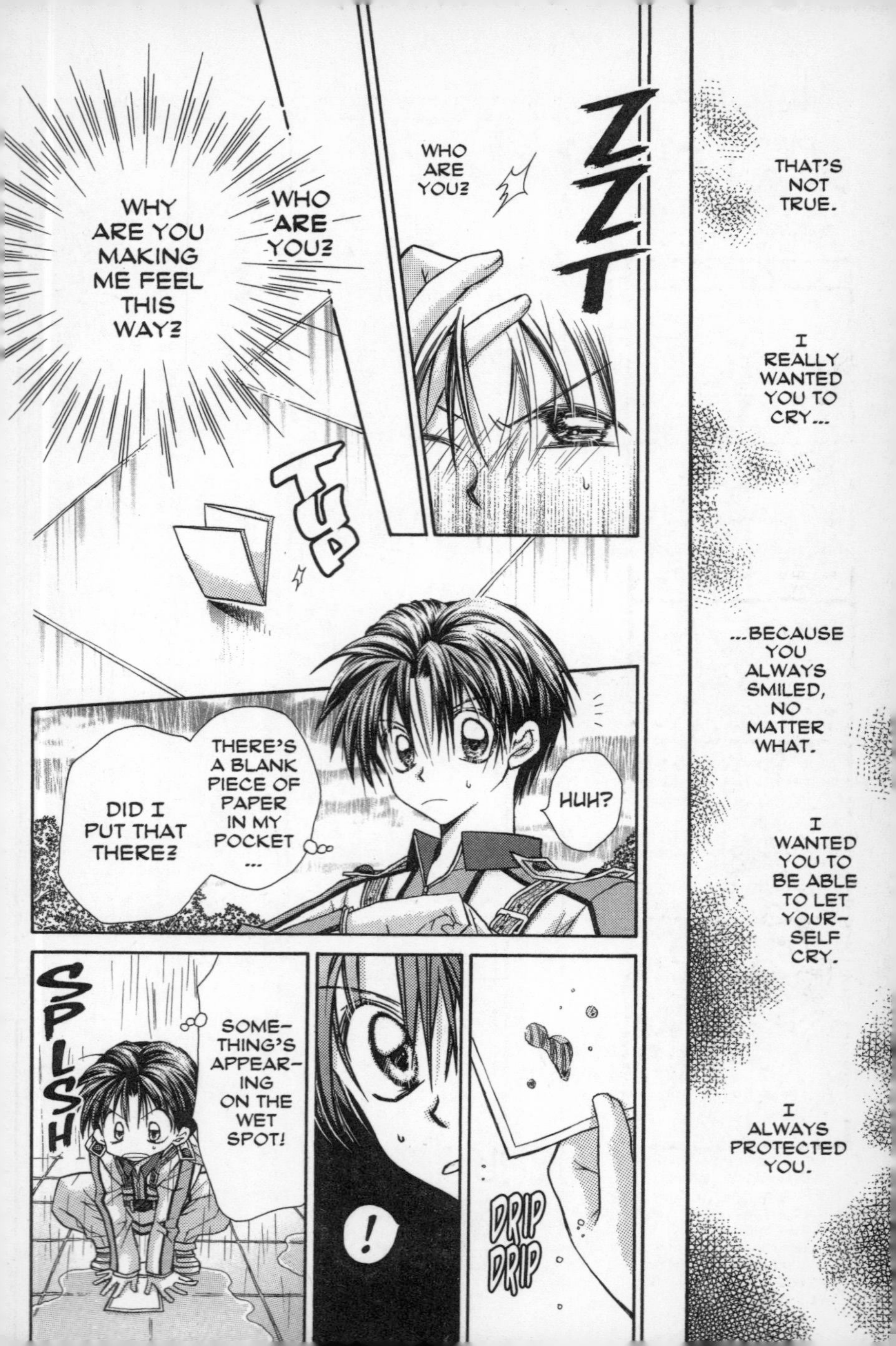
THAT'S NOT TRUE.
I REALLY WANTED YOU TO CRY...
...BECAUSE YOU ALWAYS SMILED, NO MATTER WHAT.
I WANTED YOU TO BE ABLE TO LET YOUR-SELF CRY.
I ALWAYS PROTECTED YOU.
ZZZT
WHO ARE YOU?
WHO ARE YOU?
WHY ARE YOU MAKING ME FEEL THIS WAY?
TUG
HUH?
THERE'S A BLANK PIECE OF PAPER IN MY POCKET ...
DID I PUT THAT THERE?
DRIP DRIP
!
SOME-THING'S APPEAR-ING ON THE WET SPOT!
SPLSH

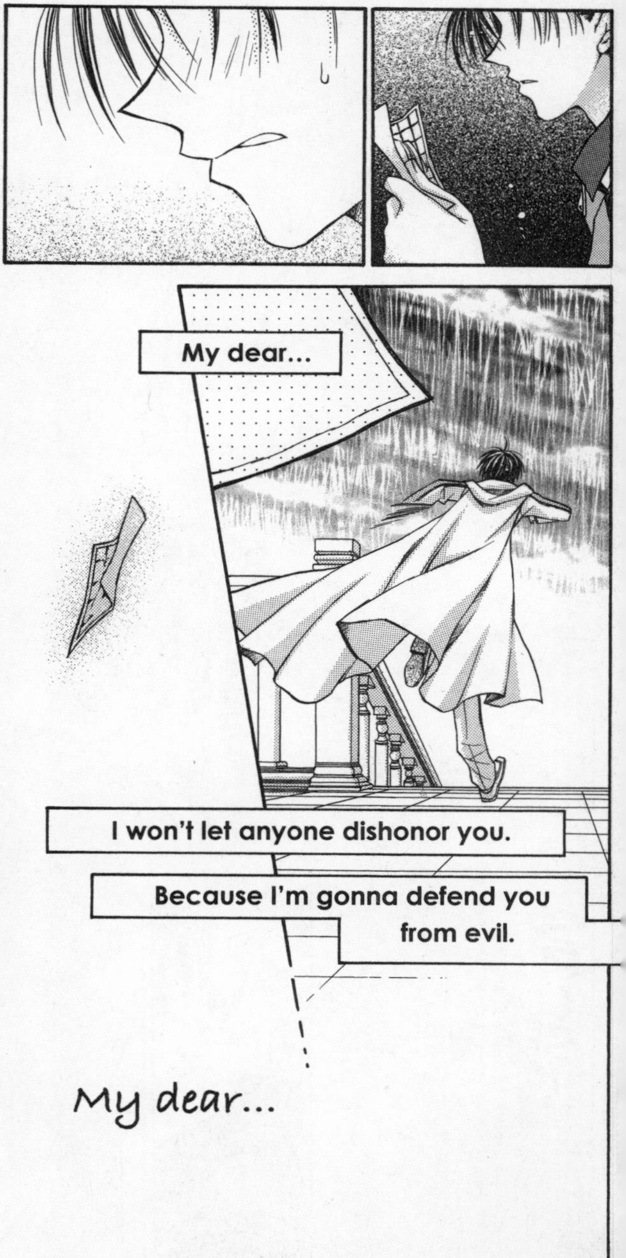

My dear...
I won't let anyone dishonor you.
Because I'm gonna defend you from evil.
My dear...

TANEPPE ARICCHO'S

PEN SAKI DE BUSUTTO

↑ THIS TITLE HURTS!

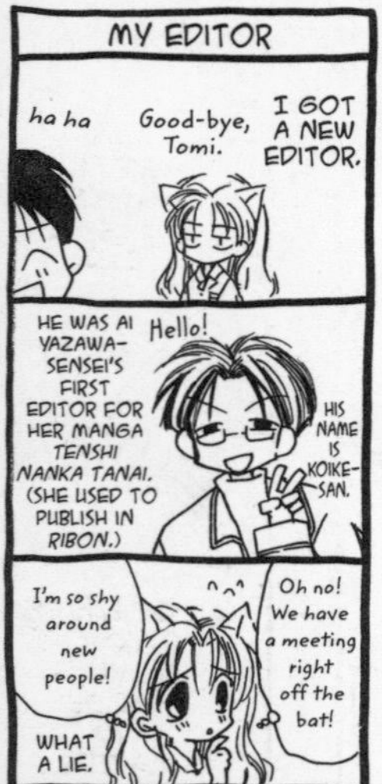

MY EDITOR
I GOT A NEW EDITOR.
Good-bye, Tomi.
ha ha
HIS NAME IS KOIKE-SAN.
Hello!
HE WAS AI YAZAWA-SENSEI'S FIRST EDITOR FOR HER MANGA TENSHI NANKA TANAI. (SHE USED TO PUBLISH IN RIBON.)
Oh no! We have a meeting right off the bat!
I'm so shy around new people!
WHAT A LIE.
I've been working on Shonen Jump, so I can get you into events.
If you want to go to the Tezuka or Akatsuka Awards or to Jump Festa, just let me know, okay?
GRMP
LIKES JUMP.

WE'RE ALREADY GETTING ALONG GREAT. (LAUGH)

TOMI WAS ONLY WITH ME FOR HALF A YEAR, WHICH WAS A REALLY SHORT TIME.

I HAD A GREAT TIME WITH HIM. HE GAVE ME GOOD ADVICE AND STUFF. THANK YOU VERY MUCH.♥

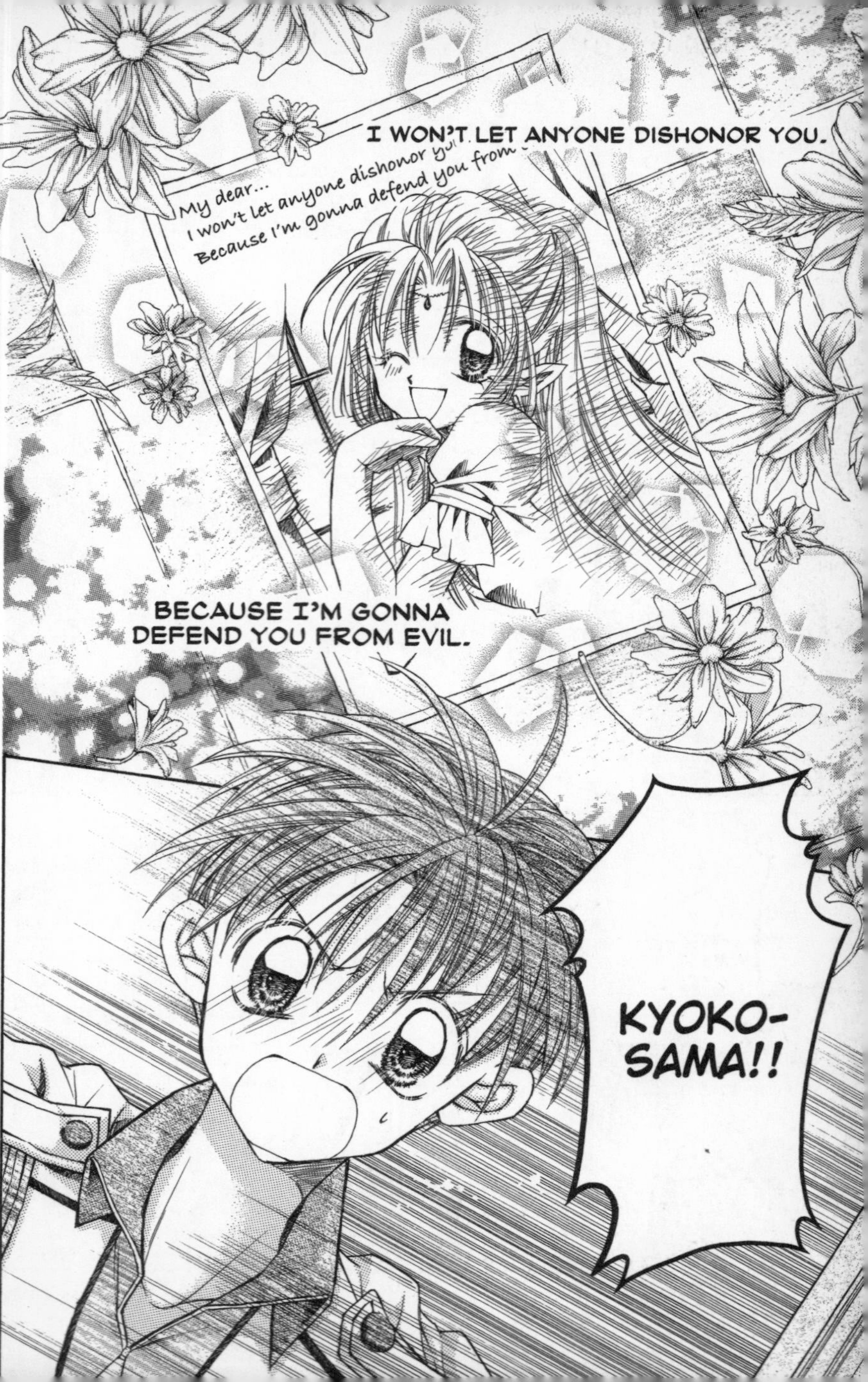
I WON'T LET ANYONE DISHONOR YOU.
My dear...
I won't let anyone dishonor
Because I'm gonna defend you from
BECAUSE I'M GONNA DEFEND YOU FROM EVIL.
KYOKO-SAMA!!

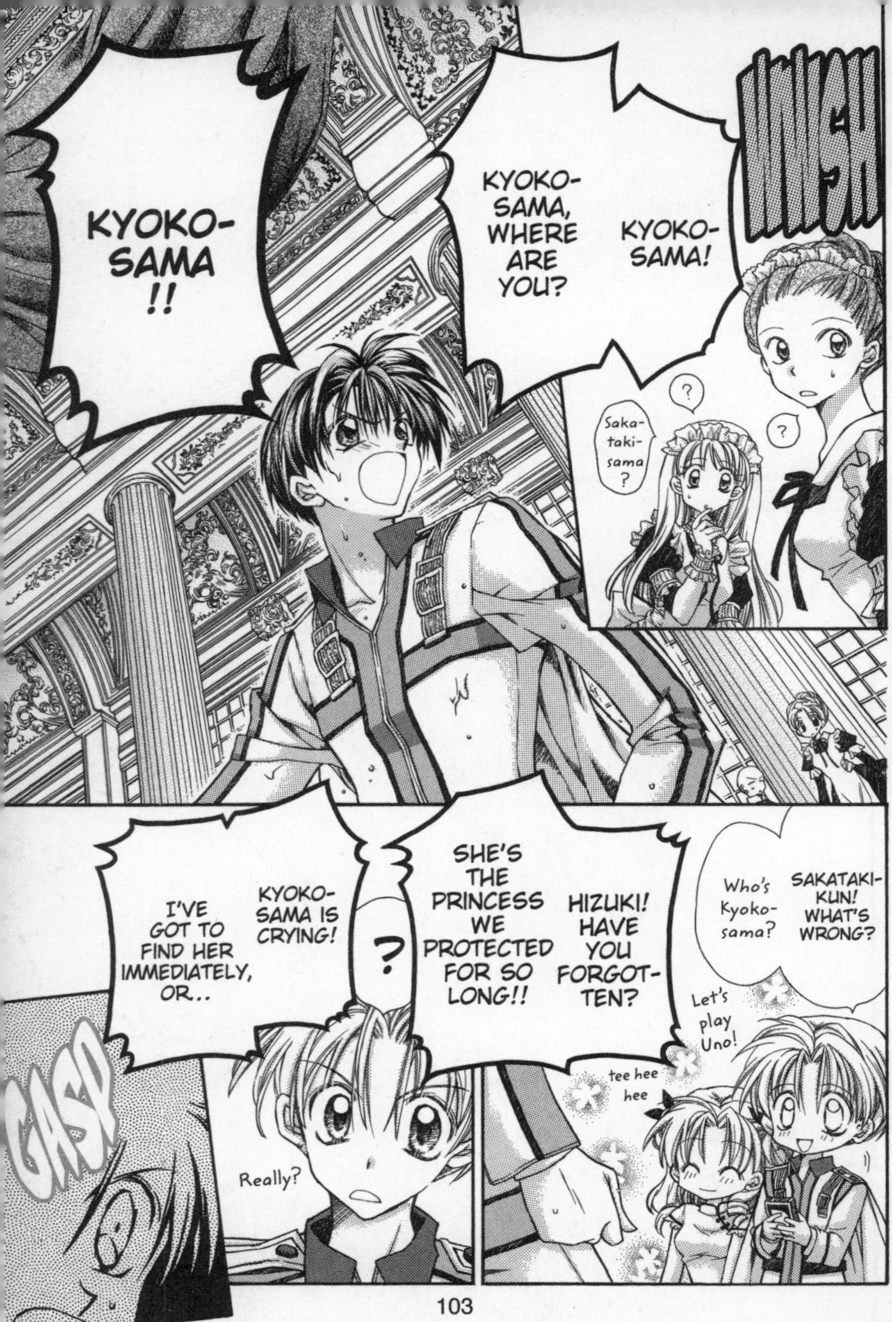
KYOKO-SAMA!
KYOKO-SAMA, WHERE ARE YOU?
KYOKO-SAMA !!
?
Saka-taki-sama ?
?
SAKATAKI-KUN! WHAT'S WRONG?
Who's Kyoko-sama?
Let's play Uno!
tee hee hee
HIZUKI! HAVE YOU FORGOT-TEN?
SHE'S THE PRINCESS WE PROTECTED FOR SO LONG!!
?
KYOKO-SAMA IS CRYING!
I'VE GOT TO FIND HER IMMEDIATELY, OR...
Really?
GASP

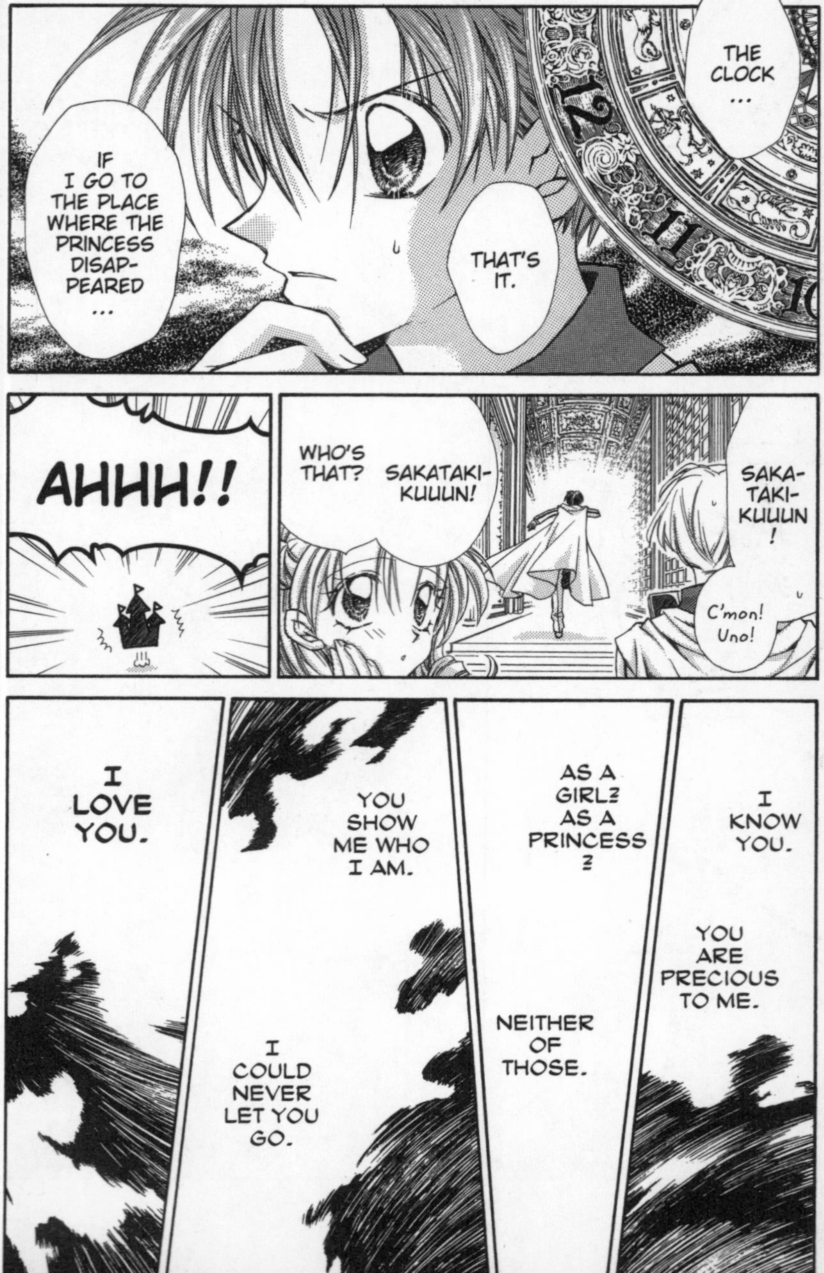
THE CLOCK ...
THAT'S IT.
IF I GO TO THE PLACE WHERE THE PRINCESS DISAPPEARED ...
SAKATAKI-KUUUN!
C'mon! Uno!
SAKATAKI-KUUUN!
WHO'S THAT?
AHHH!!
I KNOW YOU.
YOU ARE PRECIOUS TO ME.
AS A GIRL? AS A PRINCESS?
NEITHER OF THOSE.
YOU SHOW ME WHO I AM.
I COULD NEVER LET YOU GO.
I LOVE YOU.

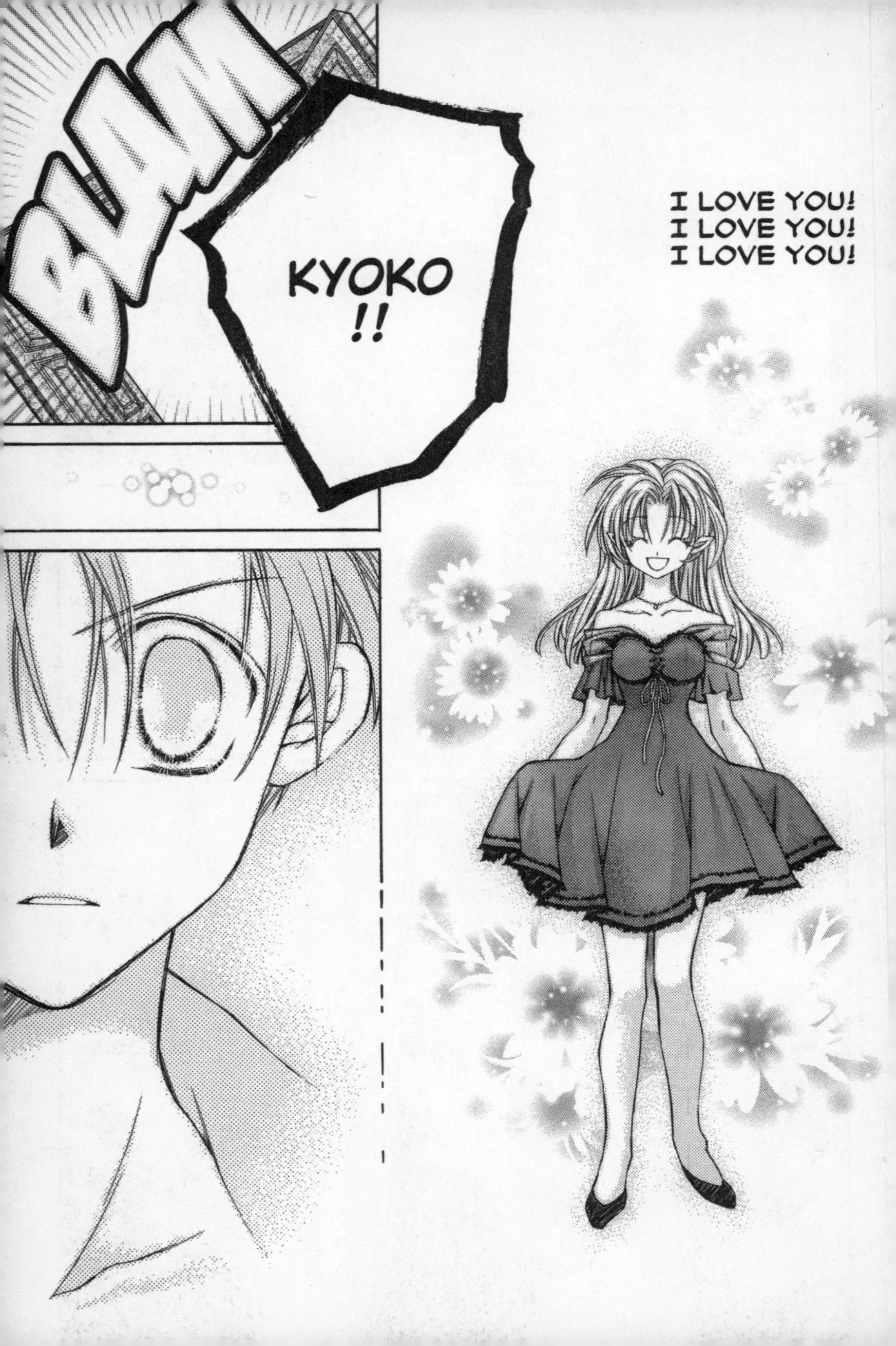

I LOVE YOU!
I LOVE YOU!
I LOVE YOU!
BLAM
KYOKO !!

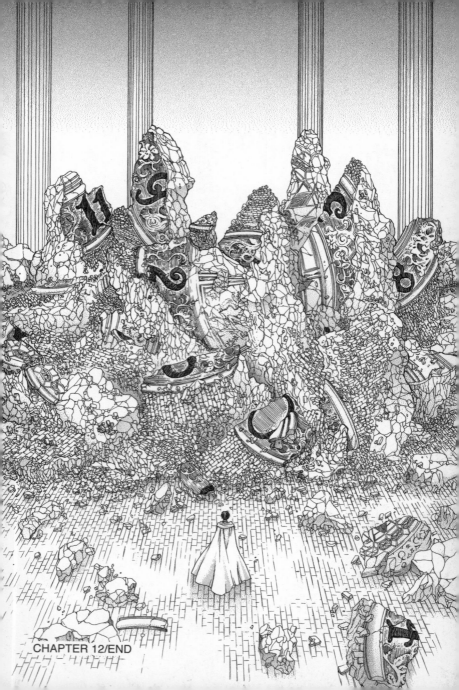

CHAPTER 12/END

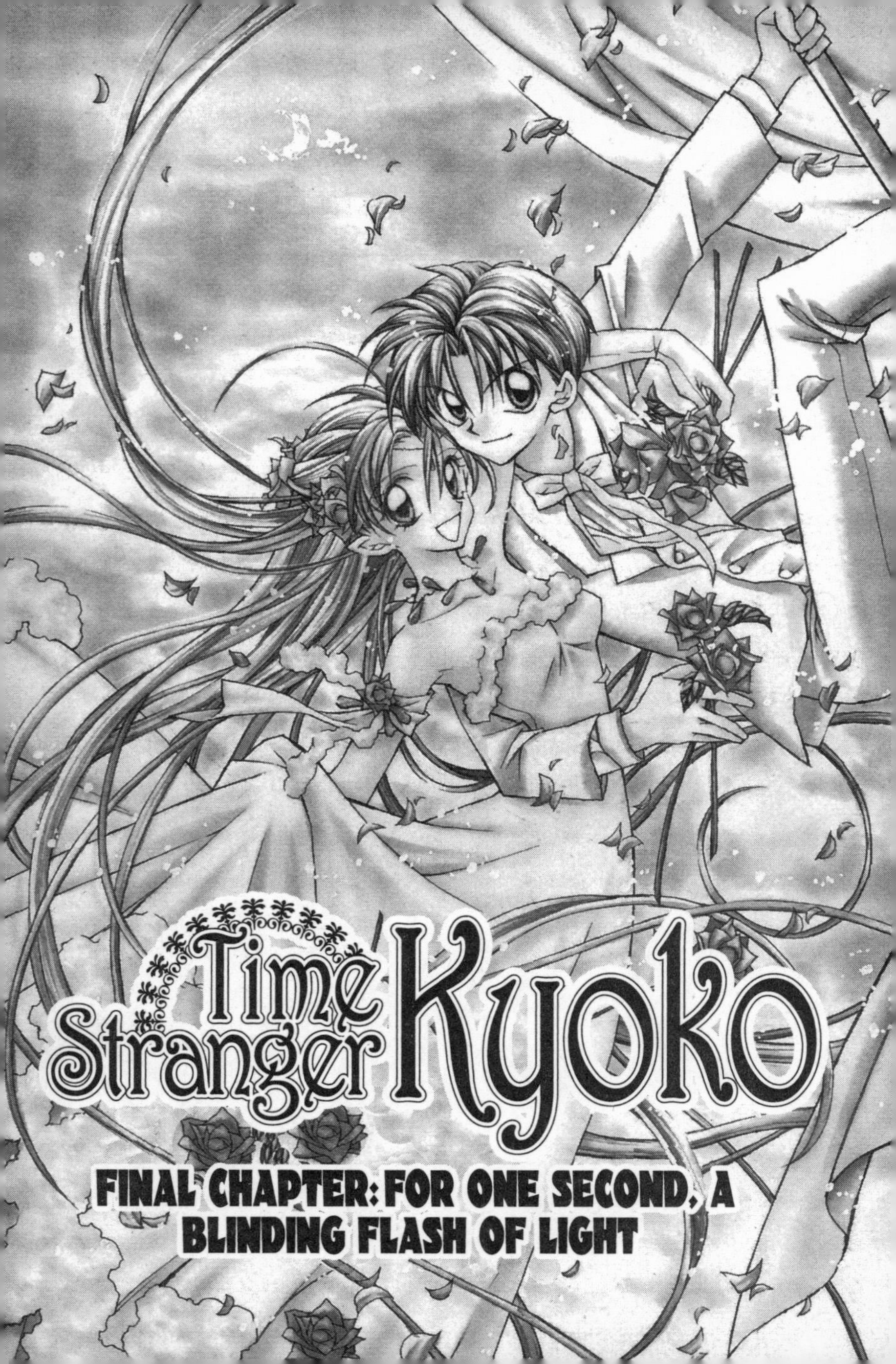
Time Stranger Kyoko
FINAL CHAPTER: FOR ONE SECOND, A BLINDING FLASH OF LIGHT

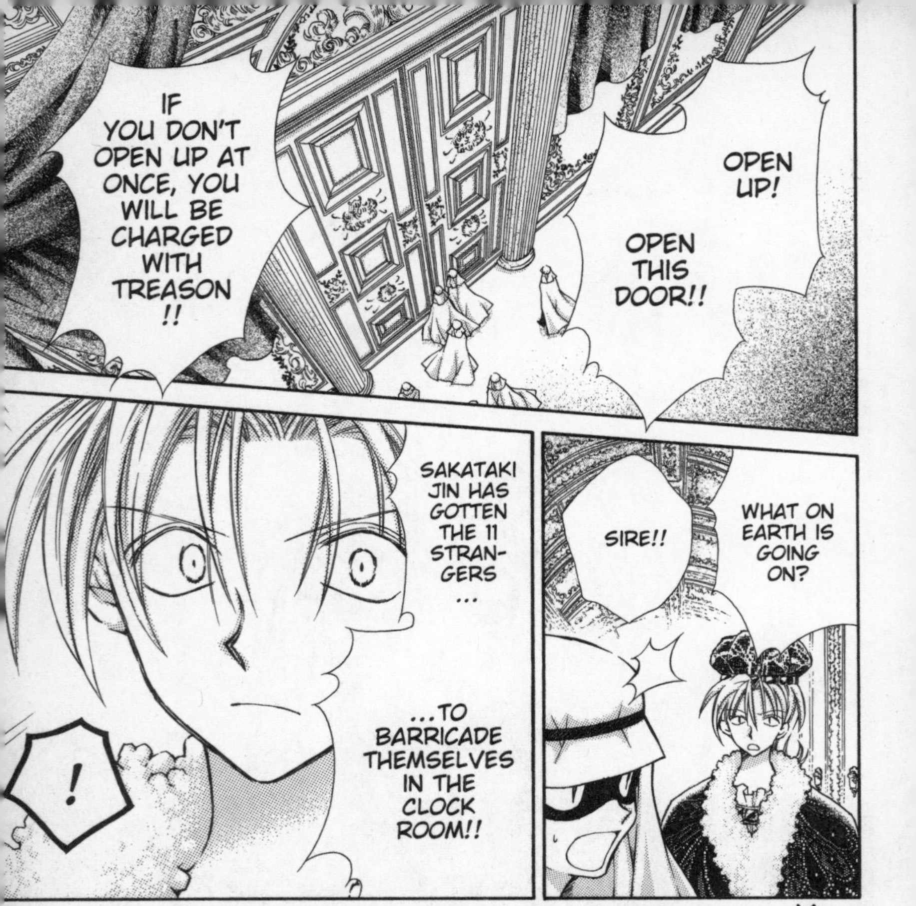
OPEN UP!
OPEN THIS DOOR!!
IF YOU DON'T OPEN UP AT ONCE, YOU WILL BE CHARGED WITH TREASON !!
WHAT ON EARTH IS GOING ON?
SIRE!!
SAKATAKI JIN HAS GOTTEN THE 11 STRAN-GERS ...
...TO BARRICADE THEMSELVES IN THE CLOCK ROOM!!
!

FINAL CHAPTER: FOR ONE SECOND, A BLINDING FLASH OF LIGHT

LEAD-IN OVERCOME TIME FOREVER... SPOILER ALERT!

THE TITLE PAGE ILLUSTRATION IS AN IMAGE FROM THEIR WEDDING DAY. BOTH OF THEM HAVE WILD SIDES, HENCE THE STYLE OF THE PICTURE. IT WAS ALSO USED IN A PHOTO ALBUM FOR THE MAGAZINE.

AS FOR THE CHAPTER, I LIKE THE LAST SEVEN PAGES (THE LETTER). I LIKE THE RHYTHM OF IT. I WAS ALSO LOOKING FORWARD TO THE ROMANTIC SCENES BETWEEN KYOKO AND SAKATAKI, BUT THE PART THAT STUCK WITH ME WAS THE SCENE WITH THE KING.

WELL, THIS IS FINALLY THE END OF *KYOKO*. THE COMIC STRIPS IN THE BACK WERE DONE FOR A SPECIAL EDITION OF THE MAGAZINE, BUT BECAUSE I ENDED THIS STORY SO ABRUPTLY, I'M INCLUDING THEM HERE AS A PRESENT FOR LONELY *KYOKO* FANS. (THE COVER ILLUSTRATION IS ALSO A PRESENT FOR MY FANS.)

WRITING *KYOKO* WAS A DREAM OF MINE FOR MANY YEARS. I HAD TO END IT LIKE THIS BECAUSE I COULDN'T DECIDE WHERE TO GO WITH IT, BUT I'M SATISFIED (FOR NOW, AT LEAST...). MY NEXT SERIES CAME TO ME IN THE MIDDLE OF WRITING *KYOKO*. (IT'S NOT ONE OF THE THREE I WAS TALKING ABOUT BEFORE.) IT'S CALLED *FULL MOON*. PLEASE READ IT!

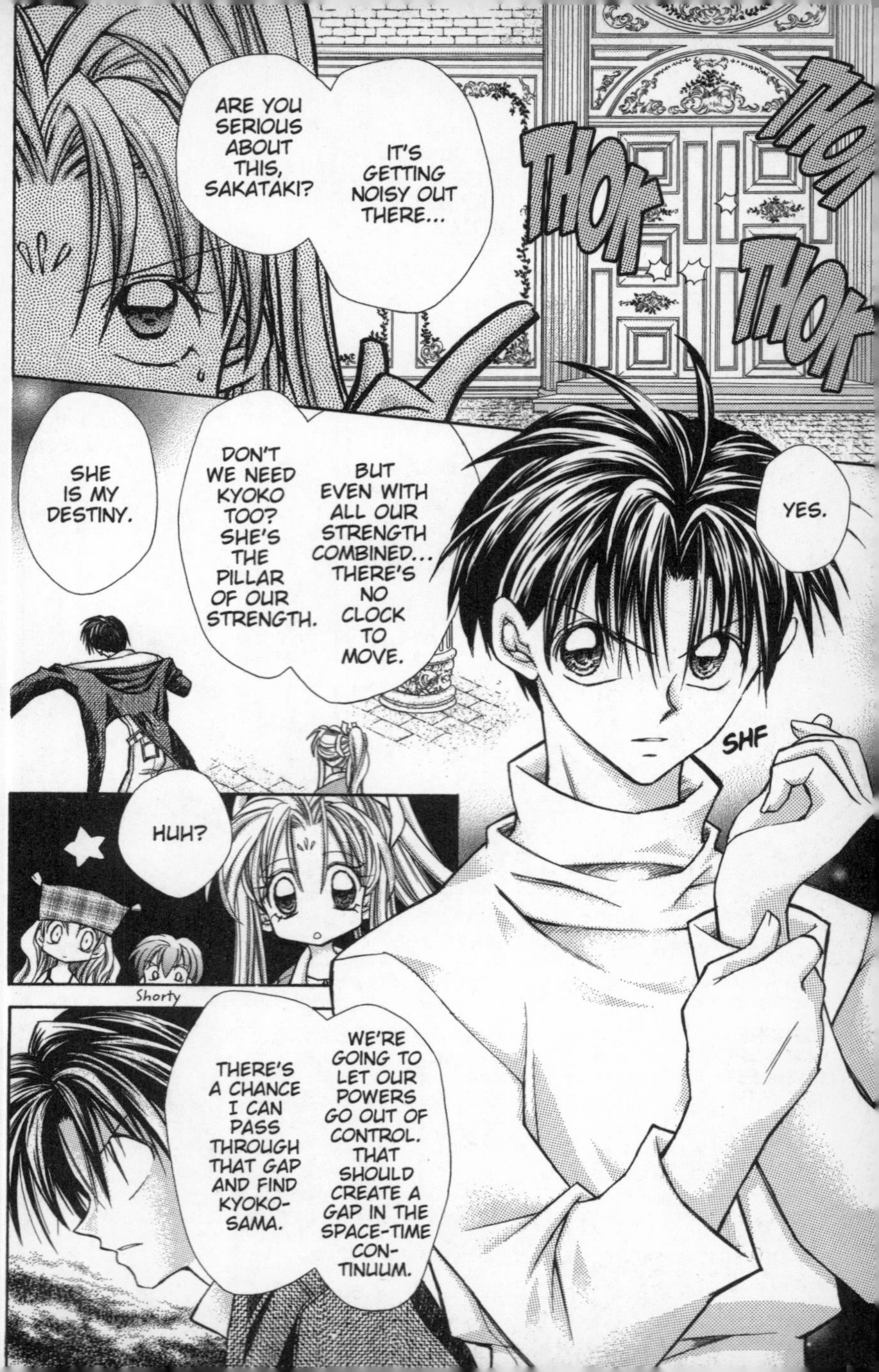
THOK
THOK
THOK
IT'S GETTING NOISY OUT THERE...
ARE YOU SERIOUS ABOUT THIS, SAKATAKI?
YES.
SHF
BUT EVEN WITH ALL OUR STRENGTH COMBINED... THERE'S NO CLOCK TO MOVE.
DON'T WE NEED KYOKO TOO? SHE'S THE PILLAR OF OUR STRENGTH.
SHE IS MY DESTINY.
HUH?
Shorty
WE'RE GOING TO LET OUR POWERS GO OUT OF CONTROL. THAT SHOULD CREATE A GAP IN THE SPACE-TIME CON-TINUUM.
THERE'S A CHANCE I CAN PASS THROUGH THAT GAP AND FIND KYOKO-SAMA.

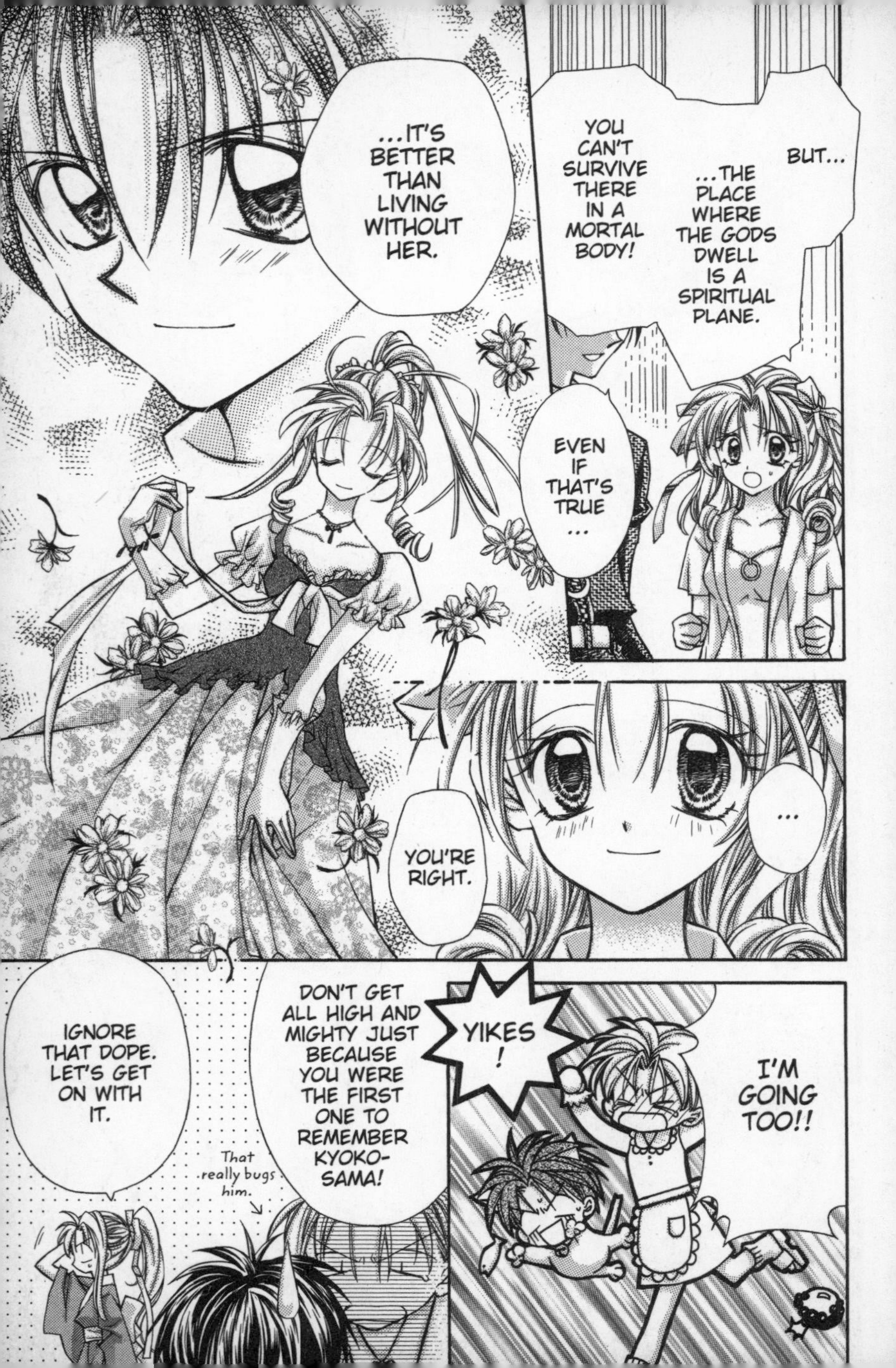

BUT...
...THE PLACE WHERE THE GODS DWELL IS A SPIRITUAL PLANE.
YOU CAN'T SURVIVE THERE IN A MORTAL BODY!
EVEN IF THAT'S TRUE ...
...
YOU'RE RIGHT.
...IT'S BETTER THAN LIVING WITHOUT HER.
I'M GOING TOO!!
YIKES!
DON'T GET ALL HIGH AND MIGHTY JUST BECAUSE YOU WERE THE FIRST ONE TO REMEMBER KYOKO-SAMA!
IGNORE THAT DOPE. LET'S GET ON WITH IT.
That really bugs him.

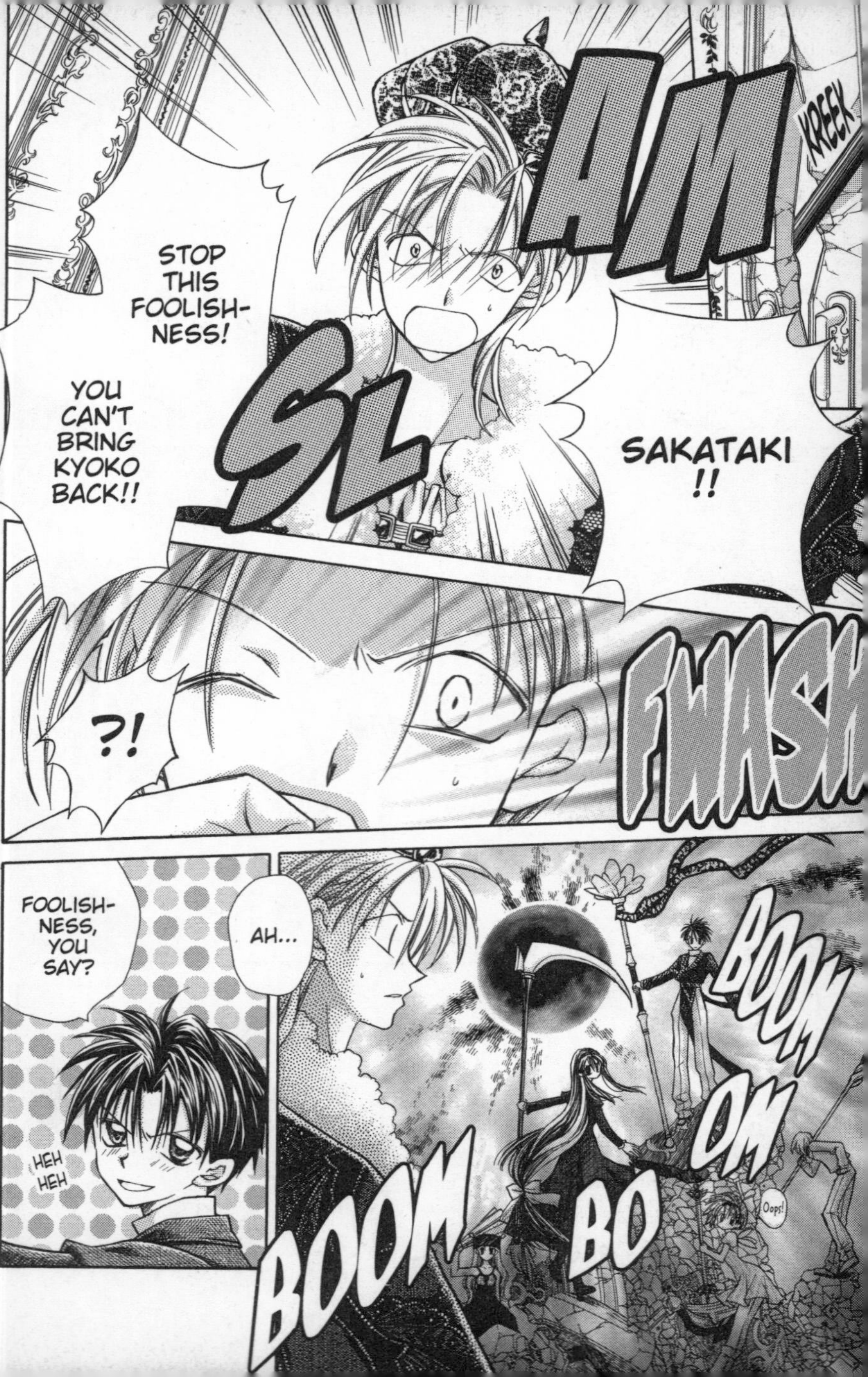
KREEK
AIM
SAKATAKI!!
SL
STOP THIS FOOLISH-NESS!
YOU CAN'T BRING KYOKO BACK!!
FWASH
?!
BOOM
AH...
Oops!
BO OM
BOOM
FOOLISH-NESS, YOU SAY?
HEH HEH

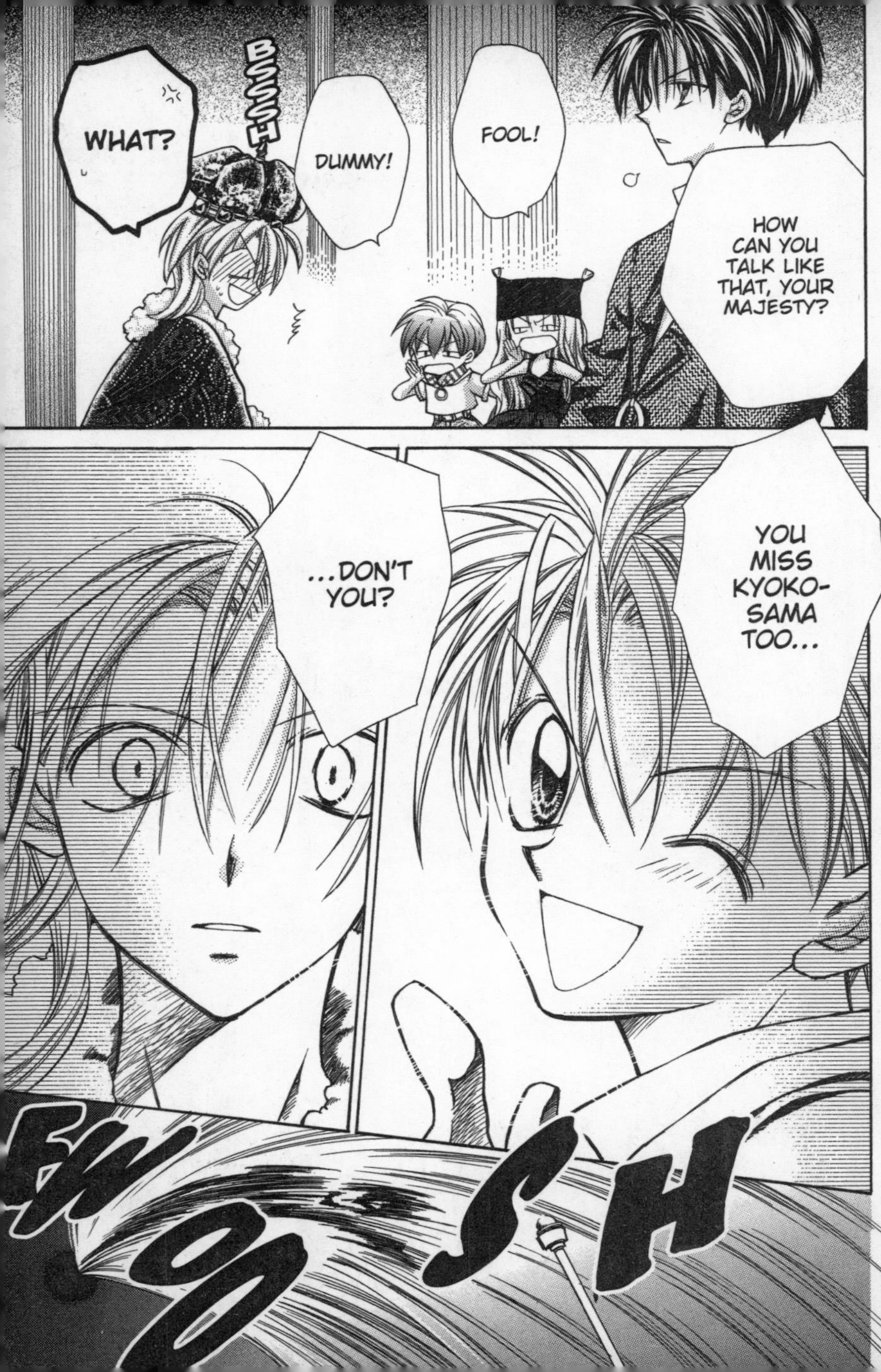
HOW CAN YOU TALK LIKE THAT, YOUR MAJESTY?
FOOL!
DUMMY!
BSSSH
WHAT?
YOU MISS KYOKO-SAMA TOO...
...DON'T YOU?
SWOSH

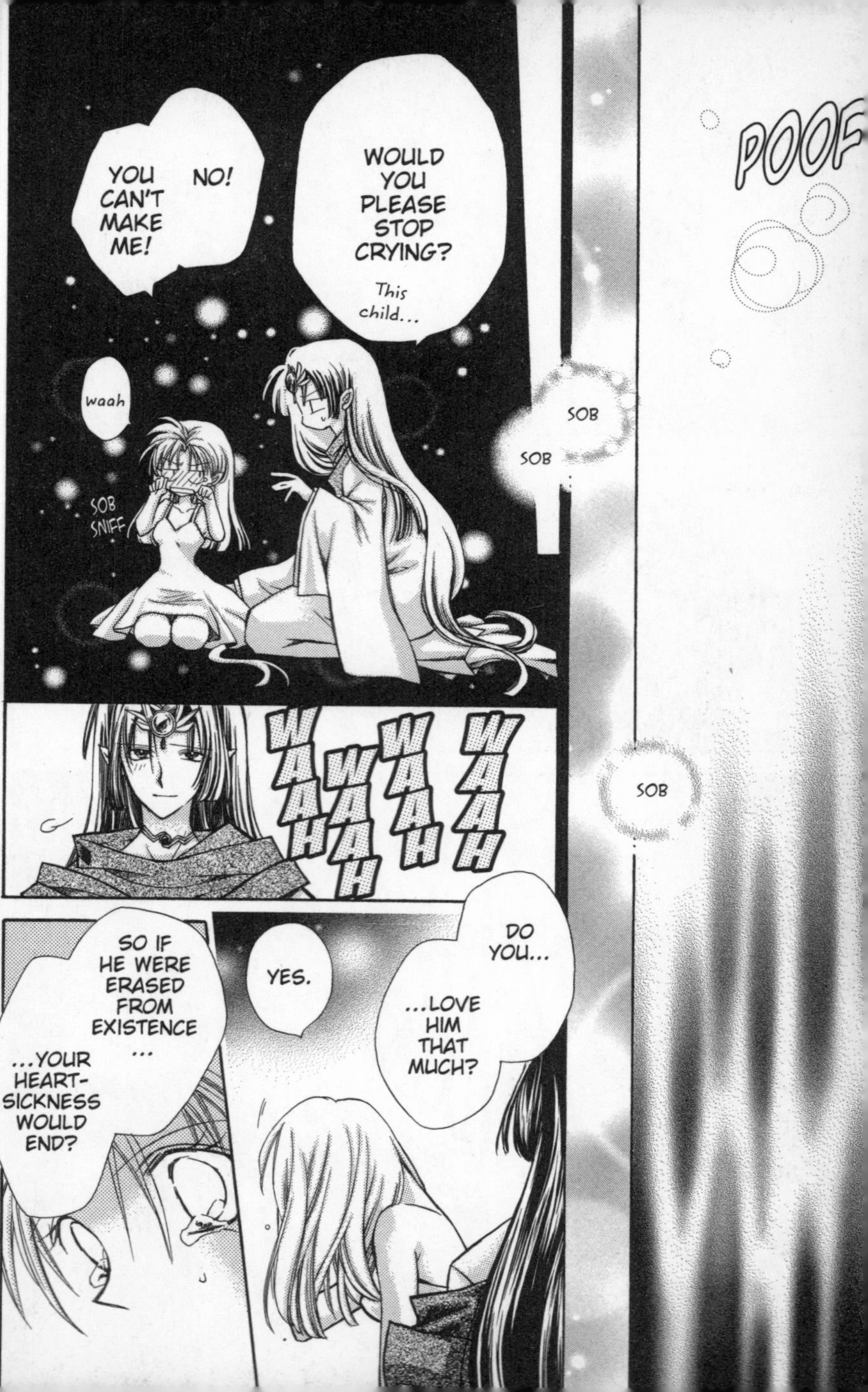
POOF
SOB
SOB
SOB
WOULD YOU PLEASE STOP CRYING?
This child...
NO!
YOU CAN'T MAKE ME!
waah
SOB SNIFF
WAAH
WAAH
WAAH
WAAH
DO YOU...
...LOVE HIM THAT MUCH?
YES.
SO IF HE WERE ERASED FROM EXISTENCE...
...YOUR HEART-SICKNESS WOULD END?

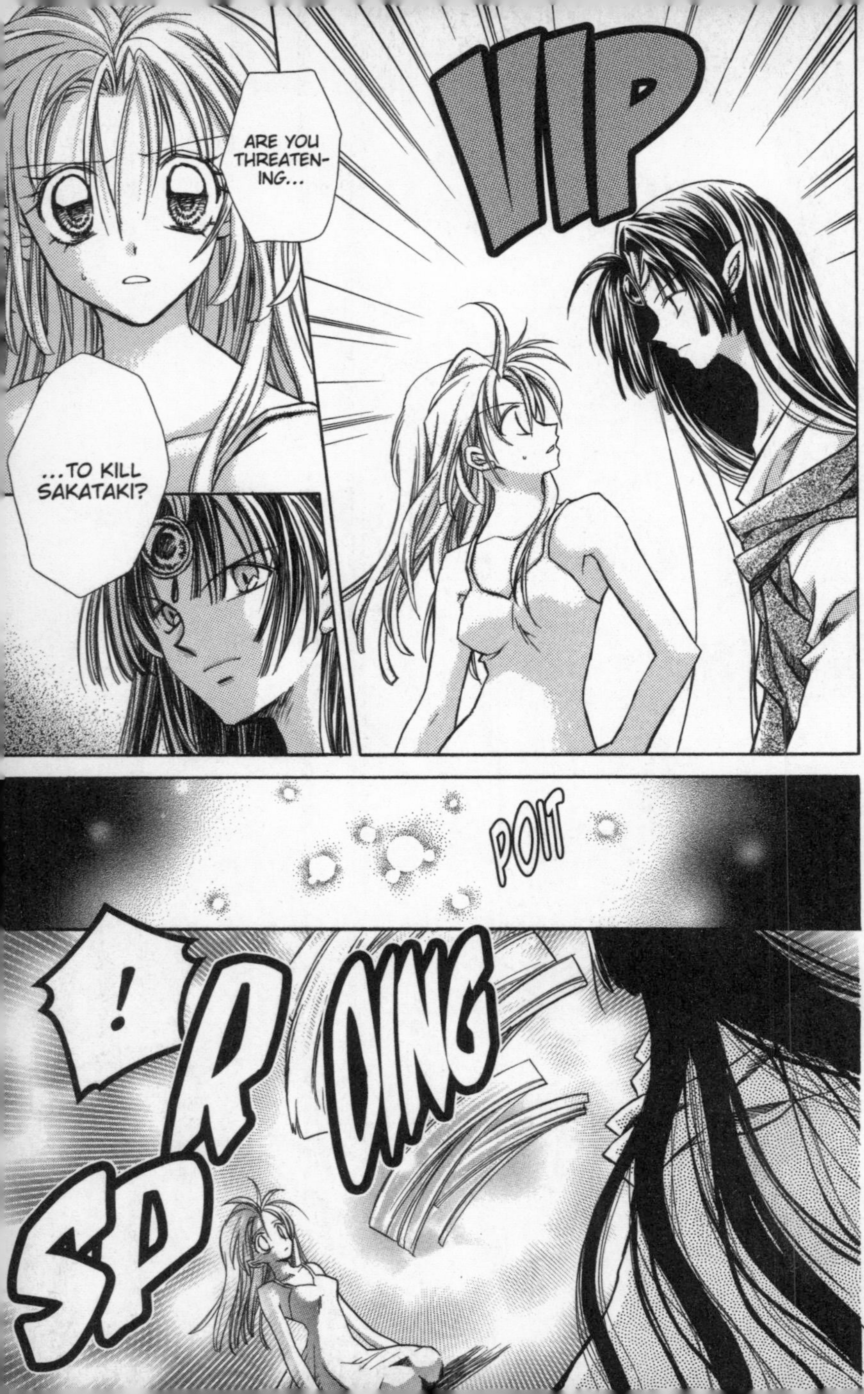
ARE YOU THREATENING…
…TO KILL SAKATAKI?
POIT
!
SPROING

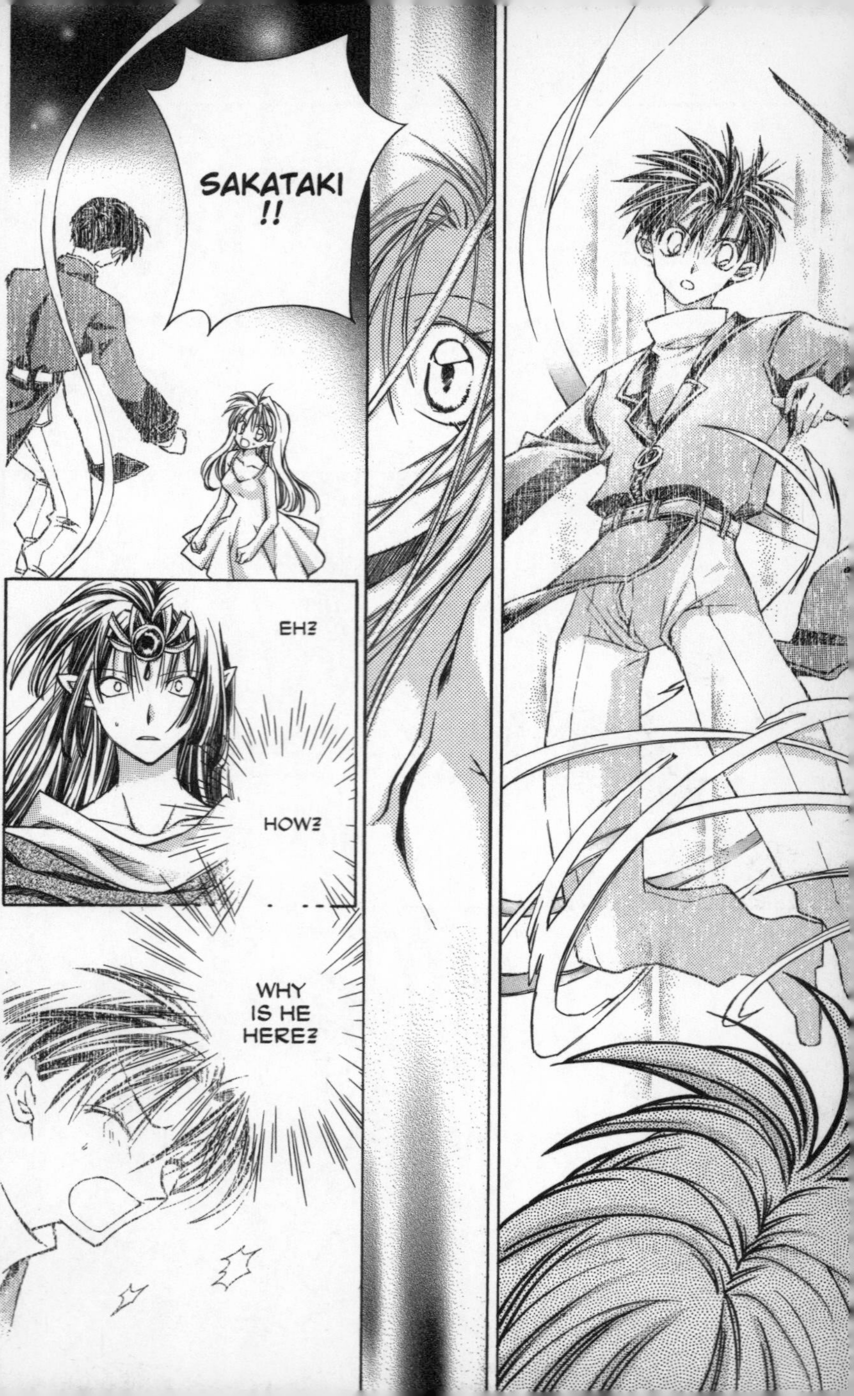
SAKATAKI !!
EH?
HOW?
...
WHY IS HE HERE?

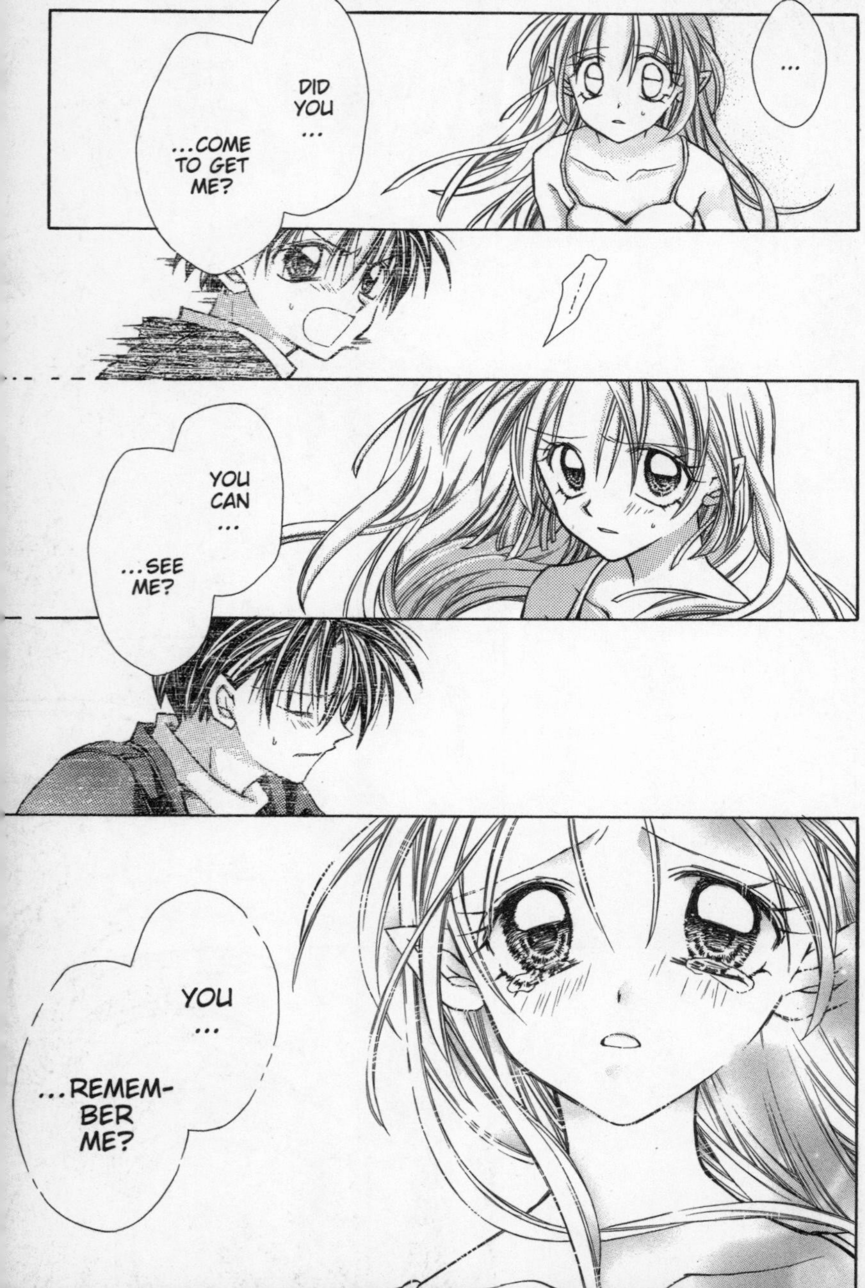
...
DID YOU ... ...COME TO GET ME?
YOU CAN ... ...SEE ME?
YOU ... ...REMEM-BER ME?

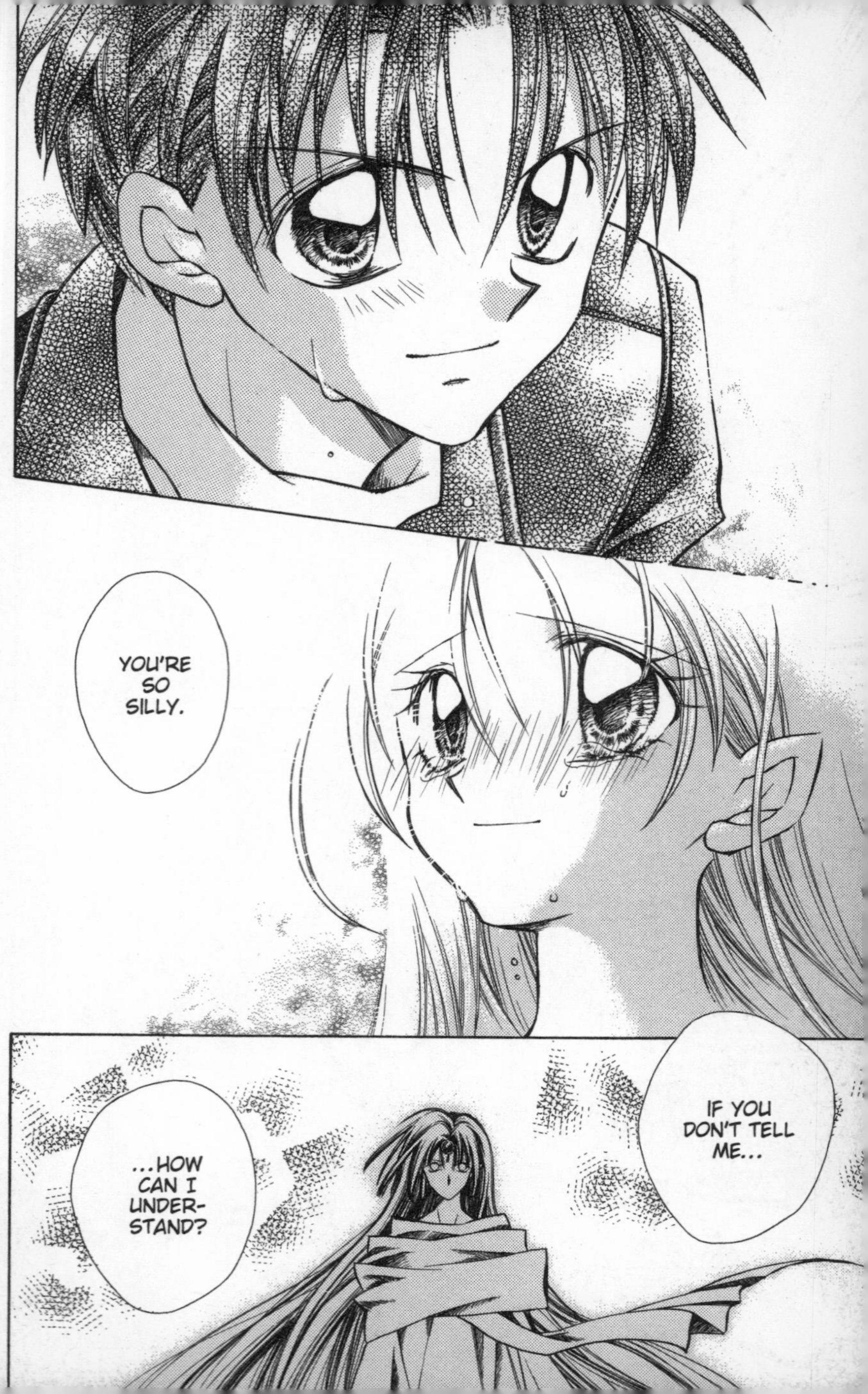
YOU'RE SO SILLY.
IF YOU DON'T TELL ME...
...HOW CAN I UNDER-STAND?

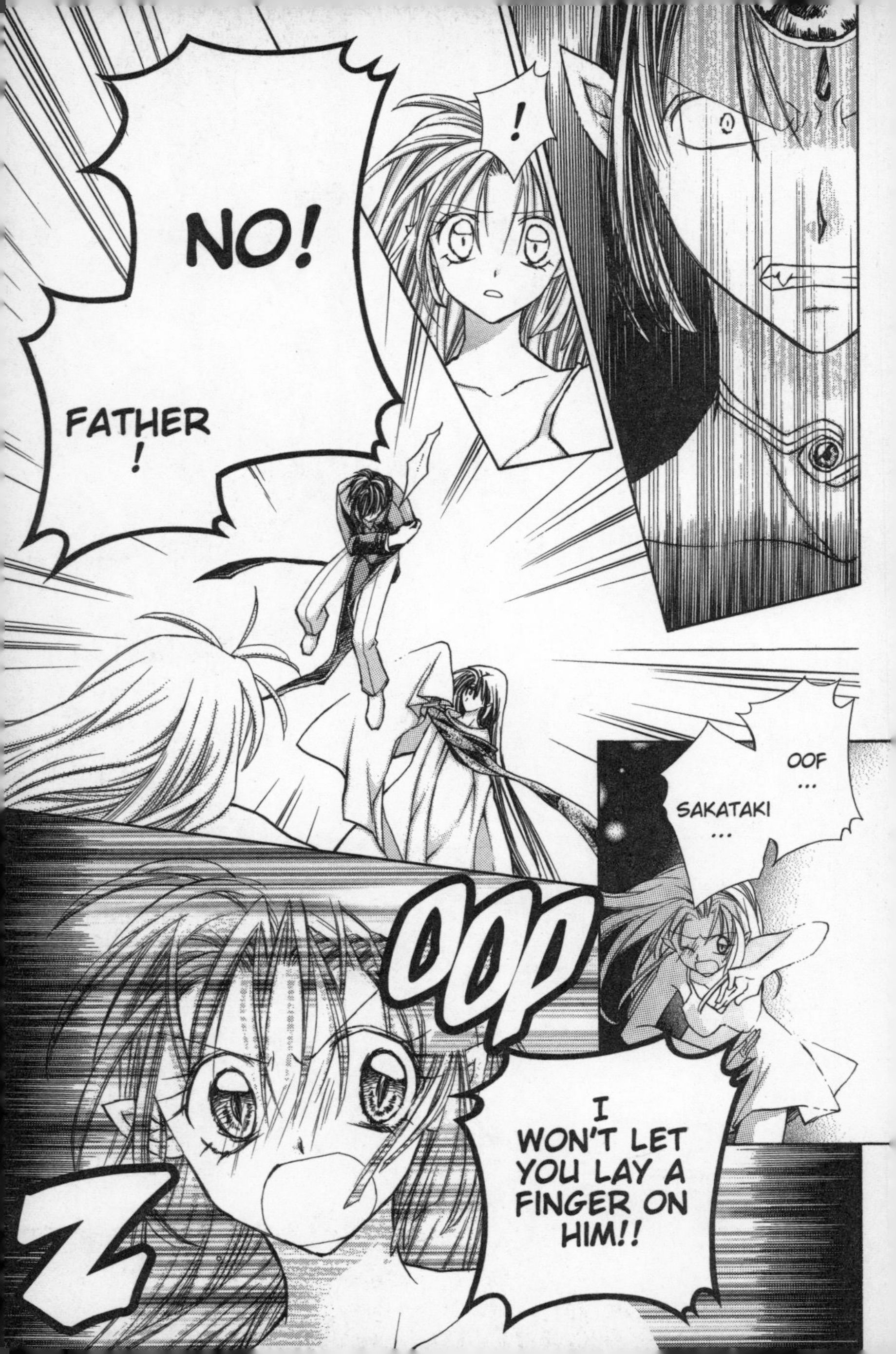
!
NO! FATHER!
OOF... SAKATAKI...
OOP
I WON'T LET YOU LAY A FINGER ON HIM!!

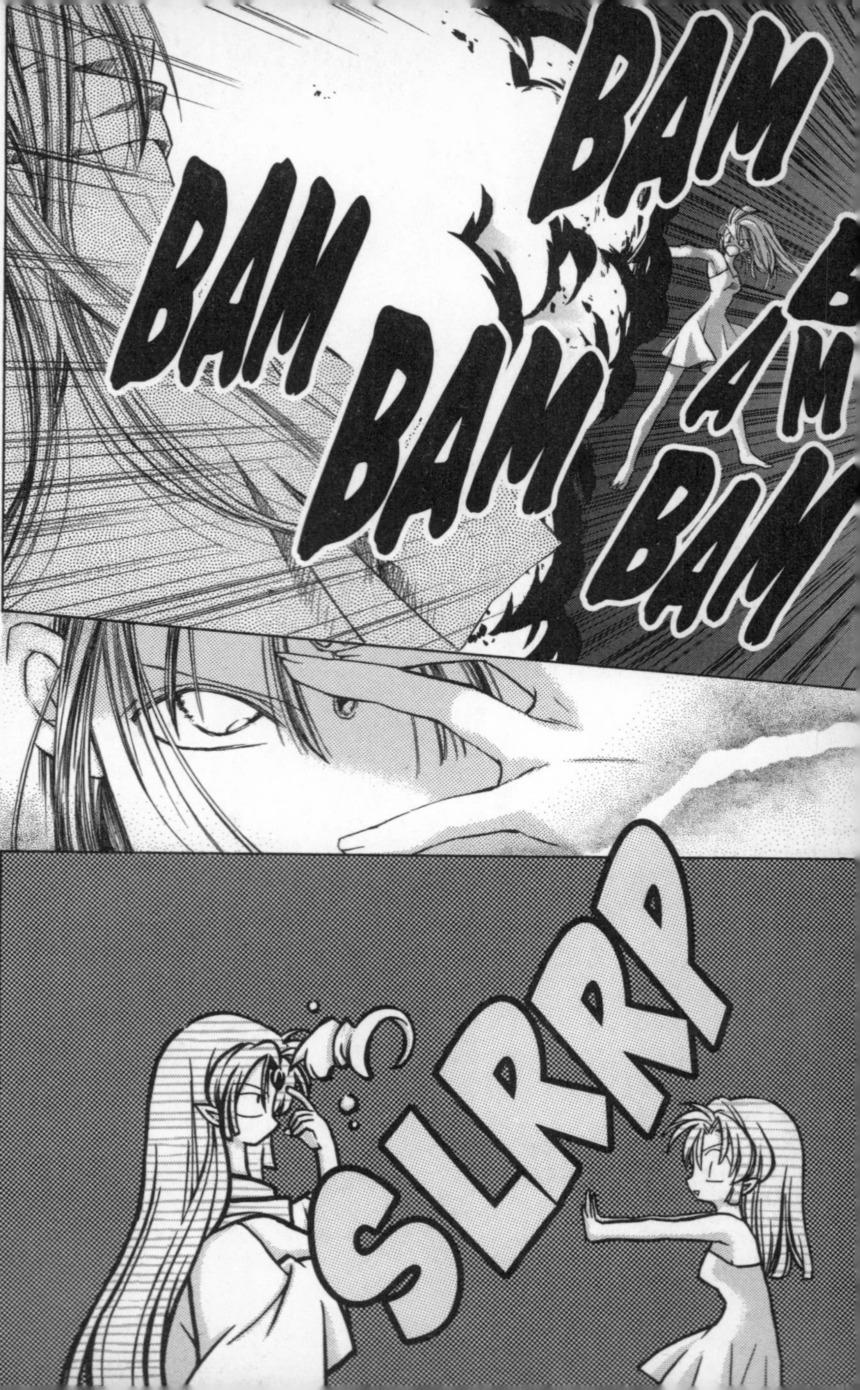

BAM
BAM
BAM
BAM
BAM
SLRRP

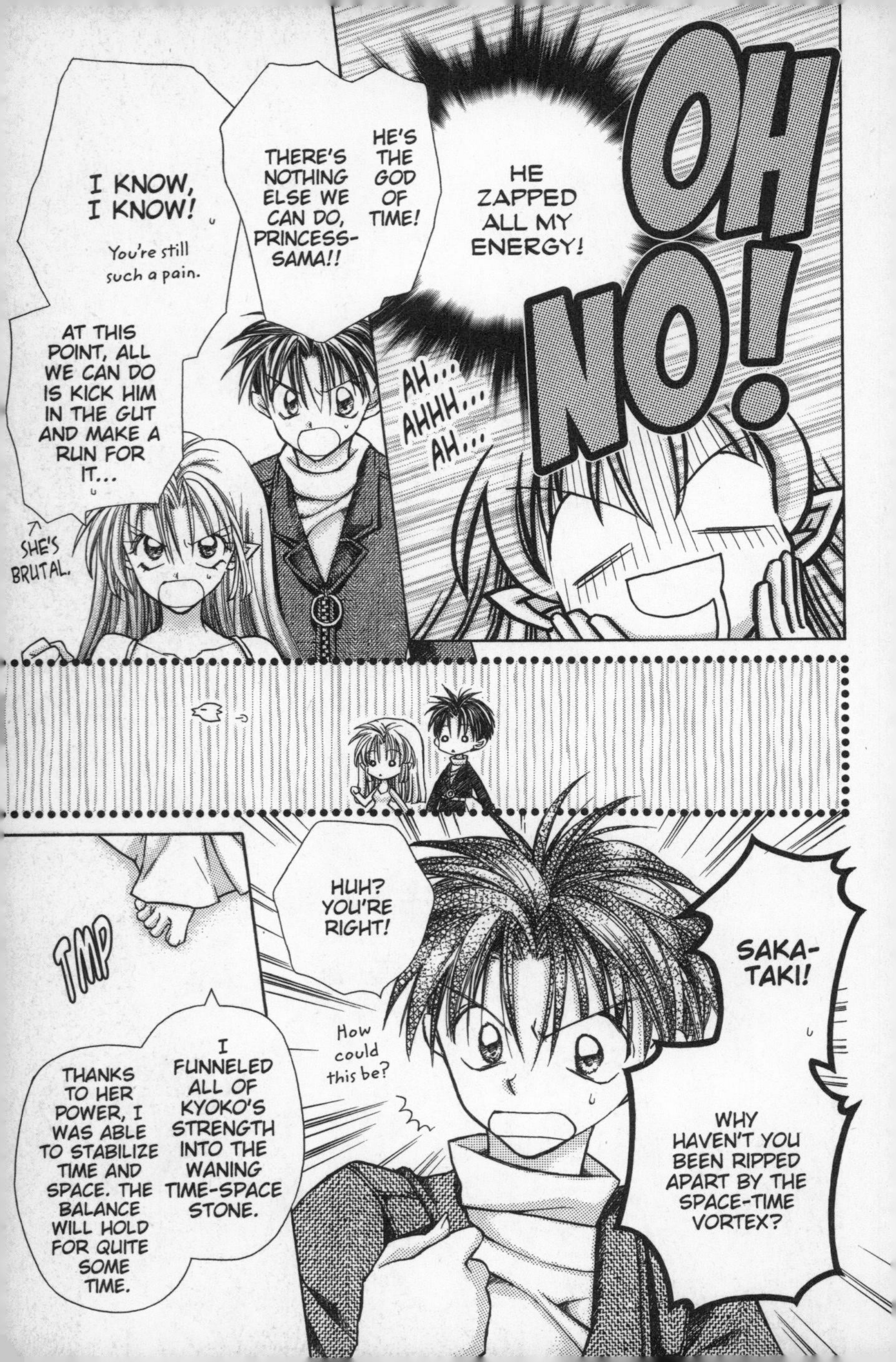
OH NO!
HE ZAPPED ALL MY ENERGY!
AH... AHHH... AH...
HE'S THE GOD OF TIME!
THERE'S NOTHING ELSE WE CAN DO, PRINCESS-SAMA!!
I KNOW, I KNOW!
You're still such a pain.
AT THIS POINT, ALL WE CAN DO IS KICK HIM IN THE GUT AND MAKE A RUN FOR IT...
SHE'S BRUTAL.
SAKA-TAKI!
WHY HAVEN'T YOU BEEN RIPPED APART BY THE SPACE-TIME VORTEX?
HUH? YOU'RE RIGHT!
How could this be?
TMP
I FUNNELED ALL OF KYOKO'S STRENGTH INTO THE WANING TIME-SPACE STONE.
THANKS TO HER POWER, I WAS ABLE TO STABILIZE TIME AND SPACE. THE BALANCE WILL HOLD FOR QUITE SOME TIME.

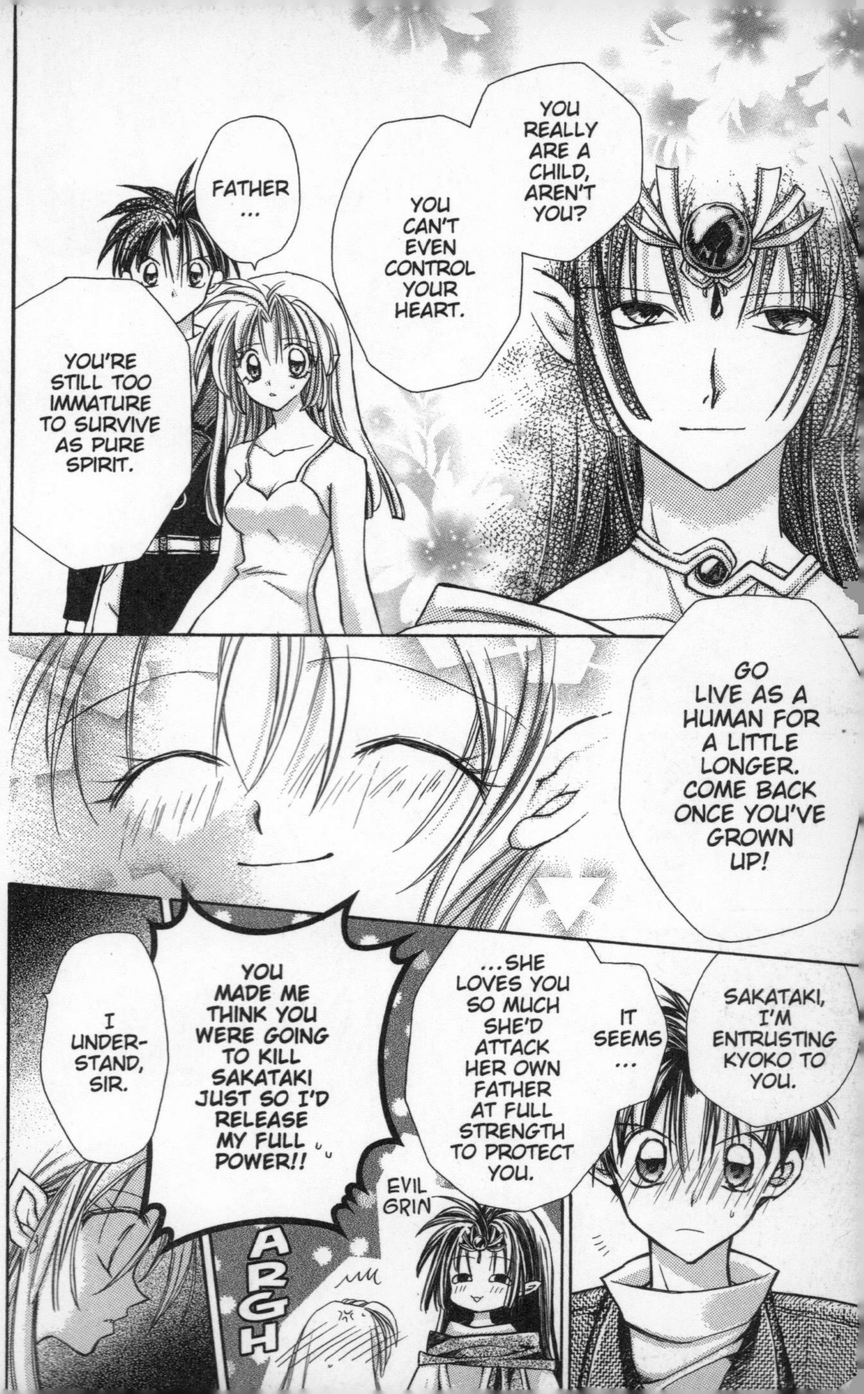

YOU REALLY ARE A CHILD, AREN'T YOU?
YOU CAN'T EVEN CONTROL YOUR HEART.
FATHER ...
YOU'RE STILL TOO IMMATURE TO SURVIVE AS PURE SPIRIT.
GO LIVE AS A HUMAN FOR A LITTLE LONGER. COME BACK ONCE YOU'VE GROWN UP!
SAKATAKI, I'M ENTRUSTING KYOKO TO YOU.
IT SEEMS ...
...SHE LOVES YOU SO MUCH SHE'D ATTACK HER OWN FATHER AT FULL STRENGTH TO PROTECT YOU.
EVIL GRIN
YOU MADE ME THINK YOU WERE GOING TO KILL SAKATAKI JUST SO I'D RELEASE MY FULL POWER!!
ARGH
I UNDER-STAND, SIR.

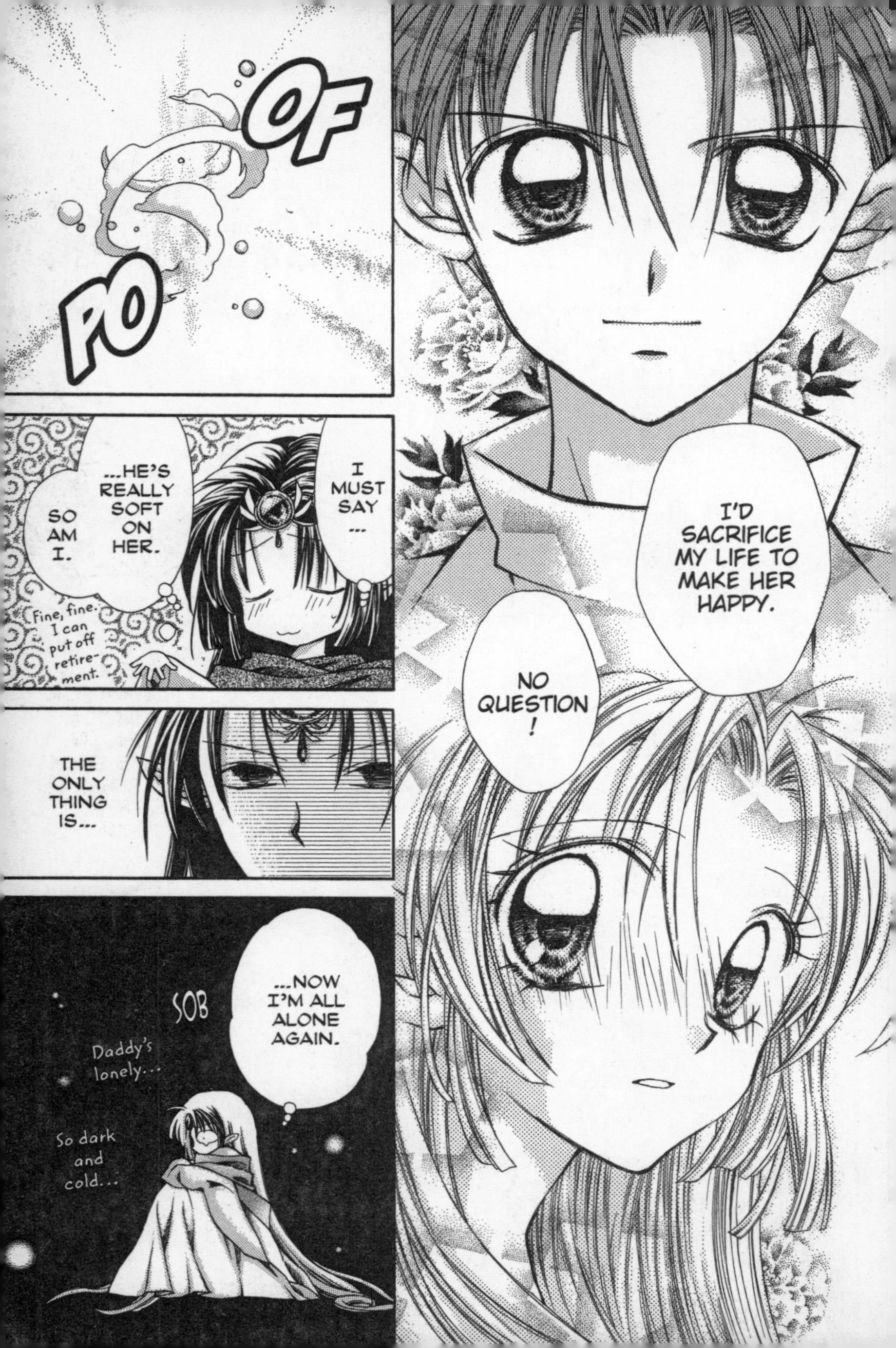
I'D SACRIFICE MY LIFE TO MAKE HER HAPPY.
NO QUESTION!
POOF
I MUST SAY...
...HE'S REALLY SOFT ON HER.
SO AM I.
Fine, fine. I can put off retirement.
THE ONLY THING IS...
...NOW I'M ALL ALONE AGAIN.
SOB
Daddy's lonely...
So dark and cold...

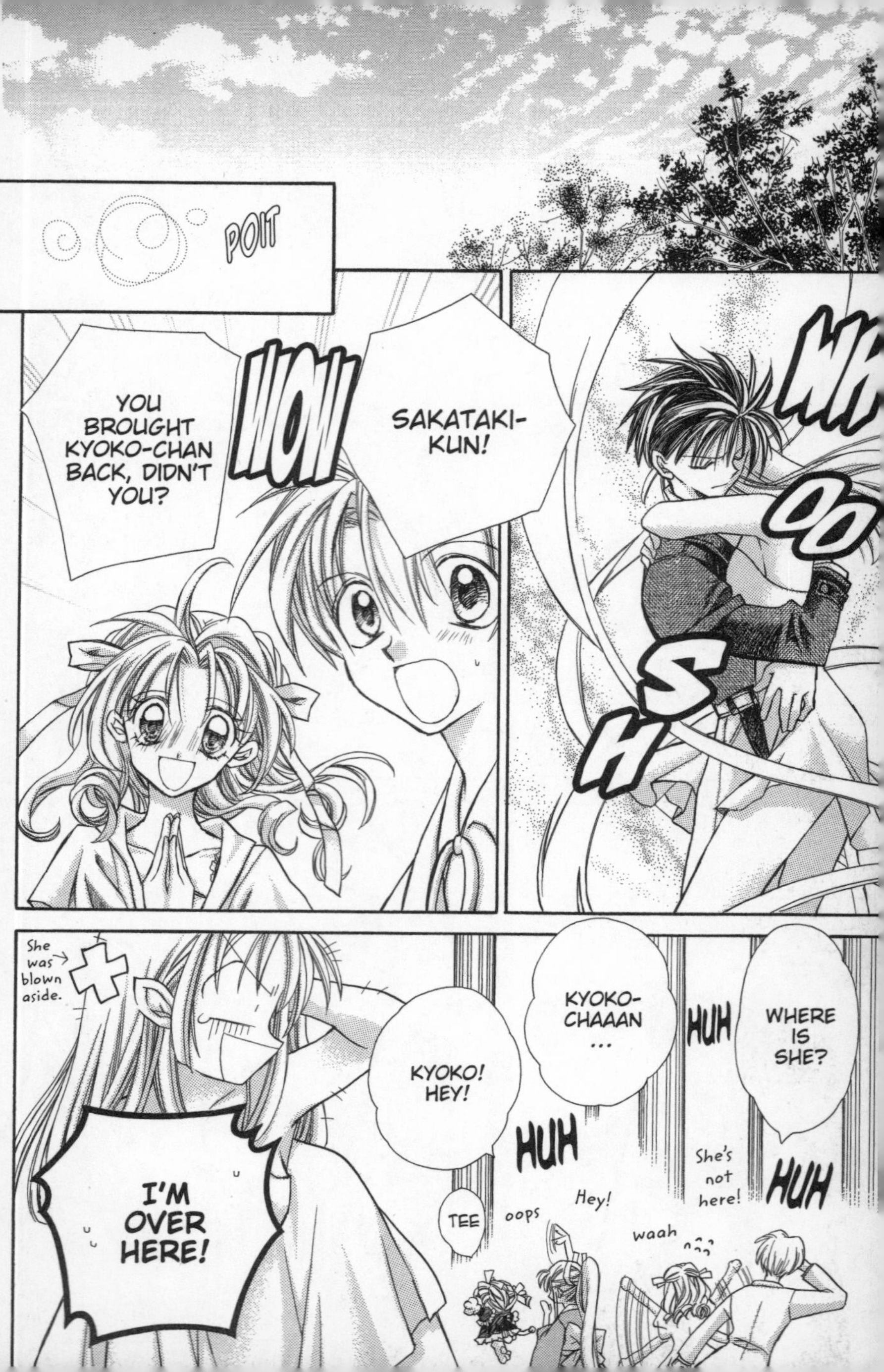
POIT
WH
OO
S
H
SAKATAKI-KUN!
WOW
YOU BROUGHT KYOKO-CHAN BACK, DIDN'T YOU?
WHERE IS SHE?
HUH
KYOKO-CHAAAN ...
KYOKO! HEY!
HUH
She's not here!
HUH
Hey!
waah
oops
TEE
I'M OVER HERE!
She was blown aside.

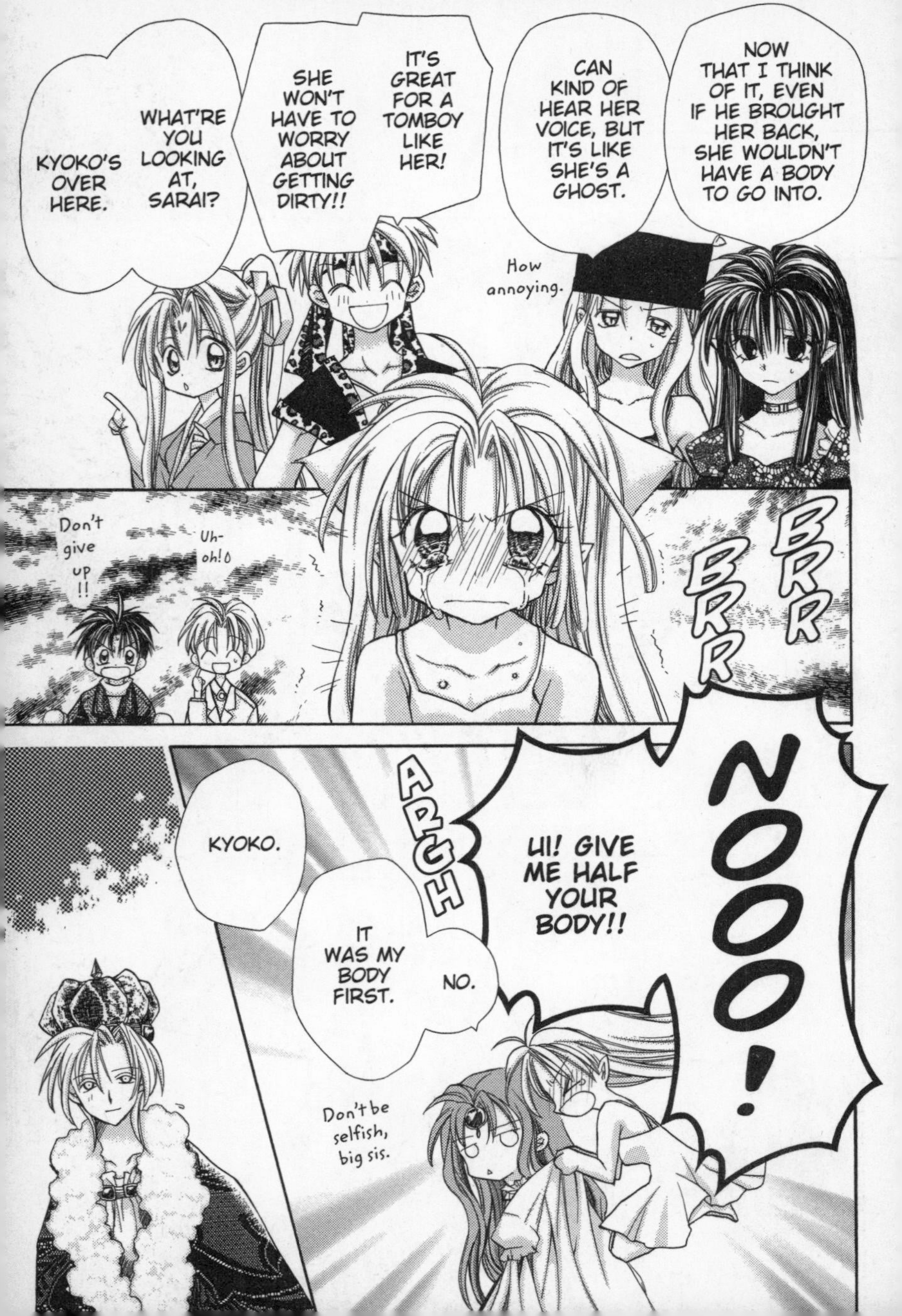
NOW THAT I THINK OF IT, EVEN IF HE BROUGHT HER BACK, SHE WOULDN'T HAVE A BODY TO GO INTO.
CAN KIND OF HEAR HER VOICE, BUT IT'S LIKE SHE'S A GHOST.
How annoying.
IT'S GREAT FOR A TOMBOY LIKE HER!
SHE WON'T HAVE TO WORRY ABOUT GETTING DIRTY!!
WHAT'RE YOU LOOKING AT, SARAI?
KYOKO'S OVER HERE.
BRRR
BRRR
Uh-oh!
Don't give up!!
NOOOO!
UI! GIVE ME HALF YOUR BODY!!
ARGH
NO.
IT WAS MY BODY FIRST.
KYOKO.
Don't be selfish, big sis.

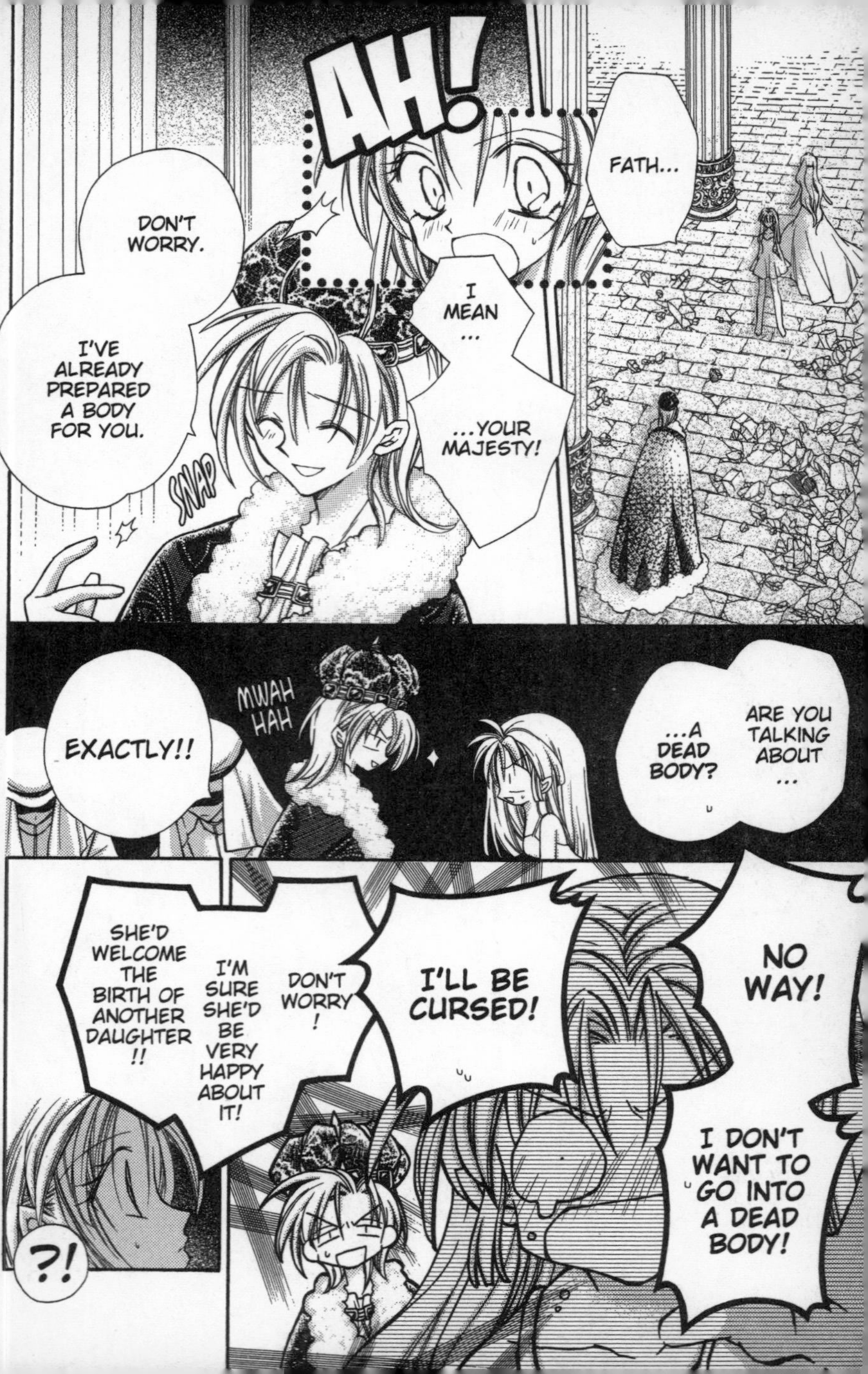
FATH...
AH!
I MEAN ...
...YOUR MAJESTY!
DON'T WORRY.
I'VE ALREADY PREPARED A BODY FOR YOU.
SNAP
ARE YOU TALKING ABOUT ...
...A DEAD BODY?
MWAH HAH
EXACTLY!!
NO WAY!
I DON'T WANT TO GO INTO A DEAD BODY!
I'LL BE CURSED!
DON'T WORRY!
I'M SURE SHE'D BE VERY HAPPY ABOUT IT!
SHE'D WELCOME THE BIRTH OF ANOTHER DAUGHTER!!
?!

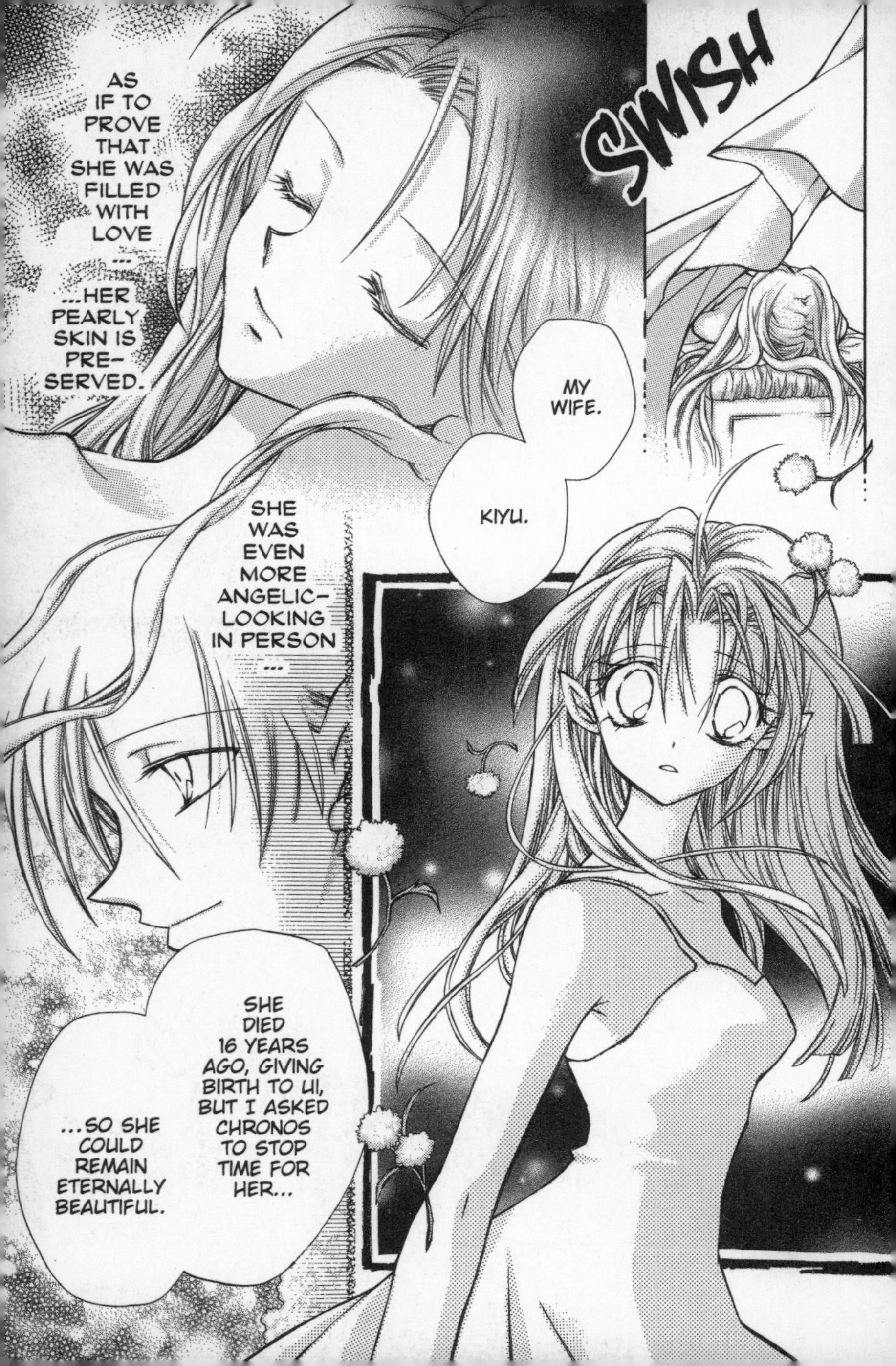
SWISH
AS IF TO PROVE THAT SHE WAS FILLED WITH LOVE ...
...HER PEARLY SKIN IS PRE-SERVED.
MY WIFE.
KIYU.
SHE WAS EVEN MORE ANGELIC-LOOKING IN PERSON ...
SHE DIED 16 YEARS AGO, GIVING BIRTH TO UI, BUT I ASKED CHRONOS TO STOP TIME FOR HER...
...SO SHE COULD REMAIN ETERNALLY BEAUTIFUL.

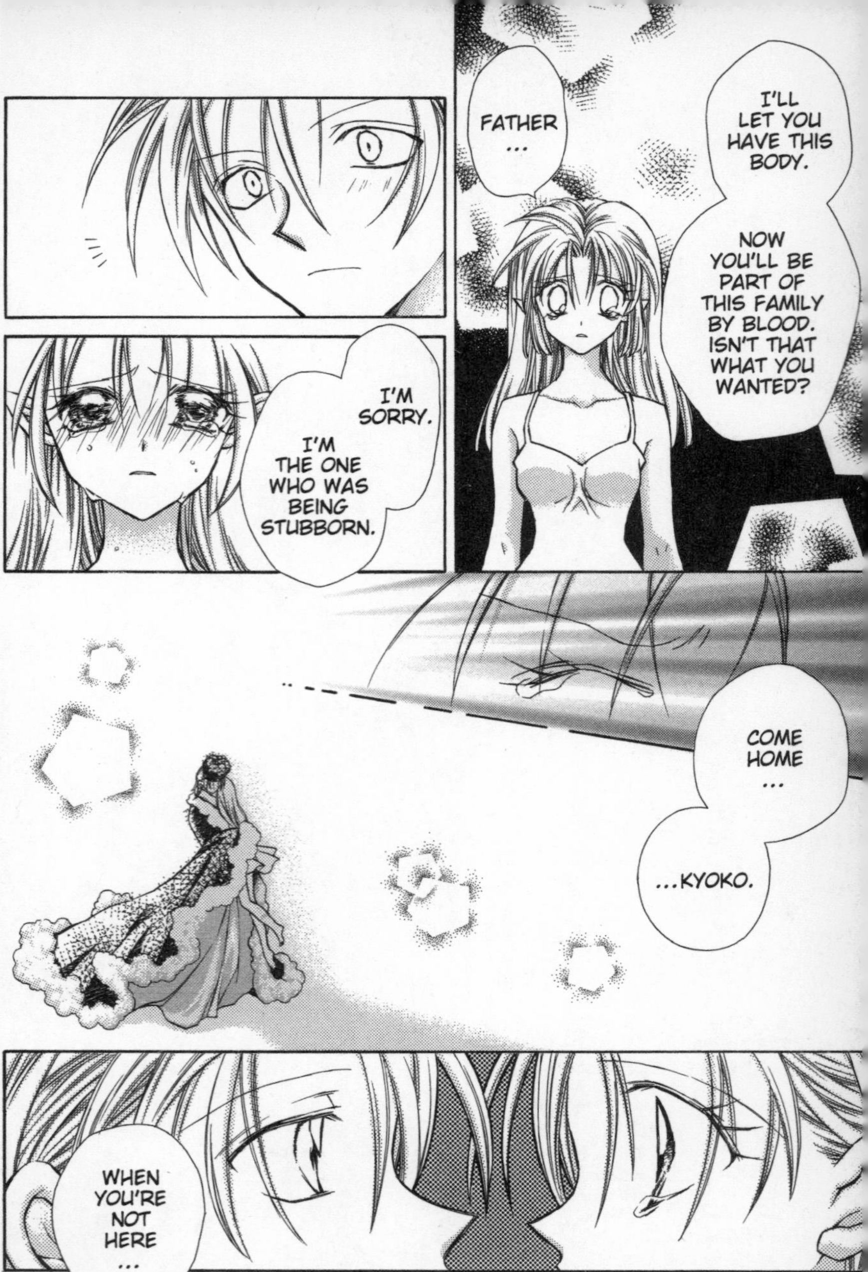
I'LL LET YOU HAVE THIS BODY.
NOW YOU'LL BE PART OF THIS FAMILY BY BLOOD. ISN'T THAT WHAT YOU WANTED?
FATHER ...
I'M SORRY.
I'M THE ONE WHO WAS BEING STUBBORN.
COME HOME ...
...KYOKO.
WHEN YOU'RE NOT HERE ...

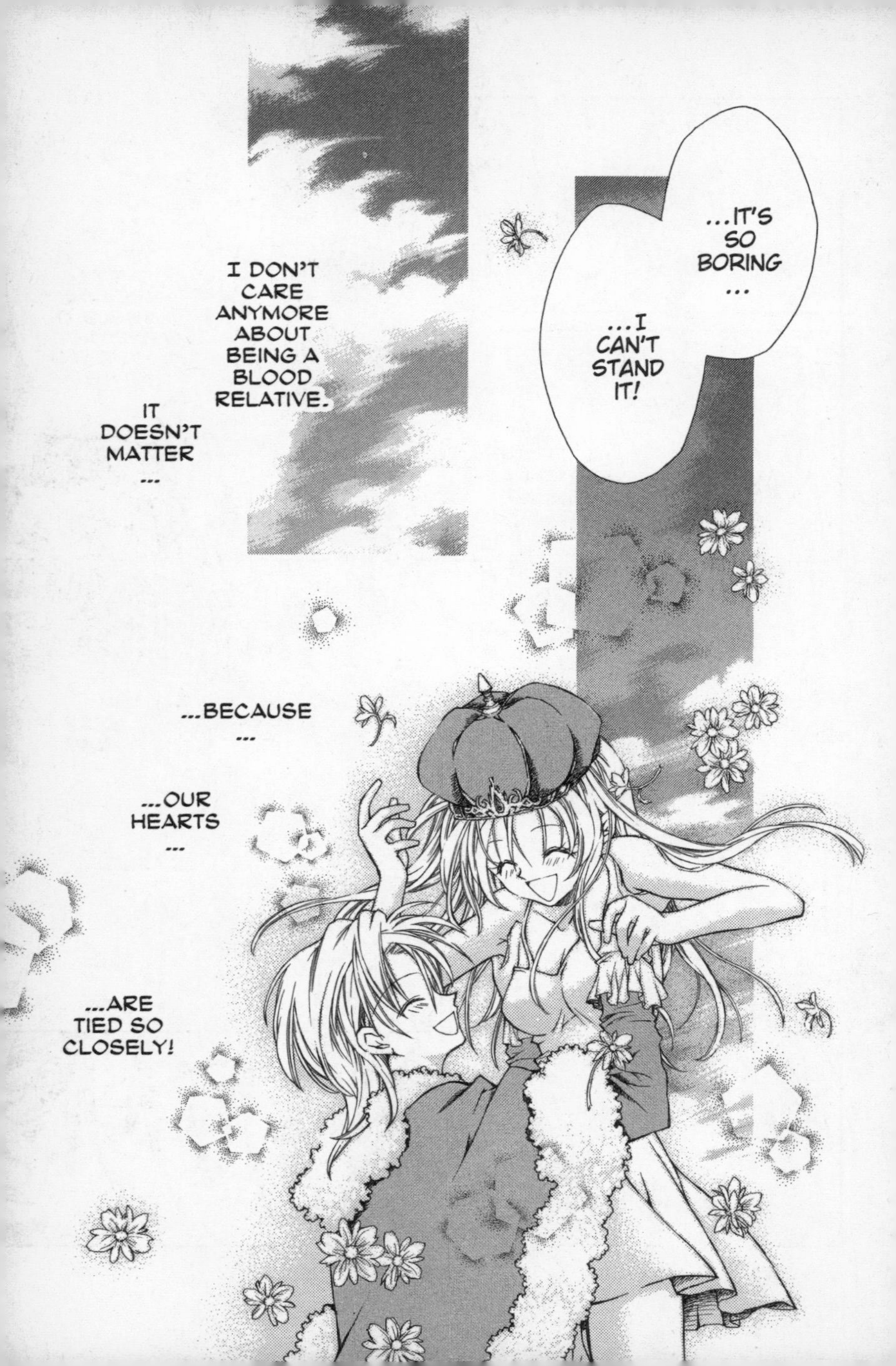
...IT'S SO BORING ...
...I CAN'T STAND IT!
I DON'T CARE ANYMORE ABOUT BEING A BLOOD RELATIVE.
IT DOESN'T MATTER ...
...BECAUSE ...
...OUR HEARTS ...
...ARE TIED SO CLOSELY!

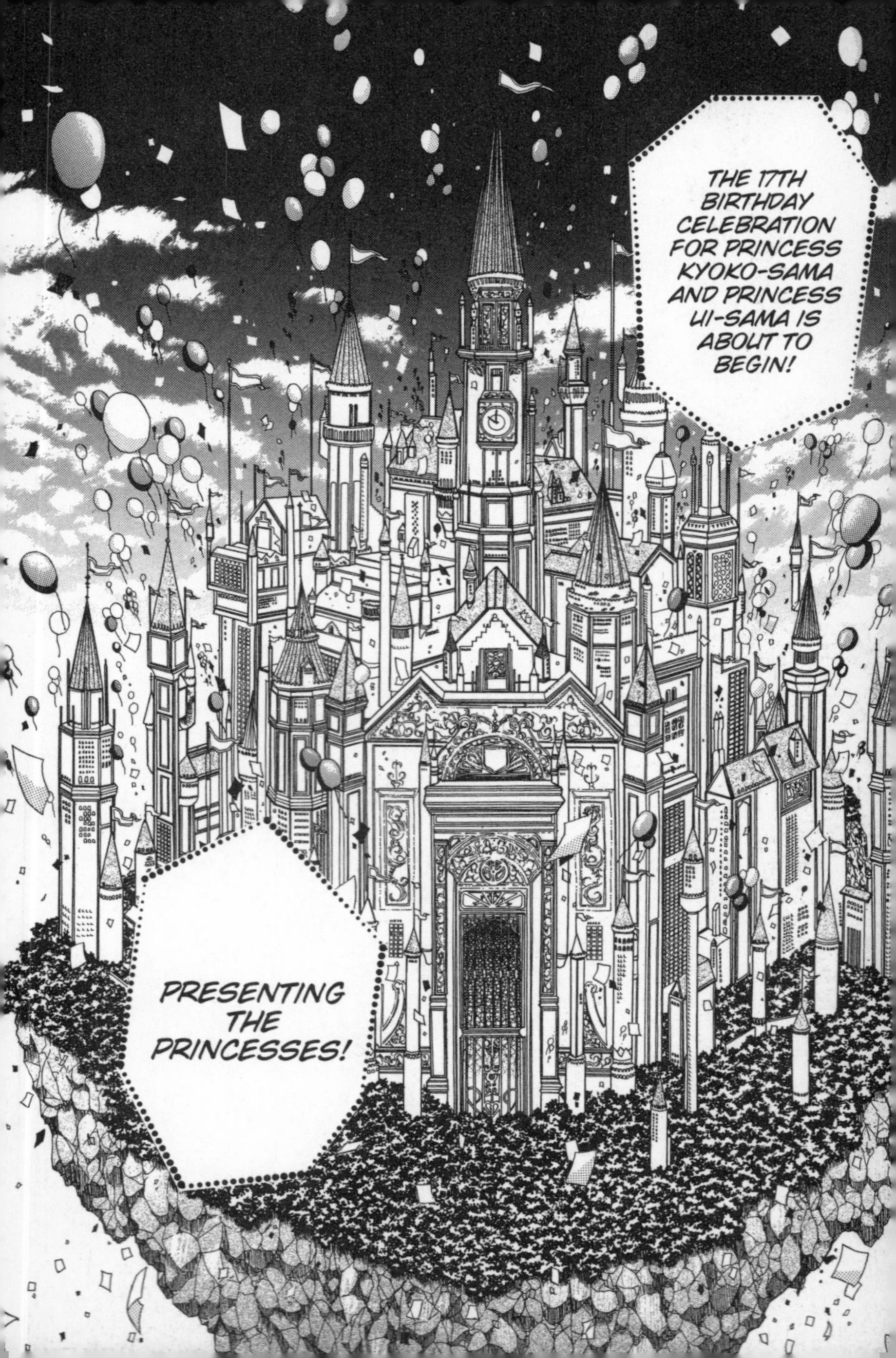
THE 17TH BIRTHDAY CELEBRATION FOR PRINCESS KYOKO-SAMA AND PRINCESS UI-SAMA IS ABOUT TO BEGIN!
PRESENTING THE PRINCESSES!

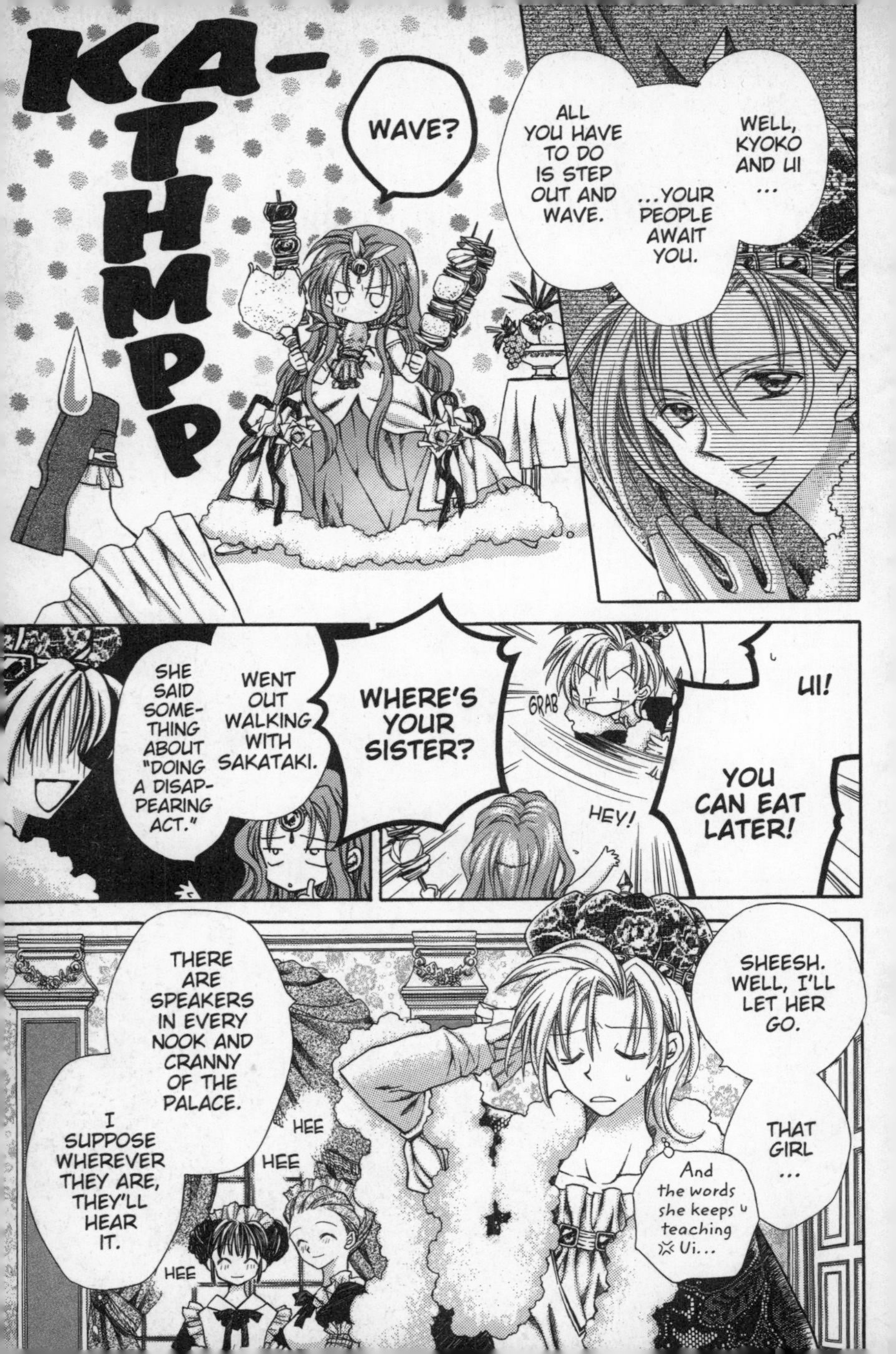

WELL, KYOKO AND UI ...
...YOUR PEOPLE AWAIT YOU.
ALL YOU HAVE TO DO IS STEP OUT AND WAVE.
WAVE?
KA-THMPP
UI!
YOU CAN EAT LATER!
GRAB
HEY!
WHERE'S YOUR SISTER?
WENT OUT WALKING WITH SAKATAKI.
SHE SAID SOMETHING ABOUT "DOING A DISAPPEARING ACT."
SHEESH. WELL, I'LL LET HER GO.
THAT GIRL ...
And the words she keeps teaching Ui...
THERE ARE SPEAKERS IN EVERY NOOK AND CRANNY OF THE PALACE.
I SUPPOSE WHEREVER THEY ARE, THEY'LL HEAR IT.
HEE
HEE
HEE

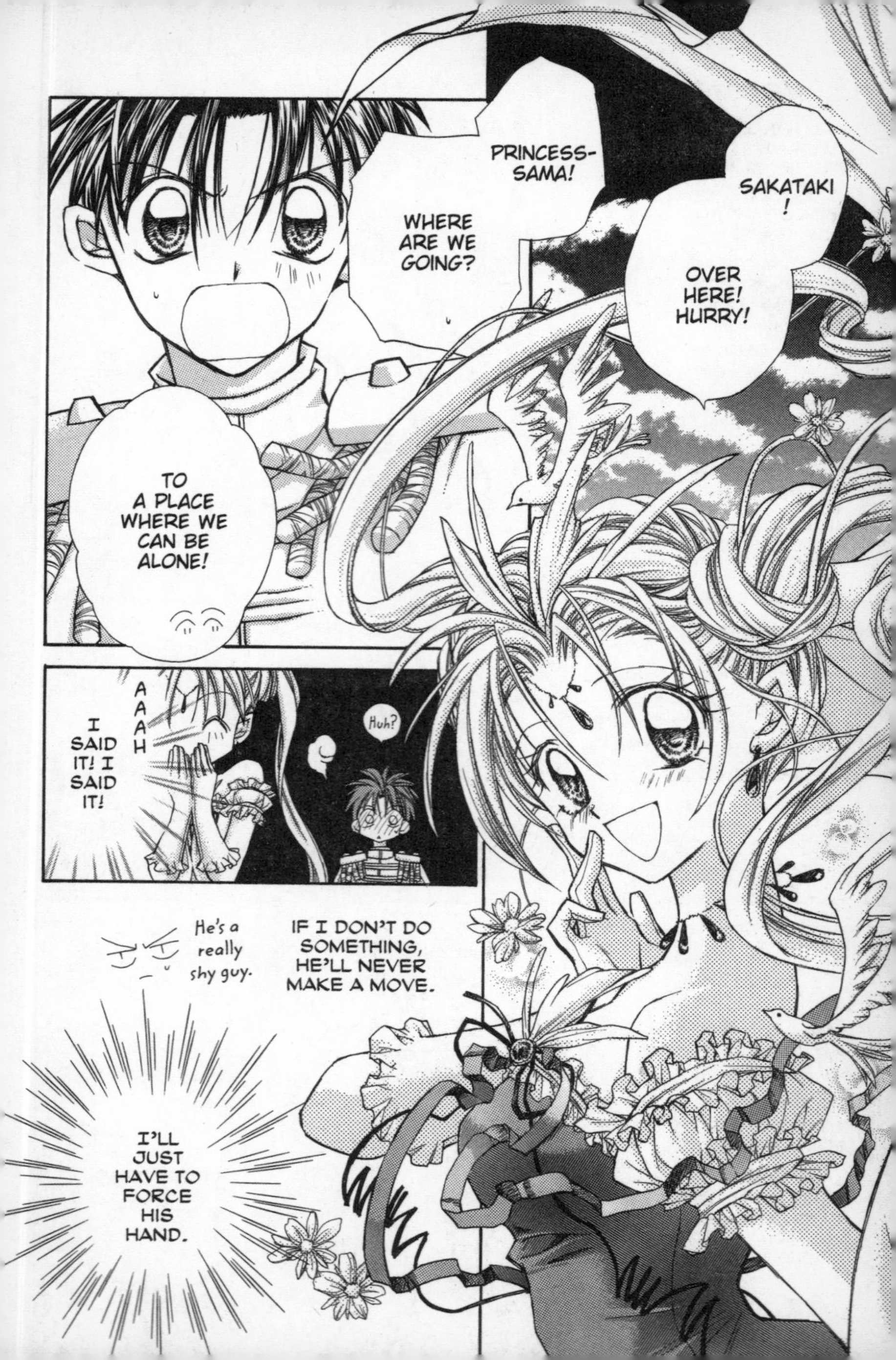
SAKATAKI!
OVER HERE! HURRY!
PRINCESS-SAMA!
WHERE ARE WE GOING?
TO A PLACE WHERE WE CAN BE ALONE!
AAAAH
I SAID IT! I SAID IT!
Huh?
IF I DON'T DO SOMETHING, HE'LL NEVER MAKE A MOVE.
He's a really shy guy.
I'LL JUST HAVE TO FORCE HIS HAND.

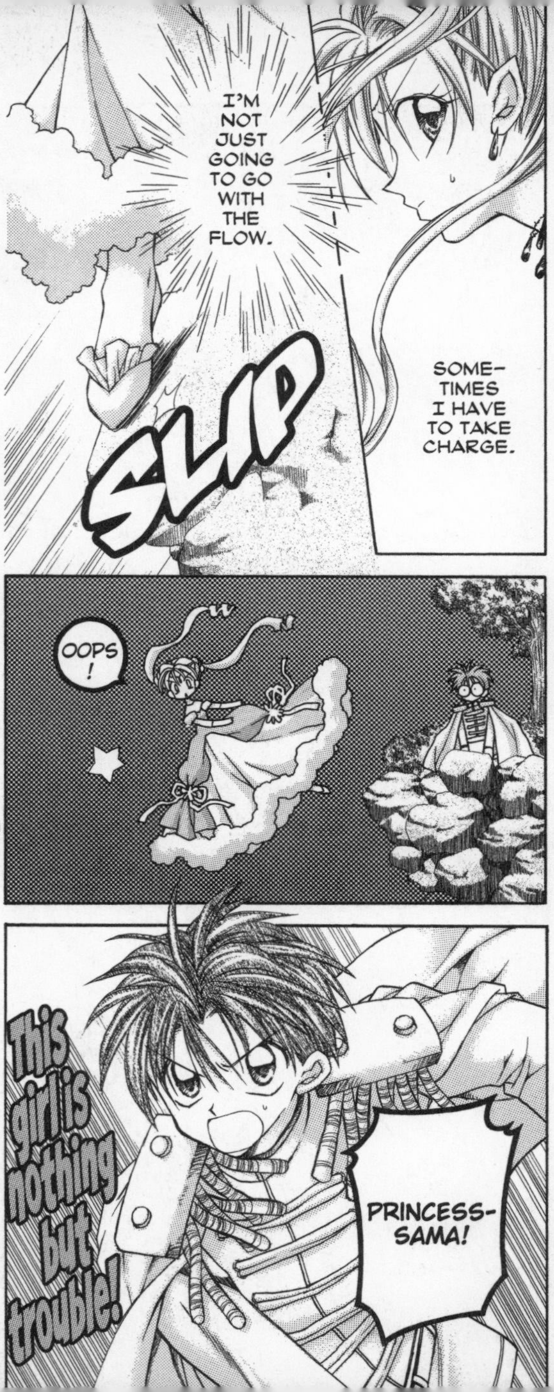
SOME-
TIMES
I HAVE
TO TAKE
CHARGE.
I'M NOT JUST GOING TO GO WITH THE FLOW.
SLIP
OOPS!
PRINCESS-SAMA!
This girl is nothing but trouble!

FAREWELL

WELL, HERE WE ARE AT MY LAST 1/3 OF A PAGE. (PENSHAKI IS ONLY 1/4 OF A PAGE. ♥)

MY NEXT SERIES IS ENTITLED *FULL MOON WO SAGASHITE*, AND IT'S ABOUT A SINGER.

I'M AIMING FOR A CUTE STORY AND CUTE ART, SO PLEASE READ IT!! IT'LL BE IN THE JANUARY ISSUE OF *RIBON*.

It's not the one I talked about wanting to write earlier.

SEND FAN LETTERS TO ↓

VIZ MEDIA
P.O. BOX 77010
SAN FRANCISCO, CA 94107

I'M GLAD I REMEMBERED TO WRITE THIS...I USUALLY FORGET.

✿SPECIAL THANKS✿

AI MINASE AND KAKA ASANO... THANKS VERY MUCH FOR THE PALACE AND OTHER SUPERB BACKGROUNDS!
RUK KAZUKI... THANKS FOR THE GIANT CLOCK!!
NIKI HOSHITUSYU... HANG IN THERE ON THOSE BACKGROUNDS! I'M EXPECTING A LOT FROM YOU!
KANA KAWASE... ALWAYS A GREAT PINCH HITTER!
KANAN KISEKI... YOU'RE JUST TOO FASCINATING...
MIWA SAWAGAMI... YOU ALWAYS CATCH ON QUICKLY. THAT'S THE SPIRIT!
AIRI TEITO... YOU STILL HAVE A LITTLE TO LEARN!
RINA ASUKA...I HAVE NOTHING TO SAY. JUST KEEP TRYING, LIKE YOU DO.
ASUKA... YOU ALWAYS SEEM SO BUSY. THANKS FOR ALWAYS COMING TO HELP.
MARI ENDO... THANKS FOR A JOB WELL DONE. PLEASE COME AND HELP AGAIN WHEN I'M IN A JAM, OKAY?

IT LOOKS LIKE A REPORT CARD ...

(ARI) AMMONITE-SAMA
TOMISHIGE-SAMA KOIKE-SAMA
RIBON'S EDITORIAL STAFF
ALL MY FANS

NEXT YEAR I'M PLANNING TO REALLY WORK HARD, SO PLEASE READ MY MANGA! ♥

I TRY TO GET MY MANGA OUT AS QUICKLY AS POSSIBLE, SO TO THOSE OF YOU WHO WAIT FOR EACH NEW VOLUME, THANKS FOR WAITING.

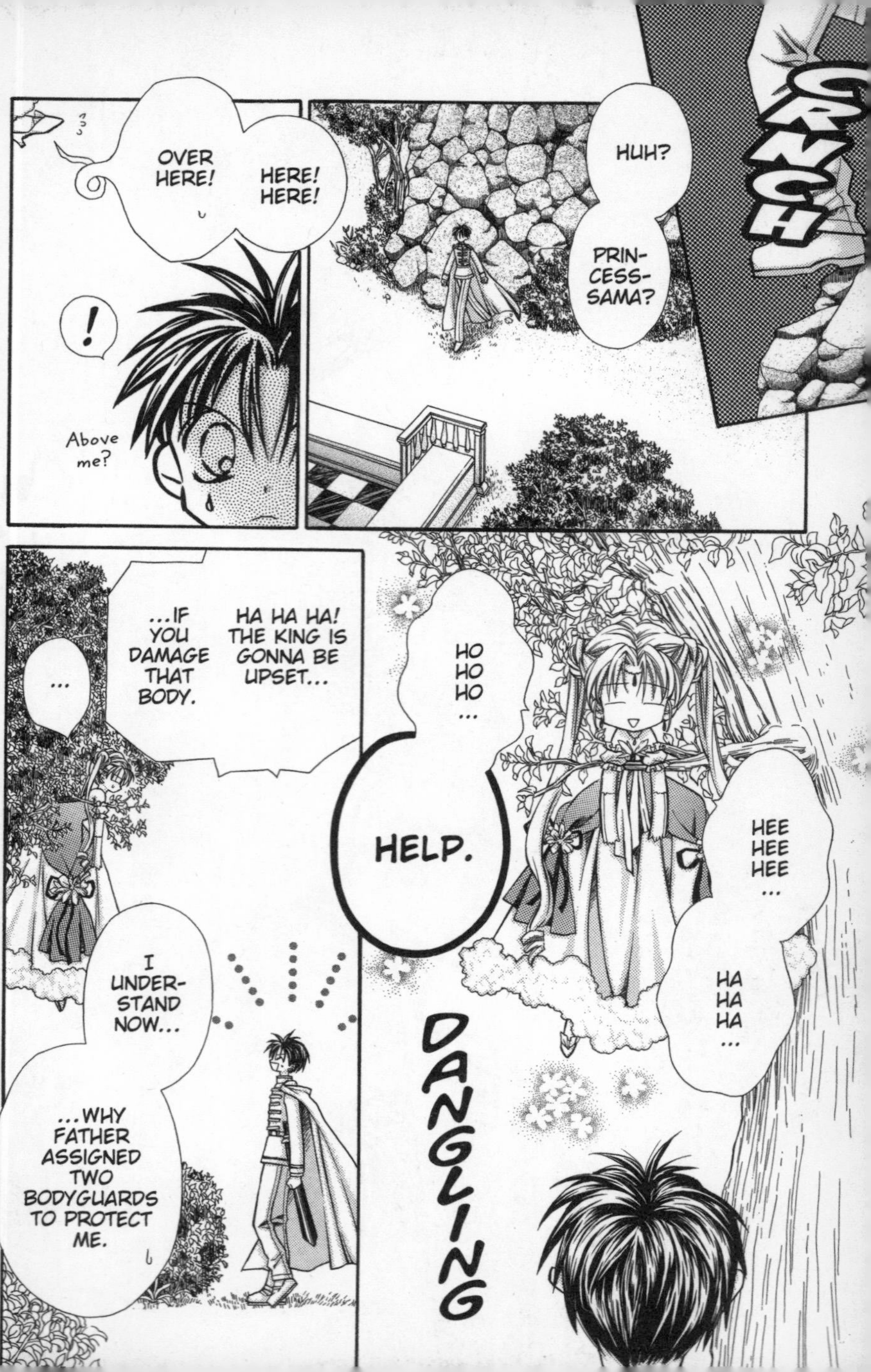
CRNCH
HUH?
PRIN-CESS-SAMA?
HERE! HERE!
OVER HERE!
!
Above me?
HO HO HO ...
HEE HEE HEE ...
HA HA HA ...
HELP.
DANGLING
HA HA HA! THE KING IS GONNA BE UPSET...
...IF YOU DAMAGE THAT BODY.
...
I UNDER-STAND NOW...
...WHY FATHER ASSIGNED TWO BODYGUARDS TO PROTECT ME.

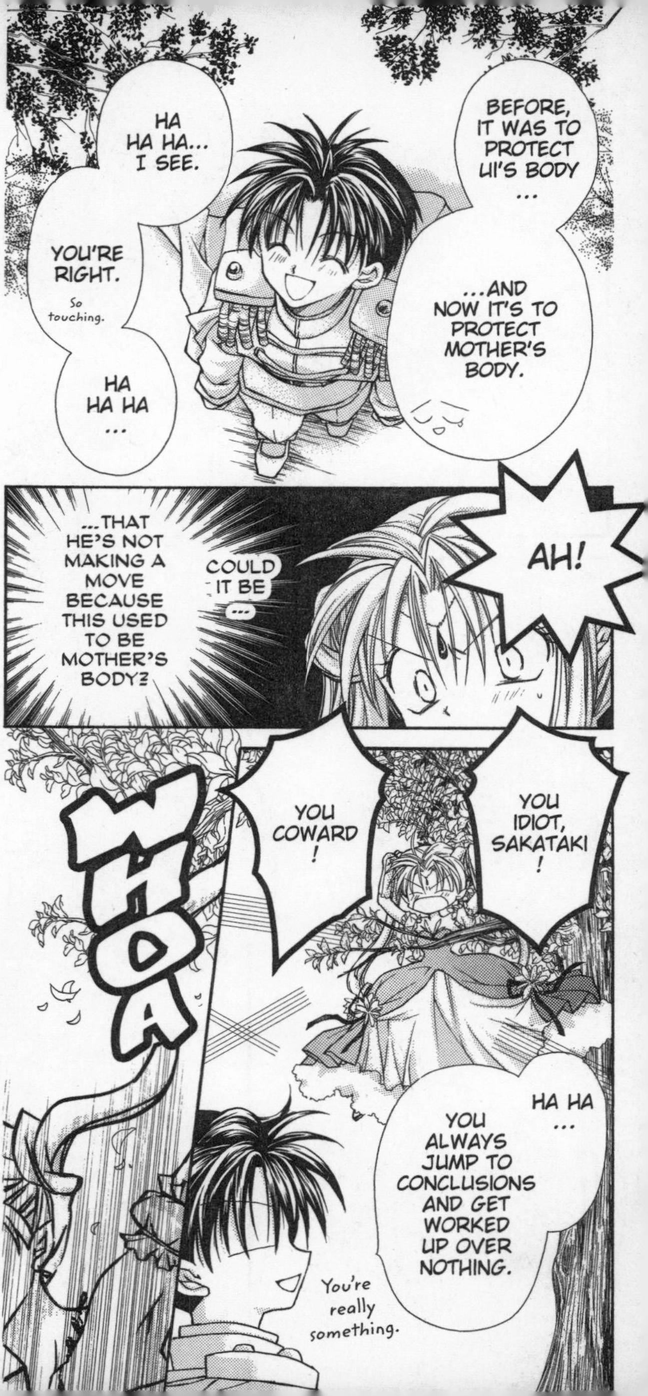
BEFORE, IT WAS TO PROTECT UI'S BODY ...
...AND NOW IT'S TO PROTECT MOTHER'S BODY.
HA HA HA... I SEE.
YOU'RE RIGHT.
So touching.
HA HA HA ...
AH!
COULD IT BE ...
...THAT HE'S NOT MAKING A MOVE BECAUSE THIS USED TO BE MOTHER'S BODY?
YOU IDIOT, SAKATAKI!
YOU COWARD!
WHOA
HA HA ...
YOU ALWAYS JUMP TO CONCLUSIONS AND GET WORKED UP OVER NOTHING.
You're really something.

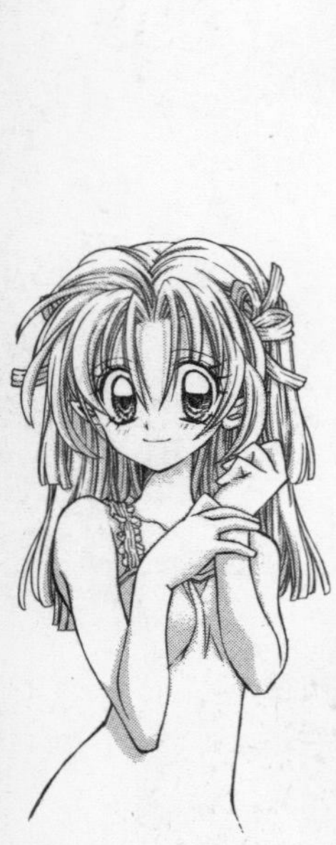

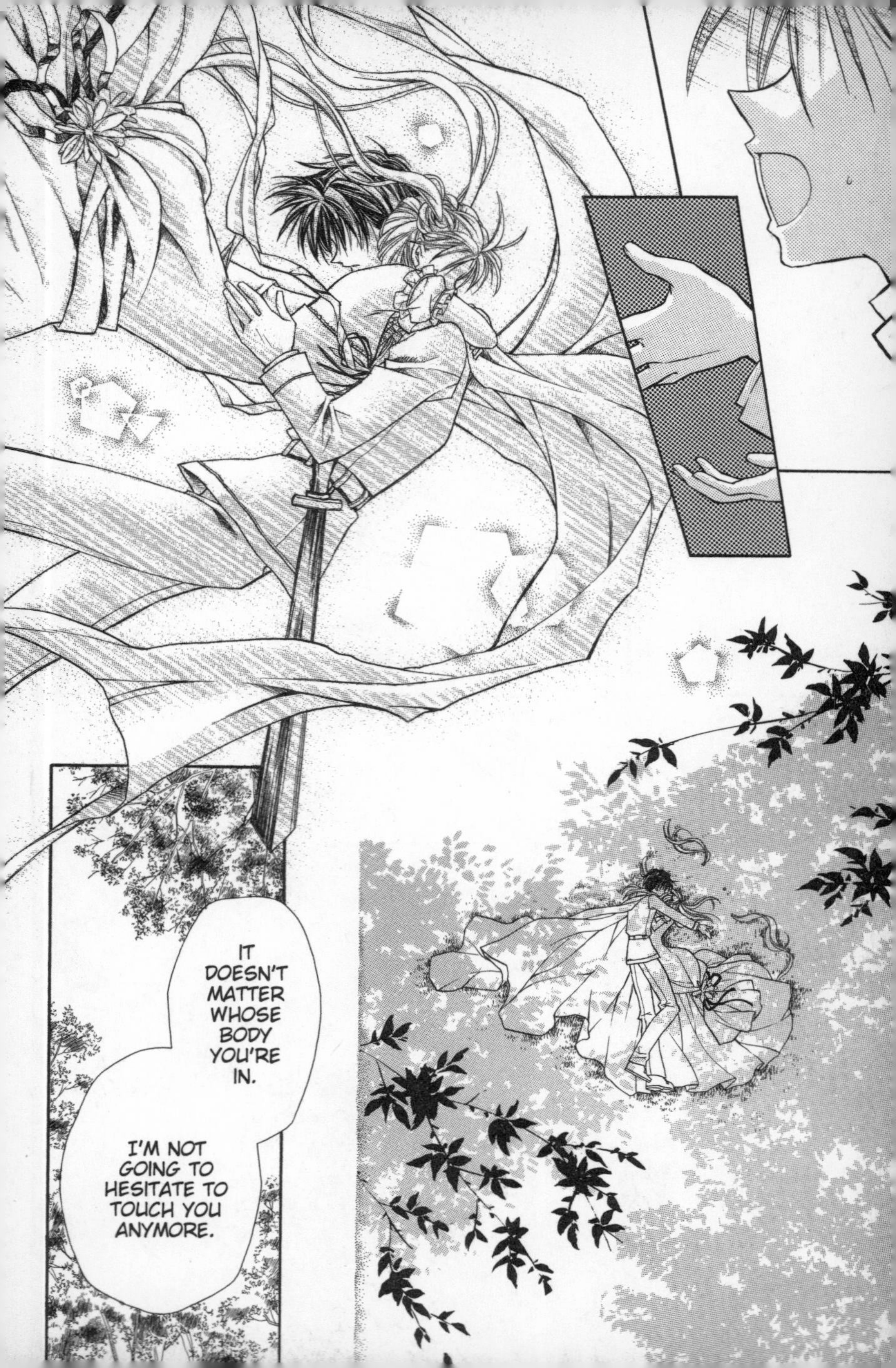
IT DOESN'T MATTER WHOSE BODY YOU'RE IN.
I'M NOT GOING TO HESITATE TO TOUCH YOU ANYMORE.

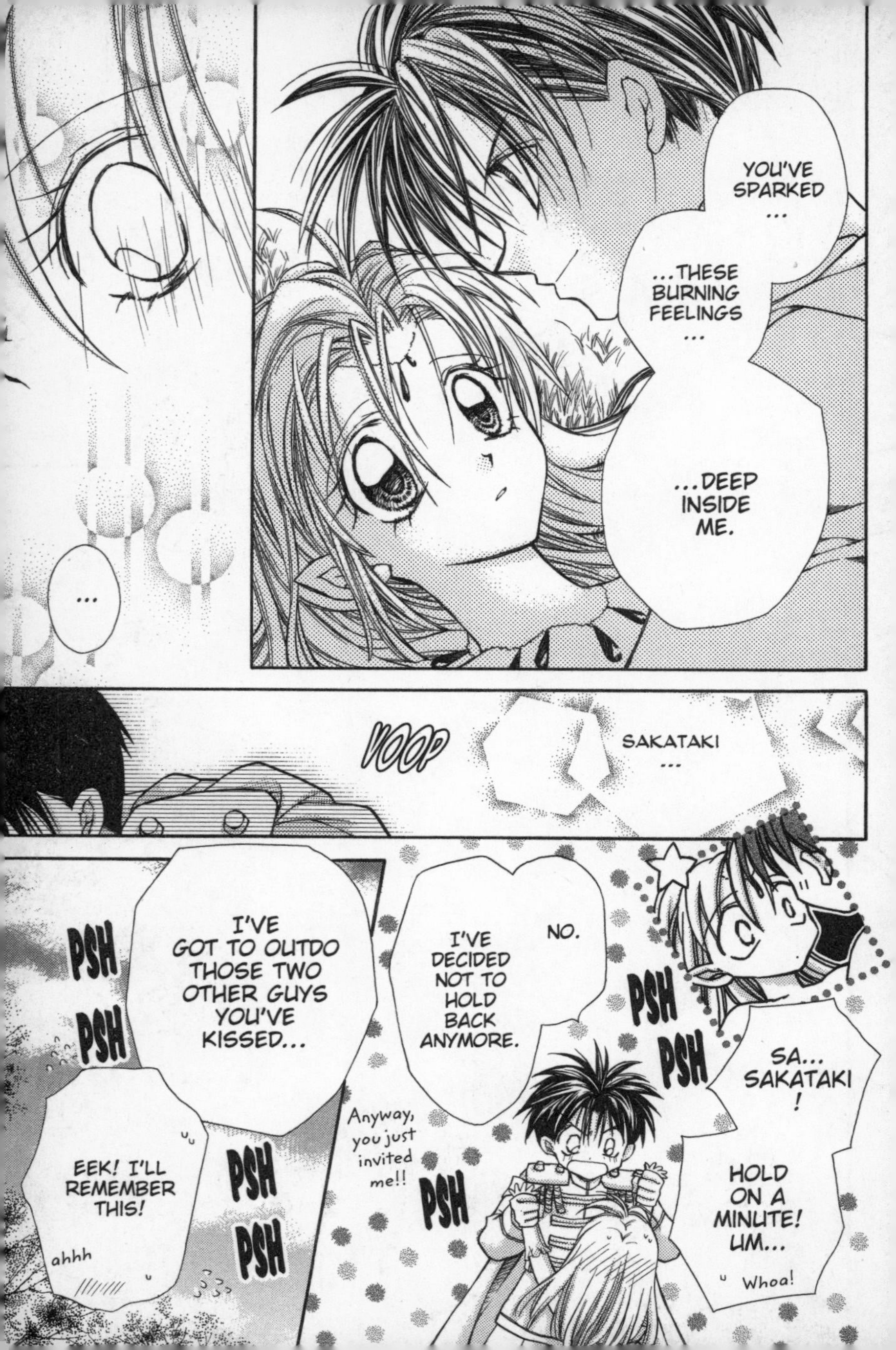
YOU'VE SPARKED ...
...THESE BURNING FEELINGS ...
...DEEP INSIDE ME.
...
SAKATAKI ...
VOOP
SA... SAKATAKI !
HOLD ON A MINUTE! UM...
Whoa!
PSH
PSH
NO.
I'VE DECIDED NOT TO HOLD BACK ANYMORE.
PSH
Anyway, you just invited me!!
I'VE GOT TO OUTDO THOSE TWO OTHER GUYS YOU'VE KISSED...
PSH
PSH
PSH
PSH
EEK! I'LL REMEMBER THIS!
ahhh

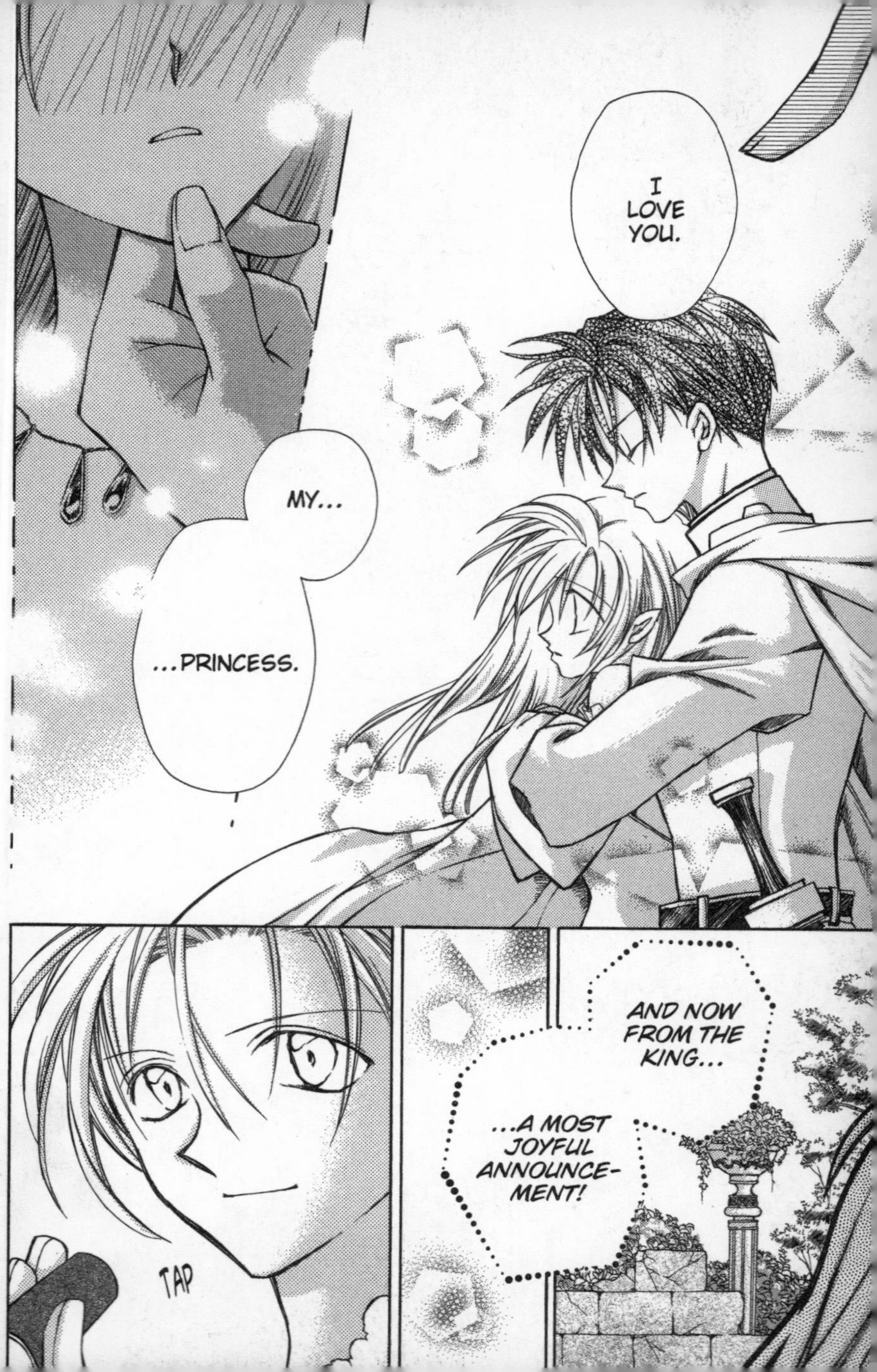
I LOVE YOU.
MY...
...PRINCESS.
AND NOW FROM THE KING...
...A MOST JOYFUL ANNOUNCE-MENT!
TAP

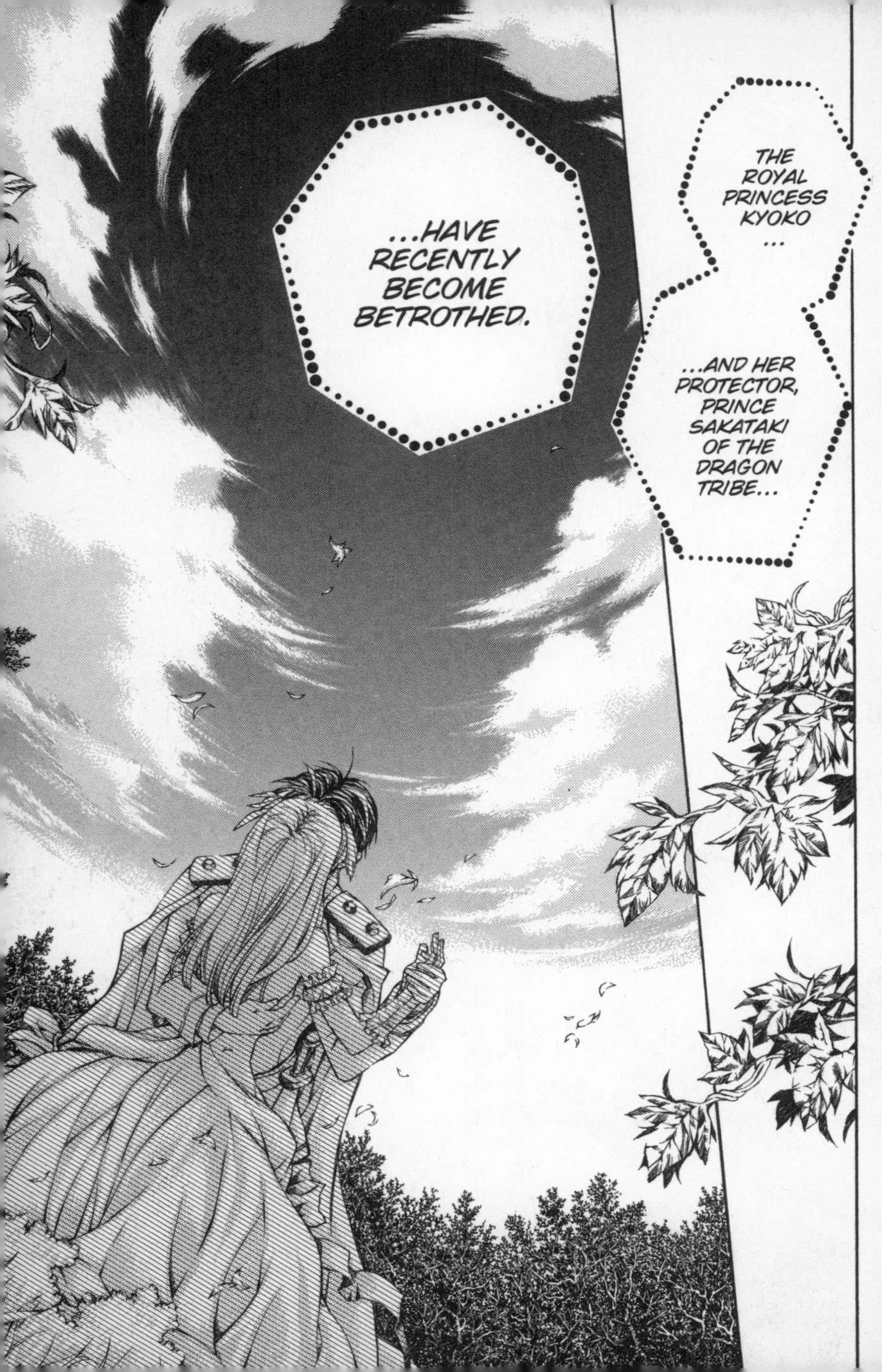
THE ROYAL PRINCESS KYOKO...
...AND HER PROTECTOR, PRINCE SAKATAKI OF THE DRAGON TRIBE...
...HAVE RECENTLY BECOME BETROTHED.

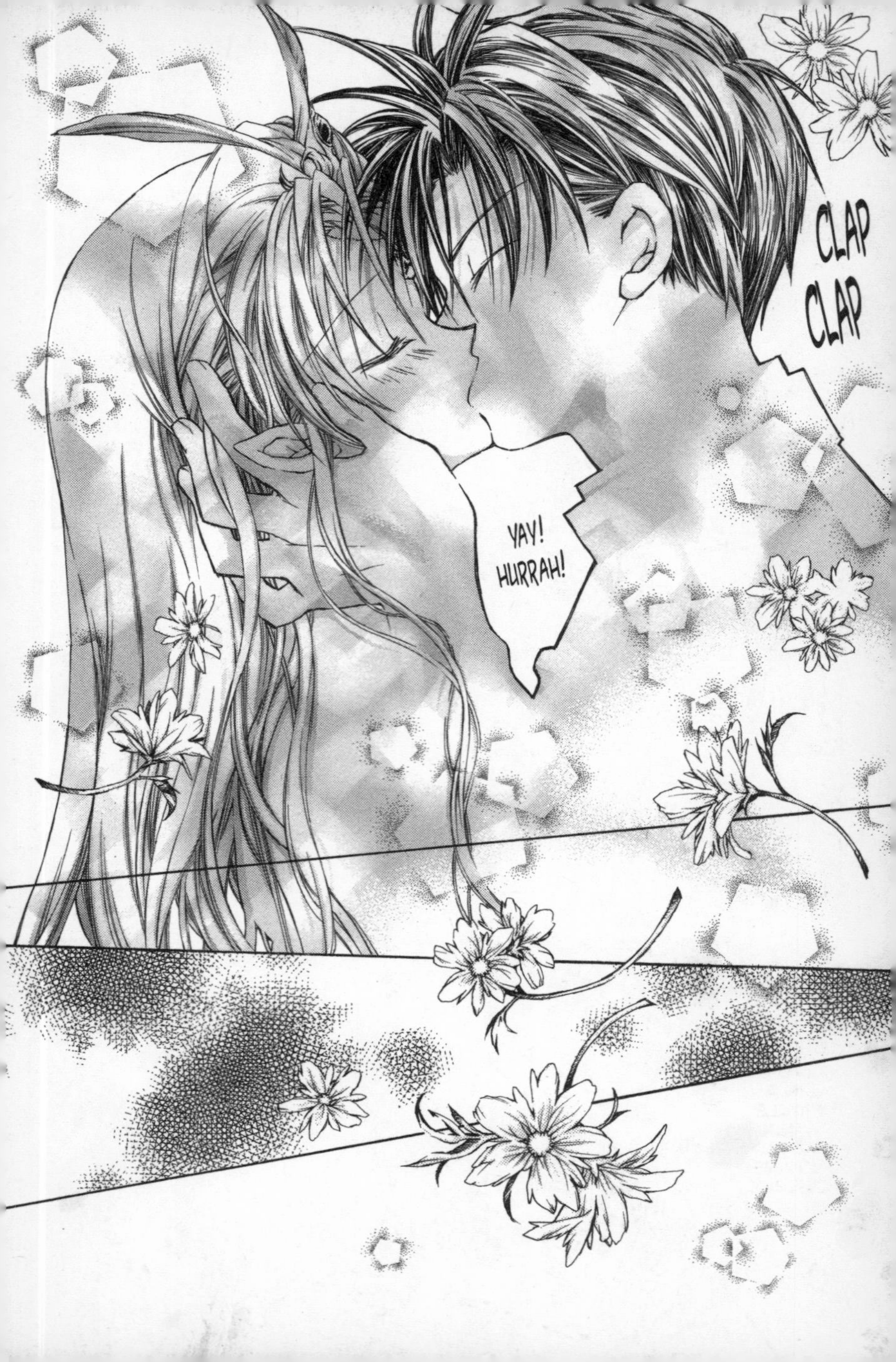
CLAP
CLAP
YAY!
HURRAH!

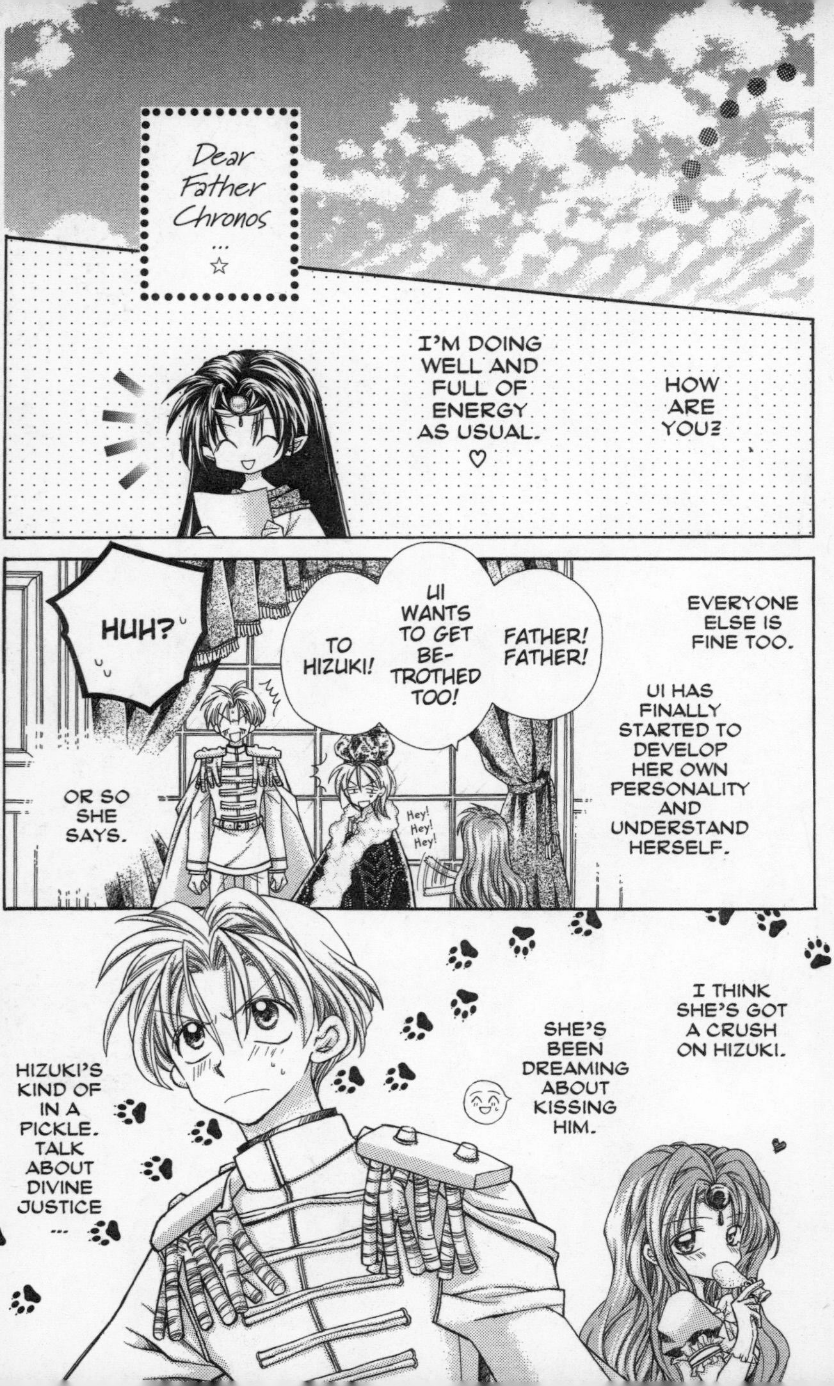
Dear Father Chronos ... ☆
HOW ARE YOU?
I'M DOING WELL AND FULL OF ENERGY AS USUAL. ♡
EVERYONE ELSE IS FINE TOO.
UI HAS FINALLY STARTED TO DEVELOP HER OWN PERSONALITY AND UNDERSTAND HERSELF.
FATHER! FATHER!
UI WANTS TO GET BE-TROTHED TOO!
TO HIZUKI!
Hey! Hey! Hey!
HUH?
OR SO SHE SAYS.
I THINK SHE'S GOT A CRUSH ON HIZUKI.
SHE'S BEEN DREAMING ABOUT KISSING HIM.
HIZUKI'S KIND OF IN A PICKLE. TALK ABOUT DIVINE JUSTICE ...

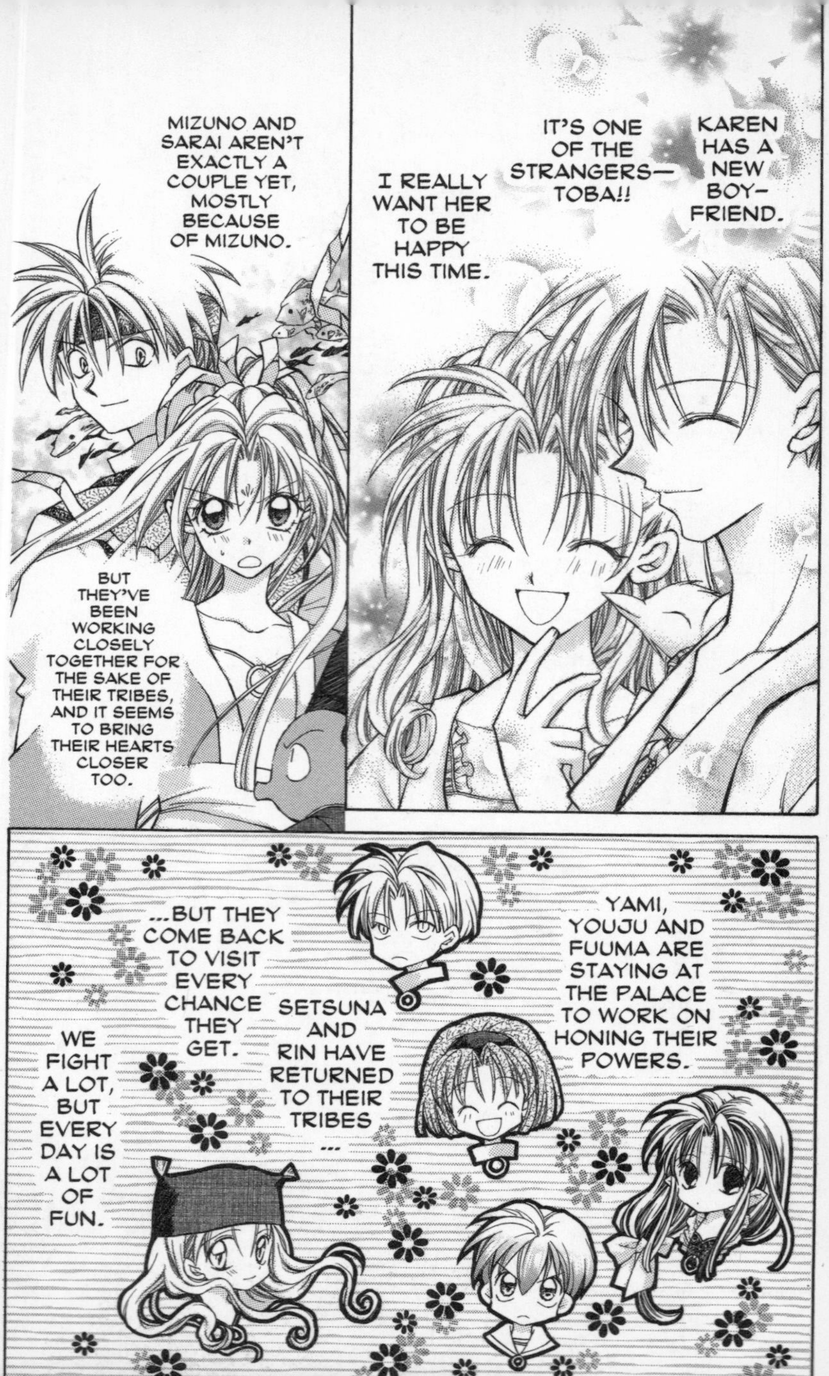
KAREN HAS A NEW BOY-FRIEND.
IT'S ONE OF THE STRANGERS—TOBA!!
I REALLY WANT HER TO BE HAPPY THIS TIME.
MIZUNO AND SARAI AREN'T EXACTLY A COUPLE YET, MOSTLY BECAUSE OF MIZUNO.
BUT THEY'VE BEEN WORKING CLOSELY TOGETHER FOR THE SAKE OF THEIR TRIBES, AND IT SEEMS TO BRING THEIR HEARTS CLOSER TOO.
YAMI, YOUJU AND FUUMA ARE STAYING AT THE PALACE TO WORK ON HONING THEIR POWERS.
SETSUNA AND RIN HAVE RETURNED TO THEIR TRIBES...
...BUT THEY COME BACK TO VISIT EVERY CHANCE THEY GET.
WE FIGHT A LOT, BUT EVERY DAY IS A LOT OF FUN.

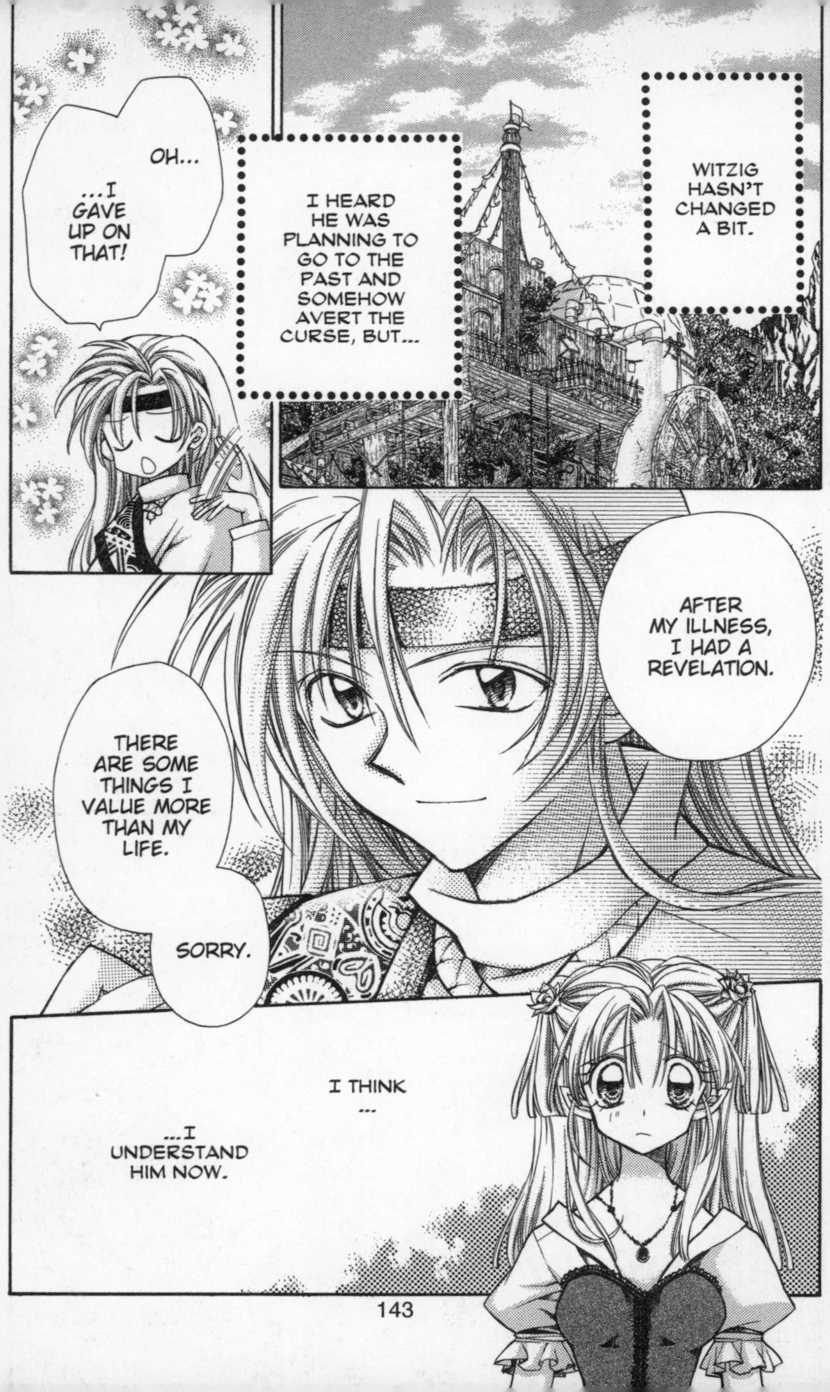
WITZIG HASN'T CHANGED A BIT.
I HEARD HE WAS PLANNING TO GO TO THE PAST AND SOMEHOW AVERT THE CURSE, BUT...
OH...
...I GAVE UP ON THAT!
AFTER MY ILLNESS, I HAD A REVELATION.
THERE ARE SOME THINGS I VALUE MORE THAN MY LIFE.
SORRY.
I THINK...
...I UNDERSTAND HIM NOW.

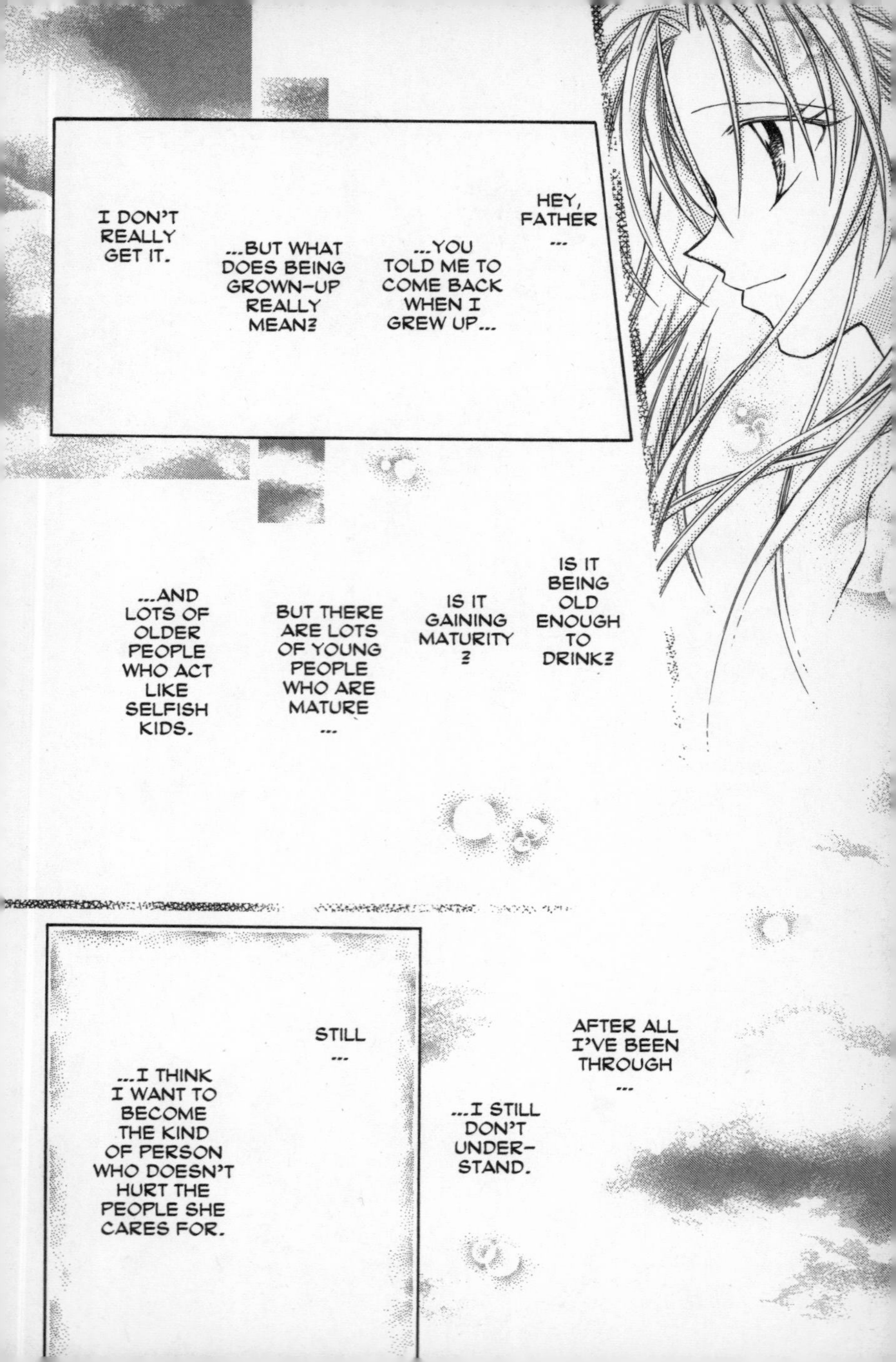
HEY, FATHER ...
...YOU TOLD ME TO COME BACK WHEN I GREW UP...
...BUT WHAT DOES BEING GROWN-UP REALLY MEAN?
I DON'T REALLY GET IT.
IS IT BEING OLD ENOUGH TO DRINK?
IS IT GAINING MATURITY ?
BUT THERE ARE LOTS OF YOUNG PEOPLE WHO ARE MATURE ...
...AND LOTS OF OLDER PEOPLE WHO ACT LIKE SELFISH KIDS.
AFTER ALL I'VE BEEN THROUGH ...
...I STILL DON'T UNDER-STAND.
STILL ...
...I THINK I WANT TO BECOME THE KIND OF PERSON WHO DOESN'T HURT THE PEOPLE SHE CARES FOR.

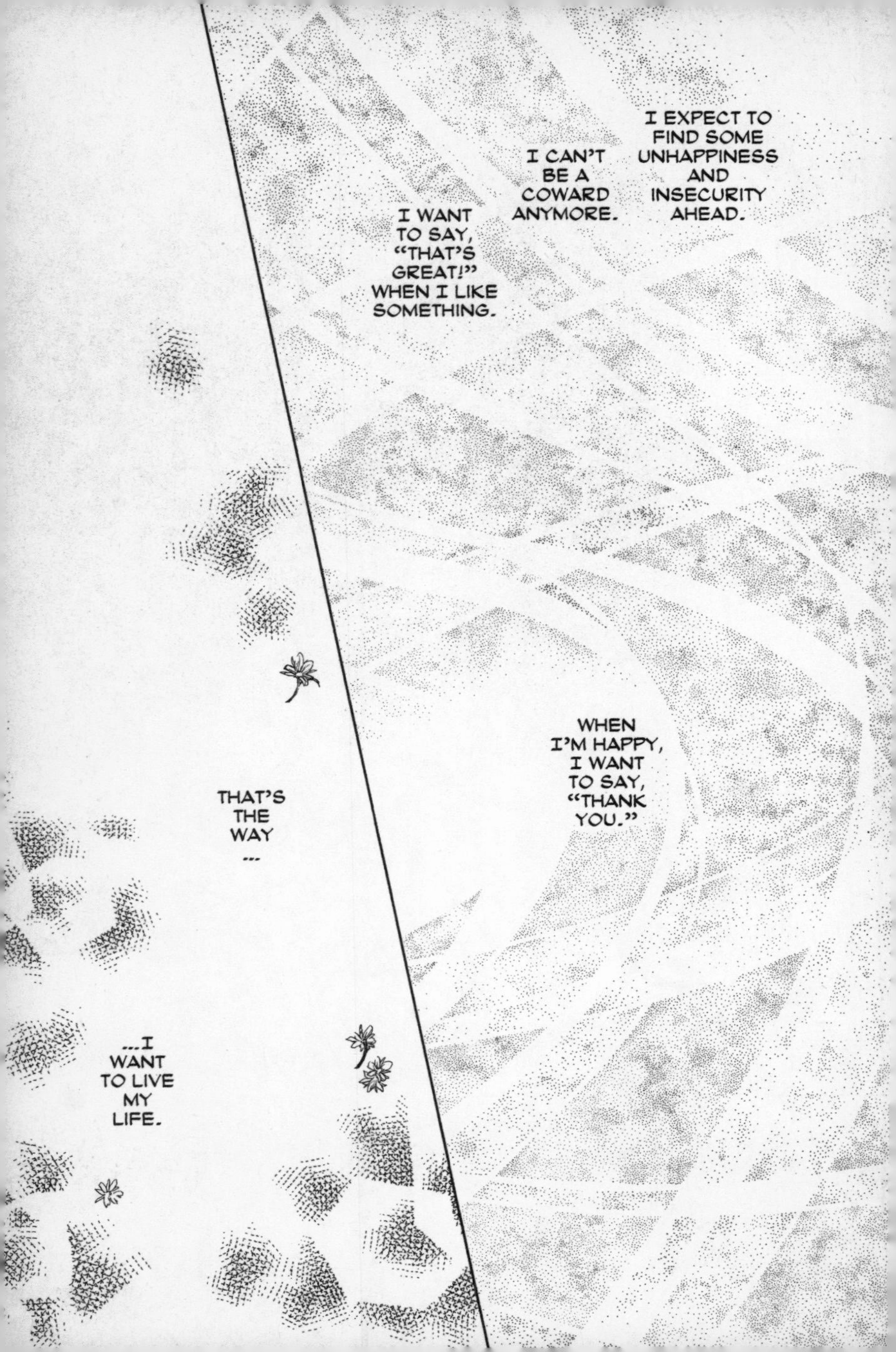
I EXPECT TO FIND SOME UNHAPPINESS AND INSECURITY AHEAD.
I CAN'T BE A COWARD ANYMORE.
I WANT TO SAY, "THAT'S GREAT!" WHEN I LIKE SOMETHING.
WHEN I'M HAPPY, I WANT TO SAY, "THANK YOU."
THAT'S THE WAY ...
...I WANT TO LIVE MY LIFE.

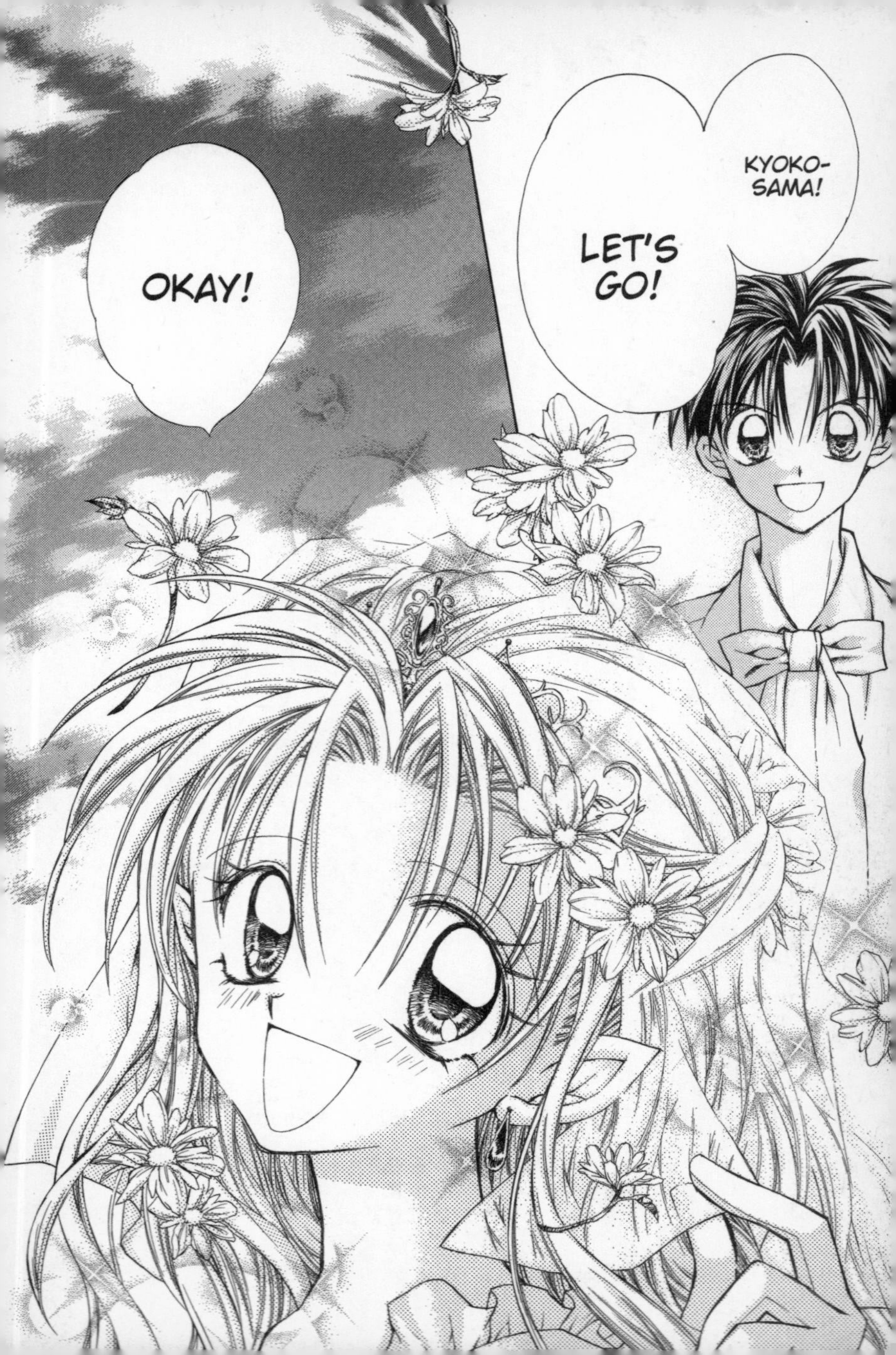
KYOKO-SAMA!
LET'S GO!
OKAY!

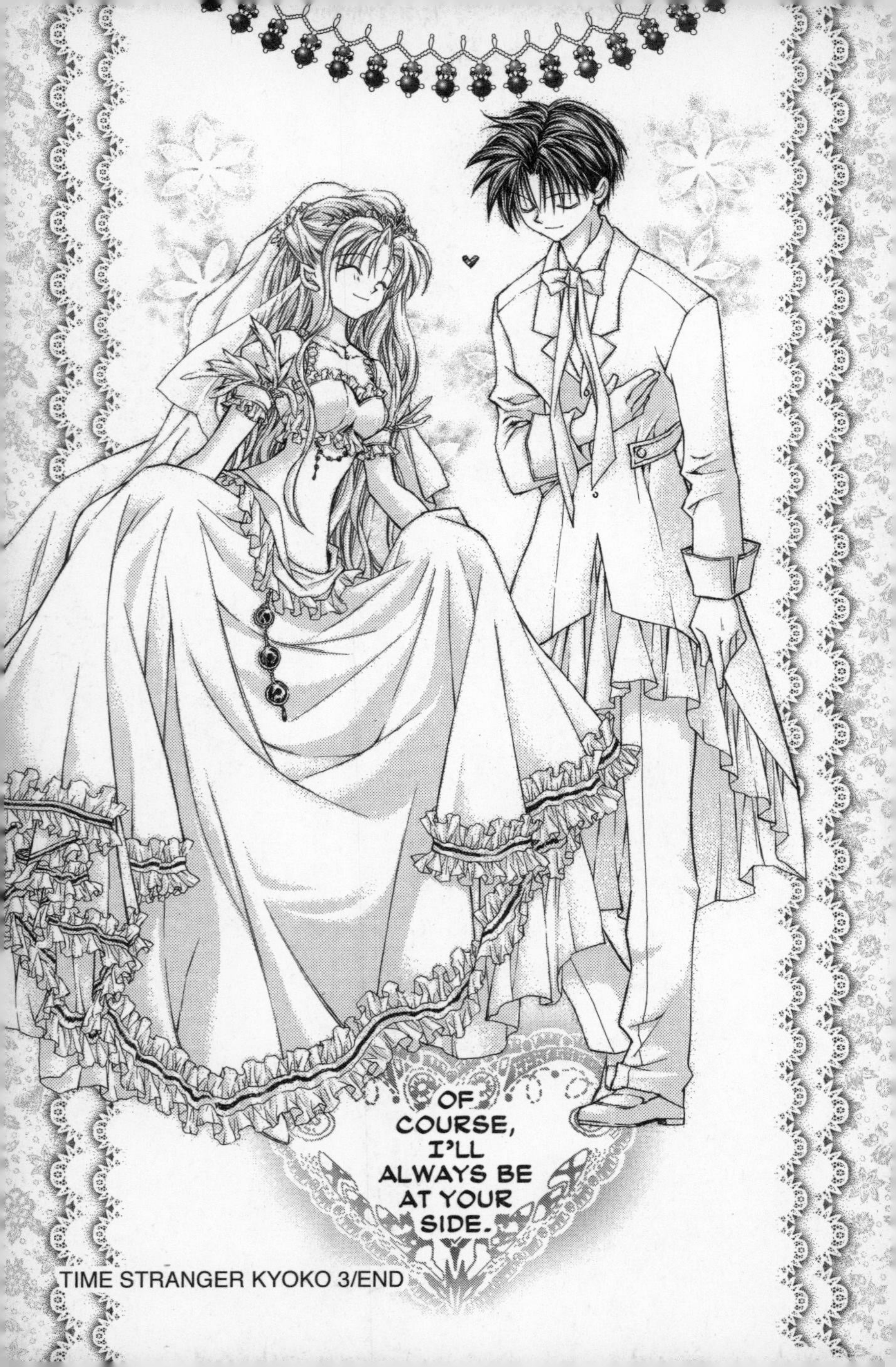
OF COURSE, I'LL ALWAYS BE AT YOUR SIDE.

TIME STRANGER KYOKO 3/END

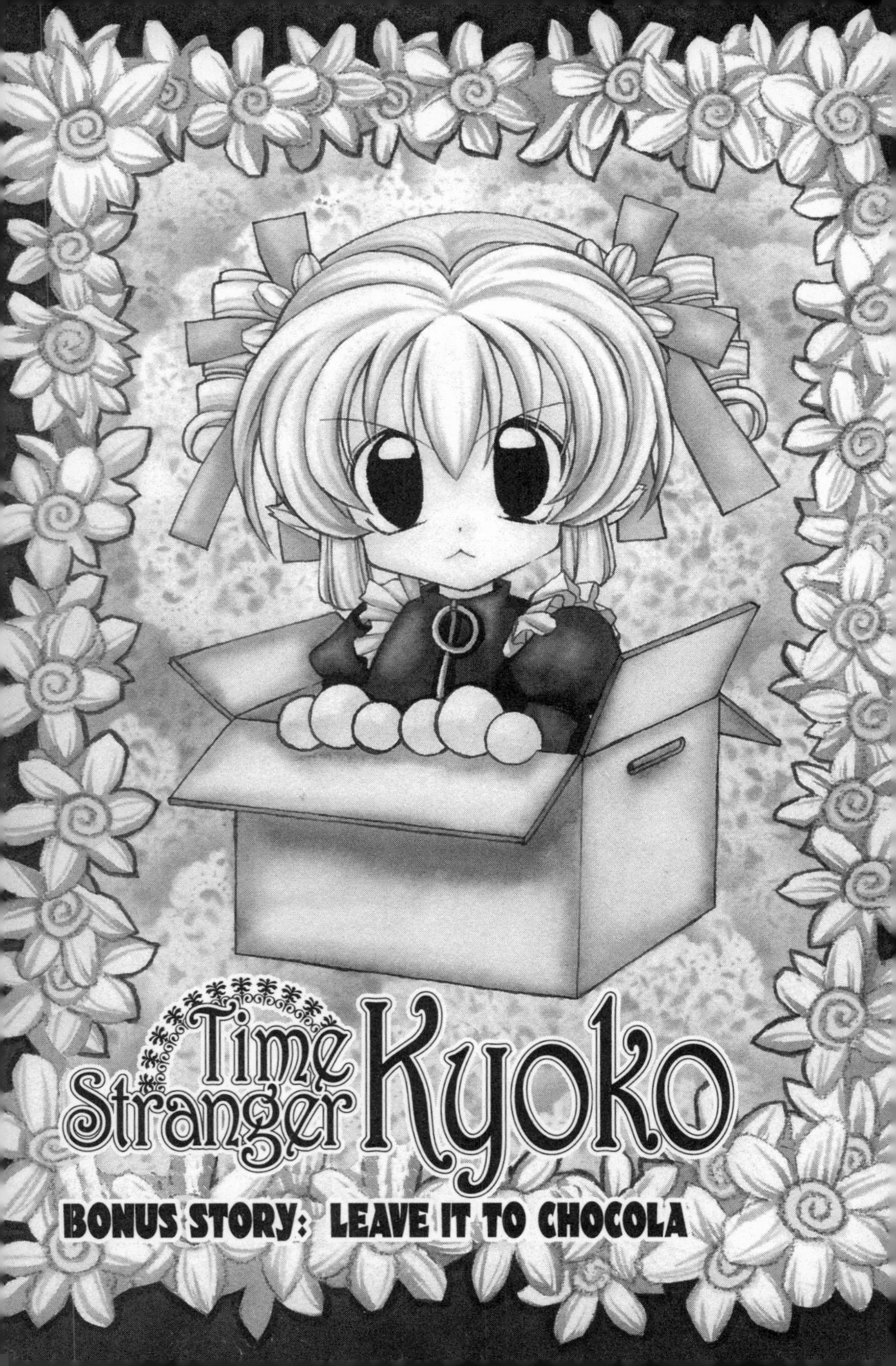
Time Stranger Kyoko
BONUS STORY: LEAVE IT TO CHOCOLA

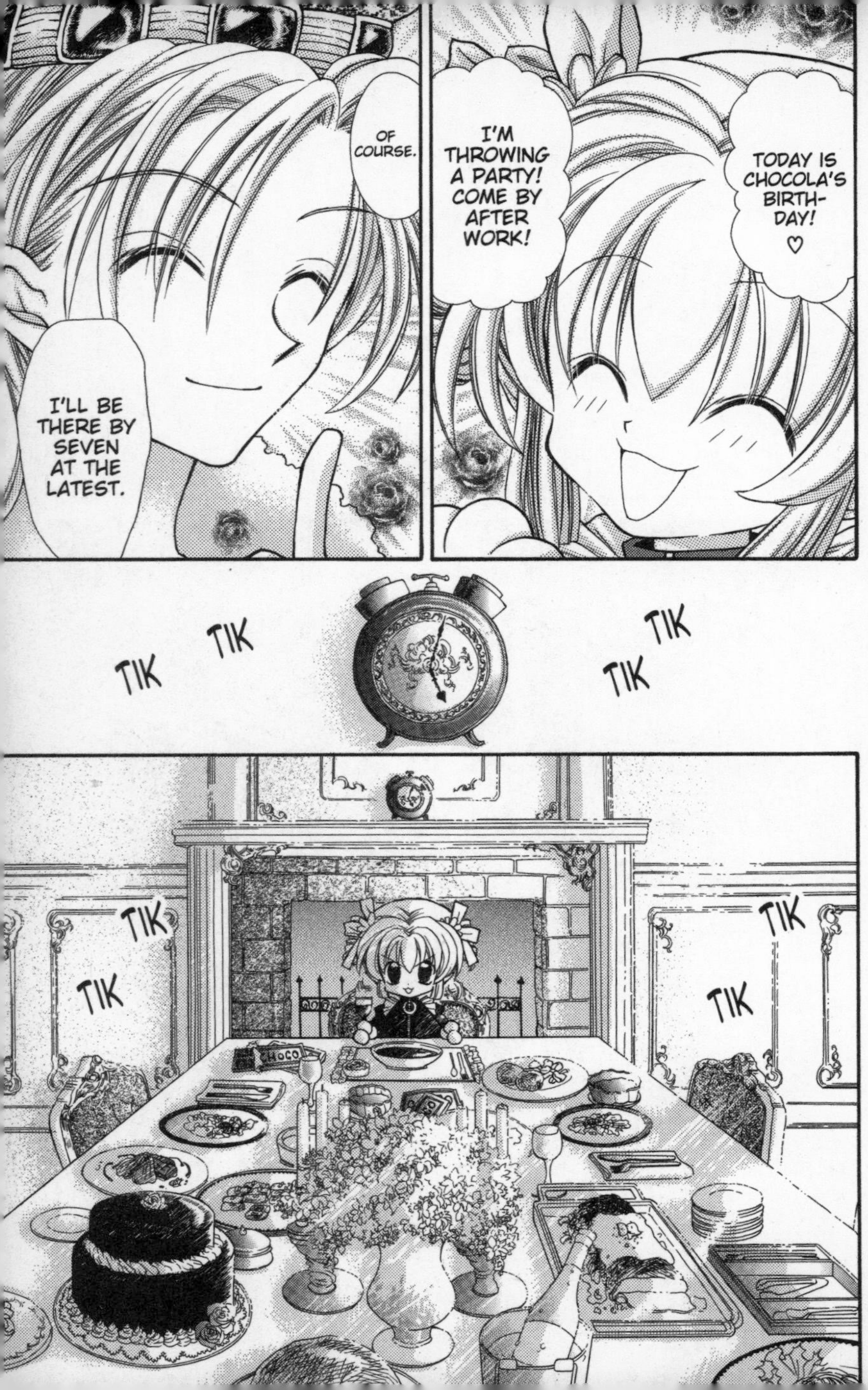
TODAY IS CHOCOLA'S BIRTH-DAY! ♡
I'M THROWING A PARTY! COME BY AFTER WORK!
OF COURSE.
I'LL BE THERE BY SEVEN AT THE LATEST.
TIK
TIK
TIK
TIK
TIK
TIK
TIK
TIK

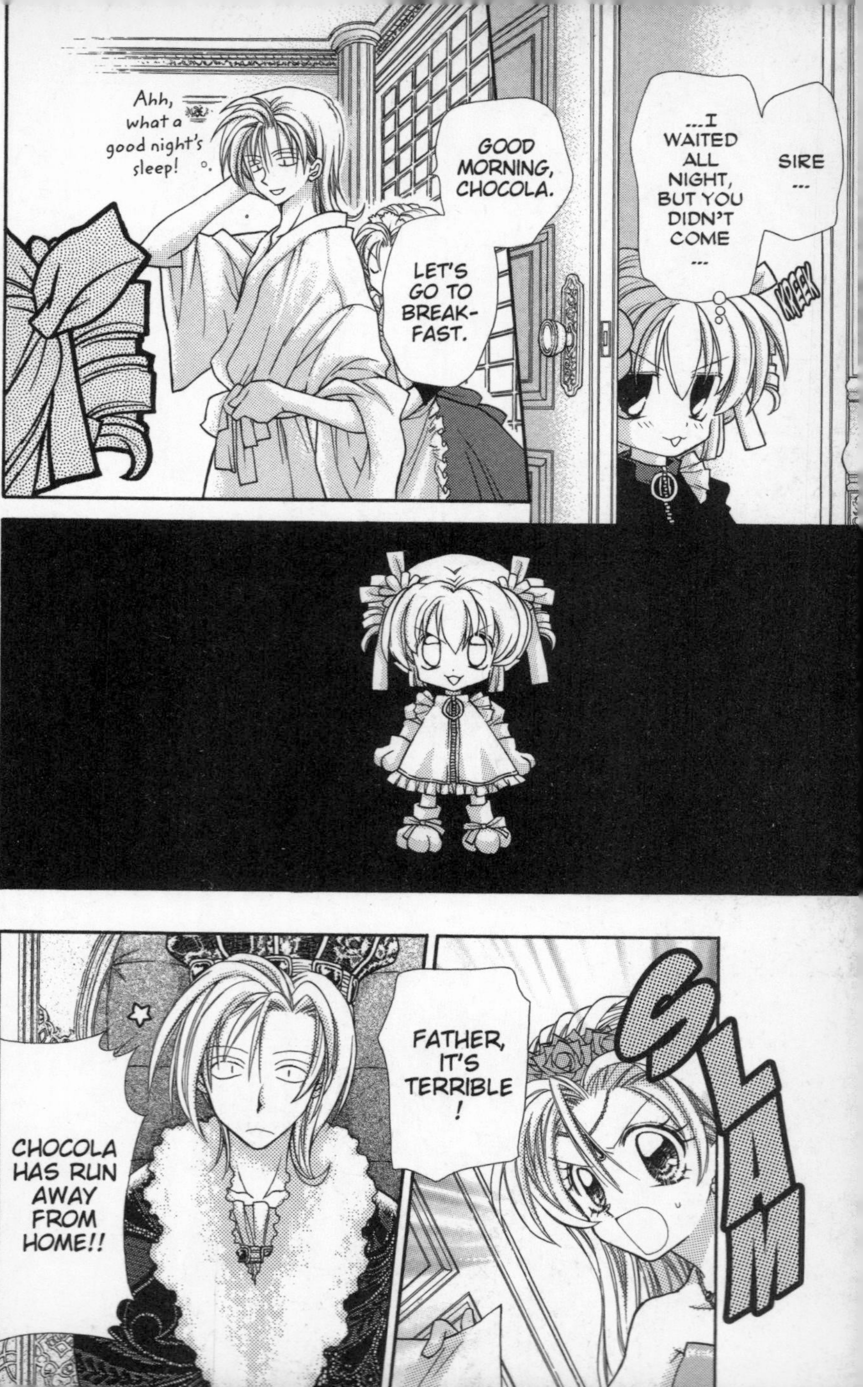
SIRE...
...I WAITED ALL NIGHT, BUT YOU DIDN'T COME...
KREEK
Ahh, what a good night's sleep!
GOOD MORNING, CHOCOLA.
LET'S GO TO BREAK-FAST.
SLAM
FATHER, IT'S TERRIBLE!
CHOCOLA HAS RUN AWAY FROM HOME!!

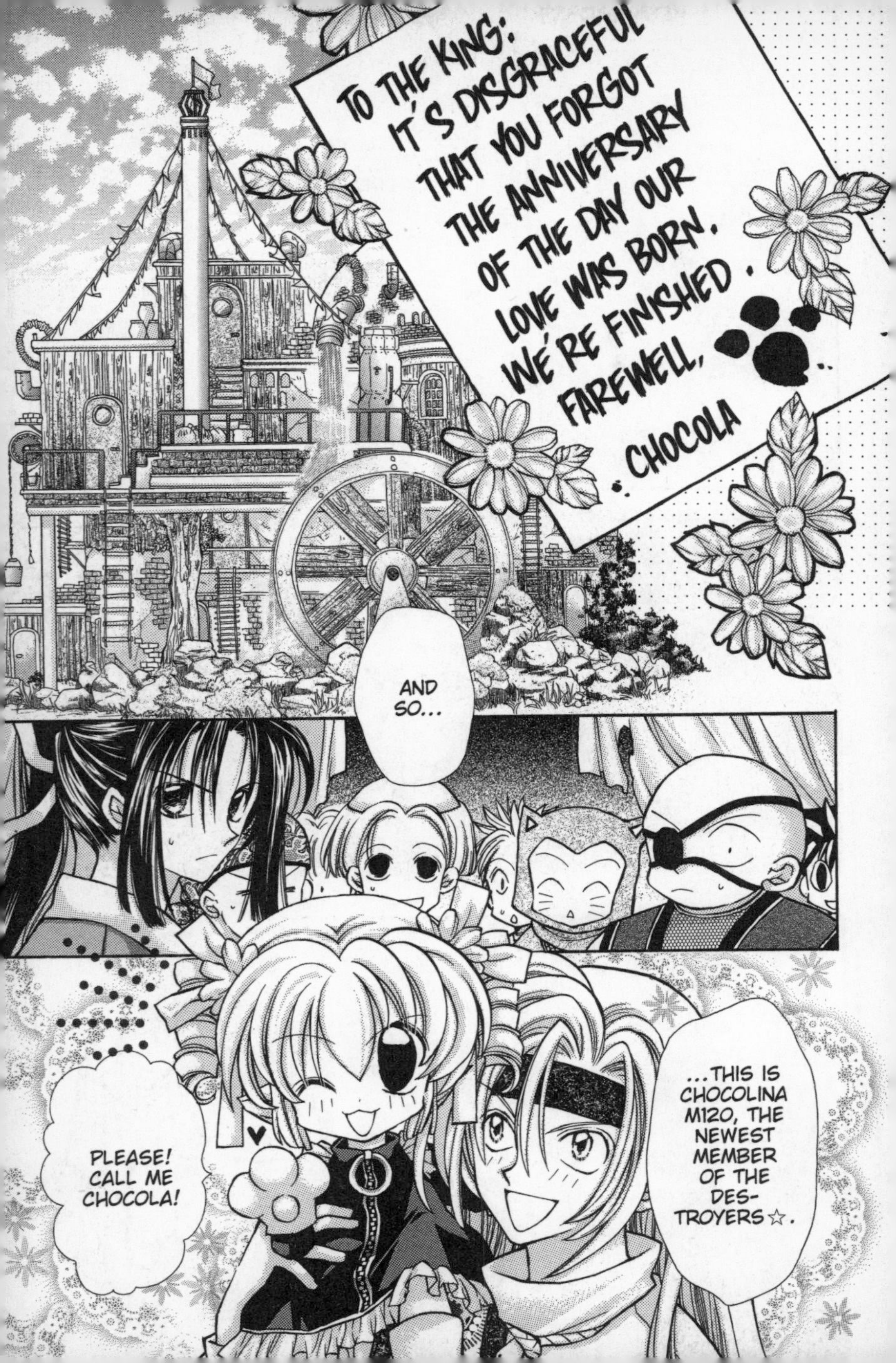
TO THE KING: IT'S DISGRACEFUL THAT YOU FORGOT THE ANNIVERSARY OF THE DAY OUR LOVE WAS BORN. WE'RE FINISHED. FAREWELL, CHOCOLA
AND SO...
...THIS IS CHOCOLINA M120, THE NEWEST MEMBER OF THE DES-TROYERS☆.
PLEASE! CALL ME CHOCOLA!

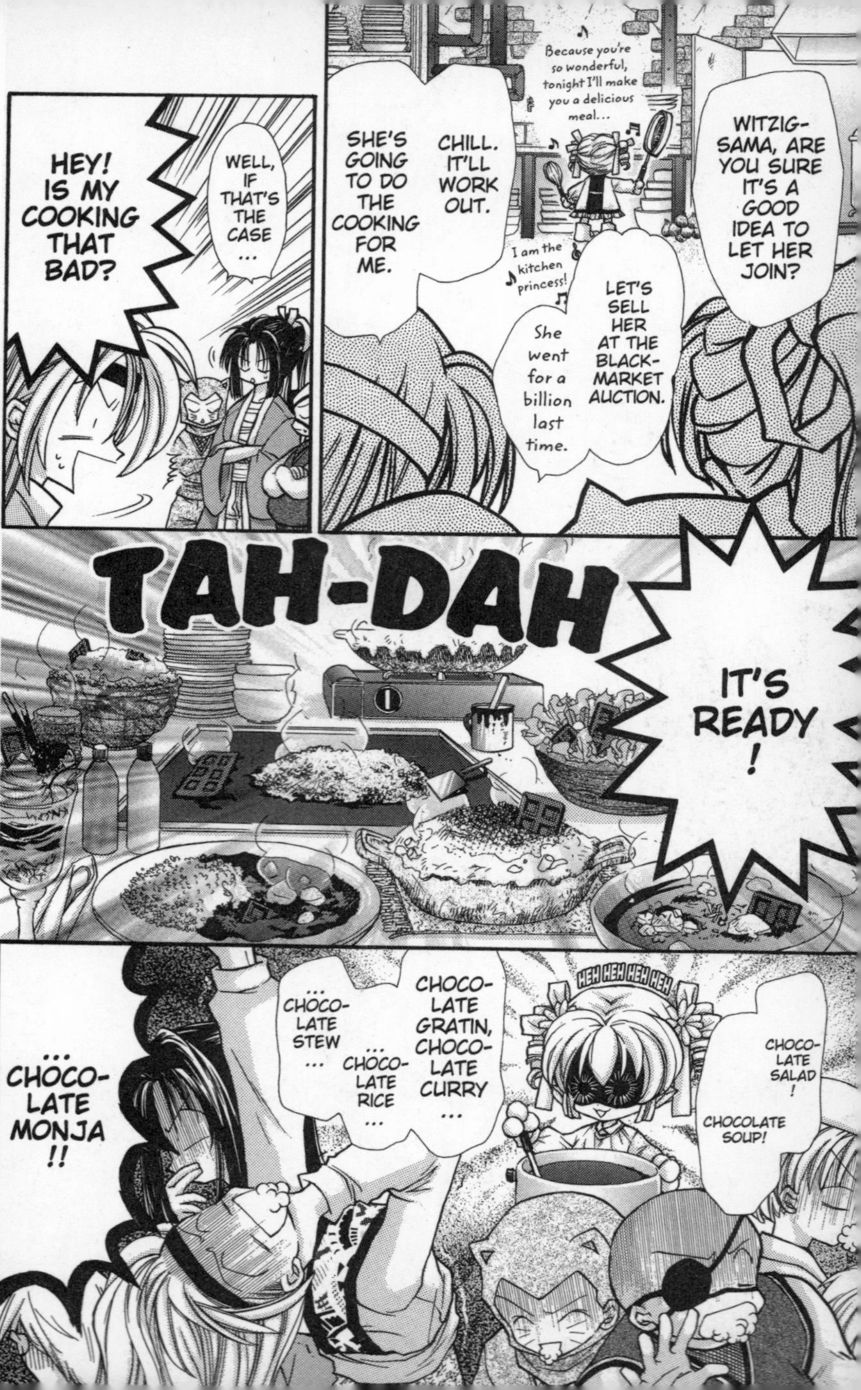
WITZIG-SAMA, ARE YOU SURE IT'S A GOOD IDEA TO LET HER JOIN?
Because you're so wonderful, tonight I'll make you a delicious meal...
CHILL. IT'LL WORK OUT.
SHE'S GOING TO DO THE COOKING FOR ME.
I am the kitchen princess!
LET'S SELL HER AT THE BLACK-MARKET AUCTION.
She went for a billion last time.
WELL, IF THAT'S THE CASE...
HEY! IS MY COOKING THAT BAD?
TAH-DAH
IT'S READY!
HEH HEH HEH HEH
CHOCOLATE SALAD!
CHOCOLATE SOUP!
CHOCOLATE GRATIN, CHOCOLATE CURRY...
...CHOCOLATE RICE...
...CHOCOLATE STEW...
...CHOCOLATE MONJA!!

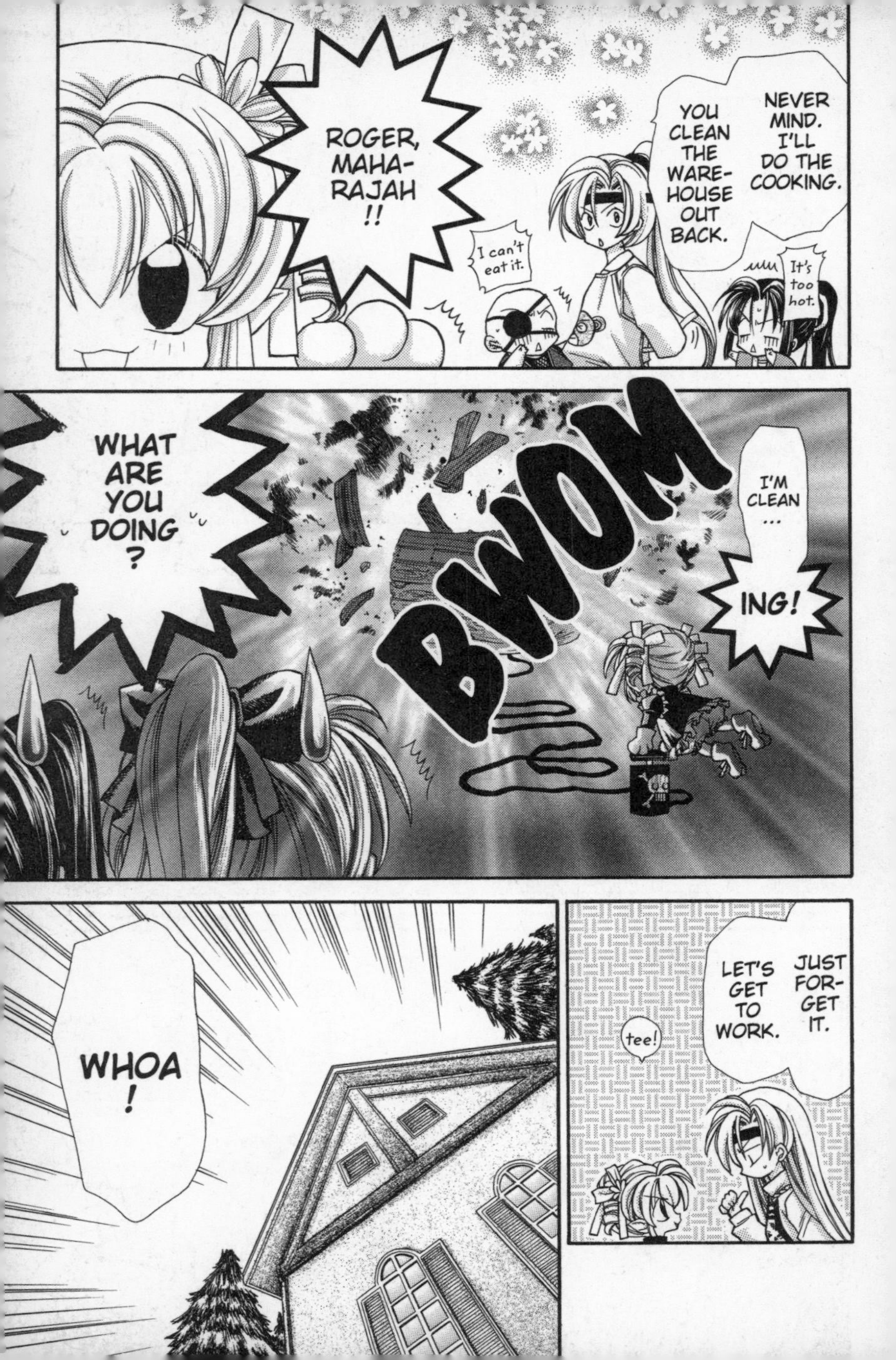
NEVER MIND. I'LL DO THE COOKING.
YOU CLEAN THE WARE-HOUSE OUT BACK.
It's too hot.
I can't eat it.
ROGER, MAHA-RAJAH !!
I'M CLEAN ...
ING!
BWOM
WHAT ARE YOU DOING ?
JUST FOR-GET IT.
LET'S GET TO WORK.
tee!
WHOA !

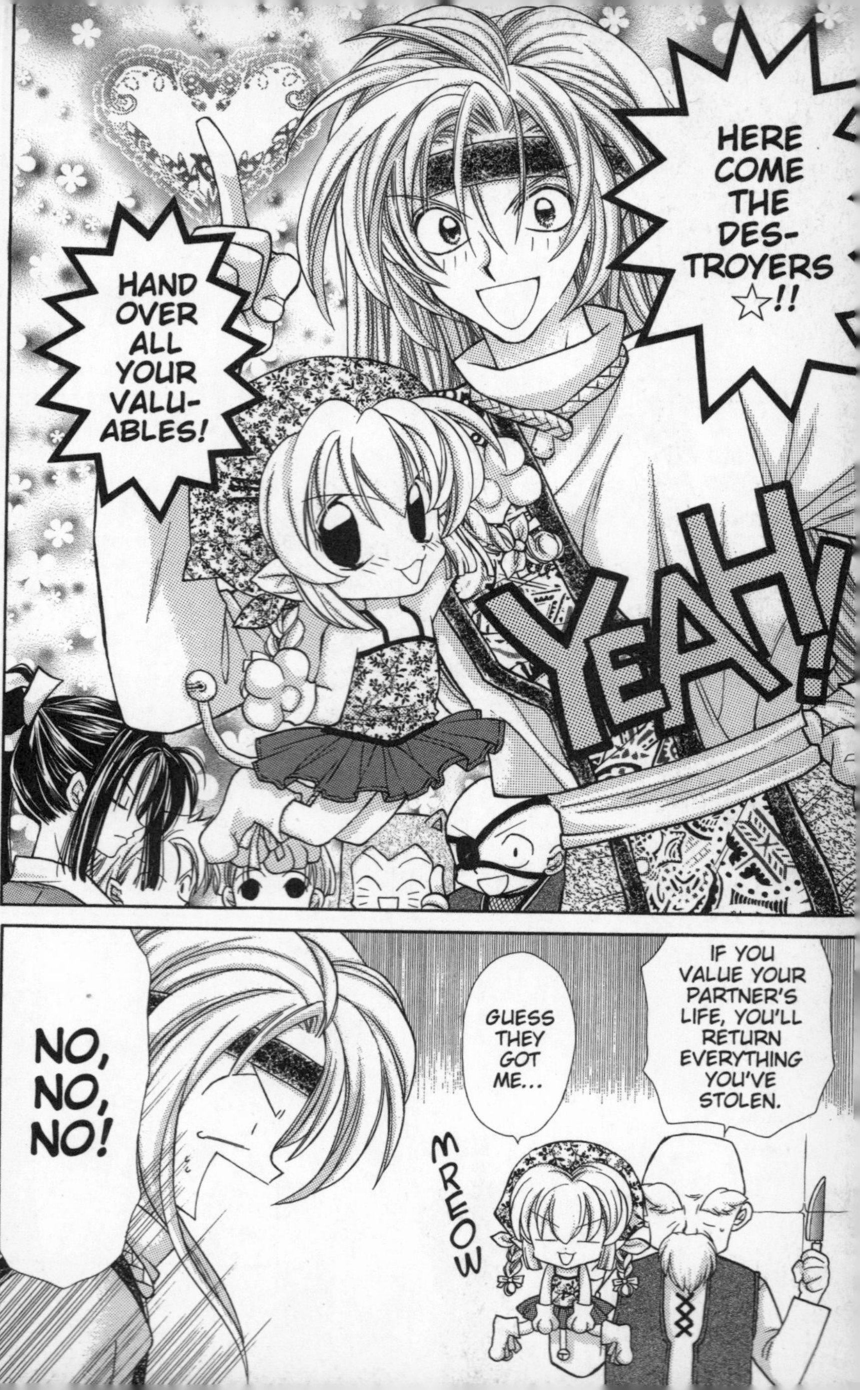

HERE COME THE DESTROYERS☆!!
HAND OVER ALL YOUR VALUABLES!
YEAH!
IF YOU VALUE YOUR PARTNER'S LIFE, YOU'LL RETURN EVERYTHING YOU'VE STOLEN.
GUESS THEY GOT ME...
MREOW
NO, NO, NO, NO!

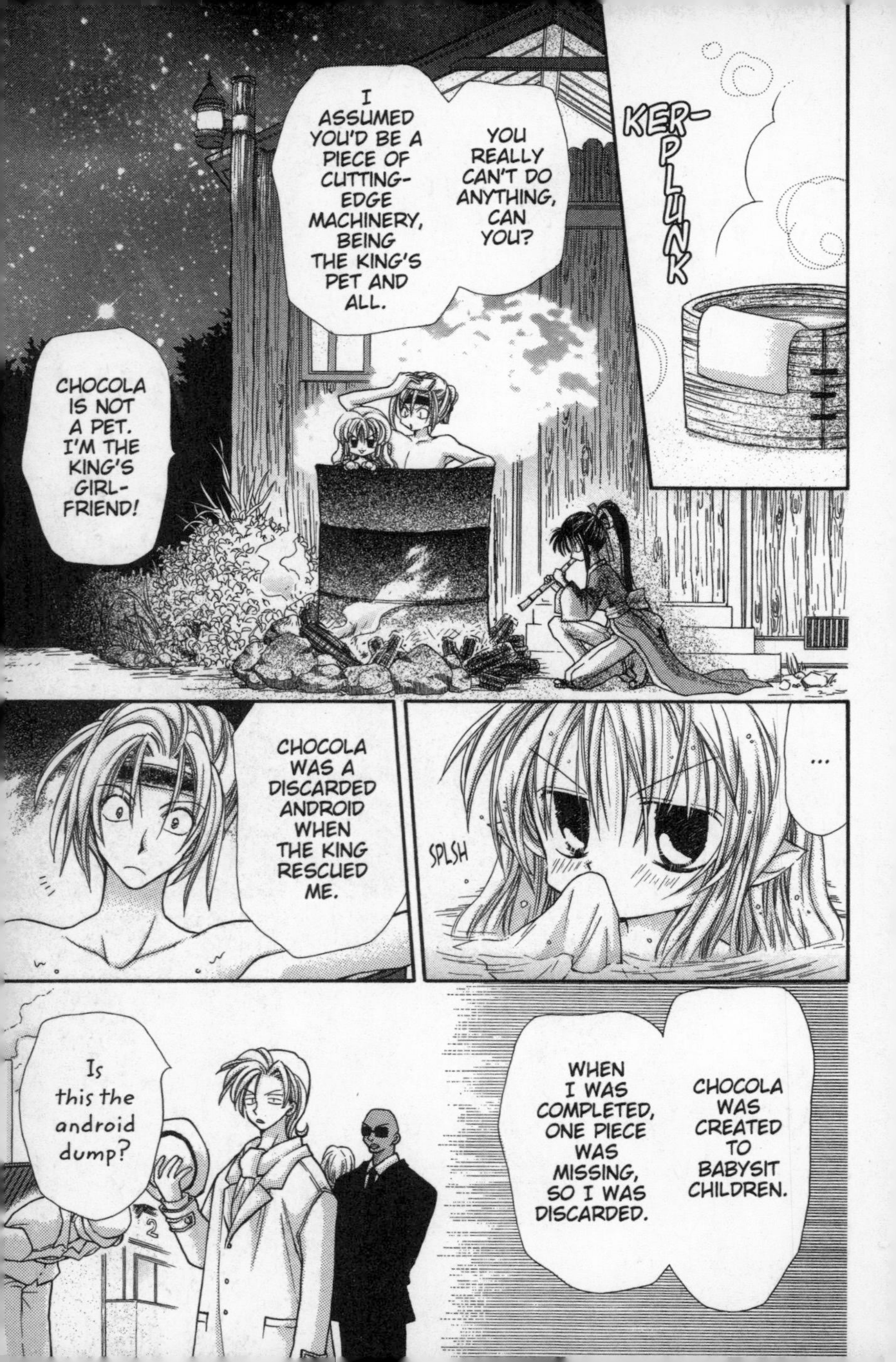
KER-PLUNK
YOU REALLY CAN'T DO ANYTHING, CAN YOU?
I ASSUMED YOU'D BE A PIECE OF CUTTING-EDGE MACHINERY, BEING THE KING'S PET AND ALL.
CHOCOLA IS NOT A PET. I'M THE KING'S GIRL-FRIEND!
...
SPLSH
CHOCOLA WAS A DISCARDED ANDROID WHEN THE KING RESCUED ME.
CHOCOLA WAS CREATED TO BABYSIT CHILDREN.
WHEN I WAS COMPLETED, ONE PIECE WAS MISSING, SO I WAS DISCARDED.
Is this the android dump?
2

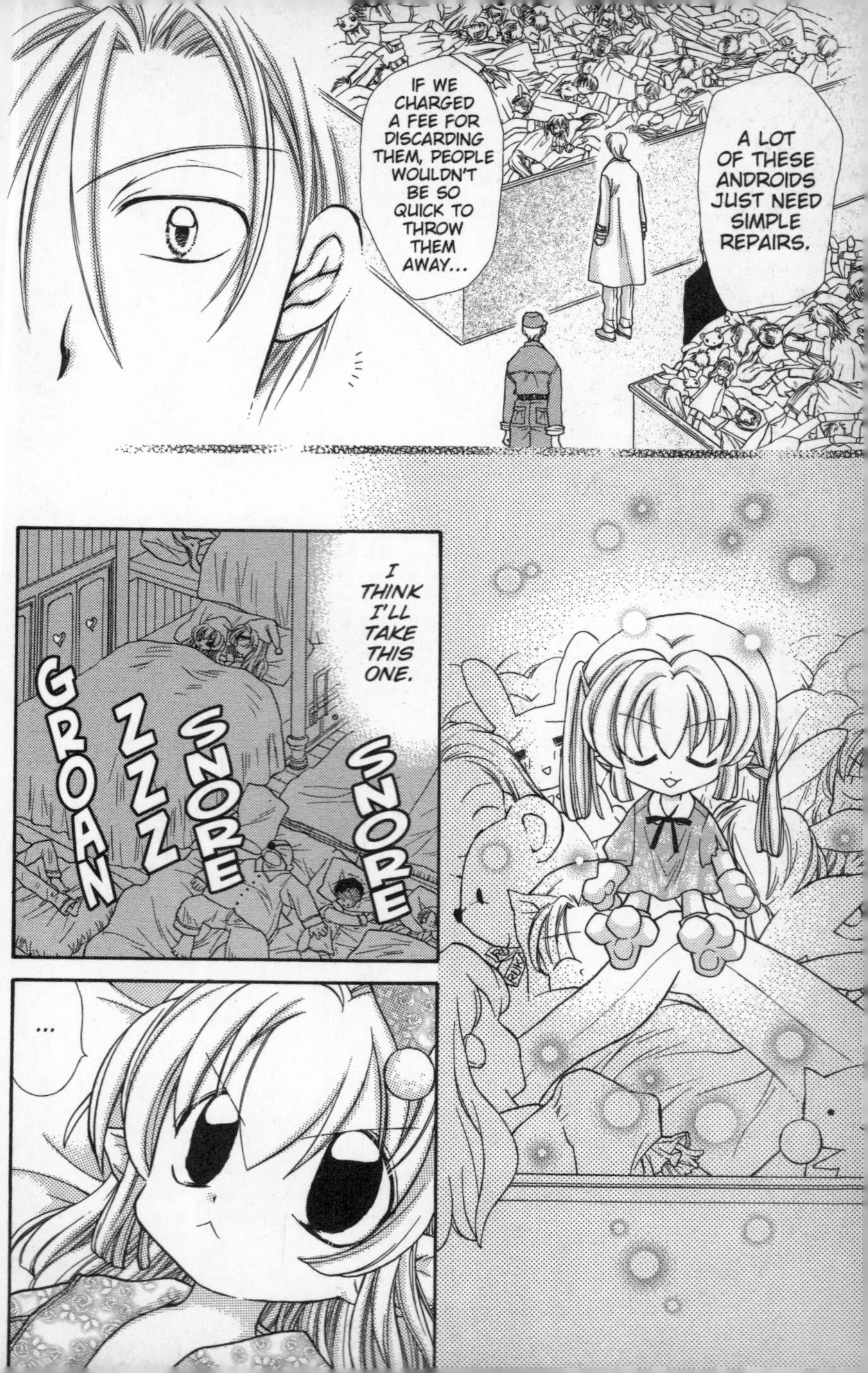
A LOT OF THESE ANDROIDS JUST NEED SIMPLE REPAIRS.
IF WE CHARGED A FEE FOR DISCARDING THEM, PEOPLE WOULDN'T BE SO QUICK TO THROW THEM AWAY...
I THINK I'LL TAKE THIS ONE.
SNORE
SNORE
ZZZ
GROAN
...

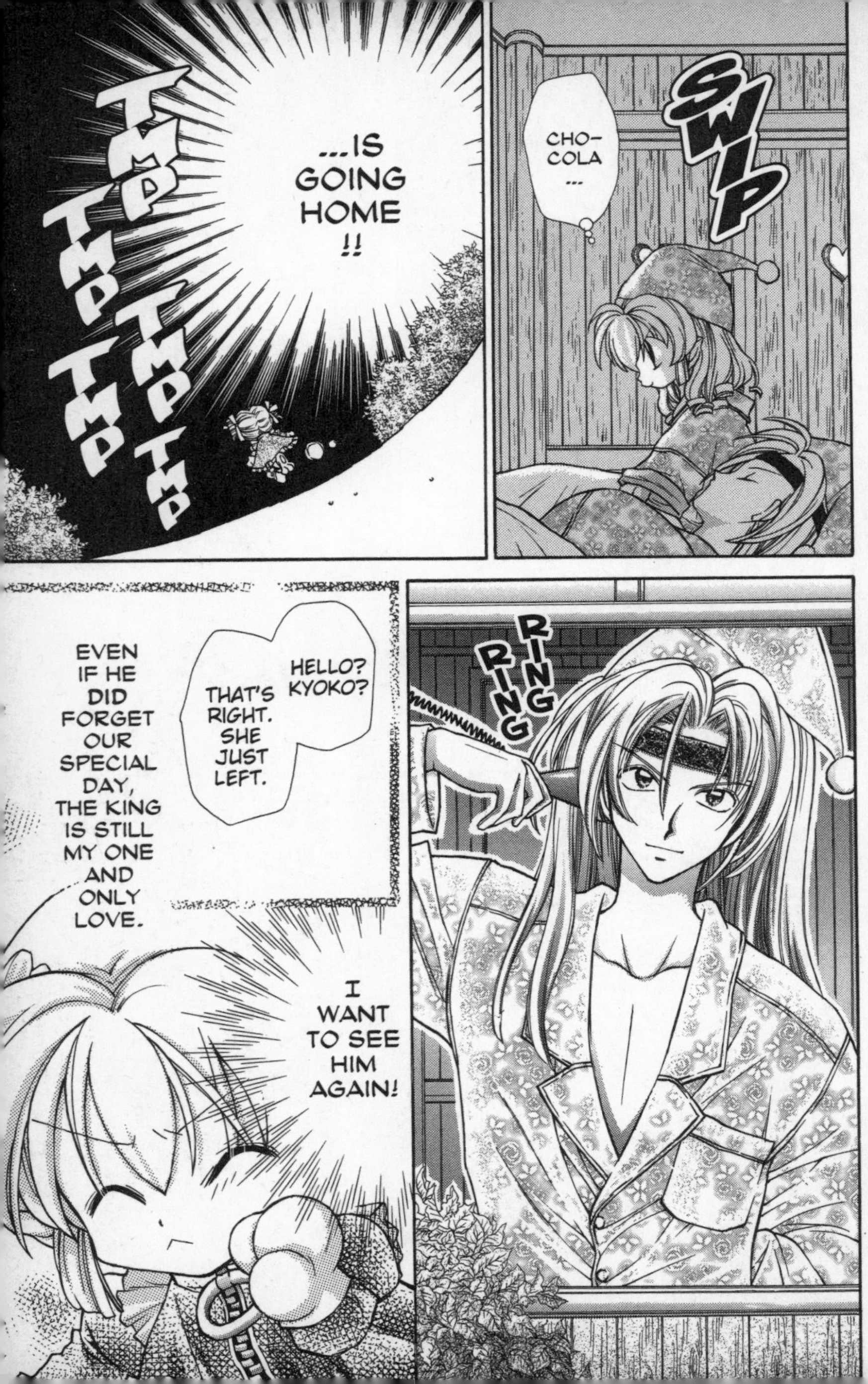
SWIP
CHO-COLA...
TMP TMP TMP TMP TMP TMP TMP
...IS GOING HOME!!
RING RING
HELLO? KYOKO?
THAT'S RIGHT. SHE JUST LEFT.
EVEN IF HE DID FORGET OUR SPECIAL DAY, THE KING IS STILL MY ONE AND ONLY LOVE.
I WANT TO SEE HIM AGAIN!

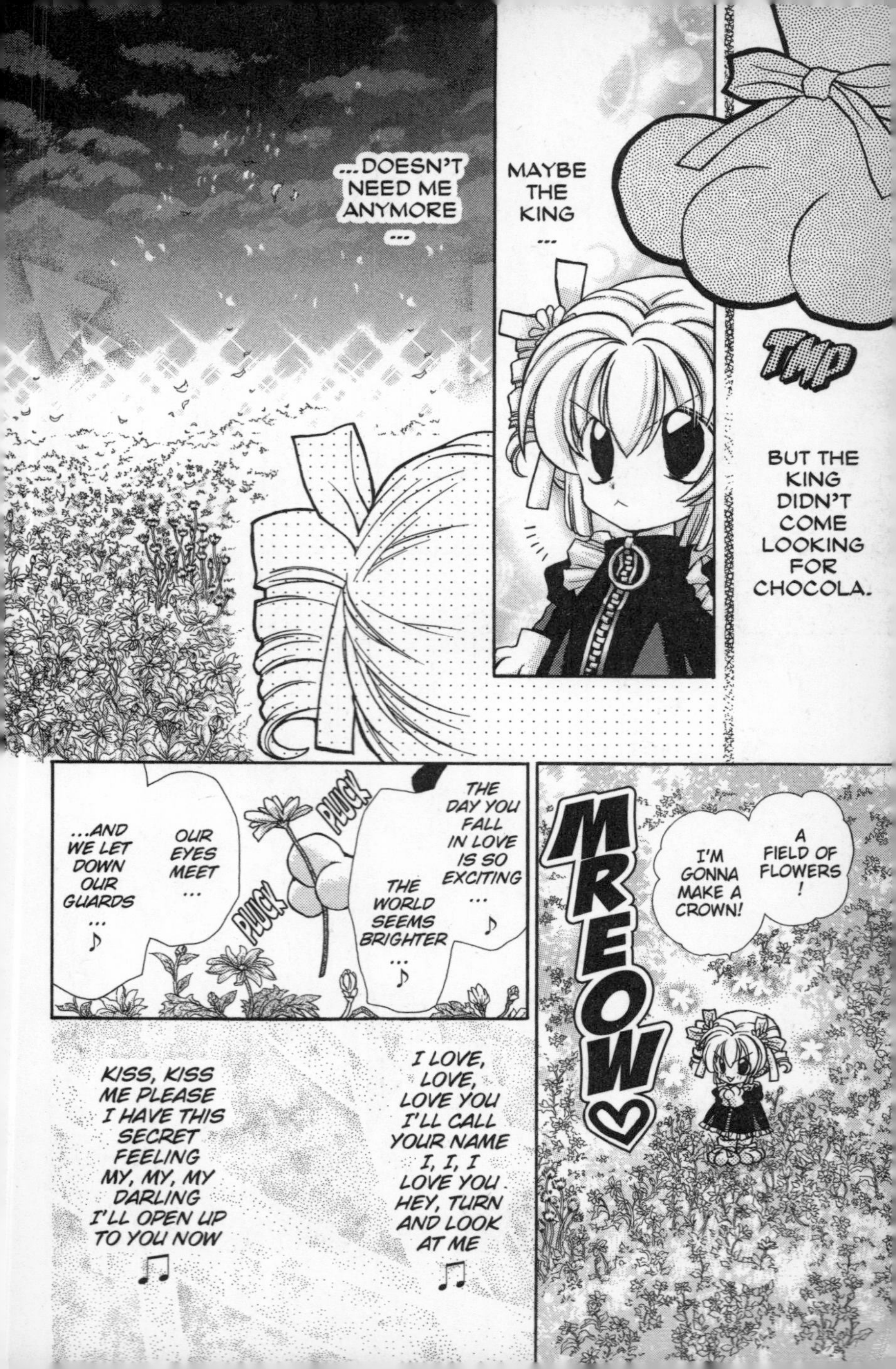
TMP
BUT THE KING DIDN'T COME LOOKING FOR CHOCOLA.
MAYBE THE KING ...
...DOESN'T NEED ME ANYMORE ...
MREOW♥
A FIELD OF FLOWERS!
I'M GONNA MAKE A CROWN!
THE DAY YOU FALL IN LOVE IS SO EXCITING ... ♪
THE WORLD SEEMS BRIGHTER ... ♪
PLUCK
PLUCK
OUR EYES MEET ...
...AND WE LET DOWN OUR GUARDS ... ♪
I LOVE, LOVE, LOVE YOU I'LL CALL YOUR NAME I, I, I LOVE YOU HEY, TURN AND LOOK AT ME ♫
KISS, KISS ME PLEASE I HAVE THIS SECRET FEELING MY, MY, MY DARLING I'LL OPEN UP TO YOU NOW ♫

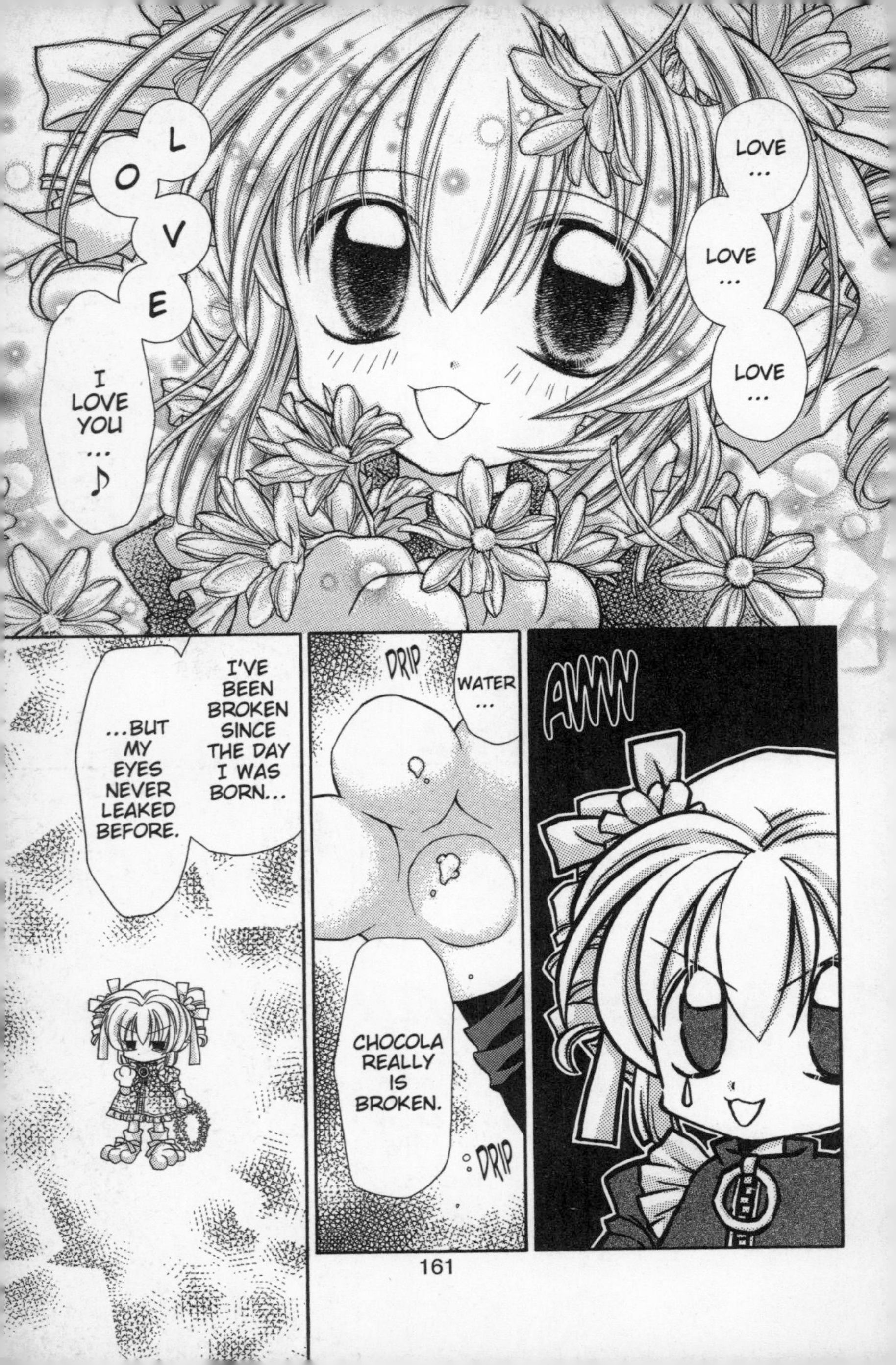

LOVE...
LOVE...
LOVE...
LOVE
I LOVE YOU...♪
AWW
DRIP
WATER...
CHOCOLA REALLY IS BROKEN.
DRIP
I'VE BEEN BROKEN SINCE THE DAY I WAS BORN...
...BUT MY EYES NEVER LEAKED BEFORE.

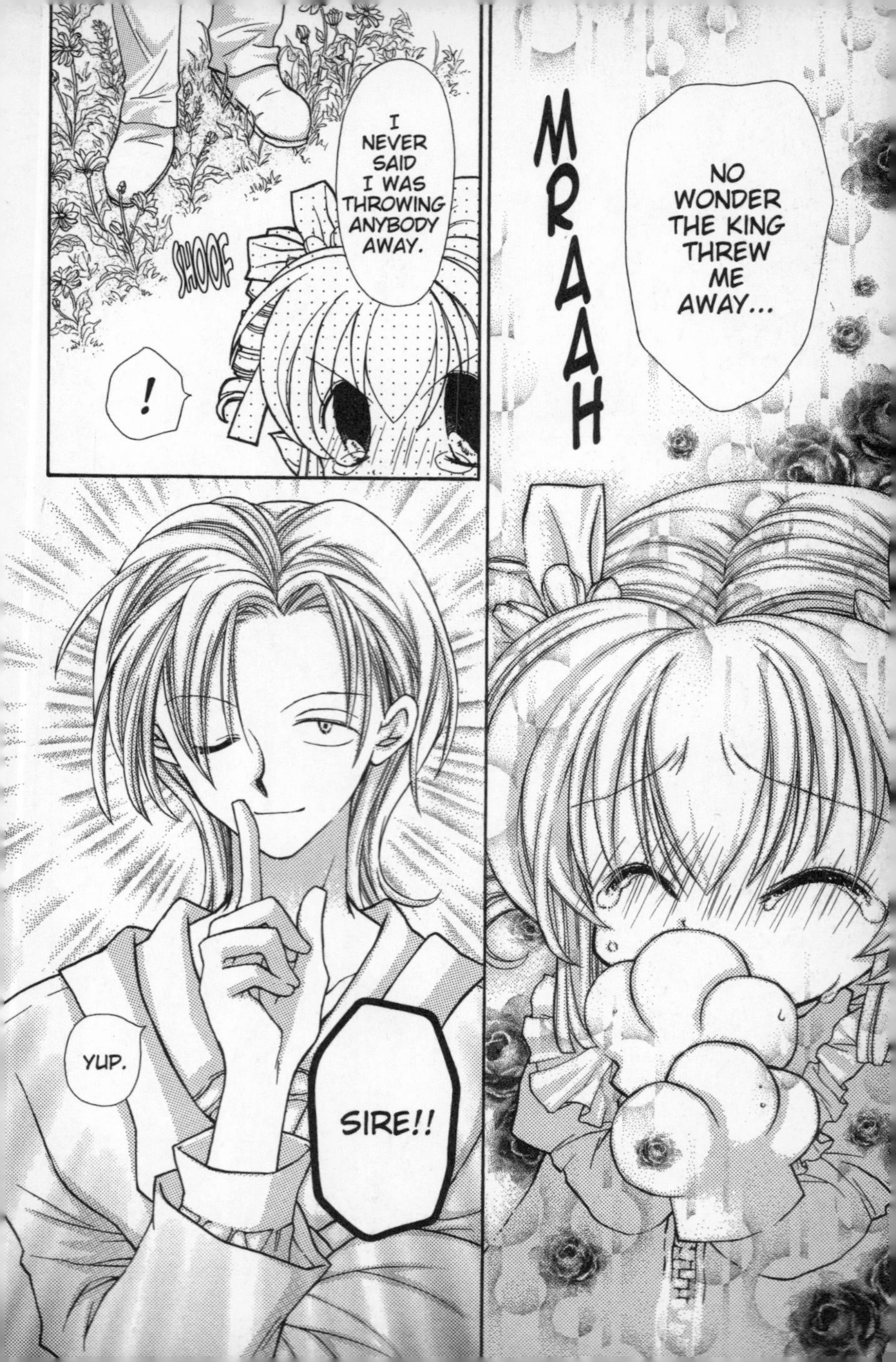
NO WONDER THE KING THREW ME AWAY...
MRAAH
I NEVER SAID I WAS THROWING ANYBODY AWAY.
SHOOF
!
SIRE!!
YUP.

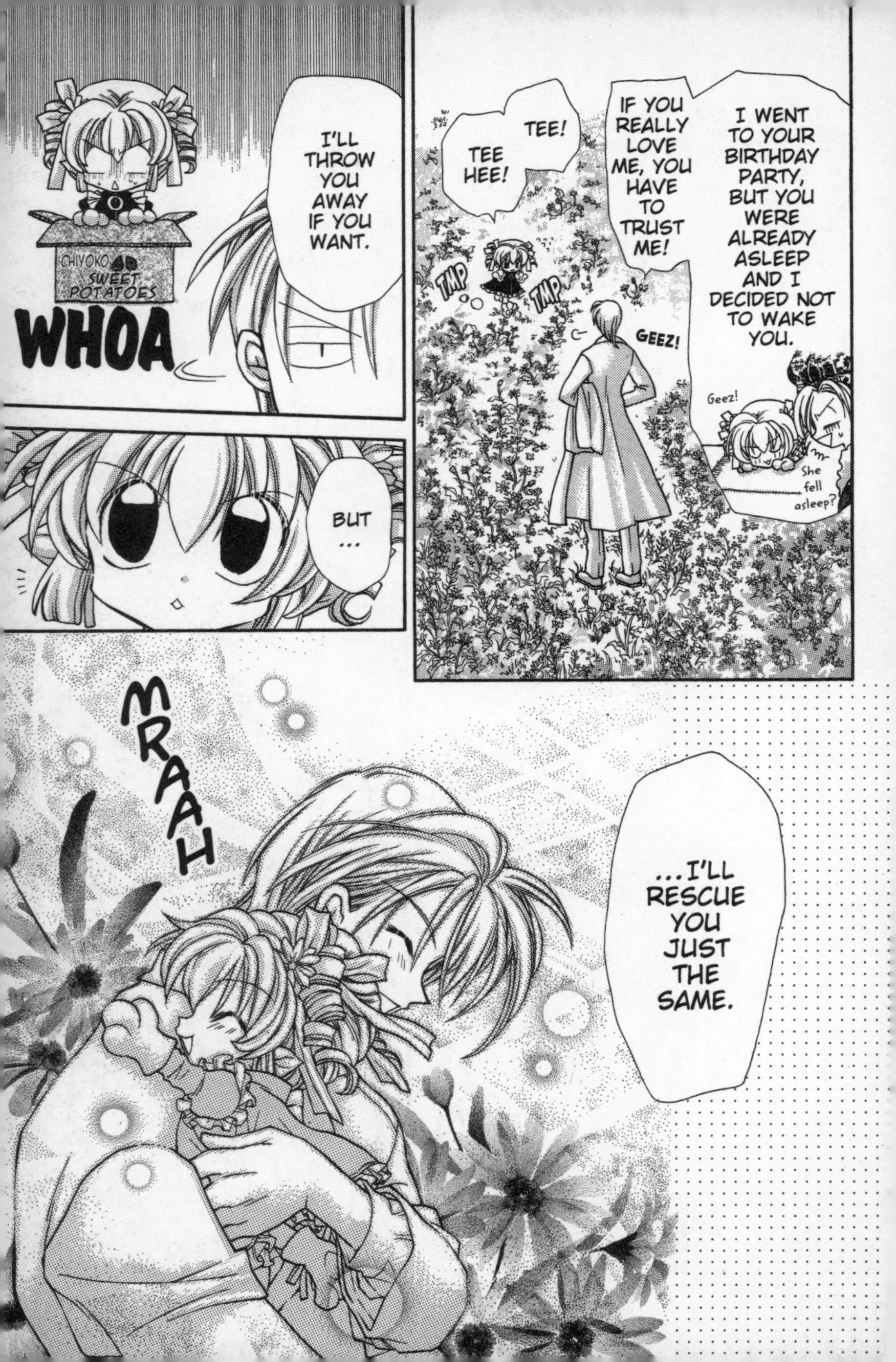
I WENT TO YOUR BIRTHDAY PARTY, BUT YOU WERE ALREADY ASLEEP AND I DECIDED NOT TO WAKE YOU.
IF YOU REALLY LOVE ME, YOU HAVE TO TRUST ME!
TEE!
TEE HEE!
GEEZ!
TMP
TMP
Geez!
She fell asleep?
I'LL THROW YOU AWAY IF YOU WANT.
CHIYOKO SWEET POTATOES
WHOA
BUT ...
...I'LL RESCUE YOU JUST THE SAME.
MRAAH

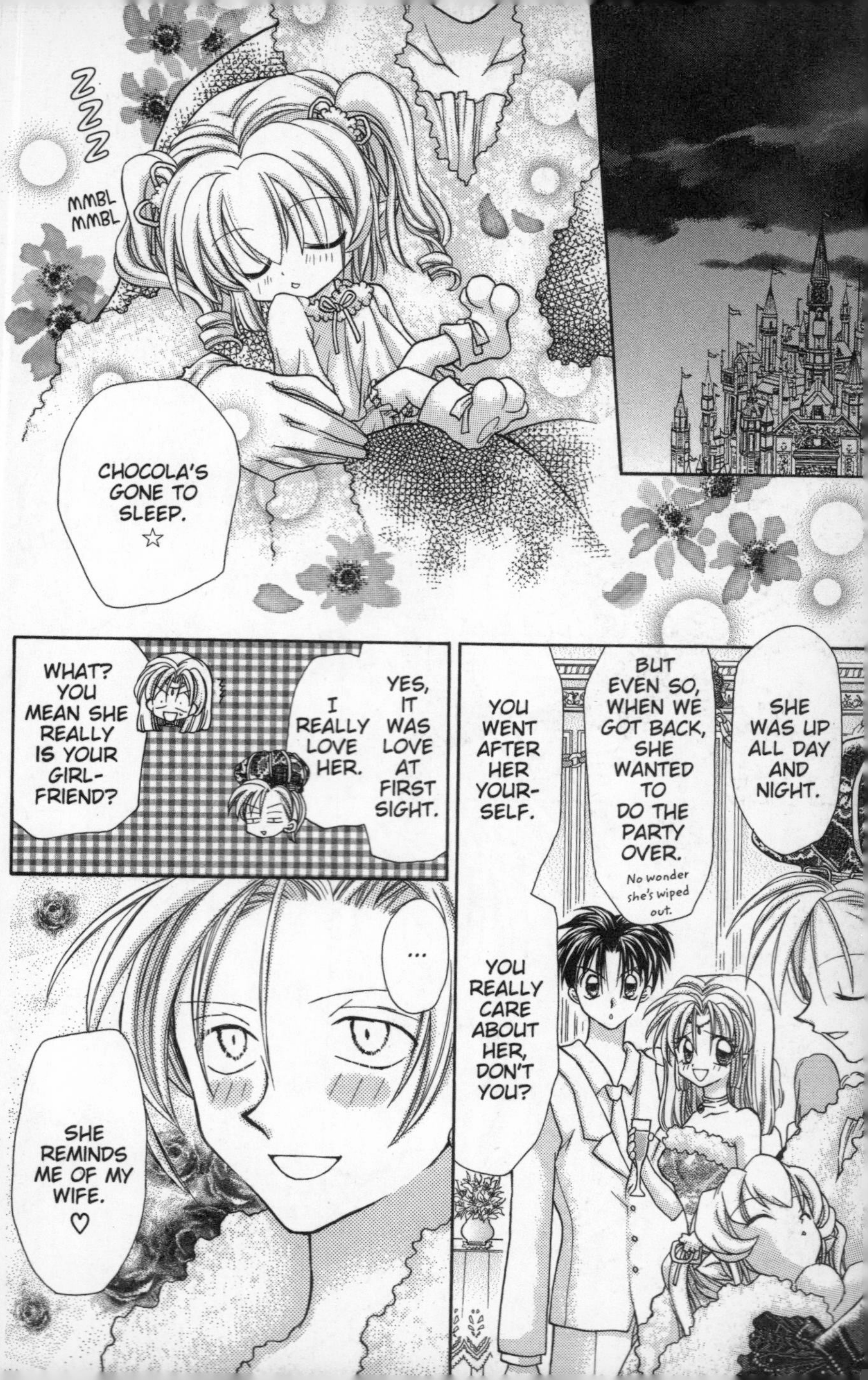
ZZZ
MMBL MMBL
CHOCOLA'S GONE TO SLEEP. ☆
SHE WAS UP ALL DAY AND NIGHT.
BUT EVEN SO, WHEN WE GOT BACK, SHE WANTED TO DO THE PARTY OVER.
No wonder she's wiped out.
YOU WENT AFTER HER YOURSELF.
YOU REALLY CARE ABOUT HER, DON'T YOU?
YES, IT WAS LOVE AT FIRST SIGHT.
I REALLY LOVE HER.
WHAT? YOU MEAN SHE REALLY IS YOUR GIRLFRIEND?
...
SHE REMINDS ME OF MY WIFE. ♡

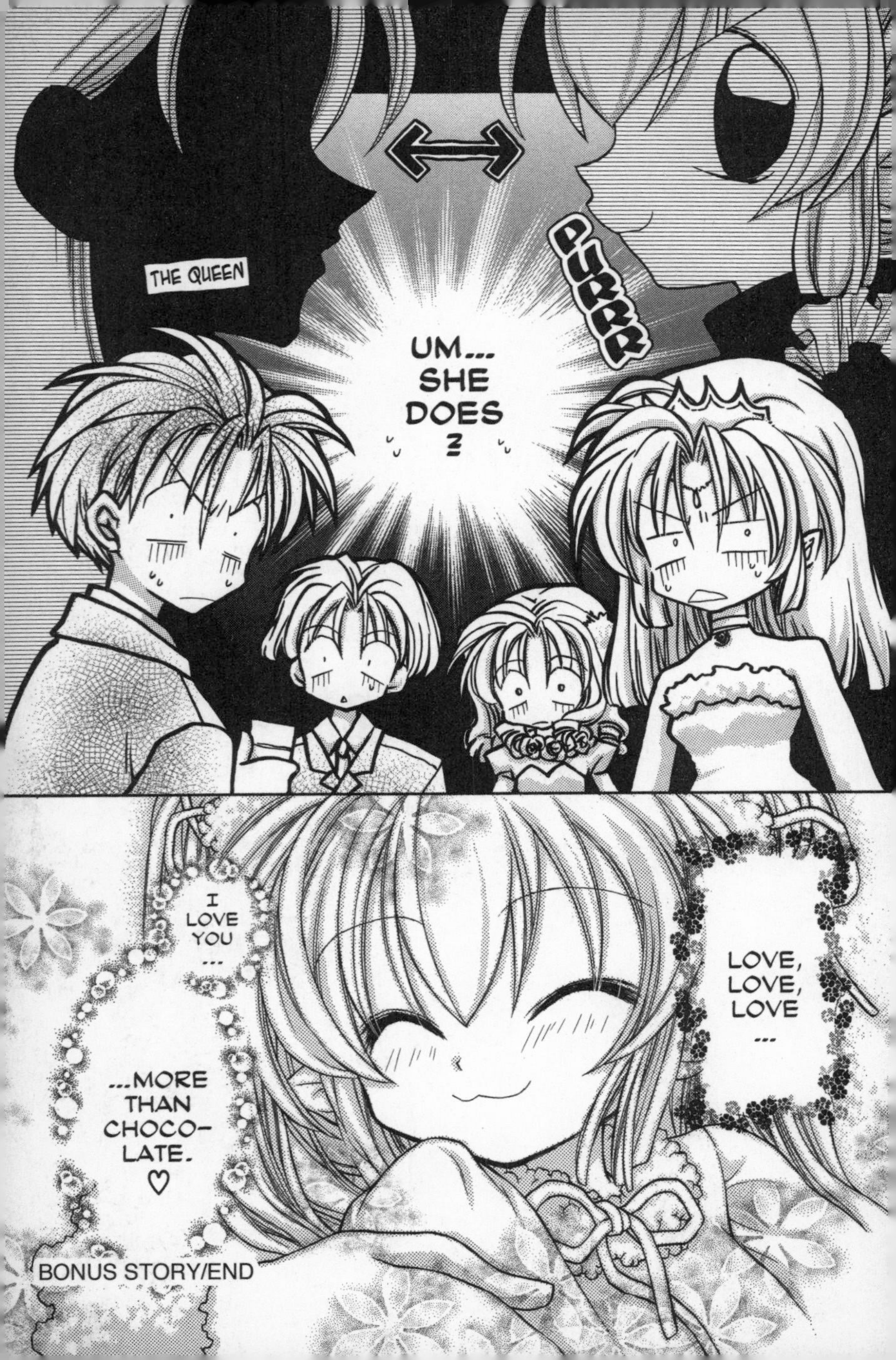
PURRR
THE QUEEN
UM... SHE DOES?
LOVE, LOVE, LOVE ...
I LOVE YOU ...
...MORE THAN CHOCO-LATE. ♡
BONUS STORY/END

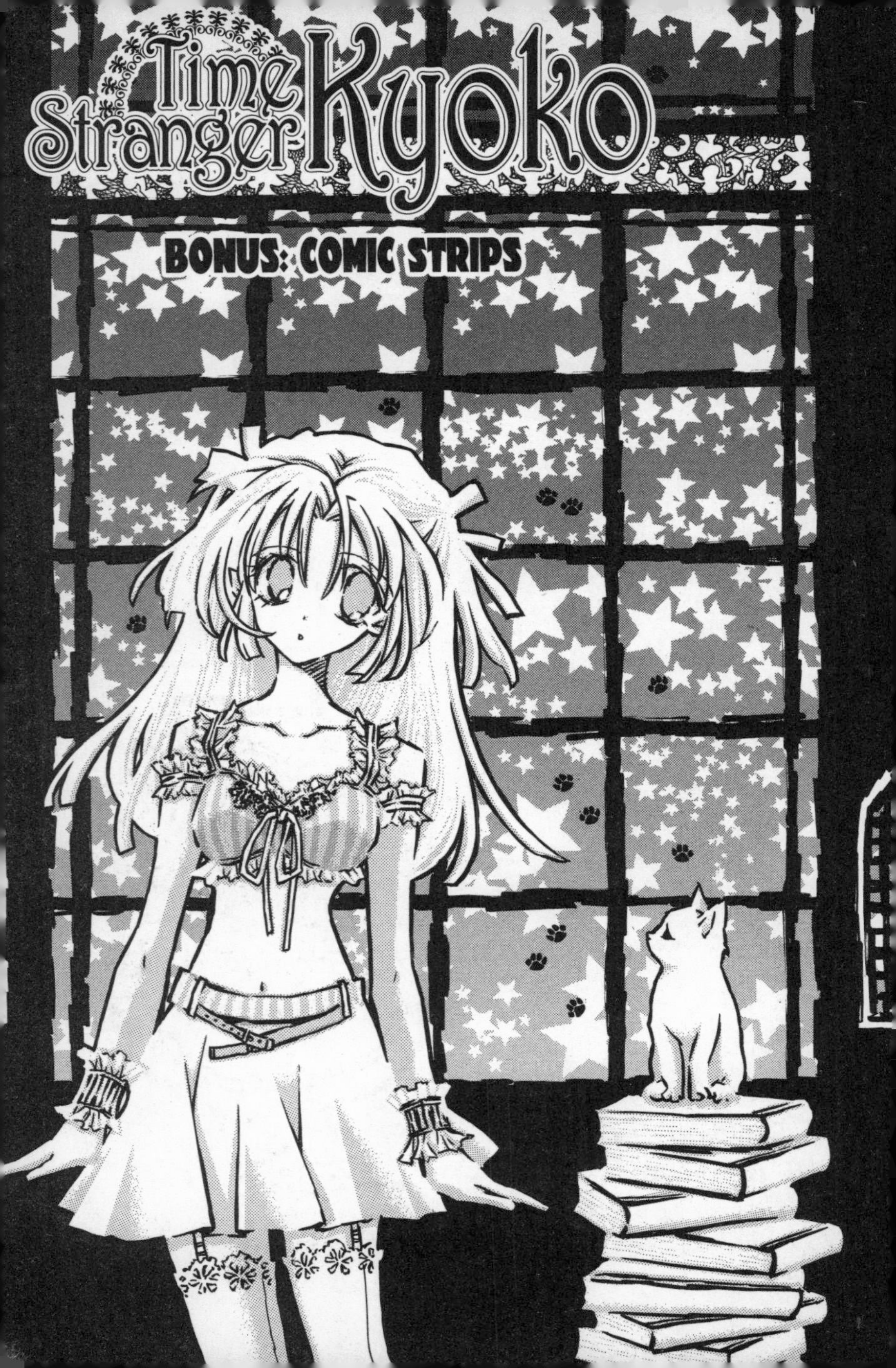
Time Stranger Kyoko
BONUS: COMIC STRIPS

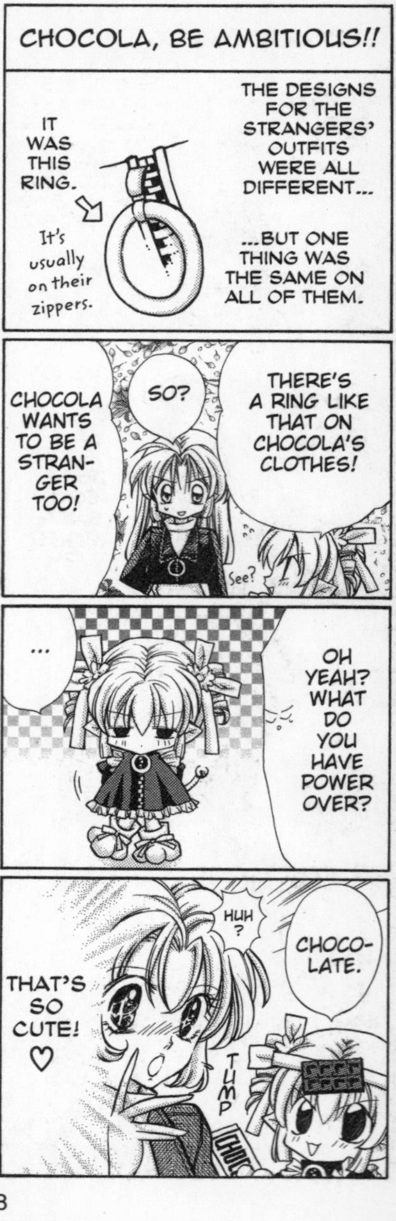
CHOCOLA, BE AMBITIOUS!!
THE DESIGNS FOR THE STRANGERS' OUTFITS WERE ALL DIFFERENT...
...BUT ONE THING WAS THE SAME ON ALL OF THEM.
IT WAS THIS RING.
It's usually on their zippers.
THERE'S A RING LIKE THAT ON CHOCOLA'S CLOTHES!
SO?
CHOCOLA WANTS TO BE A STRAN-GER TOO!
See?
OH YEAH? WHAT DO YOU HAVE POWER OVER?
...
CHOCO-LATE.
HUH?
THAT'S SO CUTE! ♡
TUMP

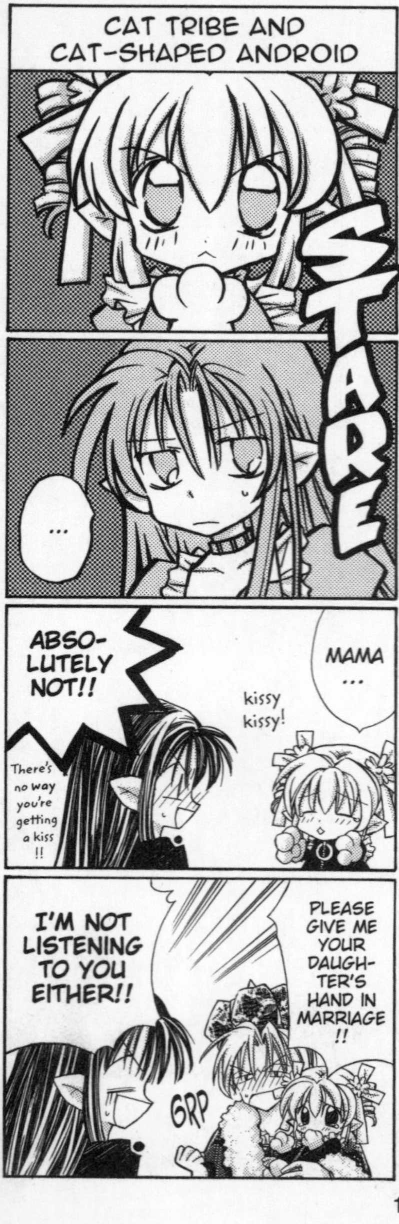
CAT TRIBE AND CAT-SHAPED ANDROID
STARE
...
MAMA...
kissy kissy!
ABSO-LUTELY NOT!!
There's no way you're getting a kiss!!
PLEASE GIVE ME YOUR DAUGH-TER'S HAND IN MARRIAGE!!
I'M NOT LISTENING TO YOU EITHER!!
GRP

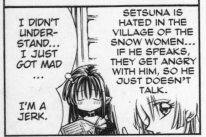

BLACK AND WHITE
OH, SETSUNA-SAN. IT'S ALMOST TIME FOR LUNCH.
AREN'T YOU GOING?
...
TODAY WE'RE HAVING SHRIMP AU GRATIN, CLUB SANDWICHES AND PUMPKIN SOUP.
IT SOUNDS REALLY TASTY.
...
IF YOU DON'T GO NOW, PRINCESS UI WILL EAT IT ALL UP.
THAT OKAY?
...
WHERE'S SETSUNA?
I HATE HIM.
SOB

BLACK AND WHITE 2
SETSUNA IS HATED IN THE VILLAGE OF THE SNOW WOMEN... IF HE SPEAKS, THEY GET ANGRY WITH HIM, SO HE JUST DOESN'T TALK.
I DIDN'T UNDER-STAND... I JUST GOT MAD ...
I'M A JERK.
EXCUSE ME, SETSUNA-SAN... HOW ABOUT SOME SAND-WICHES?
...
I MADE THEM MYSELF.
...
I'LL JUST LEAVE THEM HERE.
AH! ♡
yum

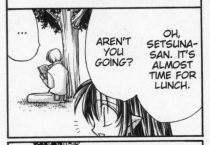

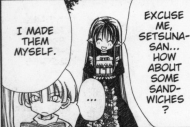

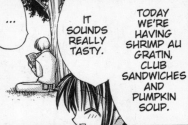

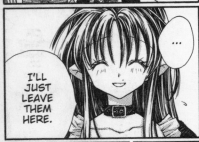

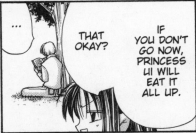

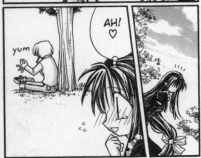

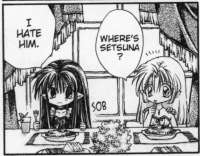

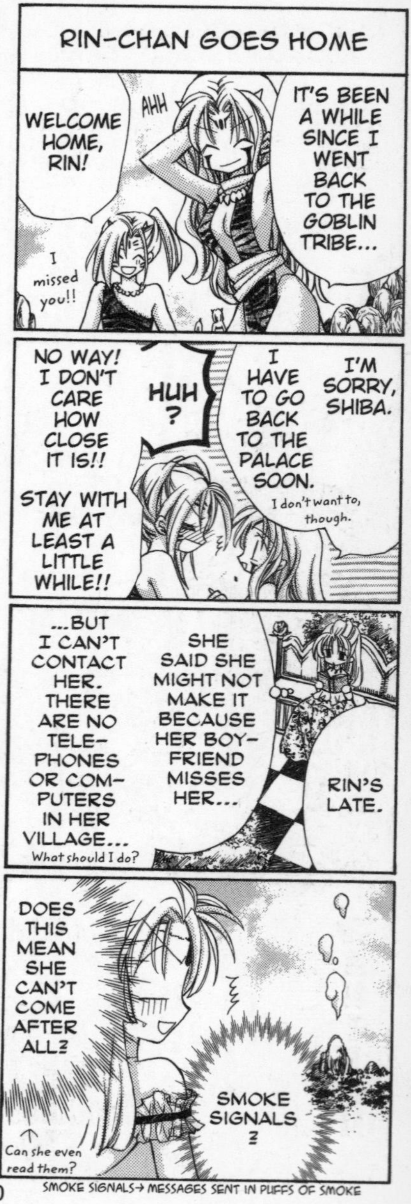
RIN-CHAN GOES HOME
IT'S BEEN A WHILE SINCE I WENT BACK TO THE GOBLIN TRIBE...
AHH
WELCOME HOME, RIN!
I missed you!!
I'M SORRY, SHIBA.
I HAVE TO GO BACK TO THE PALACE SOON.
I don't want to, though.
HUH?
NO WAY! I DON'T CARE HOW CLOSE IT IS!!
STAY WITH ME AT LEAST A LITTLE WHILE!!
RIN'S LATE.
SHE SAID SHE MIGHT NOT MAKE IT BECAUSE HER BOY-FRIEND MISSES HER...
...BUT I CAN'T CONTACT HER. THERE ARE NO TELE-PHONES OR COM-PUTERS IN HER VILLAGE...
What should I do?
SMOKE SIGNALS?
DOES THIS MEAN SHE CAN'T COME AFTER ALL?
Can she even read them?

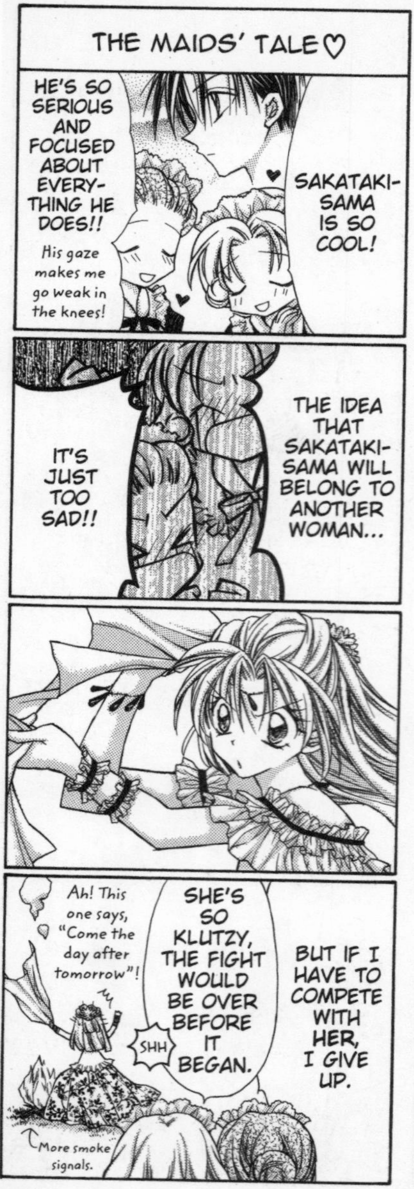
THE MAIDS' TALE♡
SAKATAKI-SAMA IS SO COOL!
HE'S SO SERIOUS AND FOCUSED ABOUT EVERY-THING HE DOES!!
His gaze makes me go weak in the knees!
THE IDEA THAT SAKATAKI-SAMA WILL BELONG TO ANOTHER WOMAN...
IT'S JUST TOO SAD!!
BUT IF I HAVE TO COMPETE WITH HER, I GIVE UP.
SHE'S SO KLUTZY, THE FIGHT WOULD BE OVER BEFORE IT BEGAN.
SHH
Ah! This one says, "Come the day after tomorrow"!
More smoke signals.

SMOKE SIGNALS→ MESSAGES SENT IN PUFFS OF SMOKE

OH, FUUMA-KUN

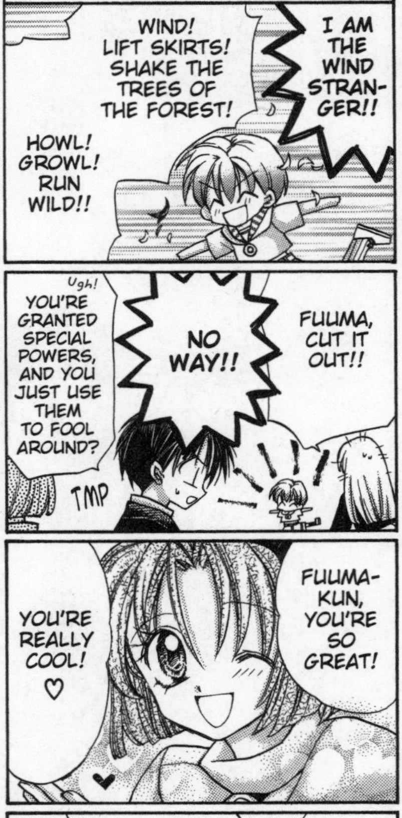
I AM THE WIND STRANGER!!
WIND! LIFT SKIRTS! SHAKE THE TREES OF THE FOREST!
HOWL! GROWL! RUN WILD!!
FUUMA, CUT IT OUT!!
NO WAY!!
Ugh!
YOU'RE GRANTED SPECIAL POWERS, AND YOU JUST USE THEM TO FOOL AROUND?
TMP
FUUMA-KUN, YOU'RE SO GREAT!
YOU'RE REALLY COOL! ♡
UM... ER...
REALLY ?
BLUSH
Yeah.
HE QUIETED DOWN! SCOLDING DOESN'T WORK, BUT FLATTERY DOES, EH?
Nah.
IT'S THE WEAK-NESS OF LOVE.
RUB RUB

BROTHERHOOD AND ALCOHOL AND MINIONS AND TEARS

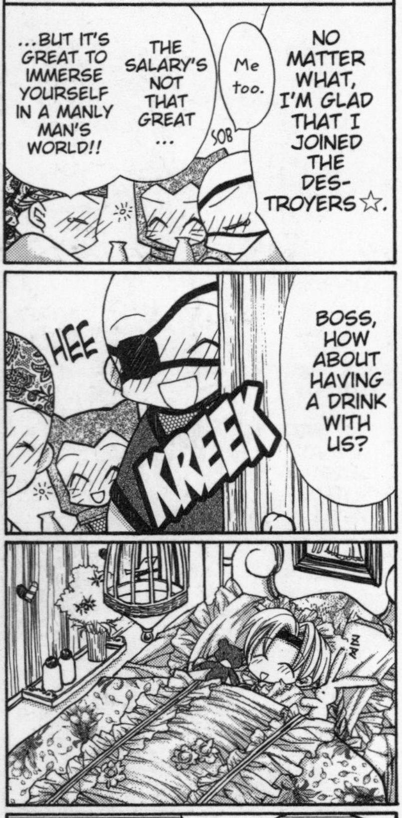
NO MATTER WHAT, I'M GLAD THAT I JOINED THE DES-TROYERS☆.
Me too.
SOB
THE SALARY'S NOT THAT GREAT ...
...BUT IT'S GREAT TO IMMERSE YOURSELF IN A MANLY MAN'S WORLD!!
BOSS, HOW ABOUT HAVING A DRINK WITH US?
KREEK
HEE
CAREER
CHANGE
WANTED!!

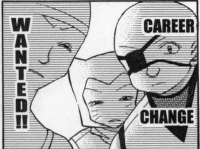

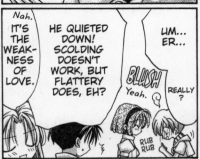

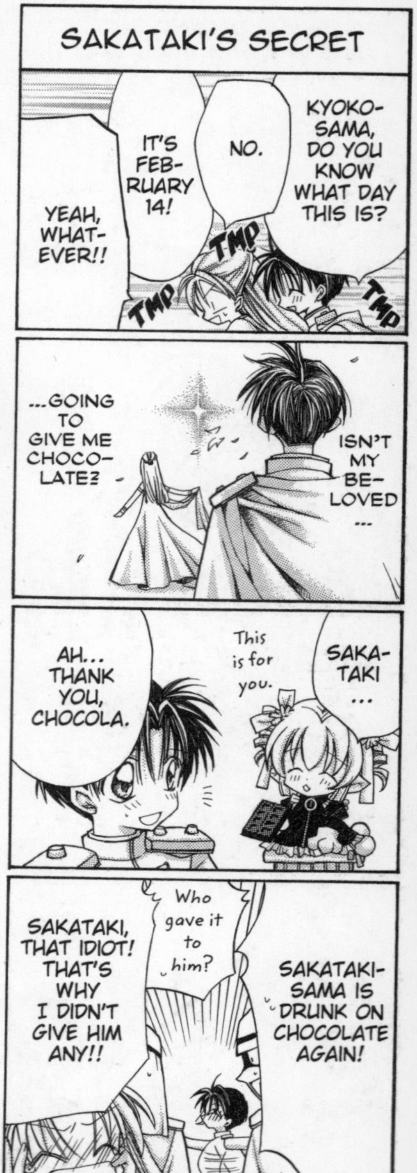
SAKATAKI'S SECRET
KYOKO-SAMA, DO YOU KNOW WHAT DAY THIS IS?
NO.
IT'S FEBRUARY 14!
YEAH, WHATEVER!!
TMP
TMP
TMP
ISN'T MY BELOVED ...
...GOING TO GIVE ME CHOCOLATE?
SAKATAKI ...
This is for you.
AH... THANK YOU, CHOCOLA.
SAKATAKI-SAMA IS DRUNK ON CHOCOLATE AGAIN!
Who gave it to him?
SAKATAKI, THAT IDIOT! THAT'S WHY I DIDN'T GIVE HIM ANY!!

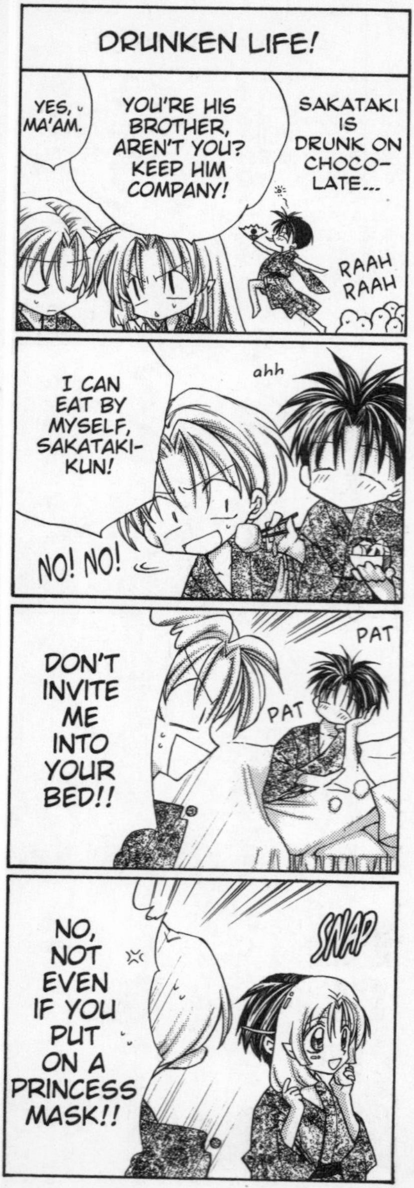
DRUNKEN LIFE!
SAKATAKI IS DRUNK ON CHOCOLATE...
RAAH RAAH
YOU'RE HIS BROTHER, AREN'T YOU? KEEP HIM COMPANY!
YES, MA'AM.
ahh
I CAN EAT BY MYSELF, SAKATAKI-KUN!
NO! NO!
PAT
PAT
DON'T INVITE ME INTO YOUR BED!!
SNAP
NO, NOT EVEN IF YOU PUT ON A PRINCESS MASK!!

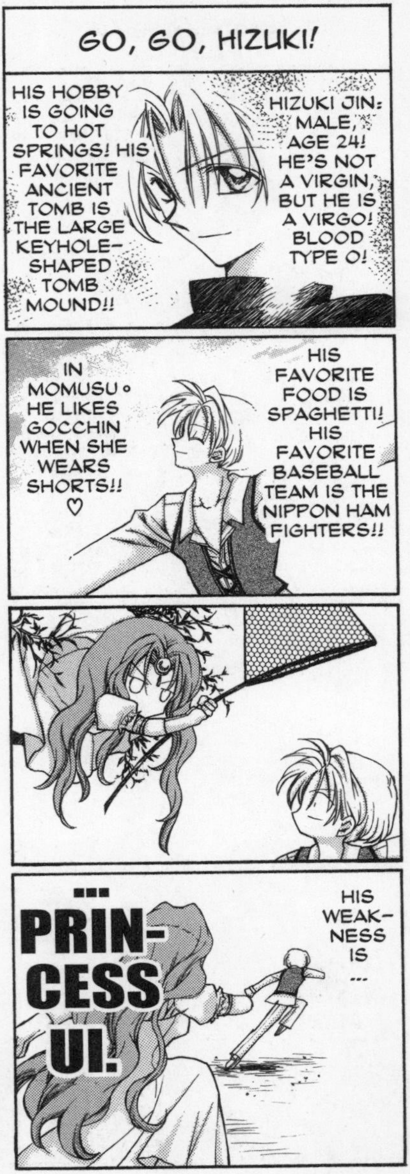
GO, GO, HIZUKI!
HIZUKI JIN: MALE, AGE 24! HE'S NOT A VIRGIN, BUT HE IS A VIRGO! BLOOD TYPE O!
HIS HOBBY IS GOING TO HOT SPRINGS! HIS FAVORITE ANCIENT TOMB IS THE LARGE KEYHOLE-SHAPED TOMB MOUND!!
HIS FAVORITE FOOD IS SPAGHETTI! HIS FAVORITE BASEBALL TEAM IS THE NIPPON HAM FIGHTERS!!
IN MOMUSU。 HE LIKES GOCCHIN WHEN SHE WEARS SHORTS!! ♡
HIS WEAKNESS IS ...
...PRINCESS UI.

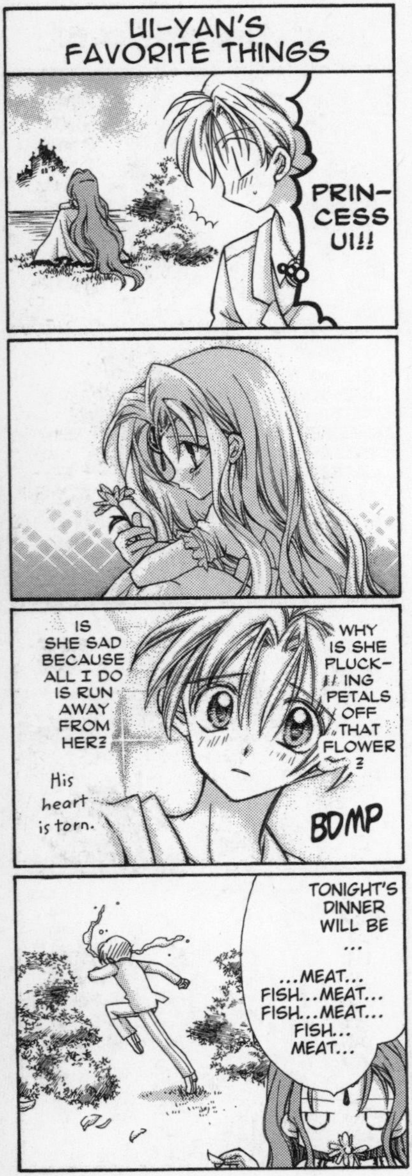
UI-YAN'S FAVORITE THINGS
PRINCESS UI!!
WHY IS SHE PLUCKING PETALS OFF THAT FLOWER?
IS SHE SAD BECAUSE ALL I DO IS RUN AWAY FROM HER?
BDMP
His heart is torn.
TONIGHT'S DINNER WILL BE ...
...MEAT... FISH...MEAT... FISH...MEAT... FISH... MEAT...

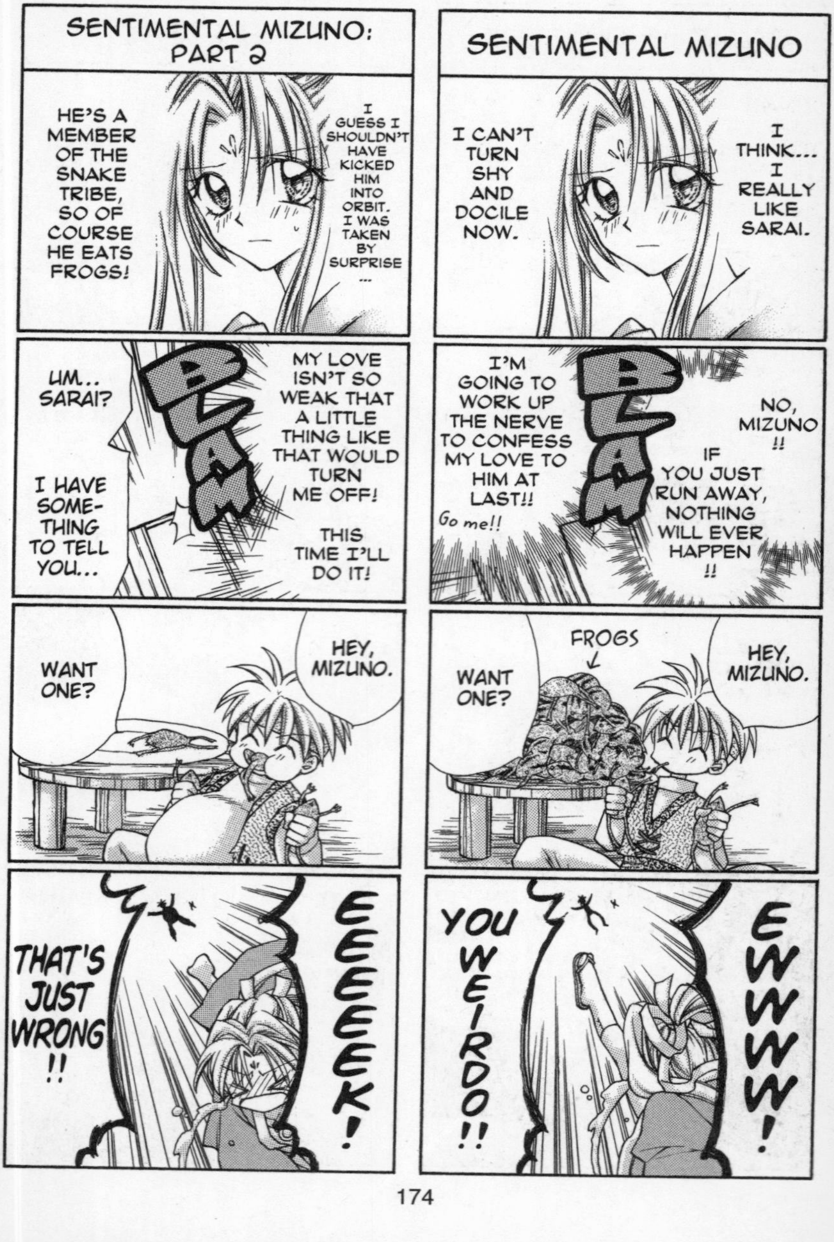
SENTIMENTAL MIZUNO
I THINK... I REALLY LIKE SARAI.
I CAN'T TURN SHY AND DOCILE NOW.
NO, MIZUNO!!
IF YOU JUST RUN AWAY, NOTHING WILL EVER HAPPEN!!
BLAM
I'M GOING TO WORK UP THE NERVE TO CONFESS MY LOVE TO HIM AT LAST!!
Go me!!
HEY, MIZUNO.
FROGS
WANT ONE?
EWWWW!
YOU WEIRDO!!
SENTIMENTAL MIZUNO: PART 2
I GUESS I SHOULDN'T HAVE KICKED HIM INTO ORBIT. I WAS TAKEN BY SURPRISE...
HE'S A MEMBER OF THE SNAKE TRIBE, SO OF COURSE HE EATS FROGS!
MY LOVE ISN'T SO WEAK THAT A LITTLE THING LIKE THAT WOULD TURN ME OFF!
THIS TIME I'LL DO IT!
BLAM
UM.. SARAI?
I HAVE SOME-THING TO TELL YOU...
HEY, MIZUNO.
WANT ONE?
EEEEEEK!
THAT'S JUST WRONG!!

LAST RESORT

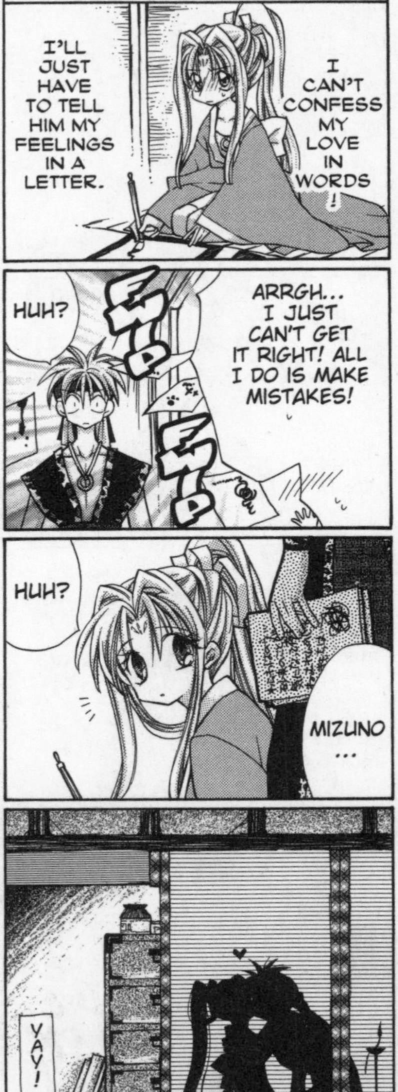
I CAN'T CONFESS MY LOVE IN WORDS!
I'LL JUST HAVE TO TELL HIM MY FEELINGS IN A LETTER.
ARRGH... I JUST CAN'T GET IT RIGHT! ALL I DO IS MAKE MISTAKES!
WHIP
WHIP
HUH?
MIZUNO ...
HUH?
YAY!

SAKATAKI AND LOVE

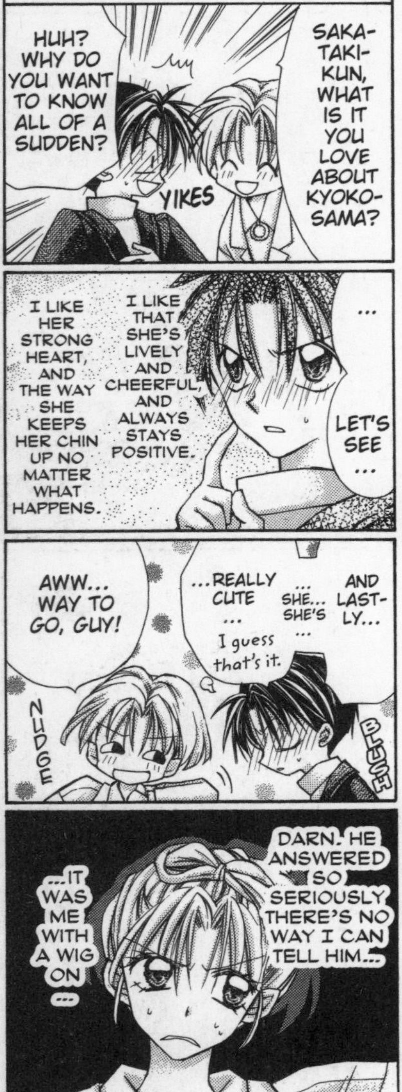
SAKATAKI-KUN, WHAT IS IT YOU LOVE ABOUT KYOKO-SAMA?
HUH? WHY DO YOU WANT TO KNOW ALL OF A SUDDEN?
YIKES
...
LET'S SEE ...
I LIKE THAT SHE'S LIVELY AND CHEERFUL, AND ALWAYS STAYS POSITIVE.
I LIKE HER STRONG HEART, AND THE WAY SHE KEEPS HER CHIN UP NO MATTER WHAT HAPPENS.
AND LASTLY...
... SHE... SHE'S ...
...REALLY CUTE ...
I guess that's it.
BLUSH
AWW... WAY TO GO, GUY!
NUDGE
DARN. HE ANSWERED SO SERIOUSLY THERE'S NO WAY I CAN TELL HIM...
...IT WAS ME WITH A WIG ON ...

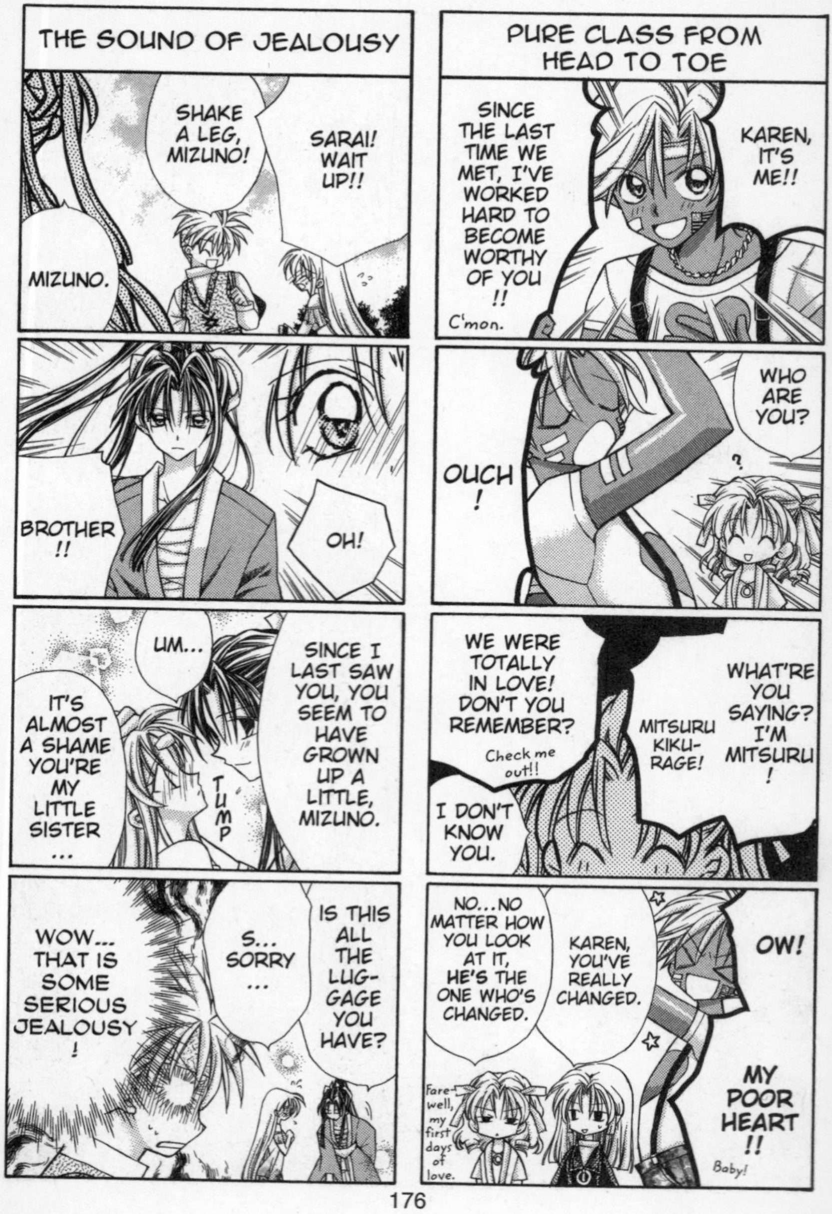
PURE CLASS FROM HEAD TO TOE
KAREN, IT'S ME!!
SINCE THE LAST TIME WE MET, I'VE WORKED HARD TO BECOME WORTHY OF YOU!!
C'mon.
WHO ARE YOU?
?
OUCH!
WHAT'RE YOU SAYING? I'M MITSURU!
MITSURU KIKU-RAGE!
WE WERE TOTALLY IN LOVE! DON'T YOU REMEMBER?
Check me out!!
I DON'T KNOW YOU.
OW!
KAREN, YOU'VE REALLY CHANGED.
NO...NO MATTER HOW YOU LOOK AT IT, HE'S THE ONE WHO'S CHANGED.
MY POOR HEART!!
Baby!
Farewell, my first days of love.
THE SOUND OF JEALOUSY
SARAI! WAIT UP!!
SHAKE A LEG, MIZUNO!
MIZUNO.
OH!
BROTHER!!
SINCE I LAST SAW YOU, YOU SEEM TO HAVE GROWN UP A LITTLE, MIZUNO.
UM...
TUMP
IT'S ALMOST A SHAME YOU'RE MY LITTLE SISTER...
IS THIS ALL THE LUGGAGE YOU HAVE?
S...SORRY...
WOW...THAT IS SOME SERIOUS JEALOUSY!

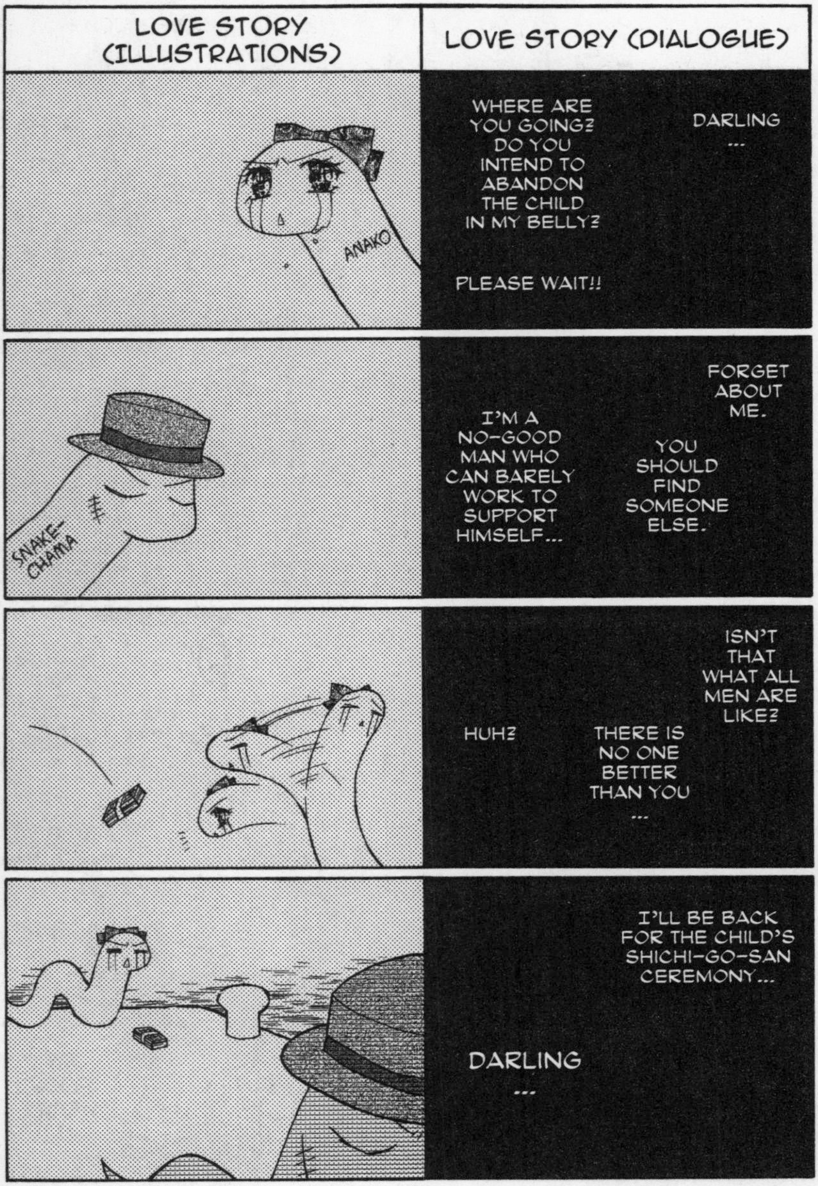
LOVE STORY (ILLUSTRATIONS)
LOVE STORY (DIALOGUE)
DARLING ...
WHERE ARE YOU GOING? DO YOU INTEND TO ABANDON THE CHILD IN MY BELLY?
PLEASE WAIT!!
ANAKO
FORGET ABOUT ME.
YOU SHOULD FIND SOMEONE ELSE.
I'M A NO-GOOD MAN WHO CAN BARELY WORK TO SUPPORT HIMSELF...
SNAKE-CHAMA
ISN'T THAT WHAT ALL MEN ARE LIKE?
THERE IS NO ONE BETTER THAN YOU ...
HUH?
I'LL BE BACK FOR THE CHILD'S SHICHI-GO-SAN CEREMONY...
DARLING ...

※ This page is reprinted exactly as it appeared in the 2001 *Ribon Summer Vacation Entertaining Extra Edition*.

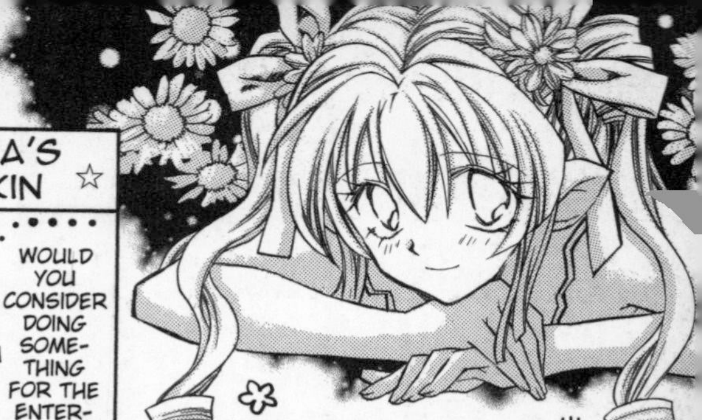

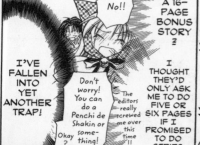

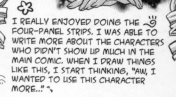

I REALLY ENJOYED DOING THE FOUR-PANEL STRIPS. I WAS ABLE TO WRITE MORE ABOUT THE CHARACTERS WHO DIDN'T SHOW UP MUCH IN THE MAIN COMIC. WHEN I DRAW THINGS LIKE THIS, I START THINKING, "AW, I WANTED TO USE THIS CHARACTER MORE..."

BY THE WAY, THE PICTURE ABOVE IS CHOCOLA AT AGE 16. THE ILLUSTRATION ON THE AUTHOR BIO PAGE IS CHOCOLA TOO. I GAVE THE ORIGINAL DRAWING AWAY AS A CONTEST PRIZE. Whoever wins it, please take good care of it, okay?

MY NEXT WORK WILL BE A ONE-SHOT MANGA (COMMERCIAL TIME...HEH). IT WILL RUN IN THE NOVEMBER ISSUE OF *RIBON*. THERE WILL BE A FREEBIE WITH THE ISSUE. !

Let me rest!

THE FREEBIE WAS FUN TO DO, AND I REALLY ENJOYED IT, SO PLEASE CHECK IT OUT.

The final version will be pretty small, though...

I WILL KEEP DOING MY BEST. SEE YOU!

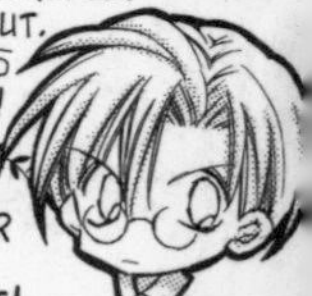

RIBON, NOVEMBER PERSONAL ADVERTISEMENT!

THE MAIN CHARACTER, AKIYOSHI-KUN

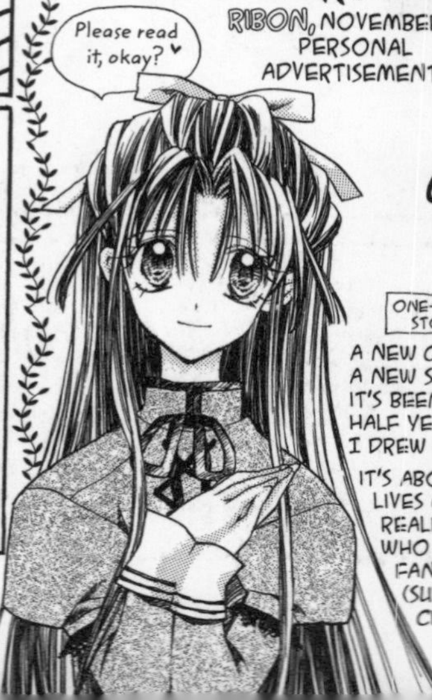

Please read it, okay?

GINYUU MEIKA

ONE-SHOT STORY

A NEW CHARACTER AND A NEW SHORT MANGA... IT'S BEEN FOUR AND A HALF YEARS SINCE I DREW ONE. B-dmp B-dmp

IT'S ABOUT A BOY WHO LIVES GROUNDED IN REALITY AND A GIRL WHO LIVES IN A FANTASY WORLD. (SUBJECT TO CHANGE...)

ARINA TANEMURA'S PENCHI DE SHAKIN ☆

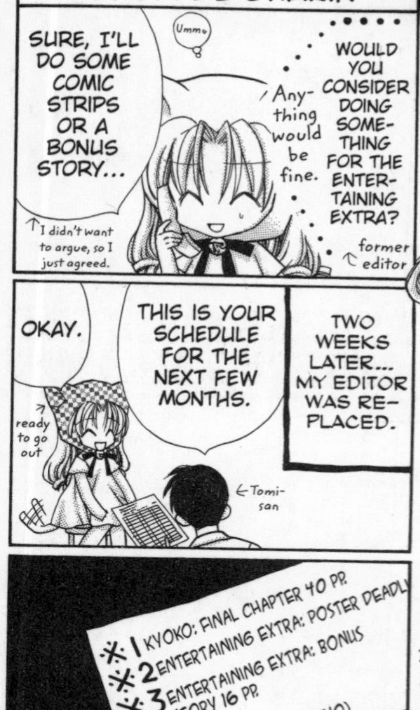

WOULD YOU CONSIDER DOING SOMETHING FOR THE ENTERTAINING EXTRA?
former editor
Anything would be fine.
Ummm
SURE, I'LL DO SOME COMIC STRIPS OR A BONUS STORY...
I didn't want to argue, so I just agreed.
TWO WEEKS LATER... MY EDITOR WAS REPLACED.
THIS IS YOUR SCHEDULE FOR THE NEXT FEW MONTHS.
OKAY.
ready to go out
Tomi-san
※1 KYOKO: FINAL CHAPTER 40 PP.
※2 ENTERTAINING EXTRA: POSTER DEADL
※3 ENTERTAINING EXTRA: BONUS STORY 16 PP.
BOOK SIGNING (TOKYO)
※4
A 16-PAGE BONUS STORY?
No!!
I THOUGHT THEY'D ONLY ASK ME TO DO FIVE OR SIX PAGES IF I PROMISED TO DO STRIPS TOO.
The editors really screwed me over this time!!
Don't worry! You can do a Penchi de Shakin or something!
Okay?
I'VE FALLEN INTO YET ANOTHER TRAP!

BONUS/THE END

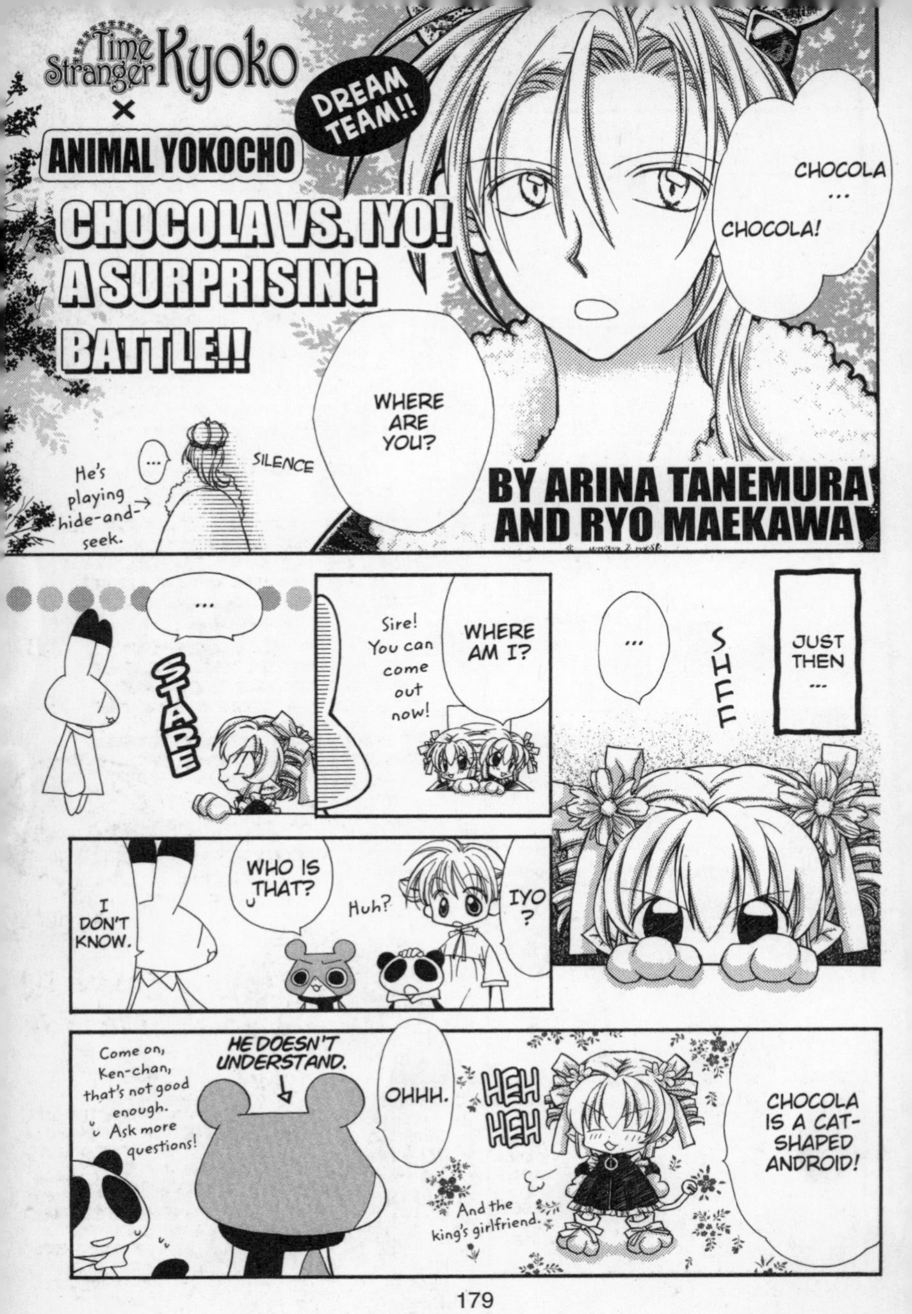

CHOCOLA ... CHOCOLA!
Time Stranger Kyoko × ANIMAL YOKOCHO
DREAM TEAM!!
CHOCOLA VS. IYO! A SURPRISING BATTLE!!
WHERE ARE YOU?
BY ARINA TANEMURA AND RYO MAEKAWA
SILENCE
...
He's playing hide-and-seek.
JUST THEN ...
SHFF
...
WHERE AM I?
Sire! You can come out now!
...
STARE
IYO?
Huh?
WHO IS THAT?
I DON'T KNOW.
CHOCOLA IS A CAT-SHAPED ANDROID!
And the king's girlfriend.
HEH HEH
OHHH.
HE DOESN'T UNDERSTAND.
Come on, Ken-chan, that's not good enough. Ask more questions!

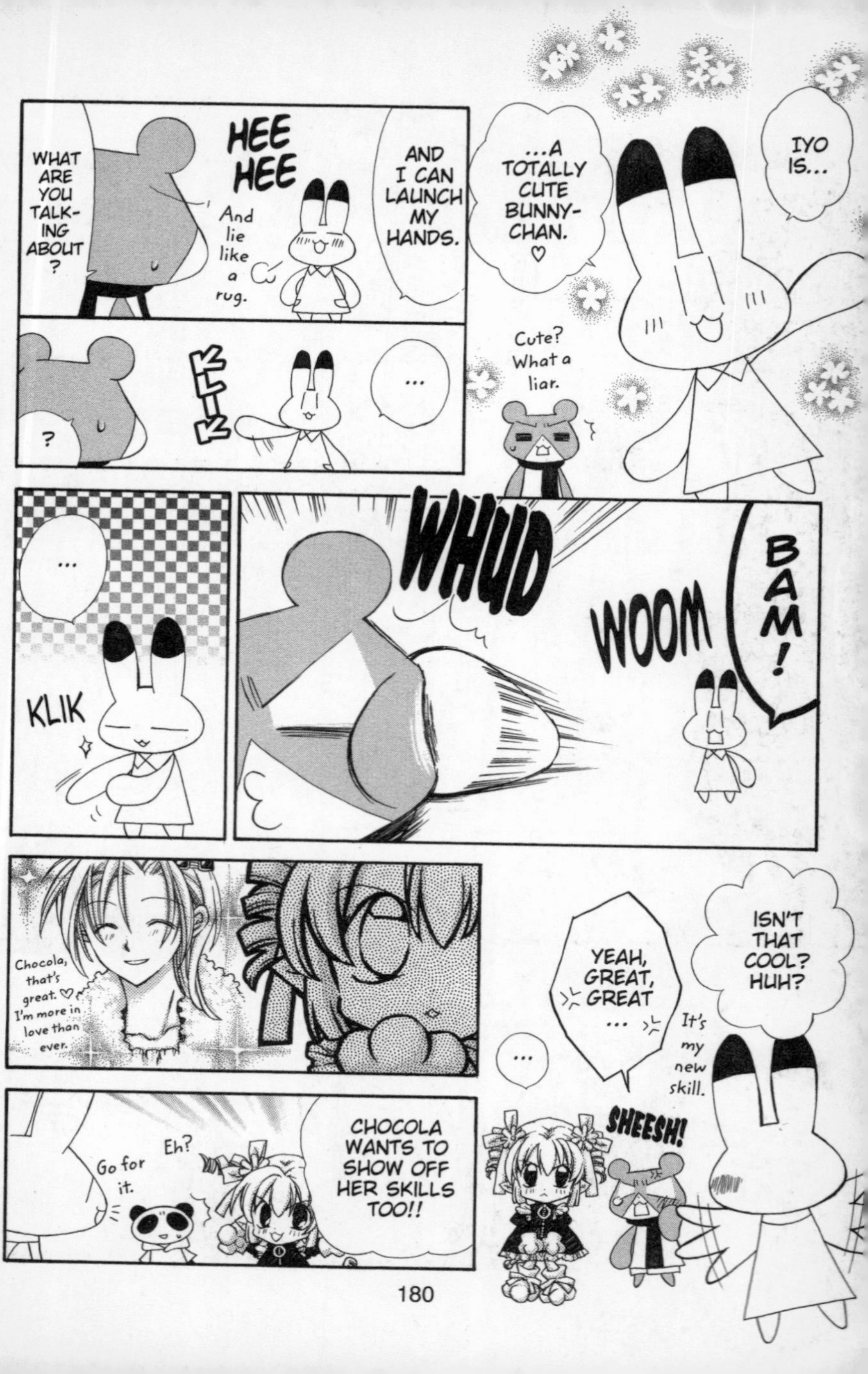
IYO IS...
...A TOTALLY CUTE BUNNY-CHAN. ♡
Cute? What a liar.
AND I CAN LAUNCH MY HANDS.
HEE HEE
And lie like a rug.
WHAT ARE YOU TALKING ABOUT?
...
KLIK
?
BAM!
WOOM
WHUD
...
KLIK
ISN'T THAT COOL? HUH?
It's my new skill.
YEAH, GREAT, GREAT...
...
SHEESH!
Chocola, that's great. ♡ I'm more in love than ever.
CHOCOLA WANTS TO SHOW OFF HER SKILLS TOO!!
Eh?
Go for it.

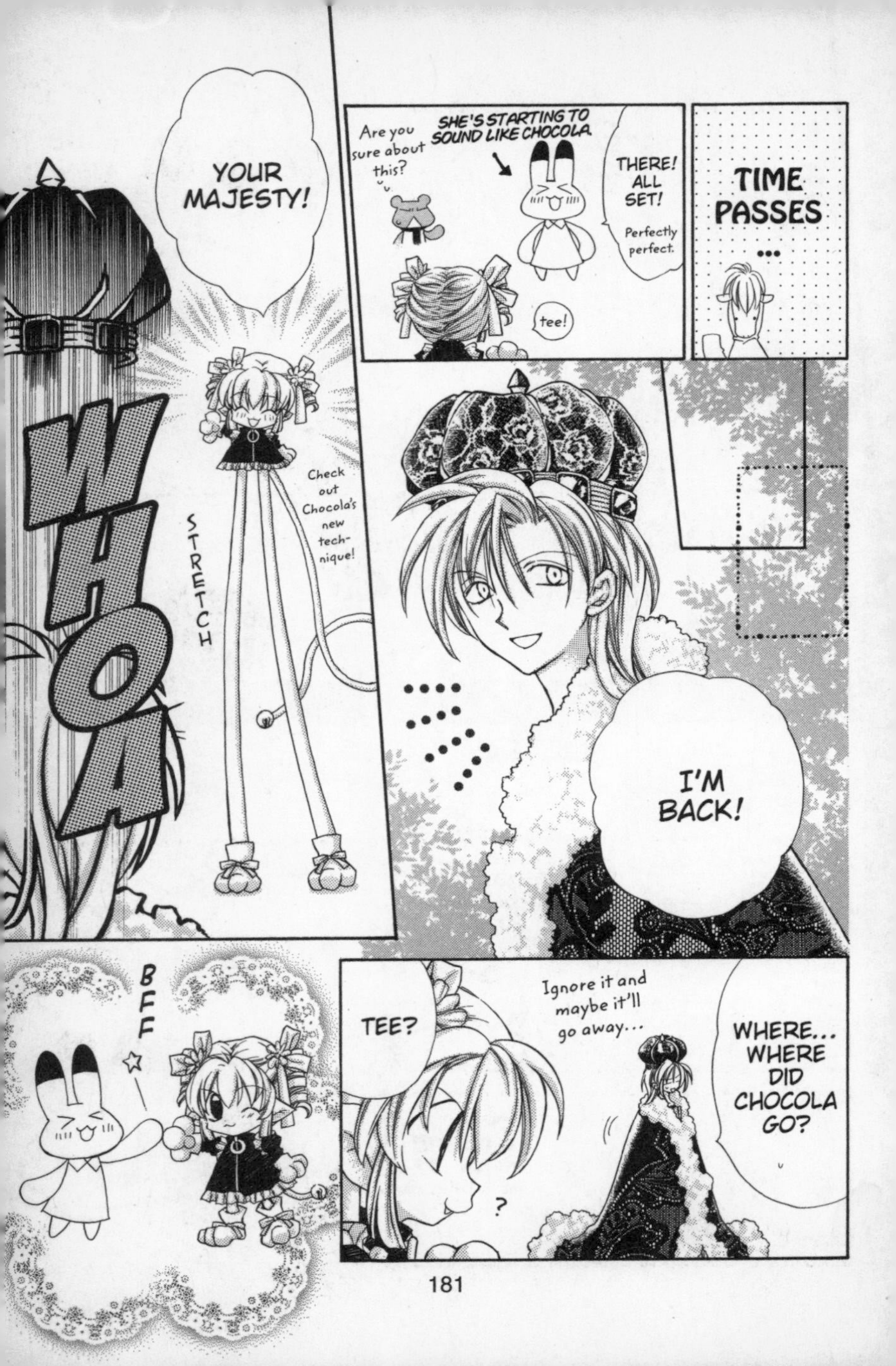
TIME PASSES...
THERE! ALL SET!
Perfectly perfect.
tee!
SHE'S STARTING TO SOUND LIKE CHOCOLA
Are you sure about this?
I'M BACK!
YOUR MAJESTY!
Check out Chocola's new tech-nique!
STRETCH
WHOA
WHERE... WHERE DID CHOCOLA GO?
Ignore it and maybe it'll go away...
?
TEE?
BFF

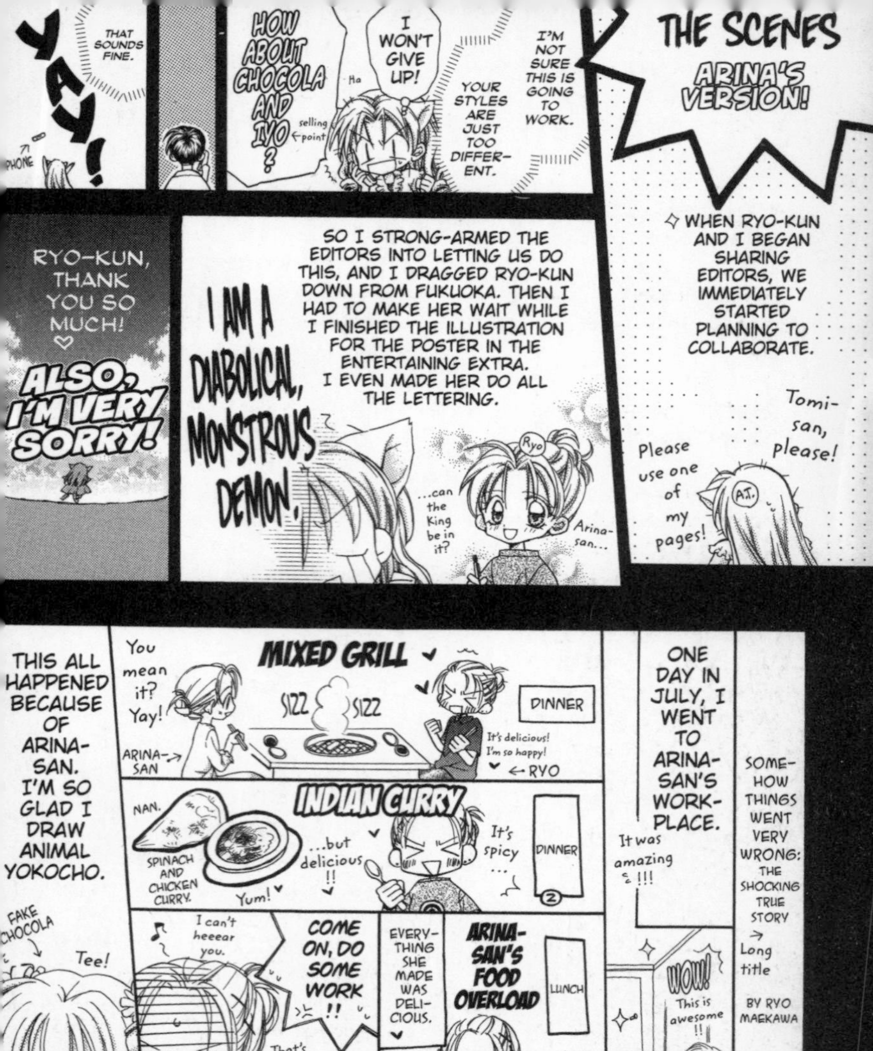
THE SCENES
ARINA'S VERSION!
WHEN RYO-KUN AND I BEGAN SHARING EDITORS, WE IMMEDIATELY STARTED PLANNING TO COLLABORATE.
Tomi-san, please!
Please use one of my pages!
A.T.
I'M NOT SURE THIS IS GOING TO WORK.
YOUR STYLES ARE JUST TOO DIFFER-ENT.
I WON'T GIVE UP!
Ha
HOW ABOUT CHOCOLA AND RYO?
selling point
THAT SOUNDS FINE.
YAY!
PHONE
SO I STRONG-ARMED THE EDITORS INTO LETTING US DO THIS, AND I DRAGGED RYO-KUN DOWN FROM FUKUOKA. THEN I HAD TO MAKE HER WAIT WHILE I FINISHED THE ILLUSTRATION FOR THE POSTER IN THE ENTERTAINING EXTRA. I EVEN MADE HER DO ALL THE LETTERING.
Arina-san...
Ryo
...can the King be in it?
I AM A DIABOLICAL, MONSTROUS DEMON.
RYO-KUN, THANK YOU SO MUCH!
ALSO, I'M VERY SORRY!
SOME-HOW THINGS WENT VERY WRONG: THE SHOCKING TRUE STORY
Long title
BY RYO MAEKAWA
ONE DAY IN JULY, I WENT TO ARINA-SAN'S WORK-PLACE.
WOW!
This is awesome!!
It's so big!!
It was amazing!!!
DINNER
MIXED GRILL
It's delicious! I'm so happy!
RYO
You mean it? Yay!
ARINA-SAN
SIZZ SIZZ
DINNER 2
INDIAN CURRY
It's spicy...
...but delicious!!
Yum!
NAN.
SPINACH AND CHICKEN CURRY.
LUNCH
ARINA-SAN'S FOOD OVERLOAD
BLUSH
I'm so happy.
EVERY-THING SHE MADE WAS DELI-CIOUS.
Yummy...
EMOTION-ALLY MOVED.
COME ON, DO SOME WORK!!
You're just eating!
That's not a shocking story!!
I can't heeear you.
Tee!
FAKE CHOCOLA
THIS ALL HAPPENED BECAUSE OF ARINA-SAN. I'M SO GLAD I DRAW ANIMAL YOKOCHO.

TIME STRANGER KYOKO 3/END

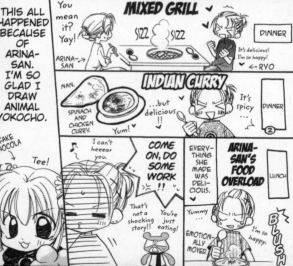

Time Stranger Kyoko Notes

The suffixes –*kun* and –*chan* are added to a person's name to show familiarity. The suffix –*sama* is added to show respect for someone who is higher up in the social hierarchy. Witzig's "snake–*chama*" is a cute nickname for his snake.

Page 33: Tanemura's manga usually run in Japan in the shojo magazine *Ribon*.

Page 44: *Osage* can mean both "pigtails" and "money down."

Page 51: Sakataki is imitating Moominpapa from the *Moomin* books, by Swedish-Finnish writer and illustrator Tove Jansson. The Moomins are popular characters in Japan.

Page 63: In the first panel, in the original Japanese, Kyoko says "Mochibachi," a contraction of *mochiron*, meaning "of course," and *bachiri*, meaning "perfectly."

Page 65: A *yakatabune* is a traditional Japanese roofed pleasure boat.

Page 65: The *ne* in Mami-ne indicates "older sister," and the *ni* in Nao-ni indicates "older brother," but Tanemura doesn't mean they're literally her siblings; they're just terms of endearment.

Page 85: The Sabotender is a monster in the *Final Fantasy* games, usually given the English name Cactuar. Auron is a character in *Final Fantasy X*.

Page 99: Momusu. is a nickname for the massive Japanese girl group Morning Musume. Mini-Moni is a spin-off group featuring the shortest girls in Morning Musume.

Page 101: *Tenshi Nanka Janai* (I'm Not an Angel) is an early manga by Ai Yazawa, creator of *NANA*. Jump Festa is a huge annual fan convention centered around *Shonen Jump* magazine.

Page 154: *Monja*, or *monjayaki*, is a type of griddle cake with vegetables.

Page 168: "Boys, be ambitious!" is a famous piece of parting advice given by educator William S. Clark upon his departure from Sapporo Agricultural College (now Hokkaido University) in 1877.

Page 177: The Shichi-Go-San ceremony, on November 15, is held to celebrate children's third, fifth and seventh years. These years are considered lucky and mark traditional childhood rites of passage.

Page 179: *Animal Yokocho* is a popular children's manga by Ryo Maekawa that runs in *Ribon* magazine. Iyo the rabbit, Kenta the bear, and Issa the panda are "the Happy AniYoko Trio," three magical animals who visit 5-year-old Ami through a doorway in her room.

The future in *Kyoko* is the future I hope for. Some people have told me it's not realistic because, even though it's set in the future, the backgrounds look like something from ancient times. But I didn't want to draw a digital future. I like analog. I guess there isn't any chance we'll really see a future of gears and clockwork, but in my manga I wanted to create the future I long for. Thank you, everyone, for supporting my dream.

Arina Tanemura was born in Aichi, Japan. She got her start in 1996, publishing *Nibanme no Koi no Katachi* (The Style of the Second Love) in *Ribon Original* magazine. Her early work includes a collection of short stories called *Kanshaku Dama no Yuutsu* (Short-Tempered Melancholic). Two of her titles, *Kamikaze Kaito Jeanne* and *Full Moon*, were made into popular TV series. Tanemura enjoys karaoke and is a huge *Lord of the Rings* fan.

TIME STRANGER KYOKO
VOL. 3

The Shojo Beat Manga Edition

STORY AND ART BY
ARINA TANEMURA

Translation/Mary Kennard
Adaptation/Heidi Vivolo
Touch–up Art & Lettering/Rina Mapa
Design/Yukiko Whitley
Editor/Shaenon K. Garrity

Editor in Chief, Books/Alvin Lu
Editor in Chief, Magazines/Marc Weidenbaum
VP, Publishing Licensing/Rika Inouye
VP, Sales & Product Marketing/Gonzalo Ferreyra
VP, Creative/Linda Espinosa
Publisher/Hyoe Narita

Printed in Canada

Published by VIZ Media, LLC
P.O. Box 77010
San Francisco, CA 94107

Shojo Beat Manga Edition
10 9 8 7 6 5 4 3 2 1
First printing, January 2009

store.viz.com

PARENTAL ADVISORY
TIME STRANGER KYOKO is rated T+ for Older Teen and is recommended for ages 16 and up. This volume contains sexual themes.
ratings.viz.com

Arina Tanemura Series

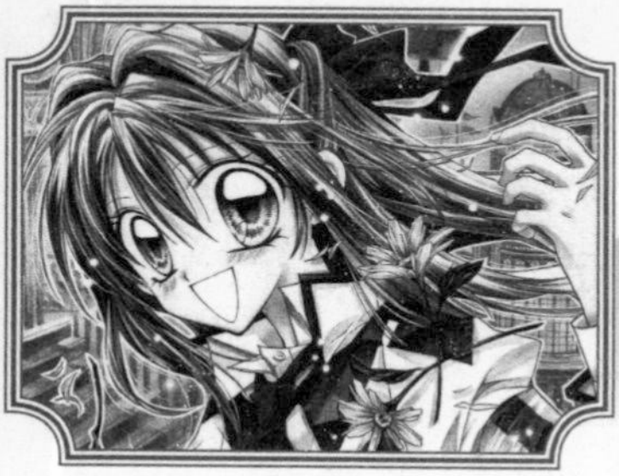

The Gentlemen's Alliance †

Haine Otomiya joins Imperial Academy in pursuit of the boy she's loved since she was a child, unaware that he has many secrets of his own.

I•O•N

Chanting the letters of her first name has always brought Ion Tsuburagi good luck—but her good-luck charm is really the result of psychic powers!

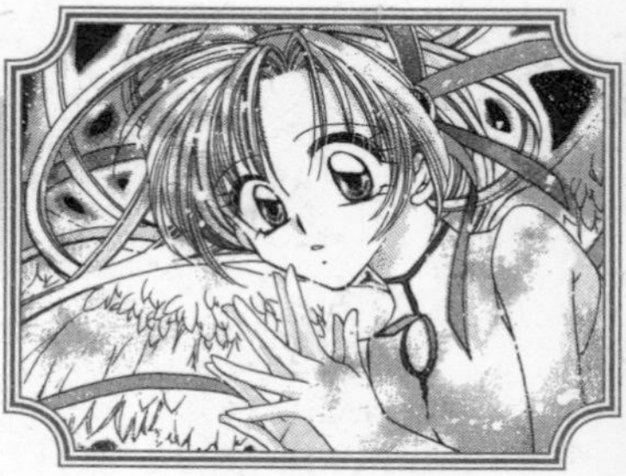

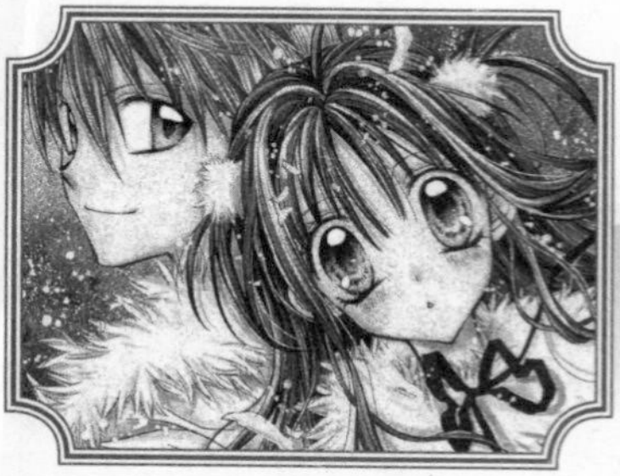

Full Moon

Mitsuki Koyama dreams of becoming a pop star, but she is dying of throat cancer. Can she live out a lifetime of dreams in just one year?

Short-Tempered Melancholic

A collection of short stories including Arina Tanemura's debut manga, "In the Style of the Second Love"!

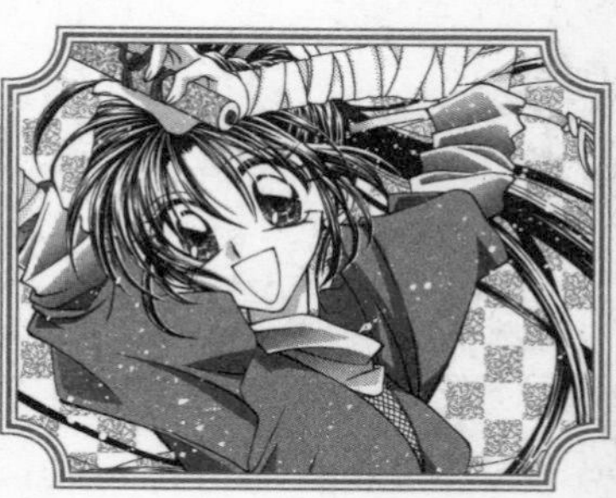

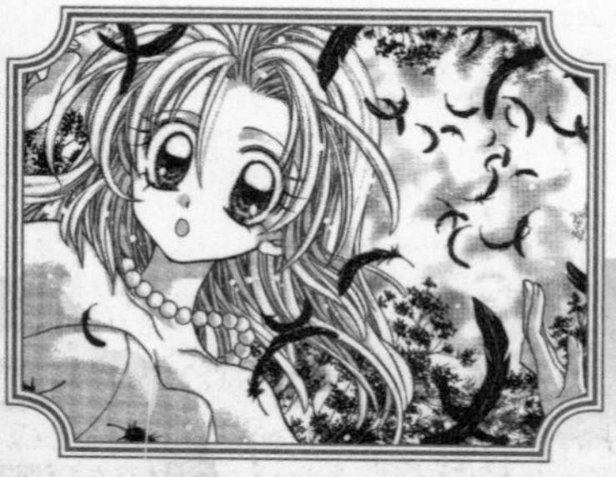

Time Stranger Kyoko

Kyoko Suomi must find 12 holy stones and 12 telepaths to awaken her sister who has been trapped in time since birth.

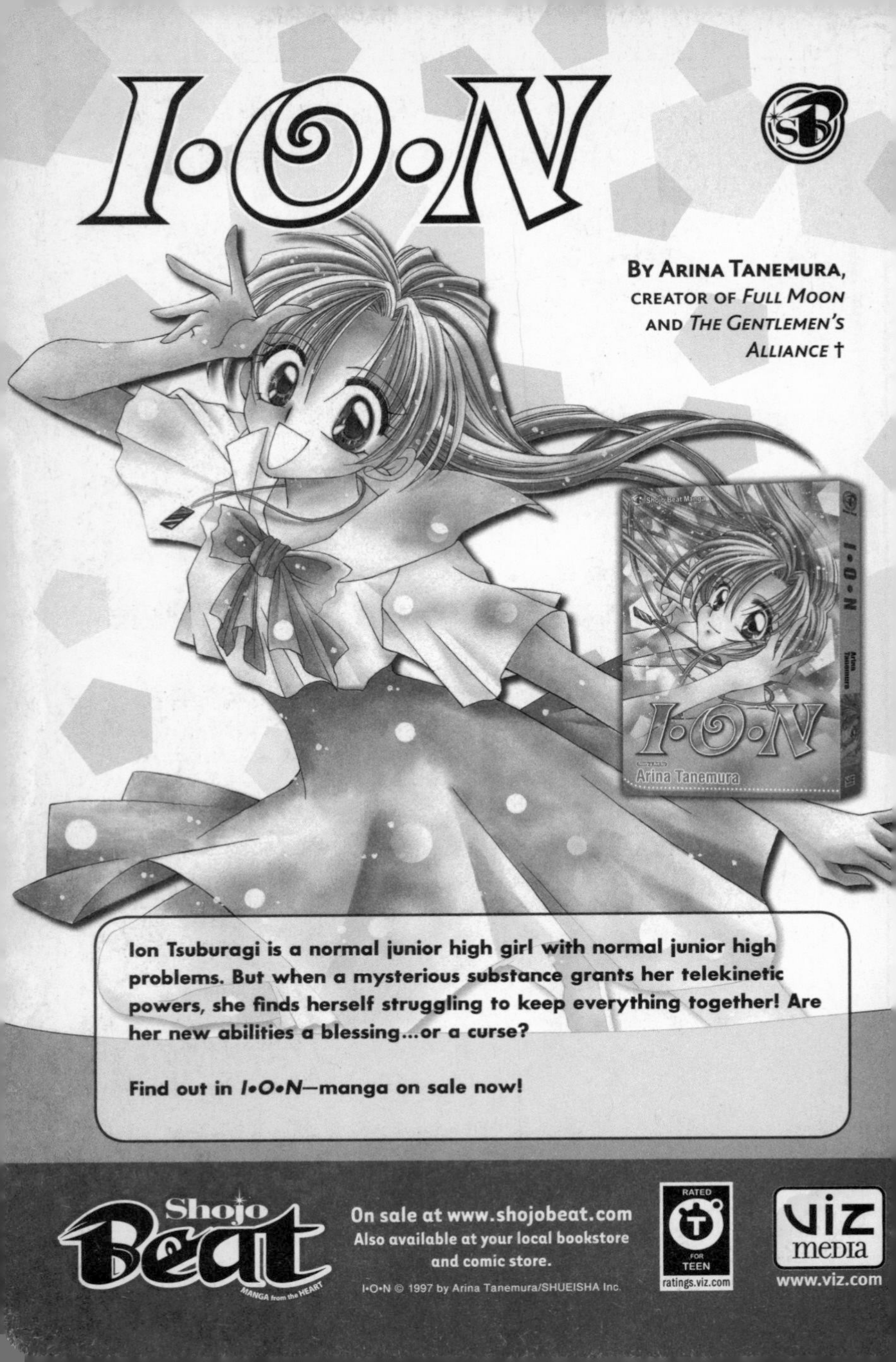
I•O•N
By Arina Tanemura, creator of Full Moon and The Gentlemen's Alliance †
Shojo Beat Manga
I•O•N
Arina Tanemura
Ion Tsuburagi is a normal junior high girl with normal junior high problems. But when a mysterious substance grants her telekinetic powers, she finds herself struggling to keep everything together! Are her new abilities a blessing...or a curse?
Find out in I•O•N—manga on sale now!
Shojo Beat
MANGA from the HEART
On sale at www.shojobeat.com
Also available at your local bookstore and comic store.
I•O•N © 1997 by Arina Tanemura/SHUEISHA Inc.
RATED T FOR TEEN
ratings.viz.com
viz media
www.viz.com

Art book featuring
216 pages of beautiful
color images personally
selected by Tanemura

Read where Mitsuki's
pop dreams began
in the manga—all 7
volumes now available

Complete your
collection with the
anime, now on DVD

RATED
T
... FOR
TEEN
ratings.viz.com

www.viz.com

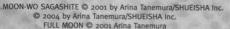

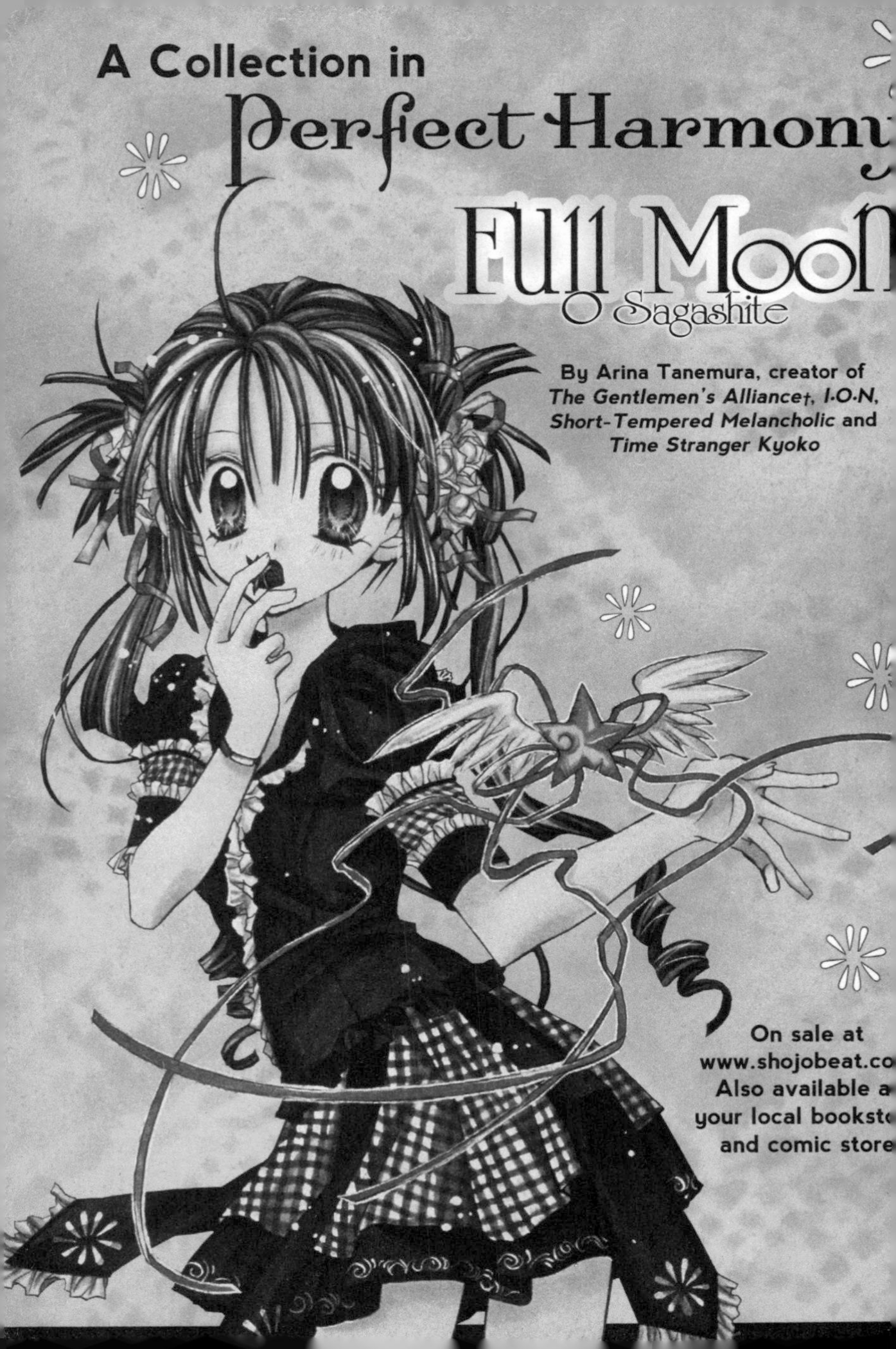
A Collection in
Perfect Harmony
Full Moon
O Sagashite
By Arina Tanemura, creator of
The Gentlemen's Alliance†, I·O·N,
Short-Tempered Melancholic and
Time Stranger Kyoko
On sale at
www.shojobeat.co
Also available a
your local bookst
and comic store